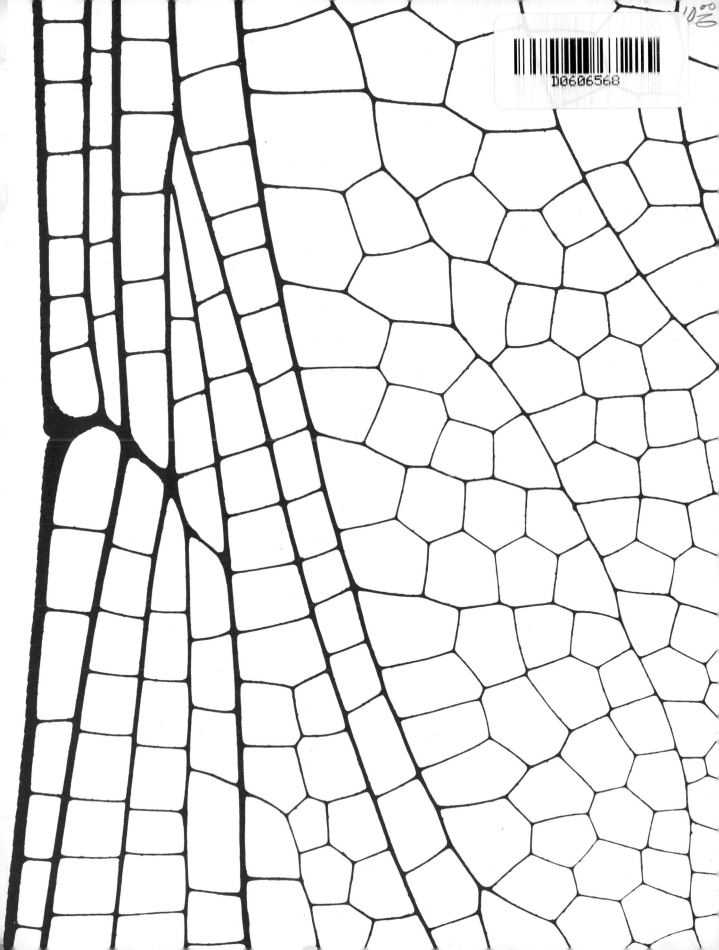

ENCOUNTER WITH ART

ENCOUNTER WITH ART

REID HASTIE
PROFESSOR, DEPARTMENT OF ART EDUCATION
UNIVERSITY OF MINNESOTA

CHRISTIAN SCHMIDT
DESIGNER–CRAFTSMAN

McGRAW-HILL BOOK COMPANY

New York, St. Louis, San Francisco, London,
Sydney, Toronto, Mexico, Panama

ENCOUNTER WITH ART

PREFACE

In the introduction to one of his books a great man of science, Linus Pauling, has said: *

> We are now living in the atomic age. In order to understand the world every person needs to have some knowledge of atoms and molecules.
>
> If you know something about atoms and molecules you can understand the accounts of some of the new discoveries that continue to be made by scientists and can find pleasure in the satisfaction of your intellectual curiosity about the nature of the world. Many scientists find great happiness through the discovery of some fact or the development of some insight into the nature and structure of the world that had previously not been known to anyone. You may share this happiness through your appreciation of the meaning and significance of the new knowledge.

The authors of this book accept this statement of the need to know about atoms and molecules for an understanding of the nature and structure of the world. Also, they would like to add that to understand art as the visual statement and record of man's response to his environment—the scientist's world of atoms and molecules— every person needs to have some knowledge of what an artist does and how he does it. His sculpture, painting, and architecture become the visual equivalent of what he sees, feels, and understands about his world.

If you know something about the art process, you can understand some of the new expressions that continue to be made by artists and some of those that were made in the past. You can find pleasure in the satisfaction of your intellectual and aesthetic curiosity about the nature of art—man's response as he examines his world. Many artists find great happiness in the discovery of some metamorphic imagery or symbolism for the presentation of their in-

---

* Linus Pauling and Roger Hayward, *The Architecture of Molecules*, W. H. Freeman and Company, San Francisco, 1964.

sight into the nature of the universe that has not been expressed by anyone. You may share this happiness through your appreciation of the meaning and significance of these discoveries.

The structure of knowledge of art has two distinct streams, one leading to the production of works of art and the other concerning the appreciation of these products. There are elements in common in these two human actions, and in part they overlap. Education in the field of art has taken account of the two parts of the knowledge structure and has given different emphases to one or the other, according to the goals set for learning and instruction. This book has attempted to meet the needs of the teacher and the student regarding the production and appreciation of art.

The introduction (Chapter 1) places the problem in space and time and then develops the rationale for the organization of the book. This is followed in an orderly sequence, beginning with (a) the artist's perception of his world (Chapters 2 and 3) and (b) his abstraction of what he considers important (Chapter 4). Next there is a discussion of (c) how significant form is given to these perceptions with the tools of his craft through the creative process (Chapters 5 and 6), and then there is an explanation of (d) how an artist obtains a fusion of the aesthetic factors of matter, form, and content in the design process (Chapters 6 through 9). We conclude with (e) how the ultimate is reached when what the artist has put into his work of art is taken out by other persons for appreciation and evaluation (Chapters 10 through 14).

Supplementary notes provided in the Appendix expand upon some of the theoretical concepts and research findings that have been incorporated into the body of the text.

In our transition from the perception of his world by the artist to the perception of the artist's visual statement of his experience by someone else, the relevant theoretical concepts and processes are examined. These include perception, abstraction, creativity, design, aesthetics, art appreciation, and art judgment. These are all quite complicated, and often there is confusion in the mind of the reader when only verbal explanations are offered. For clarity the authors have supplemented the text with a number of visual essays that parallel the discussions of processes and will, it is hoped, illustrate and expand the meaning these will have for the reader. As an artist uses visual means to present his responses to his environment for others to see and understand, the authors are employing visual statements to clarify for the reader some of what goes on as the artist does what he does.

There are also a number of examples of works of art from different historical periods which have been selected for inclusion because they have a specific reference to materials in the text. These illustrations do not follow the chronological sequence found in an art history textbook. There are many good art history books which the reader can consult in order to expand his information and knowledge of the art that has been created during man's whole history. The illustrations given here provide the nucleus or core around which the more comprehensive mass of the historical examples could be constructed.

Encounter with Art has been selected as the title for this book because it expresses precisely the true nature of man's relationship with the art product and the act of its creation. In an encounter something takes place, something happens, some kind of contact is made. In a sense one must "put his foot forward"; it is an active rather than a passive engagement. That the role of the artist involves action needs little explanation. He makes the work of art out of the coordinated effort of mind, heart, and hand. The person who looks at the material form the artist has made also has a part to play. He must prepare himself for the encounter. It is hoped that an understanding of creative-artistic behavior will open the door to an appreciation of the products of art.

Acknowledgments

When this project began, the authors held the naïve notion that they could reach their goal through their own independent efforts. It soon became apparent that this would not be the case. Assistance came from such a multitude of sources that a vast amount of type would be required to enumerate them all. We wish to acknowledge our indebtedness to all who have helped us.

Art teachers from different parts of the country allowed us to photograph the creations of their students; artists contributed photographs of their work. Many businesses, museums, and churches gave us freedom to select and record from their resources. Particular appreciation is gratefully extended to the directors and staffs of the Walker Art Center, the Minneapolis Institute of Arts, the St. Paul Art Center, and the University of Minnesota Gallery.

We wish to thank Abbot Baldwin Dworschak, O.S.B., and the members of the monastic community at Collegeville, Minnesota for their gracious assistance while photographing St. John's Abbey.

Friends and colleagues within the University of Minnesota provided advice and insight in the refinement of various sections of this book. Their comments as scientists, economists, art historians, psychologists, and philosophers broadened our view of our subject.

Bernard S. Myers of the McGraw-Hill Book Company gave us assistance beyond normal expectations. His personal library of photographs of art works, collected for his own publications, was the source of many of the illustrations included in this volume.

Photographic Credits

The photographs reproduced in this book were provided by the following individuals and institutions:

Albright-Knox Art Gallery, Buffalo, N.Y. 11-6; Alinari 4-1; Archives Photographiques, Paris 8-1, 9-36; Art Institute of Chicago 1-16, 9-37; Oliver Baker 2-46; Hedrich Blessing 6-22; Rudolph Burchhardt 8-29; City Art Museum, St. Louis, Mo. 4-5; Deutsche Fototothek, Dresden 10-1; Andre Emmerich Gallery, New York 11-7; Expo-67 Information Service 8-38–8-40; J. R. Eyerman, Black Star 3-25; Giraudon 2-32; Solomon R. Guggenheim Museum, New York 4-20, 5-19, 6-15; High Altitude Observatory, Boulder, Colo. 3-28; Hans Hinz 7-18; David Hirsch 13-5; Michael Holford 4-2, 8-19, 9-46, 14-8; Sidney Janis Gallery, New York 6-23, 11-10; Jewish Museum, New York 1-27; Roman Norbert Ketterer, Switzerland 1-5; *Leica Fotografie*, no. 6, p. 258, 1967 (A. Lenditsch, Umschau Verlag, Frankfurt am Main) 2-54; William Lockhart 9-22; McGraw-Hill, Inc. 8-36; Marlborough Fine Arts Ltd., London 1-2; Metropolitan Museum of Art, New York 8-9, 8-13, 9-34; Minneapolis Institute of Arts 1-4, 2-58, 4-4, 4-13, 4-19, 5-21, 9-14, 9-24, 9-25, 10-4, 10-5, 10-12–10-15, 10-19, 11-1, 11-12, 13-1, 13-3, 13-8, 13-10–13-12, 14-5; Minnesota Highway Department 3-24; Musée d'Unterlinden, Colmar 4-12; Musée Royal de l'Afrique Centrale, Tervueren, Belgium 10-6; Museum of Fine Arts, Houston, Texas 1-21; Museum of Modern Art, New York 1-1, 4-7, 4-11, 4-35, 5-13–5-18, 8-11, 9-26, 9-43, 14-9; National Gallery, London 4-17; O. E. Nelson, New York 8-12; Hugh Newbury 10-7; Philadelphia Museum of Art 6-27; Phillips Collection, Washington, D.C. 7-13, 9-38; Eric Pollitzer 1-10; Ad Reinhardt 1-18; Rijksmuseum, Amsterdam 8-14; Rohm-Haas Reporter 7-14; Jean Roubier 4-3, 8-35; Christian Schmidt 1-12–1-14, 1-23, 1-25, 1-26, 1-29, 2-1–2-30, 2-33–2-45, 2-47–2-53, 2-55–2-57, 2-59, 3-1–3-23, 3-30, 3-31, 3-33–3-37, 4-8, 4-21–4-34, 4-36–4-38, 5-1–5-12, 5-22–6-14, 6-17–6-21, 6-28, 6-30–6-32, 7-1–7-12, 7-19–7-38, 8-3–8-8, 8-10, 8-15, 8-16, 8-20, 8-21, 8-24–8-27, 8-30–8-34, 8-41–8-53, 9-4–9-13, 9-17–9-21, 9-27–9-32, 9-39–9-42, 9-47, 10-3, 10-8–10-11, 12-1–12-62, 13-9, 14-1, 14-2, 14-6, 14-7, left-hand chapter division pages, dust jacket illustration; © S.P.A.D.E.M. 8-2; Staatliche Museen zu Berlin 9-49; Städtische Kunsthalle, Mannheim 9-35; Eric Sutherland, Walker Art Center 1-3, 1-19, 1-20, 1-22, 1-28, 2-31, 4-15, 4-18, 6-24–6-26, 6-29, 7-15–7-17, 8-17, 8-18, 8-22, 8-23, 9-33, 9-44, 9-45, 10-2, 11-2, 11-11, 11-13, 13-2, 13-4, 13-6, 13-7; Trans-World Airlines, Inc. 8-37; Uffizi Gallery, Florence 13-13; Ullstein Bilderdienst, Berlin 9-48; University of Minnesota Gallery, Minneapolis 1-8, 1-9, 14-11; Walker Art Center, Minneapolis 1-6, 1-11, 1-17, 1-24, 4-6, 4-10, 4-14, 4-16, 5-20, 8-28, 9-1–9-3, 9-15, 9-16, 9-23, 10-16–10-18, 11-4, 14-3, 14-12, 14-13; Alvin Weber 3-26, 3-27; Whitney Museum of American Art, New York 1-7, 1-15, 4-9, 6-16, 11-3, 11-5, 11-8, 11-9, 14-10; Observatoire de Paris, Meudon, 3-29.

Additional Credits

The authors wish to acknowledge the work of Edward H. Weiss *Sun, Shell Eyes, Mirror Mouth with Rope*, which opens Chapter 10 (p. 312), and the Campbell Soup Company for permission to reproduce its label on p. 400. Also included are the following unidentified works by the authors: Reid Hastie (paintings, pastels, and watercolors) 3-3–3-37, 5-22–5-29, 6-14, 6-17–6-20, 9-41, 9-42; Christian Schmidt (jewelry and sculpture) 2-20–2-22, 5-3–5-12, 6-10–6-13, 7-11, 7-12, 7-31–7-35, 8-45–8-53, 9-19–9-21.

TABLE OF CONTENTS

ENCOUNTER WITH ART

Chapter 1

CONTEMPORARY ART AND THE ARTIST

Art has been defined as a means of conceiving the world visually and the artist as the man who has the ability and the desire to transform his visual perception into expression in a material form.[1]

This description of art and the artist helps us to reconcile the various and often conflicting viewpoints expressed through painting, sculpture, and the crafts in the twentieth century. It connects the art of our time with the products from centuries in the past. In this viewpoint the fundamental characteristic of art is that it is a personal thing. As persons differ from one another, their insights, imagination, and varying personalities should bring forth products that are uniquely different. In the last two decades, artists have employed many modes of visual perception and have seen their world in various ways. The means at their command for recording their perceptions are equally diverse.

Much has been written that describes the state of our contemporary world with its mobility, constant conflict, and change. The accelerating quest for knowledge, social and political upheavals, and the fears, successes, insecurities, and complacencies of the people of our societies have been recorded by the mass media of the nations of the world. All these happenings have been reflected and proclaimed in the arts of our time by men striving to maintain independence of thought and action.

CURRENT TRENDS IN ART

An intelligent appreciation of the creative expressions in the arts requires some knowledge of the historical situation, the social context and the prevailing thinking of the time in which these works were created. We know and have experienced the culture out of which contemporary art has been produced. The present is here for our inspection; the past is not. It should be easier for us to see or to sense the connection between the art of our time and the culture from which it has been produced. A yardstick for the appreciation and evaluation of the art from past centuries can grow out of our understanding of this connection between the art of the present and the cultural background which produced it.

In many respects, the problems of the contemporary artist are unprecedented in history, at least in degree, if not in kind. Never before has the artist been subjected to such a barrage of ideas through instant communication. Changes take place quickly and are relayed with equal speed. Events all over the world, not just in the next village, are brought to us almost as they take place, through the sounds and sights of mass-media communication. While this appears very exciting and beneficial, in reality it creates very real and unnatural pressures on the sincere creative individual. It takes a strong-willed artist to continue his development of a personal and meaningful avenue of exploration over the period of time required for mature expression. This is especially difficult when both the outer and inner worlds of the artist change directions at frequent intervals.

Abrupt changes in the style of artistic expression have created many

---

1 Herbert Read, **A Concise History of Modern Painting**, Frederick A. Praeger, Inc., New York, 1962, pp. 11–12.

1-1
Jackson Pollock, Number 1.
1948. Oil on canvas.
Museum of Modern Art, New York.

problems for the spectator as he seeks to gain a foothold on the way to a full appreciation of the contemporary artist and his products. In order to grasp the differences and similarities in the various ways in which man, the artist, has seen the world and expressed his perceptions of it for others to see, a review of current developments in art is presented. In this review the artists and their works are grouped according to the factors they have considered most important as influences on their way of conceiving the world. There are weaknesses in any classification system which attempts to place the works of artists into neat categories, because some artists and works fall outside the boundaries of such a system.

While looking at the sky on a crisp winter night, the sweep of stars massed across the whole expanse is overwhelming. There seem to be so many of them! At first, each star appears separated from all the others; but, as one looks a little longer, clusters begin to take shape, pairings appear, and groupings emerge. Single stars seem to belong with others; together they make up the constellations. Although each light spot in the constellation is distinct in size and brightness from others, it helps us to make sense of the whole if we take in clusters of light spots that are positioned in relation to each other. In a similar fashion, the sweep of individual artists across the sky of contemporary art is overwhelming and confusing to the viewer. There seems to be such a battery of different kinds of paintings and sculpture moving in different directions with little relationship to one another. But, as is true of stars in the sky, we can bring some sense of order to the whole by taking out clusters of individuals and their works which are connected by common intent. These can be related or grouped into stylistic patterns having some consistency. This procedure also helps us to see those individuals whose work falls outside our somewhat arbitrary descriptive categories.

This organized review of art developments of the last two decades enables us to identify the differences in artistic expressions. We can compare these expressions by artists with our own conceptions of this same world. Through this accent on the contemporary, we can also obtain an awareness of how art from any place and time has reflected the culture and the thinking of the people in that culture. It is also hoped that there will be a clarification of how the innovations that have come forth during the present period have had their roots and sources in the past; we can see how they are linked to the traditions of the artists who went before. The four general divisions are made according to the direction selected by the artist for his personal mode of expression. One group of artists has made inner feelings and the action of painting or sculpture itself the subject of its works. Another group has attempted to bring the symbols of our culture and its values forcibly to our attention. A third group has chosen to work toward an art of "intellectual purity." The last division includes those artists who are concerned with the expression of real time and real motion in their art.

THE INNER WORLD OF THE ARTIST

It is usually hazardous to make a definitive statement about what happened inside a man from the outward results of this inner action as seen in a work of art. In the case of works classified as abstract expressionism, we are, however, on slightly firmer ground, since the artists involved in this movement have been participants rather than observer-recorders. The act of creating a painting or sculpture has itself become the subject.

In painting, the initial slash of pigment across the canvas provokes a spontaneous and immediate response from the artist and leads to the subsequent placement of related colors and shapes. Successive applications of pigment follow intuitively as the artist responds with sensitivity to the colors and forms that have previously been established. In this manner the artist "gets into" his painting and presents a clear visual image that expresses his sensuous experience. His spontaneous impulses are guided by his intuitive sense of rightness; the intuitive applications of pigment are adjusted and changed, in effect controlled, to form a composition that for him expresses a clear statement of his sensations, emotions, and feelings. The instantaneous brushwork of pigment conveys these feelings and maintains the qualities of speed, energy, and excitement that pervade the process of creating a painting. The works of Jackson Pollock, Arshile Gorki, Hans Hofmann, Willem de Kooning, and Franz Kline, to name a few, are examples of this mode of artistic expression (Fig. 1-1).

1-2
*Mark Rothko. Mauve and Orange.
1961. Oil on canvas.
Marlborough Fine Arts Ltd.,
London.*

1-3
*Nicolas de Staël. The Red Sky.
1952. Oil on canvas.
Walker Art Center, Minneapolis.*

The artist's tools and media are often impromptu and depart from the traditional in keeping with the improvisation and loosely controlled action-reaction that are characteristics of the process of action painting. The pigment is brushed, dripped, spread, sprayed, or rolled over the canvas surface with every imaginable instrument, even the hands and feet of the painter. Wire, plastic, glass, wood, string, and paper are added to satisfy the personal demands of the artist.

Abstract art is usually without realistic content, and conventional subject matter is absent. The products are dependent upon size and texture for their impact upon the viewer. The personal style evolved by Mark Rothko consists in placing two or three soft-edged rectangles or ribbons of pigment across the canvas. The canvases of Sam Francis are constructed with a loose mosaic of free-form segments. Franz Kline's bold slashes of dark pigment against a light background suggest power and force. The works of Adolph Gottlieb keep a frozen, precariously balanced kind of instability with his symbols and pictographic images. All the artists who have worked in the abstract-expressionist manner have tended to give the spectator a clear idea of feelings and sensations through their fluid images and the ways that they are formed (Figs. 1-2, 1-3).

Abstract expressionism as an art movement is an extension and elaboration of the figurative expressionism of painters like Kokoschka, Soutine, Nolde, Rouault, and Kirchner who have transformed reality in glowing and encrusted colors (Figs. 1-4, 1-5). Their willingness to pay attention to forces inside themselves and to make the expression of their personal feelings the subject of their art has been extended by those artists who later worked in the style of abstract expressionism. Surrealist theories of automatism also had their influence; the spontaneous expression of the subconscious will relates the work of the abstract expressionist to the Oriental art of calligraphy.

THE OUTER WORLD OF THE ARTIST

Many critics believe that pop art evolved as a reaction against the ideas of the abstract expressionists. In this form of art there is little or no indication of the artist's personal involvement that can be discerned in the finished painting or sculpture. One gets the impression that the artist remains neutral and remote as he portrays the conventions, conveniences, and concerns of his society. Nobility and grandeur are bestowed on the commonplace; the trivia and paraphernalia of our contemporary world are presented as symbols of our culture. Pop bottles and soup cans, ice-cream cones and hamburgers are blown up bigger-than-life. Vegetables are cast in metals, reminiscent of the baby shoes in bronze of another era; perishables are embalmed in plastic; comic strips are enlarged. The obvious is made more obvious. With satire and humor, and often with deadly seriousness, the pop artist has thrust his selection of the symbols of our age into the field of our consciousness. With his direct use of "found" objects and his techniques of collage and assemblage, the boundary between what is painting and what is sculpture has been blurred and broken. Intention is considered more important than technique.

1-4
Oskar Kokoschka.
Tower Bridge, London. *1925.*
Minneapolis Institute of Arts.

1-5
Ernst Ludwig Kirchner.
Reclining Nude with Fan.
1908. Oil on cloth.
Kunsthalle, Bremen.

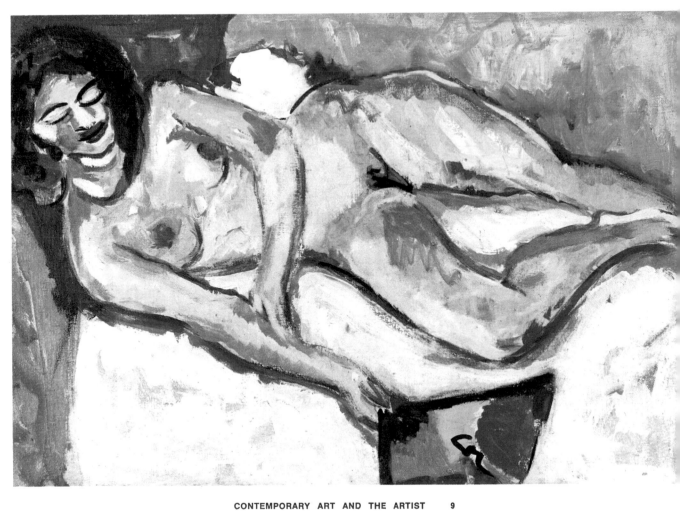

CONTEMPORARY ART AND THE ARTIST   9

1-6
Andy Warhol. 16 Jackies.
1965. Walker Art Center,
Minneapolis.

1-7
Jasper Johns. Studio. 1964.
Whitney Museum of American Art,
New York.

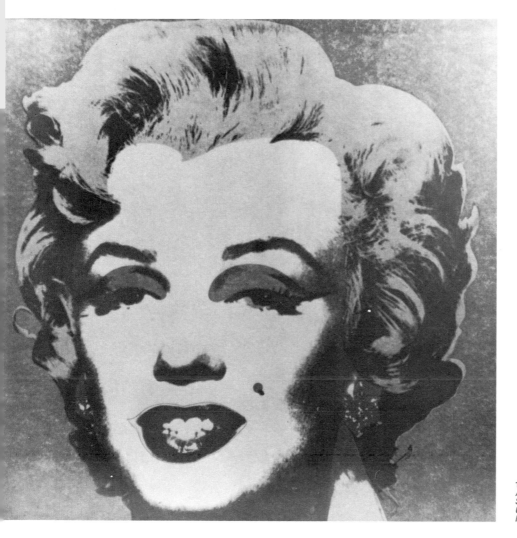

1-8
Andy Warhol. Marilyn.
Serigraph.
University of Minnesota Gallery,
Minneapolis.

The works of the practitioners of pop art demonstrate the diversity of means and methods that the artist has invented for the portrayal of the uncertainties of human experience and the ambiguity in standards of values in society. The technique of assemblage, which is a useful device for artistic expression, has been defined as "three dimensional art in a two dimensional or pictorial context which yet escapes of bas-relief."[2]

Jasper Johns with his flags, maps, and tin cans and Robert Rauschenberg with his bed, goat, automobile tire, and Bulova clocks have gained a measure of international acclaim for their assemblages. Andy Warhol has given us a new look at soup cans and Brillo boxes; his portraits of Jacqueline Kennedy, Marilyn Monroe, and Mrs. Scull were each made up of more than thirty arcade photos (three for 25 cents) that were enlarged and screen-printed in color (Figs. 1-6 – 1-8).

---

[2] See **The Artist Speaks**, *Art in America*, vol. 53, no. 4 (August–September, 1965), p. 109.

A painting by James Rosenquist, *Silver Skies*, contains images of a tire, a car windshield, a section of a pop bottle, and a girl's knee on a bicycle seat. Roy Lichtenstein has brought us giant-size comic strips (*Blam*) and a girl with a large tear dripping from her eye (*Thinking of Him*); Wayne Thiebaud has created paintings and sculptures of pies, gum-ball machines, and a windowful of cakes (Figs. 1-9, 1-10).

Sculpture has been of soft things made hard and of hard things made soft. Assemblages of found objects have been extended to the creation of almost total environments. George Segal's life-size plaster castings of friends, art critics, artists' models, and bus drivers are placed in an appropriate setting with enough walls, windows, furniture, and other objects to create the illusion of space and scale. Claes Oldenburg's sculptures glorify many unlikely subjects — the hamburger, a banana split, and two lamb chops in a frying pan. He has also promoted soft sculpture out of cloth, plastic, and other flexible materials, with household gadgets as his

1-9
Roy Lichtenstein.
World's Fair Mural.
1963. Oil on plywood.
University of Minnesota Gallery,
Minneapolis.

subject matter (Fig. 1-11). Edward Kienholz has created real environments (*The Beanery*), but in a manner that leaves the viewer uneasy and at times shocked by the memories that are forced to the surface of his consciousness.

Pop art owes much to the Dadaist movement of fifty years ago. The spirit of revolution and protest of the two movements is not quite the same, as the times and circumstances are different. Both suggest that mankind is overwhelmed by the mechanisms of its own creation. In the earlier period artists held up to ridicule the accouterments and conventions of society with an emotionalism that was intense. The pop artist does somewhat the same, but intense feeling is neutralized or absent and cynical acceptance takes its place. The symbolism and content are similar, but the purpose of the statement is different. The use of common found objects as materials from which the visual statement is manufactured is almost interchangeable from one style to the other.

1-10
James Rosenquist.
World's Fair Mural.
1964. Oil on Masonite.
University of Minnesota Gallery,
Minneapolis.

1-11
Claes Oldenburg.
Falling Shoe String Potatoes.
1965. Painted canvas and kapok.
Walker Art Center,
Minneapolis.

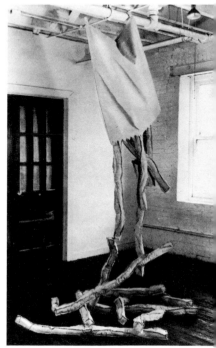

THE SEARCH FOR INTELLECTUAL PURITY

During the last few years the "freeway" of art has been congested with many styles and tendencies; some artists have taken the road that seems to lead toward an increased emphasis upon intellectualism and simplicity. Optical art, hard-edge painting, and minimal art (as it is termed by critics) exemplify this direction. Optical art — or, for short, op art — has reflected the extent to which science and technology have influenced or impinged upon our lives. The subject of this art is vision itself — visual illusions that assault, trick, fascinate, dazzle, or disturb the eye.

Many of the works of art that fall into this category remind us of color-test charts and diagrammatic illustrations of optical illusion found in textbooks on visual perception. Unlike the previously discussed styles of art, which have an aspect of the subjective and the personalized, optical art bears the stamp of formal intellectualism. It is devoid of direct social implications; subject matter is absent. The accent is upon complex, subtly repetitive patterns of line, shape, and color. It stresses mathematical order and is coldly logical without a shred of emotion — impersonalized as if it were made by a machine for other machines.

This wholly logical and nonobjective form of art does not offer much for people who feel that art should be human and deal with human activities. In it the expressions of artists are reduced to a form that could be programmed for a computer. It often gives the impression that the results can only be questioned as are the answer sheets emerging from the machine — not at all. The visual forms are often complicated and at times strangely beautiful. It is a hard-edge abstractionism. On the painted surfaces the areas are sharply defined with color that is applied evenly and smoothly. Warm- and cool-colored geometric shapes form tightly structured patterns that appear to advance and recede as they undulate across the picture plane. These compositions generate strong afterimages that intrigue the viewer, but leave him unmoved and emotionally detached.

Optical art has had forerunners in history. The "tricking of the eye" of the observer has been of serious or sometimes whimsical interest to artists at other times in the past. The designs of objects in the mosaic floors of the buildings recovered in Pompeii are so visually exact and three-dimensional in appearance that the observer is tempted to reach down and pick them up. Arches and vaulted entranceways, very narrow in actual depth, were made with structural distortions that give them the appearance of greater monumentality and thickness. There are examples of landscape drawings that change into a series of portraits when held up and viewed from the correct angle. Architectural elements — niches, windows, pilasters, and columns — were painted rather than constructed and gave the illusion of depth and volume. Paintings were planned with distortions and foreshortened perspective that could be adjusted to normality when the viewer observed the works through a carefully located peephole. Holbein's *The Ambassadors* offers this kind of distortion, and Dali's *Disappearing Bust of Voltaire* is an example of optical illusion in figurative painting.

Art with an emphasis upon mathematical order and proportionate relationships has been with us in its present form for at least fifty years.

1-12

1-13

1-14

1-12
Moiré pattern: overlay of converging circles.

1-13
Moiré pattern: overlay of perspective squares.

1-14
Moiré pattern: overlay of converging circles and perspective squares.

From the time of Aristotle, who wrote that "the chief forms of beauty are order and symmetry and precision," artists have tried to relate art to mathematics in order to obtain ideal proportions. When we consider the covers used on *Scientific American* magazine, there is little doubt about the close contact between optical art and modern science [3] (Figs. 1-12 – 1-14).

---

[3] See **Scientific American**: November, 1958; February, November, 1959; April, 1960; August, 1962; May, October, 1963. For an article by Gerald Aster and Yasunori Nishijima, "Moire Patterns," see vol. 208, no. 5 (May, 1963), pp. 54-63.

1-15
Josef Albers.
Homage to the Square: Ascending.
Whitney Museum of American Art,
New York.

The French impressionists and postimpressionists, including Monet, Manet, and later Seurat, employed a theory of optics as they painted. Their broken brushstrokes of color were resolved by the eyes of the spectator and gave their paintings a flickering quality of light and atmosphere. Josef Albers, a pioneer in the investigation of perception of color, and Victor Vasarely are given credit for initiating the optical art movement in our time (Figs. 1-15, 1-16).

Abstract expressionism and pop art have a character that is more organic and fluid in contrast to the more geometric organizations of the optical artist and the painters who prefer simplified hard-edged geometric forms. Since 1960 many sculptors have shown a preference for "primary constructions," and their art expression has been restricted to arrangements of cubes, rectangular solids, cylinders, and the like. These two types of contrasting art, the organic and the geometric, have appeared and persisted throughout history.[4]

Geometric art, by whatever special name it is called, is not entirely for

[4] See Herbert Read, **The Meaning of Art**, first published in 1931, but more recently by Penguin Books, Baltimore, 1964, p. 59.

1-16
Georges Seurat.
Sunday Afternoon on the Island
of La Grande Jatte.
Art Institute of Chicago.

optical illusion. Many of its practitioners are making the formal design elements the subject matter of art, in contrast with the abstract expressionist, who makes the act of painting the subject matter of his works. Richard Anuszkiewicz, Bridget Riley, Frank Stella, John Goodyear, Kenneth Noland, and Ad Reinhardt stress minimal simplicity and geometricity as the basis of their expressions (Figs. 1-17, 1-18). They are searching for a new classicism by using pure and precise techniques with the formal elements of color and shape, line, etc., as the subject matter of their work. This search for the essence or the minimum can be seen in painting and sculpture. Kazimir Malevich (his *White on White* series was executed in 1918) and the *Black on Black* canvases of Alexander Rodchenko employed the same devices that Ad Reinhardt used thirty years later in his series of black paintings. Subtle variations of tone appeared to the viewer who was willing to take time to contemplate the canvases. Barnett Newman also deals with nearly monochromatic art; his *Stations of the Cross* are representative of this monotonal character in painting. Other artists, although

1-17
Frank Stella.
Sketch: Les Indes Galantes.
1962. Walker Art Center,
Minneapolis.

1-18
Ad Reinhardt.
Abstract Painting Red.
1963. Woodward Foundation,
Washington, D.C.

not restricted to a single tone or color, have limited their images to extremely simplified color combinations and geometric shapes.

Since the early days of Greek philosophy there has been an attempt to find the ideal of art in a geometric law of harmony and proportion such as the golden section, which has reappeared in history in the art creations of many periods and of many places. The square is considered by many as an example of perfect harmony. As examples of this search for an "absolute," we have the paintings of Albers and Stella and the work of the sculptors Donald Judd, Tony Smith, Eduardo Paolozzi, Anthony Caro, George Sugarman, John McCracken, as well as many others (Figs. 1-19, 1-20). We find support for this concentration upon the austerity of simple and neatly edged shapes in sculpture and upon luminous flat bands of cool colors contrasted with bright colors in the point of view expressed by the 1913 suprematist movement. This group stated that "the proper means for the artist is the one that provides the fullest expression of pure feeling and ignores the habitually accepted object. The object in itself is meaningless for him and the ideas of the conscious mind are worthless. Feeling is the decisive factor and thus art arrives at non-objective representation."

1-19
*Eduardo Paolozzi. Silk.
1965. Chrome-plated steel.
Walker Art Center,
Minneapolis.*

1-20
*George Sugarman. Yellow Top.
1960. Polychrome laminated wood.
Walker Art Center, Minneapolis.*

THE ART OF REAL TIME AND REAL MOTION

As the nations of the world have become more developed through the application of science and technology, the people of these nations have become more concerned about time and movement. It is therefore quite natural that artists in the twentieth century should have expressed this concern for time and motion in their products. Kinetic art has been based upon the use of *real* time and *tangible* motion, not the suggestion of these two elements as they were previously presented in works of art. The revolutionary forms of this art of motion rest upon the following statement:[5]

> *We renounce the thousand-year old illusion in art that held the static rhythms as the only elements of the classic and pictorial art. We affirm in these arts a new element, the kinetic rhythms as the basic forms of our perception of real time.*

---

[5] Principle no. 5 of the **Realist Manifesto**, published in Moscow in 1920 by the brothers Naum Gabo and Antoine Pevsner.

Alexander Calder.
International Mobile. *1949.*
Museum of Fine Arts, Houston.

Compare the mass and stability
of Octopus with the light, airy
movement of International Mobile.
Alexander Calder, Octopus.
1965. Walker Art Center,
Minneapolis.

During the early part of the twentieth century there were many artists who were concerned with movement as a design tool. The futurist painters and sculptors, including Balla, Severini, Carrà, and Boccioni, created works in which the illusion of movement was obtained. Marcel Duchamp placed a bicycle wheel on a stool as a work of art and entitled it *Mobile* (1913). Tatlin's model for a huge tower created as a monument to the Third International was made in 1920. This huge structure of steel and glass was to have a cylinder rotating once a year, a cone once a month, and a cube once a day. In 1930 Moholy-Nagy built his *Light Machine*, which integrated light and complex movement. Alexander Calder developed his air-driven mobiles in the 1930s (Figs. 1-21, 1-22). The abstract expressionists through the vast size of their canvases gave the feeling that their paintings were to be seen as a continuing experience over a span of time. Kinetic art goes beyond implied time-motion into the realm of real time and motion.

The painting *Hockey Players* (Fig. 1-23) is an example of a work in which time and motion are implied; the illusion of an energetic action is there and can be taken in by the viewer. However, the viewer must transpose the illusion of movement into a reality. In kinetic art, motion is a real, tangible entity, and the mental effort of translation is not required.

In keeping with the dominant characteristics of the way they perceived the present period of history, and using the tools and knowledges of its technological advances, a number of individuals have been exploring the

1-23
Reid Hastie. Hockey Players.
1967. Collection of Daniel Cragg.

1-25

1-24

1-26

1-24
Yaacov Agam. Composition. 1961. Walker Art Center, Minneapolis.

1-25–1-26
Charles Huntington. Boob Tube.

potentialities of kinetic art. Their investigations have taken place in six general directions.[6]

1. *Optical phenomena* in which apparent or actual movement of the object or movement of the observer produces an intense sensation of change and motion.[7]

2. *Transformations*, where rapid movement seems to dematerialize an object, or where movement of the object or of the observer can bring about a marked change in its appearance (Fig. 1-24).[8]

These first two categories of kinetic art are essentially the same as those which has been discussed under optical art.

3. *Movable works* which encourage the observer to alter or rearrange the painting or sculpture. The sculpture *Boob Tube* illustrates this invitation

[6] George Rickey, **The Morphology of Movement: A Study of Kinetic Art**, in Gyorgy Kepes (ed.), *The Nature and Art of Motion*, George Braziller, Inc., New York, 1965, pp. 61–115. See also Katherine Kuh, **Recent Kinetic Art**, in *ibid*., pp. 116–127.
[7] See Heinz Mack's *Light Rotor*, Bridget Riley's *Twist*, and Yvaral's *Instabilité*.
[8] An example is the polyphonic painting of Yaacov Agam. Executed on a single corrugated surface, it shows a succession of distinctly different compositions as the observer moves.

to the viewer. He is invited to open the hinged section to see what happens inside. By this simple act, a completely distinct visual experience has been provided — the spectator has rearranged the sculpture (Figs. 1-25, 1-26).[9]

4. *Machines* which are motorized and equipped with gears, camshafts, cranks, and levers that push and pull, lift and turn (Fig. 1-27).[10]

5. *Movement itself*, with economy of means and with self-effacing mechanics.[11]

6. *Lightplay dependent upon movement* of either the light source or the viewer (Fig. 1-28).[12]

1-27
Duraluminum, motorized and electronically controlled.
Nicholas Schöffer. Chronos 5. 1962. Jewish Museum, New York.

1-28
Chryssa. Times Square Sky. 1962. Neon and aluminum. Walker Art Center, Minneapolis.

---

[9] See also Yashide Kobashi's *Plumbob IV* (the spectator can raise or lower ceramic balls suspended on nylon cords over pulleys in a large box)· the rearrangeable sculptures of Taliman, Munari, and Mara; or the painting *Tangential Excentric* by Karl Gerstner.
[10] The works of Jean Tinguely and Pol Bury, and *Nine Spheres in a Column* by Bruno Munari.
[11] Alexander Calder's classic mobiles, José de Rivera's rotating loops and Len Lye's rotating fountains and forests of steel rods are examples of the work of artists who design with "movement itself," rather than by using motion as an incidental accessory.
[12] Examples are *Light Forest* by Gunther Vecker, *Continuella Luminie're* by Julio Le Parc, and *Great Pulsating Surface* by Gianni Colombo.

The use of light as a medium has had a great deal of development and promotion in the 1960s and is considered by many as an independent art movement. The early researches with light by Moholy-Nagy have been vastly expanded in recent years as luminal art forms have gained prominence. Incandescent light, tubes and coils of colored fluorescent lights, projected, reflected, and programmed sequences of light and filmstrips have been coordinated as technology has become the tool for the invention of optical and kinetic creations. In this age of technology, the artist has become a technician and has used many of the devices provided by the scientists for his visual statements. Shapes and colors are created with corrugated glass, polarized film, and rotating disks.

This kinetic art form is sometimes dependent upon the chance "involvement" of an audience, or relies upon the power of a motor to make the parts of a machine dangle, sway, and jiggle. In addition there are projected beams of light thrown upon moving surfaces, steel ribbons that move in magnetic fields, miniature sculptures with coiled springs that vibrate and swinging latticework, swaying rods, prism projections, and polarized-light and water sculpture. These are some of the media and experimental tools that are being explored and exploited.

THE ISSUE OF AESTHETIC VALUES

This review of current trends has shown how far the artist has gone in his search for images. The variety of expressions produced by artists in a short period of time has filled many people with excitement and satisfaction. They feel that they are part of a "golden age" in which creativity is recognized, nurtured, and valued. Others are more reserved in their enthusiasm and with sincerity are trying to sort out novelty from innovation and temporary facts from lasting visual statements of aesthetic merit.

There is difficulty in determining a set of universal aesthetic principles against which this diverse stream of expression in the art of today may be given a sense of unity and order. It has come about as the artist has gained independence. Liberation of the artist came with the advent of impressionism just before the start of the twentieth century. As the older rules were disregarded, the artist was permitted great liberty and was able to do what he wanted to do; yet this freedom required him to re-create an entire language. He gained his freedom but lost in the way of order. Other ages, other times and peoples — the Egyptians, the Greeks, and the Romans — all had their artistic order and standards. All of their artistic productions were subject to a set of rules. Their canon was inescapable because their sense of beauty was by definition contained in those rules.[13]

At present, artists alone or in groups have been taking advantage of the absence of any precise set of rules for measuring the quality of their productions. Some even feel that a product of their endeavors is and should be recognized by the critical viewer as art *because they intended it to be art.* Others argue that the work in question is good because by loose defi-

---

[13] Picasso expressed somewhat the same idea in Françoise Gilot and Carlton Lake, **Life with Picasso**, McGraw-Hill Book Company, New York, 1964, pp. 174–175.

nition it fitted into the currently popular category, trend, or tendency. This sort of reasoning, even with the individual freedom granted to the contemporary artist, bears little or no relationship to the realities of the situation. Quality still depends upon the individual artist and the merits of his product, not upon the style or tendency in which his product belongs. General styles do exist and means of evaluation also exist. There can be good or bad painting, sculpture, and crafts in any style based upon judgment consistent with the limits and intentions of a particular movement.[14] The problem of making value judgments about the quality of a work of art is one which confronts artists, critics, students, and laymen alike.

1-29
Abraham Isitshit. Medal of Honor.
St. Paul Art Center.

THE "Medal of Honor" EPISODE

This extremely personal account of an experience with judging works of art, as a member of a jury for a major national exbition,[15] is presented in order to dramatize the problem. It shows clearly the sort of personal philosophies and values that come into conflict even when the participants have national recognition for their personal accomplishments as producers of art in the fields that are being considered. The area for judgment was crafts. Although this situation might be extreme, the same events have happened and may occur again when judging exhibitions of painting or sculpture. The report follows:

Needless to say, it was an honor to be selected as a juror for this exhibition and the coming event was looked forward to with great anticipation. Here was an opportunity to view thousands of objects done by America's finest craftsmen. I was excited by the prospect of a vital exchange of ideas with my fellow jurors; it was an opportunity to stretch the barriers of one's own mind.

Since there were four jurors any decision on a two-to-two deadlock was awarded to the expert in the field under consideration. After being outvoted on a particular wall hanging, which for me had no apparent artistic justification for the inclusion of a wide variety of objects and which was so poorly fabricated that it was virtually falling apart, I made the mistake of asking my colleagues to justify their choice. This brought an immediate outburst, "What's there to talk about, you gotta' feel it in your guts, or it doesn't have it!"

During the rest of the day we completed the fiber section. One jury member preferred to judge most fabrics from the reverse side because "they were more exciting that way." Any attempts on my part to question function, craftsmanship or design were rejected.

We (the jury) selected wall hangings of loose burlap with marbles woven into the fabric (of course they fell out), conglomerations of leather, raffia, tinsel, old clothes, etc. — anything bizarre — and few things serving an honest function, done with restraint and using an intellectual subtlety of color and texture.

The judging of pottery added to my confusion. It seemed to go according to the rule that "if it's been done before — it's not any good!" This automatically ruled out most functional wheel-thrown pots because of their general similarity. What was left

14 James Schinneller, **Art: Its Present Condition**, *Art Education*, 64th Yearbook, National Society for the Study of Education, University of Chicago Press, Chicago, 1965, p. 19.
15 Fiber, Clay and Metal (1964), The Seventh Biennial Craft Exhibition, sponsored by the St. Paul (Minnesota) Art Center.

were dropped pots put back together — and other Medusa-like constructions of pots and dropped pots. Occasionally a symmetrical pot was accepted, but only if it was the background for a totally unrelated glaze painting. It was explained to me that "pornography on pots was good because it was a satire on the whole competition."

On the last day we were to jury metal — my area. The events of the previous two days seemed like a nightmare. The situation was discussed with my family the last night. They sensed that I was greatly upset and were sympathetic listeners. As the experiences of the day were related, it occurred to us that perhaps we could shock this jury back "to reality" by some ridiculous joke. We hit upon the idea of creating a monstrous piece of jewelry for this purpose. We swung into action with gusto, beginning with the outer shell of an old rusted fly-fishing reel. My sons began donating their prize possessions for the lark. A homemade sheriff's badge was placed in the center of the reel, an imitation cameo was clamped to the star, rough turquoises were crudely bound on with iron binding wire, and other dime-store trinkets were dangled from the base. This was suspended from a crude "dog chain" that my six-year-old son had handcrafted some years before and which had decorated the scarecrow in our raspberry patch until this fateful night. The "thing" was tagged with an official entry blank and entitled "Medal of Honor" (Fig. 1-29), and attributed to the artistry of the fictitious Abraham Isitshit. It was so absurd that we laughed until the tears flowed.

I could visualize the scene on the following day when someone would discover it and begin laughing — showing it to everyone as a big joke! Then, I would agree with them and after our big laugh could begin the serious business of drawing a parallel between this piece of junk and the other "junk" that we had been accepting for the show. What could better prove the point? Then, I hoped that we would return to work inclined to use our intellect as well as emotion in making decisions.

There was no problem slipping my "entry" among the other work the next morning. When the jury arrived we began circulating among the work preparatory to judging. After a bit of browsing, my creation was discovered. Someone held up the pendant for all to see — I was choking with mirth and only hoped that the craftsman could remain anonymous until the situation could be thoroughly enjoyed. But! They liked it! "It turned them on." However, to her everlasting credit, one jury member, although conceding that it would "wear well," remained somewhat skeptical.

When I had regained my composure and saw that my little joke was being taken seriously, I decided to see how far it would go. The gallery staff was rather perturbed because the master entry blank could not be found and there was no record of the entry fee. We were told that it could be judged with the other objects, but if it was found to be a fraud the gallery was not obligated to display it.

When the "Medal of Honor" was considered by the jury it was hailed as a "delightful satire" and a valuable expression in terms of the pop art movement.

The rest is history. Needless to say this was a most controversial show. After coverage in *Craft Horizons*, using a half-page illustration of the "Medal of Honor," the controversy raged through letters to the editor for months.

The "Medal of Honor" was perhaps the first piece of pop art jewelry to receive wide recognition unless the earlier works of Salvador Dali are classified as such. During ensuing discussions with artists and art critics, those who were fascinated by its brazen statement defended it stoutly against my protests that it was but worthless tripe — their argument being that I was a victim of my own talent and incapable of doing something worthless. This was not only amusing, but highly speculative as well. However, operating upon their thesis of infallible talent . . . it should be pointed out that the "Medal of Honor" was a completely conscious repudiation of everything that I believe in. It was a hoax that failed.

IMPLICATIONS AND QUESTIONS

This "inside story" takes its place in the long line of similar ventures in the history of art that have plagued the critics and added to the doubts of the public about the validity of art when even the juries of artists and critics can be confounded and fooled. It increases the suspicions of the "man in the street," coming at a time when reams of publicity are given to accounts which hail monkeys and earthworms as painters and when Brillo boxes and sculptured hamburgers are enshrined in galleries of art.

From the "Medal of Honor" incident, we can see that experienced individuals who had become more or less confident and sophisticated judges through their experiences with the production of art still had serious disagreements among themselves about the merits of an art product. Their solutions of their own art problems as producers were made through a continuous process of making judgments, intuitively, or by logical analysis or some other means, regarding the relative "rightness" of alternative courses of action. They were experienced in judging, yet there was a fundamental conflict, to say the least, among the members of the jury in their personal philosophies and theories of the nature of art and its place in human affairs.

A CONFLICT OF PHILOSOPHIES

In retrospect It would seem that the situation that spawned the "Medal of Honor" episode could be reduced to a conflict between personal philosophies of art with the concept of *art as emotion and feeling* [16] on the one hand, and of *art as experience* (intelligence plus emotions)[17] on the other.

The following excerpt from an article on the show by the weaver-juror illustrates an extension of the philosophy of art as emotion and feeling as it is applied to the judgment of art:[18]

> You either do or you don't get the idea. I cannot speak for any other member of the jury, but for myself; I LOOK AT THINGS WITH MY INSIDES — and that is all there is to it!

By contrast another juror made this statement to explain his action:

> Art is the ordering of elements in one's environment through an *intellectual* and *emotional* process. It is a process of selection and rejection . . . modification and accentuation of these elements for the purpose of expressing an idea or feeling. Is it asking too much of a juror or artist to bring his intellect as well as his emotions into play when passing judgment? The production of

---

[16] This viewpoint can be found in the writings of Freud and Conant and can be noted in the expositions of the ideas of Santayana, Russell, and others.

[17] This is in accord with the general ideas of Dewey, Edman, and others who have written about the function of arts in education, such as Broudy, Counts, and Munro. These men believed that art as the aesthetic dimension of experience is a facet of intelligence and as such is subject to cultivation and ethical assessments.

[18] Dorian Zachai, **Fiber-Clay-Metal**, *Craft Horizons*, vol. 25, no. 1 (January–February, 1965), p. 17.

art is a thinking process. Each step along the way has many alternate routes and judgments must be made constantly. Gradually certain criteria are set up by the individual which guide and aid in the selection of the precise response required for the intended effect. This is the basis of self-criticism without which an artist cannot develop. Those who do not develop this ability for self criticism join the legions of perpetual students who must always work under the direct supervision of an instructor.

In order to teach art and design, it is necessary to communicate to students how certain effects can be achieved ... point out relationships between ideas, materials and techniques. Criticism of their work must be done in terms of specific relationships and should certainly not be a flat approval or complete condemnation. When there is no attempt or willingness to discuss the problems involved, judgment has been made only on the superficial whim of the moment.

These and other philosophic bases are relied upon to construct, support, and explain our actions in producing and evaluating a work of art. There are also inconsistencies and somewhat irreconcilable differences among the basic philosophies as can be seen from our example. This is not a weakness peculiar to art and its area of knowledge. There are many theories advanced by psychologists as explanations of perception, personality, and all manners of things in the behavioral sciences. This situation exists to a lesser extent for some aspects of the physical sciences.

QUESTIONS OF IMPORTANCE

Our example of an experience with the judging of art has brought some fundamental questions to our attention. Some of these are:

1. What is there about art which distinguishes it from the random or arbitrary actions of man (and other animals)?
2. What is or should be involved in the process of making art judgments?
3. What characterizes the art process (what does an artist do and how does he do it)?
4. How does an understanding of the art process, of the creative process in general, and of aesthetic theory aid us to produce and appreciate art (and to help others as teachers)?

It is to these questions that the remainder of this book is directed.

A DEFINITION: WHAT DOES AN ARTIST DO?

Some of the best examples of how the concise meaning of an extremely complex interrelationship may be put down in symbol form are to be found in scientific writing. The essence of Albert Einstein's theory of relativity was given in the now historic formula $E = MC^2$. Thousands of scientists have tested this; millions of words have been written to explain, clarify, and expand the applications and implications of this brief statement of a theory. Countless man-hours of scientific expertise and of technical skill have been expended upon endeavors that have been released through insights gained from the view of the interrelationships of nature's forces embodied in this theory. What does this have to do with art and the artist? Simply that as Einstein took a number of seemingly unrelated elements and brought them together into a scientifically satisfying unity, the work of the artist, at its best, brings together a number of seemingly unrelated elements into an aesthetically satisfying unity. Einstein's example suggests that it would be profitable for us to look for factors or elements that all art and all artists have in common — the relationships rather than the differences. Since we call what these men do art and, despite all their differences, we call them artists, there must be something about them, their actions, and their products that is the same. They must have something in common. It is to this common denominator that attention is directed.

On the first page of this text there was a definition of art and the artist. We would like to expand this into the following:

The artist looks at his world deeply and sensitively, and he abstracts, or takes out, from this seeing of his world that which he feels is important (the essence, meaning, and significance it has for him). Then, through the tools of his craft, he gives concrete physical form to his perceptive vision so that others can take out — see, feel, and understand — that which he has formed.

Like its predecessor, this is a deceptively simple statement, until we start at the beginning and take it apart. Consider the phrase "looks at his world." Looking, or seeing, means sensing plus selecting plus perceiving, and perceiving involves the associations of all of our accumulated memories in order to gain some meaning from new sensations. The definition spreads out when "world" can be anything and everything, from the outer reaches of space to the inner reaches of the microcosm of a single man.

With the next part of the action, "he abstracts, or takes out, that which is significant," we become engaged with the complex process in art known as abstraction. When the phrase "with the tools of his craft" comes under examination, we find that we are not talking only about hammers and brushes. The artist's tools include not only all of the media and the process through which they are shaped, but also the design elements and the principles for their structural organization as the work of art is formed.

Finally, there is the evaluation and appreciation by other people of what the artist has created. The validity of his solution is given its most critical test when others look at it and are able to apprehend its significance. Thus we have made a full circle from the artist looking at his world to the viewer looking at the artist's expression of his perceptions. In our original definition we have brought together the two streams of knowledge in the field of art — the one leading to the production of a work of art, the other to the appreciation of art.

The ideas that are presented on the following pages of this book have been organized according to the stages in this definition of the art process, which begins with how an artist looks at his world and culminates with how others look at, judge, and appreciate his products as works of art.

Chapter 2

THE ARTIST LOOKS AT HIS WORLD

Let us go along with an artist as he looks at a small segment of his world and follow him through his own words and with the photographs he has taken.

A BIG VIEW OF A SMALL WORLD

I live and work in a studio-home located in an isolated valley near Jordan, Minnesota. This is a quiet farming community forty miles southwest of the Twin Cities (St. Paul-Minneapolis). The surrounding landscape is hardly spectacular, but within a few yards from my back door is to be found, by looking closely, all of the drama and the pattern of order of nature at work — of living, growing, and dying. Here is all of the quiet excitement, a striving to find a place to live and grow in the sun, wind, and snow.

I stepped out my back door and looked across the expanse of weeds and gardens. One patch of high weeds stood out as a lighter green from the surrounding foliage (Fig. 2-1). Although there were many weeds in this patch, it seemed to hold together as one distinct mass. The separate weeds combined to appear like a single plant; the individual stems were extremely erect and appeared more precise than the surrounding greenery (Fig. 2-2).

Moving in closer, I noticed that these plants had an overall conical shape; their leaves were largest at the base and gradually diminished in size as they mounted up the stock. Each single plant stock, square in cross section, stood like a steel rod, tapering from base to tip. Along this stock Siamese pairs of spade-shaped, deeply scalloped leaves were arched directly opposite each other like the wings

2-1
A clump of weeds.

2-2
A single plant.

2-3
Like a bird of prey.

2-4
With a mighty thrust.

2-1   2-2

2-3   2-4

of a bird of prey (Fig. 2-3). As the leaf pairs moved upward, they were rotated ninety degrees from one another as they ascended toward the top.

Each leaf had no separate stem, but flowed out from the main stock, so tightly held that the shaft appeared to pierce each pair of leaves with a mighty thrust (Fig. 2-4). The pocket formed by leaves and stem dropped moisture gathered from the wide, sloping leaf surfaces. Although the leaf-to-stock relationship was a formal design (each leaf being directly opposite its partner), the lateral leaf veins had a staggered, or alternating, pattern.

When seen from beneath, the main leaf veins were a heavy riblike structure supporting the more fragile skin (Fig. 2-5). The translucent capillary system leading from the veins divided the enclosed leaf areas into irregular but related blocks much like the patterns of cracks in sun-dried mud.

Viewed against sunlight the leaf revealed an infinite variation of form — each a modified miniature of the preceding theme (Fig. 2-6). Perhaps this rhythmic pattern is continued into the microscopic structure. The leaves had a rough, coarse feeling. Their surface was covered with sharp hairlike fuzz.

The stalk shaft was crowned with pairs of buds bursting from the deep well formed by shaft and leaf (Fig. 2-7). Each pair of buds was again at right angles to the other, following the same sequence that marked the leaves emerging from the stock. The bud sheath was tightly rolled, yet covered the petals, giving the appearance of an eminent explosion (Fig. 2-8). The few open blossoms were yellow-orange with slim, irregular, radial thrusting petals (Fig. 2-9). Each blossom had an inner core surrounded by a ring of stamenlike rows of pins with their heads up. The heavy massive base beneath each of the blossoms was remindful of an upside-down hat crown (Fig. 2-10).

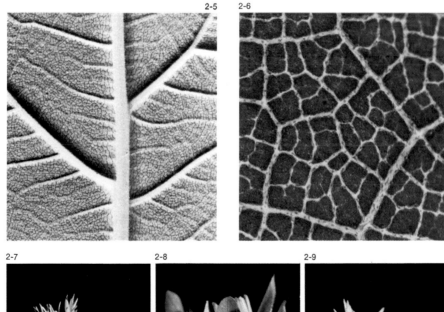

2-5
2-6

2-5
When seen from beneath.

2-6
Patterns revealed by sunlight.

2-7
Shaft crowned with buds.

2-8
A tightly rolled bud.

2-9
Explosion.

2-10
Radiating petals.

2-7

2-8

2-9

2-10

AN ANALYSIS OF THE PERCEPTUAL ACTION

This is a descriptive record of an artist looking at and really seeing with meaning a fragment of the world which is within the experience of most adults and children in our culture. The same experience could be duplicated by human beings elsewhere, with slight differences in the subject matter of flora and fauna. This is far removed from the laboratory situation in which the researcher limits the visual field of the subject to a single variable of sensory data. Here we have a situation of great complexity, with an array of sensory stimuli acting upon the artist-observer simultaneously as is the case in the usual situations encountered in everyday life. Note that our artist was at first confronted with the total configuration of this slice of the universe. Then, by selection he narrowed his field of focus to a group of wild flowers, a spray of wild grasses, a bunch of weeds and seedpods. He then moved to a single object which commanded his attentive interest. He made this one flower or weed the whole unit of his interest. He filled in the gaps in his knowledge of the relationship of the parts that make up this unit of nature — the petals to other petals, then the flower to its stem and leaves until a new whole was organized. From these cycles of sensory data, gradually decreasing in scope — from a whole backyard to a group of wild flowers, to a single wild flower, to a pattern of petals radiating from a center or leaves branching from an axial stem — the observer obtained an understanding of the meaning of the structural principles of growth which occur repeatedly in nature and in the design of art. Figures 2-1 through 2-10 show this sequence of perceptive analysis in which the "whole character" of each focus area is maintained as the artist moves from looking at the backyard to looking at a single flower. He has moved from the general to the particular until he has obtained a unit of information which he can absorb fully.

From the psychologist we receive an explanation of perceptive activity similar to that of the artist as he looked at his backyard. Allport, in a discussion of the various classes of perceptual phenomena, concludes: "These facts show that perception proceeds by interrelationships within definite wholes, one part affecting other parts. Nothing ever occurs by itself; *and a whole 'character' is formed by the ensemble that cannot be experienced in the parts when they are perceived separately.*"[1]

In our description of an "experience in seeing" we have also tried to emphasize that the artist's perception was from the whole to the parts. Each part in turn became a new whole in which each new assortment of elements was seen in relationship to other parts, to form a unified structure. The unity of organization of the whole structure of the landscape was established. It was a penetration layer by layer with appropriate meaning. The essence of the interrelationship of many diverse and seemingly independent elements was held constant.

In the confines of his backyard, the artist or any other individual has available for his inspection most of the design organizations and structural patterns found in nature. These can be found in plants, insects, animals,

---

[1] Floyd H. Allport, **Theories of Perception and the Concept of Structure**, 6th printing, John Wiley and Sons, Inc., New York, 1965, pp. 62–63 (italics supplied).

rocks, and water. In the ways these are formed, grow, move, and change can be discovered examples of all the design principles and elements which he will use in his art. In the course of a lifetime packed with similar meaningful contacts with things and events made by man and by nature, he will gather a storehouse of raw materials for his use. They are readily available to him for abstracting, contemplating, reasoning, remembering, and shaping and for all his other "actings" as a person and an artist.

There are many parallels to be found between the structure of natural growth and that of art. In nature we discover that some things grow by expanding out from a central core (Fig. 2-11); in art there are compositions that radiate from a centered unit. When planning a design, artists will occasionally connect small units to an axis in much the same way that leaves or branches are connected to the main stem of the plant (Fig. 2-12). The spiral occurs in both artistic and natural forms (Fig. 2-13). Geo-

2-11
Razor coral: radial growth.

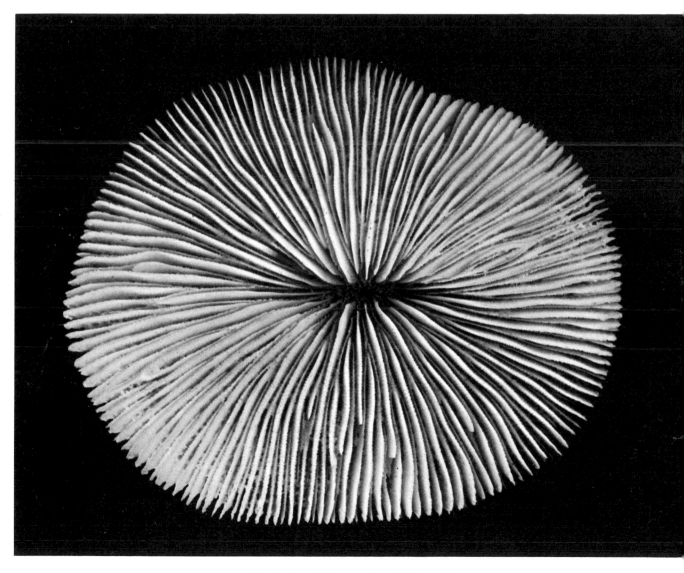

2-12   2-14   2-15

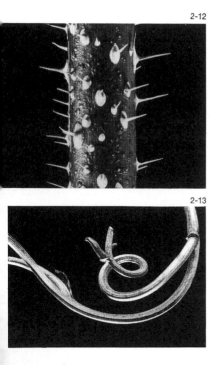

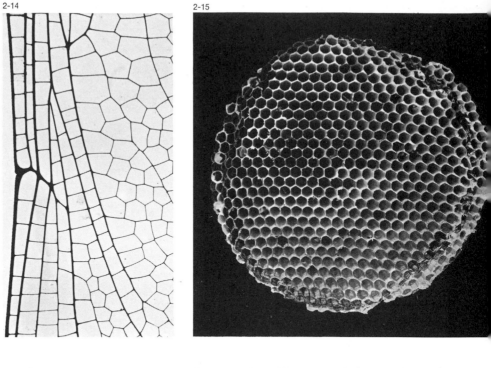

2-12
Rose stem: axial growth.

2-13
Plant form: spiral growth.

2-14
Dragonfly wing: geometric
progression in growth.

2-15
Hornet's nest: modular growth.

metric progressions are to be discovered in biology, painting, and archi-tecture (Fig. 2-14). Nature and art often depend upon modularity for the creation of a unified whole; the repeated addition of small identical basic units make up the organization of a very large whole structure (Fig. 2-15). Awareness of this structural relatedness adds a new dimension for the viewer of art and nature.

THE ACT OF SEEING

Huxley[2] has simplified the definition of the act of seeing to equal *sensing* plus *selecting* plus *perceiving*. He noted that with adults the three phases occurred, for all practical purposes, simultaneously. There are some dif-ferences among individuals in their eyes and nervous systems, which do the sensing; however, the greatest differences will occur in our selecting and perceiving faculties.

Selecting is the process of discriminating or focusing more intensely upon one part of the total visual field. It utilizes the physiological functions which allow the eye to record its clearest images at the central point of the retina. The individual, by his own decision and in his own interest, tends to discriminate something in the visual field more clearly than any of the other elements in this field (Figs. 2-16 – 2-18). When we say, in a somewhat oversimplified way, that "people only see what they want to see," we are going back to this aspect of seeing which allows the individual to select

2 Aldous L. Huxley, **The Art of Seeing**, Harper and Brothers, New York, 1942, pp. 41–51.

2-16
Seedpods isolated from background.
Selection from the visual field.

2-17
Seedpods lost in background.
Selection from the visual field.

2-18
A unified composition formed by selective framing with a camera.
Section of a flute.

2-18

out of the total visual field those elements that he deems important in his own personal interest.

Perceiving is the mental process — an activity of the mind intermediate between sensation and thought. It gives meaning and significance to a sensation. As a cognitive process, perception involves a stimulating object or event, an attentive adjustment (set), and the arousal of some degree of meaning. Through this process the individual apprehends the significance of an object or event for some act or adjustment. The perception is made of a "whole," and it occurs immediately and unanalytically. In visual perception the object or event is sensed in accordance with the structure of the eye; it is given meaning and significance in accordance with the existing fund of knowledge which is stored in the memory of the individual. Memory includes all of a person's previously experienced sensations to which he has given meaning. Because of differences in the memory of one individual as compared to that of another, the same phenomena — a wild flower, a painting, or a piece of sculpture — may be perceived by two people in a somewhat different way. This happens because the information which he receives directly through the senses accounts for only a part, and perhaps the lesser part, of the way the world appears.

DEVELOPMENT OF AWARENESS

Recently the importance of the development of perceptual awareness has been given more emphasis as a key to full involvement of the individual with nature and art. Awareness consists of much more than casual observation of objects and incidents, although taking in the visual sensations

2-19
Milkweed pod.

of the environment is a starting point. It means regarding with attention in order to see the familiar with clearer eyes. It is observation through which the eye is aided by the mind to see how a thing is made and the pattern of its design. This kind of awareness brings a deep sensitivity to our physical world and its ongoing events. It adds to our fund of knowledge, through which our imagination is exercised and our ideas are formed. It extends to our observations of people in their environments and includes the moods and undercurrents of emotion generated by the interlocking relationships they have with each other in various environmental settings — man with nature and man with man. Thus by using insight and memory our understanding of the structure of the object or event is opened up to reveal its pattern of order and the cause-and-effect relationship of the parts to the whole of it. We can then move from a passive to an active involvement. Consciously, by putting our imagination to work, we can manipulate or transpose the object or event. We can change its content and see it against other backgrounds and in other relationships and conditions of environment.

When the designer of jewelry observes a milkweed pod, he is aware of more than a drying, drab, gray shape. He is aware of the overall form, of the gently swelling curves and the dynamically changing thrust from the rounded mass to the tapering end which turns upward. He sees the texture change from a pronounced roughness to a smoother surface. He looks for the attachment of the pod to the main stem, along with the others of its own kind. From previous experience he knows that in the tensions caused by drying the pod will burst, breaking open and forcing the light, feathery seeds up into the air, where they are caught by the wind and carried along to another place as the cycle of life in nature moves on. In his imagination he slices the pod open, replaces the material of the shell with silver and its center with a semiprecious stone, and it becomes a pendant. In this manner the cycle of art moves on from the awareness of nature to a form in precious metal. (Figs. 2-19 – 2-22).

The painter follows the same road, but his imaginative manipulations of the seedpod are transferred from metal to pigment, his tools from saw and torch to brush and palette knife. His participation with the sight of the pod, as he watches it dry in the sun, leads from the surging shapes seen against the blue sky to pigmented patterns of curving wedge shapes interwoven with symbols of the earth and sky. Casualness is gone, and his observation takes on depth and meaning.

AWARENESS AND VISION

So that the reader may understand its reason and purpose and derive much meaning from the material on perception and awareness, whether it be related to reports of scientific investigations or to the way an artist sees his world, some explanation is necessary. Let us start with the assumption that knowledge of how and why we see as we do under the practical conditions of everyday life is useful and interesting knowledge to have. We then proceed a step further and suggest that visual training is possible. All of us can improve our understanding of the environment and our ability to respond to it effectively. In addition, this knowledge of perception and the training of vision based on this knowledge can make a difference in our production of art and our appreciation of it.

Practical vision. A distinction can be made among the different levels of intensity of vision as these are exemplified by different individuals under different conditions. We can start with that kind of seeing which is generally practiced by all people and which is necessary for their survival. It is this very "practical" kind of vision which is necessary for the identification of objects and for decision concerning relevant actions in response to this identification. Through association with prior learning from all previous experience, objects and events are given names or labels, are placed in categories, or are otherwise classified and stored away in our memory. This is the kind of visual perception that has had the broadest

2-20
Pendant with agate. Pod.

2-21
Pendant with jade. Twin Pod.

2-22
Pendant. Hollow Pod.

2-20

2-21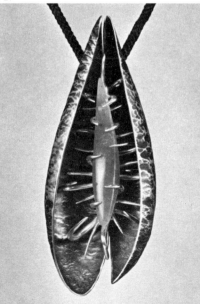

2-22

interest for researchers, and to a large extent the studies that they have made relate to this level of vision. It is this practical vision that we employ most of the time in day-by-day living.

Curious vision. There are times when an adult or child will single out an unfamiliar object for much closer attention than he will pay to the visual stimuli which are normal and expected by him under usual conditions. This kind of vision — "curious vision" — is exercised by scientists and by specialists in many fields of endeavor. With this kind of vision they look at objects with more thoroughness and with keener interest in detail.

For practical vision "a rose is a rose," yet the variety of coloring in flowers of the same species and the shapes and sizes of their petals are infinitely different. Smudges spotting the surface of the wall or table are seen by the housewife as fingerprints. To the specialist in criminology, these marks can identify one individual out of a multitude. Each of the countless snowflakes is unique. This is nature's insistence on creativity. Mechanical things from the assembly lines of industrial plants appear identical until examined under a microscope, where additional information points up the difference of one refrigerator, typewriter, or pen point from the rest of its kind.

This level of seeing, though accurate and deep in its analysis, is limited, however, to the unit or object under observation. The pattern of relationships between the unit being observed and other units in the same category, but more especially between it and other things and events, may not be seen with any degree of significance. This lack of sensitivity to interrelationships sometimes handicaps an expert in one field. For example, the archaeologist, when he examines fragments of Greek pottery, may be able to arrive at a precise dating and chronology from the markings and decorations on the fragment. His knowledge of the historical and ethnological significance may be sound and informative. At the same time, however, the artistic quality and the significance of the story this fragment tells about the cultural attainments of a people may be omitted entirely from this curious vision. Thus we have a case of depth of vision without comprehensiveness.

Imaginative vision. Advancing a step further, we come to the kind of vision used rather extensively by artists which has been called "imaginative" or "reflective" vision. It occurs when the individual is able to manipulate the object of his vision by the free play of his imagination and by recall of many associated images to the present situation. It allows the artist to add to or change the initial visual image at will; he modifies parts and adjusts relationships of elements by a free play of imagination and with the associations from his memories of past experiences. This is done in two ways, either by a process of "mental sketching" or by actual delineation on paper or in some other art medium. The need for overt action such as sketching, drawing, or note-taking varies with conditions and the customary habits of the artist.

Aesthetic vision. Of importance to both artist and the person looking at art is a less commonly developed level or kind of vision: a sort of "aesthetic," or "pure," vision. This is the stage at which the object observed is seen as a thing or experience with aesthetic worth in itself. All associations involving utility and human practicality (Figs. 2-23, 2-24) formerly given to it are disconnected, and the object is sensed for the qualities of beauty it possesses. It is at this stage that a wall of a weather-beaten frame house in the sunlight and shadow with the paint layers peeling away becomes a thing of beauty, and a billboard with its bits and pieces of old election posters, torn and splattered, is perceived as textured patterns and colored shapes. The perception is of the aesthetic qualities of form, color, texture,

2-23

2-24

2-23
Rusted boiler plate.

2-24
Pattern of concrete blocks.

2-25
Burned wall.

2-26
This composition was achieved
by burning holes in paper.
Jack Sonenberg. Of Minos.
St. Paul Art Center.

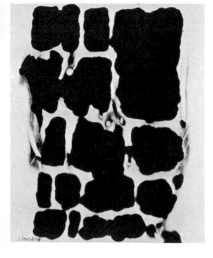

and patterns of the light falling upon the surfaces which have been weathered by nature and man (Figs. 2-25, 2-26). A piece of driftwood, the sagging door of a deserted homestead, a covered bridge — all will be seen as things of beauty rather than worthless relics.[3]

The four levels of seeing are best illustrated with reference to the object in the photograph represented in Fig. 2-27. This photograph of a chestnut burr, the protective hull that covers the seeds, is perceived by many people in a mode of practical vision. It means to them something that should be raked up and cleared away. In a practical way it is also something to remove in order to get to the chestnut itself. To the botanist, with his curious vision, the burr has an important function in the reproduction of the tree and other seeds. The artist with an imaginative vision looks at the chestnut burr and brings to his perception associations connected with its aggressive, grasping image; it might remind him of the thrust of powerful jaws, or of the claws of an earthmover, or of machines used for clearing trees and stumps from the land. He sees the harmless burr as something powerful and devouring. When we see the object in the photograph with aesthetic vision, we are mainly concerned with its shapes and the repetition of linear patterns; we are also attentive to the texture of its surfaces and the gradations of color without reference to utility.

ART AND VISUAL PERCEPTION

Like many others involved in teaching, learning, and producing art, the authors find that much of their psychological thinking, if it might be so dignified, moves out from gestalt theory. The artist and the teacher of art feel comfortable with the kind of reasoning which concludes that the value and meaning of the whole cannot be obtained by adding up the separate parts or that nature and art cannot be explained adequately by dissecting them into little bits and pieces. This accounts for the artist-producer's negative reaction to the art critic because he feels, rightly or wrongly, that the art historian-critic is too involved with the trivia of detail and misses the meaning of the whole. Gestalt theory deals principally with spatial and other configurations, that is, with only one class of phenomena in perception. However, its emphasis on organization — form, wholeness and relationships, closure and symmetry — is a major concern of the artist and the viewer of a work of art.

There have been many contributors to our knowledge of perception and to an understanding of the basis for our reactions to the world in which we live.[4] That perception of space and other visual relationships is based upon the physical properties of the eye and upon the past experience of the observer may, at first glance, seem to be of little direct assistance to the artist. Nevertheless, he faces the problem of translating his knowledge into visual form; to achieve this goal, he and his craft are inex-

---

3 Credit should be given to Ralph Pearson, who in **How to See Modern Pictures**, Dial Press, Inc., New York, 1925, pp. 29–42, establishes four categories of vision in explaining the way in which an artist analyzes his environment.
4 A summary of Allport's Event-Structure Theory can be found in Appendix 1.

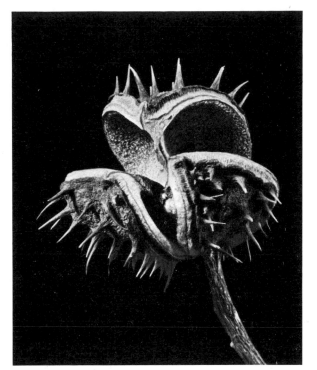

2-27
Chestnut burr.

tricably tied up with these factors of visual perception. The quantity and quality of spatial depth within the object he creates and the apprehension of these qualities by others is dependent upon the shapes, sizes, light gradients, and colors and their relationships to each other. This is the stuff of which visual perceptions are made. The artist must understand how the viewer will function while looking at art products in order to help or hinder him.

It must be granted at this point that, unlike the psychological researcher, the artist, viewer, teacher, and student are not concerned with discrete isolated contacts with simplified visual experience. They are faced with situations in which many complex, interrelated images are striking the sensitive membranes of their eyes simultaneously. These cannot be broken down easily and divided into small chunks for leisurely examination. It is understandable that the artist and layman are impatient with reports of experiments which deal with the maneuvering of a few colored disks, controlled spots of light, and simple diagrams containing one or two geometric shapes. These seem far removed from reality as they know it. However, the fragments of knowledge gained from these experiments are the starting point of our understanding of how things appear and even of why things appear as they do. This aggregate of knowledge —about what goes on inside ourselves in order to bring in a multitude of objects and events from the outside — makes possible the integration of our vision and lies at the very roots of our whole perceptual process.

In his book *Art and Visual Perception*, Arnheim covers this topic of perception most comprehensively and authoritatively from the viewpoint of art and the artist.[5] For the purposes of this writing, only those aspects of this very broad field of knowledge which are most directly relevant to the work of the artist will be discussed. As a method for organization, we will follow (roughly) the six broad classes of perceptual phenomena used by the psychologist and relate under these headings specific implications for producing and looking at art, The classes of phenomena to be discussed in order are:

1. Sensory qualities and dimensions
2. Figural or configural aspects
3. Perceptual constancy
4. Dimensional frame of reference
5. Concrete object character
6. Effect of prevailing set or state

SENSORY QUALITIES AND DIMENSIONS

The light rays that strike the retina of the eye furnish the information for vision. The retina of the eye has about 130 million receptor cells and sends more than a million nerve fibers to the brain. Information comes to us over this very complex and efficient network without much conscious effort from us. In our perception of light we distinguish whether it has hue or color (chromatic) or whether it is without hue and is achromatic in varying values of gray from white through black. The intensity increases as the patch of light appears brighter. The wavelength of the light affects our perception of its hue; as the wavelength of the patch of light is varied, the patch changes from red through orange, yellow, green, blue, indigo to violet. Next there is clarity and saturation. In a single wavelength of light, the hue appears strong and intense; as other wavelengths are added, it will become diluted and less saturated.

Variation of hue, saturation, and any combination of them will cause contrast in our visual field. From these contrasts we build our perceptions of volume and form. Although he seldom gives much direct thought to the physical properties of light, the painter is in effect manipulating these basic characteristics of light to create the images that others will see. His choice of hue, value, and intensity assigned to any patch upon his canvas or paper, plus all of the othe surrounding areas and their effect upon each other, builds the visual image of light which comes through to the eye of the observer. The sculptor, architect, and craftsman also control the physical properties of light to create contrasts in the visual field of the observer. These contrasts of light give volume, pattern, and shape to his work as it appears to his audience.

When the direction of a plane or wall surface is changed, the amount of reflected light changes. Thus forms are created which appear to move backward and forward in space. They undulate, break abruptly, or appear to be shallow or deep. By changing the texture of the surface the bright-

5 Rudolf Arnheim, **Art and Visual Perception**, University of California Press, Berkeley, Los Angeles, 1954 (paperbound, 1965).

ness or dullness of the reflected light is adjusted; by making it rougher or smoother the surface is given the property to absorb or reflect more light. To articulate form and space through control of the visual properties of light, the artist-craftsman can select from all the material assets of modern technology. In addition to the traditional clay, stone, bronze, and wood, such materials as aluminum, steel alloys, glass, plastics, fiber, and wire can be selected according to the demand for light-reflecting quality. Selections are made in accordance with the needs of a particular problem and control the kind of visual contrasts that are reflected back to the eyes of the observer.

CUES RECEIVED BY THE EYES

A cue is a stimulus that gives us the information needed to respond in a particular way. The term "monocular" is given to cues or signs received by one eye alone; the term "binocular" is used when both eyes are involved with a particular cue. When these cues are related to our existing fund of knowledge (memory), we obtain our perceptions of space, position in depth, apparent size, and the relative distance of the various items within our visual field. Monocular cues include: (1) position with respect to the horizon; (2) the distribution of shadows and illumination (light and shade); (3) interposition and overlap; (4) familiar size; (5) color saturation; and (6) clearness of detail.

Binocular cues are caused by the dissimilarity of the retinal images received when we look at a three-dimensional object; the nearer the object, the greater the difference in the two images received by the eyes separately. Another aspect of binocular vision is the convergence or eye accomodation which is accomplished according to the distance of the object from the viewer: the nearer the object is located, the larger its angle of convergence, and the greater the accomodation required.

Pictures taken by an ordinary camera with a single lens are examples of monocular, or one-eyed, vision; photographs taken with a stereoscopic camera are examples of binocular, or two-eyed, vision. The difference in depth obtained with two eyes as compared to one is made dramatically clear when we have our first encounter with the movie technique called Cinerama or see our first stereo slide projected. The stereoscope, which fascinated our parents and grandparents with its double photographs mounted side by side on cards, made Niagara Falls and other scenic marvels incredibly "real." The interpretation of aerial photographs for intelligence data in war and for exploration and mapping in peace is based on the increased depth obtained from binocular vision. Vertical photographs are taken with a single-lens camera at spaced intervals from a plane flying on a carefully plotted course at high altitude. The camera shutter is synchronized with the speed of the plane in order to ensure that the same area of the ground appears on two or more photos. This overlap is much the same as we get from our two eyes when looking at an object or scene. From each eye the angles of the observation are slightly different. Then by using a stereoscope, which allows the left eye of the interpreter to see only one photograph and the right eye to see the other, the photographed area and objects are brought into high relief.

With this technique accurate, contour maps are made, depth of water can be determined, and the natural and man-made features of the land are opened up for inspection by the cartographer, the geologist, city-planner, and military intelligence personnel.

SPACE IN DRAWING AND PAINTING

In going about the business of daily life, we seldom give thought or any serious consideration to these details of the physical aspects of the operations of our eyes. However, it is interesting to note that what we call the visual arts are built up from the same set of cues that come to our eyes as we look at the "real" physical world while walking along a city street, driving in our automobiles, or wandering through a garden. The devices used by the child or artist for representing three-dimensional space on a

2-28
The illusion of depth is achieved by position in the picture plane. *Child art.* Picking Cotton.

two-dimensional surface employ the same cues. Spatial depth in drawing and painting is indicated by the following devices.

Contrast and gradation in size. Objects which are intended to appear farther away to the viewer are made smaller than those intended to be closer. This corresponds to visual size relationships or appearances as we know them and have experienced them.

Position in the picture plane. Objects intended to be seen in the foreground, closer to the observer, are placed lower; those farther away are raised toward the top of the pictorial space (Fig. 2-28).

Overlapping planes. There is an interposition of near figures and objects over those intended to be behind or further back in the picture space. The tree overlaps part of the house when it is intended to be in front; the house overlaps the tree when the house is closer (Fig. 2-29).

Diminishing detail. In foreground objects clear and distinct details are rendered, just as we see near objects more clearly defined than distant ones. There is also more detail shown in these closer objects than in those intended to recede into the distance of pictorial space. In painting and drawing the greatest definition is usually found in the foreground. This can be altered, however, and any place in the spatial depth my be identified as the focal point from which all elements of the composition expand (Fig. 2-30).

Advancing and receding color. Though the wording is not entirely precise, it is often stated that "warm" colors tend to advance and "cool" colors tend to recede. When two colors are placed side by side on the canvas, the hue on the warmer side of the spectrum (toward red) tends to approach and appears to be closer to the observer, while that on the cool

2-29
The illusion of depth is achieved through the use of overlapping planes.
Child art. In the Forest.

2-30
The illusion of depth is achieved by the use of greater detail in the foreground.
Child art. Circus.

2-29   2-30

side of the spectrum (blues and violets) appears to be farther away by comparison (Fig. 2-31).

Josef Albers, who feels that "art is seeing," set out to explore the reaction of different colors on the same forms in a series of paintings entitled *Homage to the Square* (Fig. 1-15). In all of these he uses the same compositional format: a series of three or four superimposed squares. Color is flatly applied and changes the emotional and visual effect of the squares for the observer. This procedure emphasizes the characteristics of color, how it changes in different lights, and the effect of one color upon another. By a juxtaposition of colors the central squares can be made to jump out or recede into space. Squares of the same measured dimensions appear larger or smaller, darker or brighter, depending upon the backgrounds against which they are placed.

Aerial perspective of color. This incorporates the effect of the intervening atmosphere upon our vision of objects in space. The object becomes paler and less distinct as the distance from the observer increases. It is transferred directly into our manipulation of pigment. Objects close up are stronger in hue, saturation, and value; the contrasts of light and shade are greater and more distinctly marked. Objects farther away become paler and more grayed, less intense and lighter in hue. Contrasts of light and shade are less distinct and less clearly marked (Fig. 2-32).

Converging diagonals. The use of this effect to create an illusion of spatial depth is most effectively employed in parallel and angular perspective drawings. The parallel lines of the railroad tracks and of the road are caused to converge (rather than to remain parallel) at a vanishing point on the eye-level horizon of the observer. In examples of Oriental art the diagonal projection is also used to indicate position in space. Although

2-31
Note how the colors of the three circular shapes appear to affect their position in space.
Adolph Gottlieb. Trio. *1960. Walker Art Center, Minneapolis.*

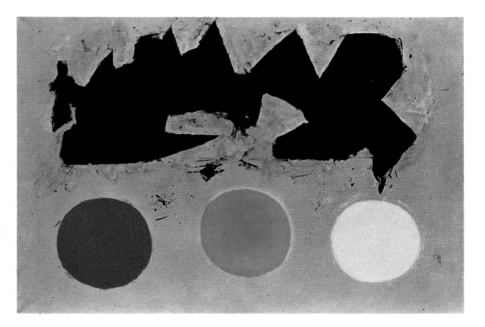

2-32
Jan Van Eyck.
The Madonna with Chancellor Rolin.
Ca. 1435. Louvre, Paris.

there may be no difference in the actual size of near and distant objects or figures, their positions on the diagonal line indicates to the viewer which are intended to be closer and which farther away (Fig. 2-33).

Transparency. When this device is used, part or all of one object or shape may be seen through another in the composition (Fig. 2-34). When transparency is used in child art, the viewer can see what is going on inside and outside at the same time, as if the solid walls of the building were removed and replaced with a sheet of glass, allowing the observer to see into each apartment and follow the actions of the occupant while still being able to see things and events that are happening outside on the street. This is also a device much used by contemporary artists. It allows them to set up the quality of ambiguous space which keeps the observer uncertain; he moves backward and forward according to the patterns laid down by the artist. An illustration of how transparency works as a device for increasing the amount of depth perceived by the viewer can be seen in the photograph of St. John's Abbey in Collegeville, Minnesota (Fig. 2-35). Although this is a photograph, much the same thing is employed as a device in painting.

THE USE OF VISUAL CUES BY THE ARTIST

These aids for perception and devices for artistic creation seldom appear or are employed separately. What is perceived is based upon some combination of cues and the relationship of one to another. Although in a given situation one set of cues is more dominant and contributes most, all of them together give the sensory data to construct the perception of a scene, object or event.

In art and life, regularity and gradual change in the pattern of a single visual cue or multiple visual cues contribute most to our perception of distance and depth. Gradual increases or decreases, a change in the perceptual quality of size, color, light and sharpness of a shade, definition of detail, angular thrust away from normal vertical and horizontal axis. and so on, work together to enhance a transformation of the space of our physical world into the symbolic pictorial and sculptural space of artistic expression.

With the exception of transparency, all the spatial devices noted above are to be found in paintings of those we classify as "visual realists." These men have developed and refined the technical devices for rendering an illusion of spatial depth known as "perspective." The Renaissance artists with mathematical precision and logic worked out a system for recording what is seen with the eye onto the two-dimensional surface of a wall or canvas. Perspective, with its vanishing point and horizon line, gives an accurate delineation of what could be seen by an observer located in a fixed position for one instant of time — as is the case with a single exposure of the camera. This rational system, combining intuition and reasoning, provides a solution for the unity of a pictorial or sculptural composition. It is only one solution, and one which has been altered both subtly and violently whenever the eye and mind of the artist felt that it did not fit the subjective needs of his concept of what was real. However, because of the controlled correctness of its distortions away from objective truth of size, distance, and shape, it opened the way for the experimental attitude toward space of Cézanne and all contemporary artists.

The abstract artist, although not interested in a visual representation of objects and events, is still involved with space and depth or the lack of them in his imagery. Whether the artist working in a particular style favors or avoids a depth effect in his compositions and constructions, he uses the same spatial devices: diminution of size, angular projection, advancement and recession of color, definiteness of detail, overlap, transparency, and position. The purpose and arrangements differ from the fixed formula of central perspective. These artists use many "eye levels" and do not view their subject from one point. They tend to move around and up and down, seeing from many angles and viewpoints. Their space representations, often ambiguous and fluid, require adjustment on the part of the observer who has been accustomed to art in the Western tradition that developed out of the Renaissance. This art is more in agreement with the appearance of things, but it is hardly consistent with what the observer knows about them.

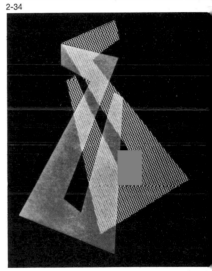

When we use central perspective, the road is drawn with lines that converge to a vanishing point off in the distance; the railroad is shown with rails coming closer together and with a row of boxcars becoming smaller as they move farther away in space. We accept this even though we know that boxcars do not shrink and that no engineer would construct a road or railway in this fashion; this is contrary to the facts as we know them.

When a contemporary artist paints the top of a vase as a circle and the bottom of the same vase as a straight line or flat, he is stating physical facts correctly. Many people are reluctant to accept this, but prefer a vase with an elliptical top and a curved bottom. Although these are in agreement with the appearance of things, they are also distortions of measured fact. Thus, in looking at art or objects in the environment, our perception is made up in part of that which comes to us directly through the senses

2-33
Photogram illustrating
the depth effect
of converging diagonals.

2-34
Photogram illustrating
the illusion of transparency.

2-35
Window reflections.
St. John's Abbey,
Collegeville, Minnesota.

THE ARTIST LOOKS AT HIS WORLD   51

and in part of that which is derived when these sensations suggest concepts and images to the brain, which has been conditioned by other experiences and education. There is always this association and interpretation based on the memory of past experiences with both art and life.

CONFIGURAL ASPECTS OF PERCEPTION

In the preceding section some of the sensory qualities and dimensions (one of six broad classes of perceptual phenomena) were discussed not only in terms of their effect on vision but also in relation to their employment in creating a work of art. These were experiences arising from the things in the environment. Configural perceptual phenomena have more to do with the effect of one thing upon the other. They are concerned with relationships that take place inside the organism rather than with physical sensory data received directly. In this case we are interested in statements of different but characteristic ways in which things appear as they do.

FIGURE-GROUND RELATIONSHIPS

This is a concept that is used freely by both the psychologist and the artist when discussing the relationship of an object to its background. The relationship between what is known as "ground" and what is known as "figure" is a primary concern in the production of a work of art; it is also equally important for looking at and understanding both art and nature (Fig. 2-36).

To provide a basis for future discussion, it seems essential that we establish certain basic characteristics of the figure-ground relationship. These are the following: (1) ground is usually larger and simpler than figure; (2) figure is usually perceived on top of or in front of ground; (3) ground may be perceived as a surface shape or a space; (4) ground areas have form, but it is the negative form of space left over from the figure's space, insubstantial and almost shapeless. In art we often call the ground area the negative space and a figure area the positive space.

In the complex scene in which everyday experience exists, the following may be given as an example of the interchangeable relationship of figure and ground (Fig. 2-37). Let us take the example of a man standing in front of a house surrounded by trees with hills behind and the sky above. In this case the walls of the house become the ground for the figure of the man; the trees become the ground against which the shape of the house is defined. The distant hills become the background against which the form of the trees as "figures" are seen. The total complex — man, house, trees, hills — is seen against the "ground" of the sky. In painting, shape and form are perceived and defined against various layers of background. However, the rules that determine which part shall be figure and which ground are less precise, and there is often a shifting backward and forward.

When we consider designing as the process which organizes seemingly unrelated elements, or parts, into an aesthetically satisfying unity, or whole, the importance of the configural aspects of perception, the effect

2-36
Photogram: the white area appears as figure on the black ground.

2-37
Photogram: an example of the interchangeable relationship of figure and ground.

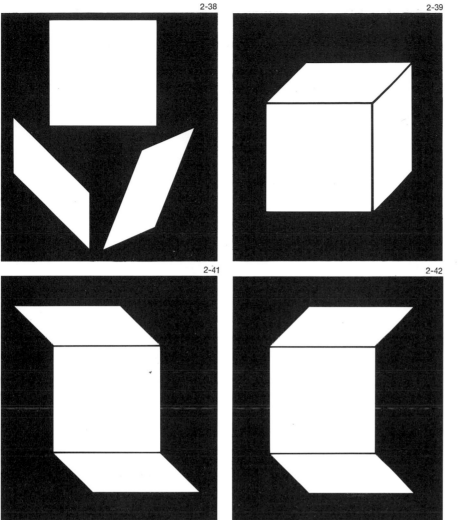

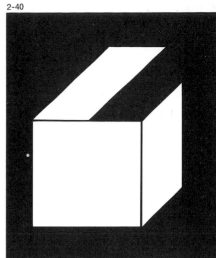

of one thing upon another, becomes a matter of primary concern. There are many factors that effectively influence perceptions and an artist's ability to translate them into evocative symbols for others. Among these factors are those which relate to the figure-ground relationships of our world as it is perceived. The visual sense patterns from which we get part of our data consists of figures appearing against ground.

Often, however, the visual data is at odds with the physical facts of a situation (Figs. 2-38–2-42). For example, a telephone pole stretched horizontally on the ground appears smaller, shorter in length, than the same pole or one of the same measured length when placed upright in a vertical position. Identical squares cut from a sheet of colored paper appear different in color and size when pasted on different colored backgrounds. Although all are identical, some appear larger, smaller, brighter, duller, darker, or lighter. Painters are aware of how a change of color and texture in one area can radically affect the overall impression.

Tests have been made to show that different color combinations, one for figure and one for background, have different measured distance at which the details of the symbol or figure may be identified and read. Recognized geometric figures, circles and squares, appear as distorted shapes when part of their contours are overlapped at an oblique angle by a grid of straight lines. The test items of examinations for "color blindness" are illustrative of how difficult it is to perceive a "figure" when it is embedded in a "ground" of closely related units. Numbers made up of small color spots, which are easily identified when seen against a plain background, are very hard to distinguish from their background of similarly shaped spots that have only subtle variations of hue, intensity, and value from the figure.

Figure units appear to go together into a single larger unit when they are perceived as having similarities of color, shape, size, and texture; this relationship is stronger in proportion to the closeness of the similarities. A figure unit, although it appears simple and clear by itself, will be difficult to perceive as part of a larger closely unified whole; the part when embedded in the whole appears different from when it stood alone (Figs. 2-43, 2-44). The person who is perceiving tends to search for a continuity of pattern, or closure, which joins the parts into some kind of configuration, unique in itself, but taking a character of direction, movement, position, and shape from the dominant order of the related parts. This relationship between parts in the new "wholeness" of a perception remains recognizable even if the proportionalities of the parts are changed.

Nothing ever occurs by itself. In painting, the total compositional pattern is formed by joining parts that cannot be experienced separately with meaning. We are familiar with the many cases in nature of the operation

2-43   2-44

2-43
Photogram: the part
when seen alone.

2-44
Photogram: the part embedded
in a complex whole.

of protective coloration and broken color patterns that allow an animal or insect to merge with its background until it cannot be detected as a distinct figure against the ground of its natural habitat. The insect which looks like a twig in color and shape can hardly be detected against the bark or branches of the tree. Some have natural markings contrasting in color and conspicuous in shape, which form patterns to disguise the fact that they are animals at all. The chameleon changes color to suit its background (Fig. 2-45).

Camouflage in time of war has become a complicated art. The broken color patterns applied to warships or tanks were intended to break-up or jumble the contour delaying recognition of vulnerable target spots and to disguise the speed and direction of movement. The shape and orientation of a building were adjusted to make it less conspicuous, shadows were added or erased. These natural and man-made examples show how the various operative rules of figure-ground relationships can be purposefully adjusted in order to delay or confuse the normal process of perception.

PRINCIPLES OF ORGANIZATION

In the perception of things in our world and also in the creation of art there are certain laws of organization noted by the researchers in psychology and employed by the artist which govern the figure-ground relationships which we perceive. These are:

1. *Area* — the smaller a closed region, the more it tends to be seen as a figuro.

2-45
Insect camouflage.

2. *Proximity* — dots, shapes, and objects that are close together tend to be grouped together.

3. *Closedness* — areas with closed contours tend to be seen as figures more than do those with open contours.

4. *Symmetry* — the more symmetrical a closed region, the more it tends to be seen as a figure.

5. *Good continuation* — the arrangement of figure and ground that tends to be seen will be that which makes the fewest changes or interruptions in straight or smoothly curving lines or contours.

These laws of area, proximity, and closedness are amenable to measurement and to quantitative statements. The other laws of organization, such as symmetry and good continuation, may also be treated quantitatively, but are more qualitative in character.

The artist or the casual spectator does not interrupt his creation or observation of visual stimuli to analyze all of the details of why things are seen as they are. A camera will register details clearly and distinctly, but our vision will not. In our seeing we tend to grasp a few outstanding features of the object, and we do not go through a mental analysis of why we see things as we do — that a shape appears as it does because its areas are small and closed, that it is seen as a figure because the dots or objects are close together, or that it is a continuing smooth curve and has a continuous contour with all of the outlying parts tied together. We simply see it as a unit and go on to the next visual experience. Knowledge of the above laws of organization and of the meaning of figure-ground relationships can be helpful in evaluating one art form as compared with another and in offering suggestions to students for improvement of the organization of their art expressions.

ATTRACTION OR ATTENTION VALUE

We have mentioned the faculty of the eye and the predisposition of the individual to discriminate and concentrate more on some elements in the visual field than upon others. In any work of art there are key elements that have been arranged to attract and hold the attention of the viewer. With this in mind, it seems appropriate to examine some of the physical and psychological properties present which attract and hold the concentration of our eyes.

The attention and attraction value depends upon several elements. These are: (1) degree of total contrast; (2) degree of visual texture contrast; (3) size of an area; (4) shape of the figure elements; (5) position of the figure in the ground; (6) dynamic effect of balance; (7) effect of association and representation; (8) eye movements in the design; (9) linear relations of an element in the field structure.

The degree of tonal contrast is also at work when looking at sculpture and causes our perceptive consciousness to be focused upon the highlighted ridges of the bronze or the deep, darkened cavity of the sculpture piece in contrast to the middle values of the other surfaces. Attention through degree of texture contrast is involved in the visual counterplay of the rough against the smooth and the patterned against the plain. Usually the eye is attracted to the spot, shape, or area which is different from the average texture of the total field. A smooth-surfaced area within a fully textured surrounding or a fully textured spot surrounded by or adjacent to a mass which is visually smooth causes greatest attraction. A boldly patterned spot attracts when it is surrounded by or adjacent to shapes without pattern.

Following is a description of an experience involving all the factors that work toward discriminating one element within the total visual field:

It was a drab spring day. The overcast sky made it seem cooler than the temperature given by the weather bureau. Looking out over the backyard, the point of greatest attraction was obvious without resorting to item analysis. One lonely tulip stood up bright and tall! As a nearly perfect example, this situation illustrated how a combination of factors work together to cause the eyes to focus attention and to discriminate upon one element in the total visual field. The bright red-vermilion of the tulip rising out of the dark-brown soil was seen against the background of a dull-green strip of lawn (degree of tonal contrast, value, and color). The waxy, smooth texture of the flower was accented by the mottled surfaces of grass and the loosely broken earth (degree of visual texture contrast). Although relatively small, the flower was larger in size than any other single unit, and its shape had a closed, definite contour, while everything else was open, indefinite, and without distinction of shape (size of an area and shape of the figure elements).

Moving the eyes back and forth to change the position of the tulip with relation to the rest of the visual field changed the balance pattern from symmetrical to asymmetrical, but did not change the attention-attraction or throw things out of balance. The single bright flower placed far to the edge was still able to act as a counterweight for a very large expanse of neutral, flat ground and grass (position of figure in ground and dynamic effect of balance). On close examination one other factor had an effect on attention. This was the long straight vertical line of the stem of the flower — longer and straighter than anything else and of a lighter green than any of the greens surrounding it. And this long green line led the eye directly and without interruption to the strong color spot of the tulip (eye movements in the design and linear relation of elements in the field structure).

The effect of association and representation was left until last. Anyone familiar with the weather of Minnesota when seasons hesitate between summer and winter for a rather reluctant spring can understand. The one lonely flower represented a kind of victory and deserved to stand up and be admired. In a rather nebulous way it is associated with all of those deeds of bravery and the "Horatio Alger" spirit of fighting upward against almost insurmountable obstacles to achieve "success" and a moment of glory.

The attraction of the size of an area has been utilized effectively by artists linked with abstract expressionism. In their works the element of size of area is not only employed to attract and hold attention, but is also calculated to impress the viewer by its monumentality. Everything about the work is large in scale, including the size of their canvases. This bigness is further emphasized by the size of areas of the color shapes as well as by the reduction of the number of shapes within the canvas. This provides impact. The same effect has been obtained in contemporary sculptures, in which very large slablike shapes are unbroken by patterns or textural articulation. This bigness of shape and area in paintings and sculptures counteracted the disruptive visual phenomena which are usually present in the surroundings when a work of art is placed in a gallery, home or office.

When more emphasis is placed upon the definition of a shape or figure element, there will be a greater clarity in seeing it. The normal eye usually grasps shapes immediately and can take in simple regular figures more quickly than those which are ambiguous and broken with their boundaries interrupted. This simplicity of form or shape is achieved in child art and with ease and distinction in the art of primitive people. In more mature styles of art, an illusion of simplicity is often achieved by a very complicated process and by taking infinite pains to hide this complexity. An effort is made to organize a wealth of meaning and to reduce a mass of detail into a clear and relatively simple straight-forward statement. The modern abstractionists — Josef Albers, Piet Mondrian, and Ben Nicholson, Hans Arp, and others — use elements as simple as any to be found anywhere in a work of art. The simplicity they achieve is obtained by the small number of structural features they include within their designs.

The attention value which can be attributed to the location of the figure within its background can hardly be minimized. If it is somewhat centrally located, less accommodation by the eye will be required to give it a place of prominence at the center of the retina and as such receive more attention. Also, objects positioned in the foreground because of size, clearness of definition and strength of reflected color achieve greater prominence than those located farther back.

Great pains have been taken to discover the ideal position in the picture plane, the place which will have the greatest degree of focus and which aids the centering of attention. At one time in the history of art, four spots known as the "eyes of the rectangle" were carefully measured and located. It was stated as a basic rule that one of these points should be used as the position for the center of interest in the composition. The eyes of the rectangle are obtained by drawing diagonals to touch the four corners of the rectangle and then raising perpendiculars from each corner to the diagonal lines. At the crossing point, where perpendiculars from the corners cross the diagonals, four spots would be established. Few, if any, artists today use this particular technique to establish the center of interest for their compositions. Nevertheless, it has been claimed that the points of greatest attraction and for controlling eye focus of the observer may be found slightly above or below and slightly to the right or left of the exact center of the canvas.

PERCEPTUAL CONSTANCY

In our discussion of perspective drawing as a device for recording three-dimensional space on a flat surface, mention was made of the tendency of adults to feel comfortable with and to accept readily a vase or cylindrical form even when its known circular shapes were represented as ellipses. This tendency of the individual to identify things in their true form, regardless of any changes of appearance in size, shape, and color caused by seeing it to the right or left or above or below his line of vision is known as perceptual constancy. These constancies help us to have a clear knowledge of what a thing is in spite of its distance or angle from the viewer.

From prior learning and past experience we assign permanent constancies that tend to resolve variations due to light conditions, distance and angle of vision. We think of things by general quality designations as in the case of blue for sky and green for grass regardless of the color that might be identified if a closer inspection was made. The rectangular walls of a room or of the outside of the house appear trapezoidal in shape when seen from different positions, but we think of and know of them as rectangular. The circular top of a can or jar is seen as a circle when we look at it head-on or from directly above. From all other angles its shape is changed through varying fullness of an ellipse to the straight line of its appearance when viewed exactly at eye level. We know of it as circular, regardless of its different appearance as observed from various angles of vision. This shape constancy is a compromise between what we see and what we know from many experiences.

Perceiving objects as the same size, a row of telephone poles or of box cars for instance, and attributing the differences in visual sizes to the difference in the distances between these objects and our viewing position is another type of perceptual constancy. Color constancy is at work when we see the grass as green and an orange as orange regardless of the kind and degree of light and shade or time of day. These constancies of shape, size, and color of the appearance of things help us to identify and recognize things in our environment when they are seen from different angles as our positions change and under different conditions of illumination. To do this, we take into consideration cues given by the object and its surroundings and adjust these to our past experiences with the object.

ILLUSIONS, DISTORTIONS, AND ART

The value of our ready acceptance of perceptual constancies is apparent. It is our means of coping with the varied cues and sensory data which we receive in the course of a day or hour of our daily pursuits. We often receive sensory data which give us ambiguous or deceptive perceptual images; they are not in agreement with our established cognitive understandings and assumptions. Often, for the pursuit of a particular goal, the artist will present visual cues which create illusions that distort and circumvent reality as it is known to and accepted by the viewer. Psychological literature is filled with references to illusions. An illusion is defined by Luckeish [6] as "any visual perception which does not harmonize with physical measurements." He also states, "Our past experiences, associations, desires, demands, imaginings, and other more or less obscure influences create illusions." Psychologists believe that in such situations the visual sensations received are subjected to an overlay of unconsciously achieved conclusions. These give an explanation or meaning to the visual image that is not consistent with physical measurement or facts of the situation.

The psychologist has developed many techniques and devices in this category of illusion to test the responses of people when there is a discrepancy between the actual situation and the assumptions they are

---

[6] M. Luckeish, **Visual Illusions**, Dover Publications, Inc., New York, 1965.

likely to make out of their past experience. The best known of these is the experiment with a distorted room. The subject is not given any information about the facts of the situation; he must depend upon his perceptual constancies about rooms and windows for the meanings he will give to his observations. This gives rise to unexpected happenings, bewildering relationships and a stimulating but irreconcilable confusion in the experience for the observer. In the design of one of these distorted rooms the left wall is made larger than the right. The floor slopes, and the rear wall is set at an oblique angle and has trapezoidal windows of different sizes. The observer, when he looks through a peephole into the room, sees what is to him a normal rectangular room. On the assumption that he is looking into a normal rectangular room, many strange and mysterious things happen. A man standing at a point close to the front edge of the left wall (which is very high) looks like a midget compared to the gigantic size of a boy standing at a point farther back along the lowest wall on the right. The face of the person looking through the window at the right appears enormous compared with the face of the man seen through the window on the left.

This phenomena is puzzling only if we continue to hold to our assumption of the normal rectangularity of the room and forget that we are looking with one eye through a peephole and are dependent upon our single-eye cues or vision. Viewed with one eye alone, the interior of the distorted room produces on the observer's retina the same projected spatial pattern as a normal rectangular room. If we should take away the framing and see with two eyes all that is concealed — the sloping floor, the unequal walls, the oblique rear wall, the trapezoidal windows — it is an easy matter to make adjustments. The firmness of our assumption of normality and rectangularity of the space, like most other rooms we have known, is removed and we regain our poise and sense of order.[7]

When art produced by children and adults replaces the experimental items as the subject for observation, we have a parallel situation. The visitor to the gallery or exhibition is not given a scorecard which informs him of the artist's intentions and procedures. He is not told in advance that the artist has painted a common object as it might appear if observed simultaneously from three different eye levels. He does not know in advance that the sculptor has taken an object, exploded it, and then reassembled the parts — making some smaller, some larger and joining them to one another in different relationships than those which are commonly observed by the human eye or the camera. It is natural for the observer to be uneasy and uncertain if he comes to this situation with assumptions based only upon his past experience with the object and the perceptual constancies he has developed from these previous contacts. It is difficult for him to adjust his unconsciously achieved conclusions of the way things should be. Although we know that many things we observe in everyday life are not in exact correspondence with physical measurement and that some aspects are omitted or distorted, we are somehow less willing to accept these same distortions, omissions, and additions when we find them in art. We are often more likely to accept the work of artists of the Renais-

---

7 See Appendix 2 for an analysis of the experiment with the trapezoidal window.

sance or of the modern visual realists — Hopper, Sheeler, Wyeth, and others — because the perspective devices they use are closer to that which the eye sees or the camera photographs (Fig. 2-46).

It is necessary to make many visual and mental adjustments when viewing the works of a number of contemporary artists as well as the art of children. Both use more experimental devices for representing space and form. Sometimes the space of a "room" is distorted from the normal rectangle, as is the case with the Ames experiment; the ambiguity of the objects in it is resolved only after the frame of reference, the key, is accepted. Optical illusions are the basic tools for many artists. Through these devices the eye is "tricked" and deceived; perceptual constancies and the laws of configurations are abrogated. Circles and squares appear distorted and "lumpy" because of an overlapping grid of straight lines; figures apparently change, are equivocal, and are seen first as one thing, then as another. Things happen to an apparently stable composition as the observer moves and changes his viewpoint or as his attention fluctuates.

If the teacher looks at child art with the perceptual constancies and assumptions of perspective space, he may be confused and unfair — missing most of the imaginative solutions invented by children for getting their ideas down on paper. To them it is perfectly natural to fold up space, combining plan-view and elevations as in Egyptian art, or to reverse perspective and change eye levels in the middle of their work period. The

2-46
Charles Sheeler. Midwest. 1954. Walker Art Center, Minneapolis.

viewer often has to walk around the composition or is forced to adjust the painting in order to see each part in its "correct" orientation.

When the art work of young children is encountered by the adult without the bias of a set of constancies based on adult standards of experience the productions can be exciting and revealing. In his picture making the child employs many of the same devices that are used by the mature artist to create the illusion of depth upon a flat surface. He is perhaps less sophisticated, but at the same time more experimental and exploratory. Illustrated are a selection of the space devices employed by children in their art expressions (Figs. 2-47–2-53). These represent a child's-eye view of his world; they are also his attempts to adjust to the tools of art and perception in order to express his own ideas and feelings about his environment and his reaction to it.

2-47–2-53
Note the various ways in which children represent the spatial depth of their world.
Space concepts in child art.

2-47

2-48

2-49

2-50

2-51

2-52

2-53

THE ARTIST LOOKS AT HIS WORLD   63

DIMENSIONAL FRAME OF REFERENCE

Individuals engaged in the process of creating art are constantly confronted with the problem of making judgments concerning alternative courses of action. Should one area or mass be made brighter, duller, heavier, lighter, stronger, or weaker as compared with others in designs for paintings, sculptures, and crafts? Judgments are not made with references to some objective standard. Through numerous experiences with many comparable situations each individual forms his own personal, subjective scale for judgment. This is called the "dimensional frame of reference" of perception. For him, it becomes the reference base from which more or less absolute judgments are determined.

In situations involving judgment of the quality of a work of art or of the art work of children this subjective reference scale will be determined after a series of examples of products has been experienced. Using this reference scale, judgments are made of a series of products, rating them in a scale of values from "very best" through "average" to "very poor." Research into various aspects of education in art is often dependent upon the ability of a group of judges to arrive at ratings of the end products with no significant difference among judges. Researches along this line have given conclusions which indicate that such consistent judgments can be made. Evidently there is more agreement than was formerly assumed among the individuals in the dimensional frames of reference which they have established.

Quite often overlooked by the teacher and by most adults is the effect of this aspect of perception (individual frame of reference) when dealing with young children. Since the young child is much smaller in stature and therefore "closer to the ground," he notices and is attracted to smaller things; in a sense he prefers them and examines them more closely. While walking through the woods or along the seashore, the impatient adult wonders how the child can spend so much time poking at a small puddle of water caught in a rock crevasse or picking over a clump of seaweeds. For the child these are complete worlds of exceedingly interesting living things. They are large to him, although small and unexciting for the adult who finds the things like ships, dead fish and a grove of Sequoia more to his liking. In the small puddle the child perceives tiny bugs skittering, seashells resting, seaweed swaying, scum, seeds, and tiny blossoms moving. It isn't until the child's selection for seeing has been enlarged and captured by the closeup lens of the camera and has been published in a magazine that the adult begins to be aware of the beauty and magnitude of the child's frame of reference.

The individual interprets things he sees in relation to his own position in space; his body becomes the central axis for his judgment of location, direction, and interval. It is from his own axis that he establishes the relationships of up–down, right–left, and forward–back. With his ability to control visual cues presented to the observer, the artist sometimes forces an adjustment in the viewer's orientation to space. The image presented is apprehended with meaning and security after this adjustment has been made.

CONCRETE OBJECT CHARACTER

Gertrude Stein's poetic statement "A rose is a rose is a rose" refers to the concrete object character of a thing in nature. We recognize it as *a rose.* It is something more than a certain texture, an arrangement of petals fastened to a stem, a color experience, a figure against a ground, a continuous contour and a size, large or small. The meaning it represents is that of *what* the object is. This is an obvious and universal aspect of perception especially when the definition of "object" is expanded to include actions and situations and when the scope of interest is broadened to include the *concrete meaning* we give to things and events.

In writing about the growth of children in their art expression, Arnheim makes the following statement:[8]

> Doggishness is perceived earlier than the particular characteristics of any one dog. If this is true we can expect early artistic representations, based on naïve observation to be concerned with generalities — that is with simple overall structural features, which is exactly what happens.

The mature artist at his best does not produce a replica of an object. He forms a representational concept that embodies the significance and meaning of the universal derived from individual experiences with objects and occurrences. Thus in a still-life painting by Cézanne we have an expression of the "apple-ness" of the apples.

This concrete object quality is achieved by many artists by the use of the object itself in their art. Popular techniques include the collage of "real" material and objects and the assemblages of "found" objects in sculpture, as well as the castings of vegetables, people, and so on. However, aside from this direct inclusion of the actual object in the work, artists have sought to achieve the fundamental or universal quality of their subject by other and less direct means — to paint the "mountainness" of the mountains.

The clusters of spots and varicolored splashes of paint seen close-up on canvases by the impressionists Monet, Childe Hassam, and Manet do not take on concrete object character of a haystack, church, railway station or water lily until the observer moves back to the correct viewing distance. These impressionists set up a visual situation with strokes of broken color, usually based on a triadic harmony of three hues equally spaced around the color circle. The range of hues and the values and intensities of these form areas of contrast which give definition to the subject matter. At an appropriate distance the eyes of the observer fuse these broken areas of color to resolve the visual forms established by the artist. In this manner, concrete object character is given to the subject matter — landscape, figures, still life. At the same time the observer receives an effect of the intervening atmosphere and light as it falls on the subjects selected by the artist.

---

[8] Rudolf Arnheim, *op. cit.*, p. 160.

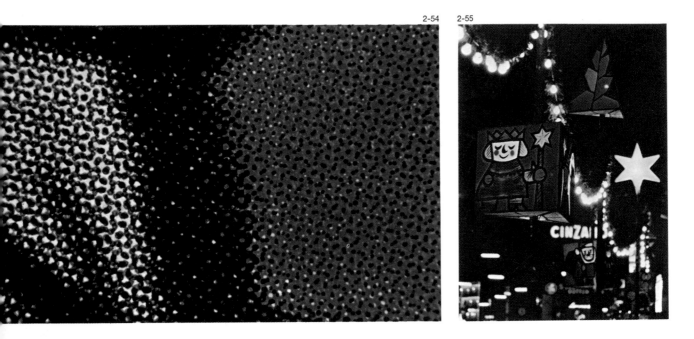

**Note the grid of separate colors
used in the printing process.**
*Magnified section
of magazine reproduction.*

2-55
*Magazine color reproduction.
(Courtesy Leica Fotografie,
Umschau Verlag, Frankfurt am Main.)*

This same effect is used in four-color printing as employed commercially for color illustrations in books, magazines and other publications. When seen under the magnifying lens, a colored illustration in a magazine is revealed as a composition of tiny dots of magenta, blue, yellow, and black. The proportions of these are mixed in the eyes of the observer under normal viewing conditions. The overall color pattern is established to define the subject matter seen by the reader (Figs. 2-54, 2-55).

EFFECT OF PREVAILING SET

The aspects of perception which have already been discussed under sensory qualities and dimension, and as configurational and constancy features, hold true for most individuals at all times. The discussion of factors included under the topics frame of reference and concrete object character are generally the same and have validity for all individuals who have a common background of experience. However, the personal qualities of the perceiver insinuate themselves into every act of perception and at every stage of the process.

Individual differences and the *state* of a person at different times play a major role in determining the selection of the objects and events that are to be perceived and the readiness with which they are perceived. This state or attitude is called a "set." It is defined as a state that is preparatory for or facilitative of some definite act of behavior — in this case, a perception. Set is not considered as part of the perception itself, but rather as a force for preparing and sustaining the organism and for facilitating or strengthening what is perceived. This readiness results in greater attentive clearness during perception and helps us to see more vividly as we look for meaning in the stimulating object or event.

Readiness, induced by needs and determined by emotional states, affects the perceptual process through selective emphasis. This in turn controls what objects we are to "see" and what we are to ignore in our environment — the world around us. In her discussion of the first point of her Perception-Delineation Theory, June King McFee has noted the following:[9]

> Readiness is a term used to describe our overall preparation for performing a task. Part of total readiness to perform is the "response sets" we have learned, the habitual tendencies to respond in certain ways to things in our environment. The culture we belong to, the ways we have learned to relate to space, our flexibility or rigidity in accepting new things, our past perceptual training, all contribute to our sets and readiness to perceive. The overall physical development and condition of a person also contribute to his readiness.

Psychological experiments have revealed some findings concerning set as a condition of perception. It has been shown that set has two aspects. First, it is a preparatory or facilitating state for perception. Next, this facilitating condition has the operational effect of making perception occur sooner, quicker, stronger, and to a greater degree of magnitude than when proper attitudes are absent or less firmly established. In some cases the condition of set seems merely to prepare the individual, making him ready for perceiving, in others it prolongs and sustains perception during its entire course.

When one is set for a certain experience, the response always represents exactly the same behavior as that for which the individual is prepared. Thus the problem of perception is tied up with the problem of other acts of behavior. Set will always appear as a selective process: we are prepared for "something" and our subsequent actions and reactions are toward this end. When there is competition for attention — one or more stimuli appearing more or less simultaneously — the stimulus for which the subject is prepared to attend is experienced first. This provides the built-in filtering device for focusing our attention upon what, in our own interest, we want to see. Its functions are both selective and productive.

The first night on the job in a rolling mill of a steel plant is a bewildering and ear-shattering experience; the sounds battering the eardrums are discordant, loud, and piercing, with little meaning for the newcomer. After a short time on the job they sort themselves out or are sorted out. The workman hears only the bells, signals, and whistles meant for him and for which he must take some responsive action. As we drive along the streets of our city environment, the complexity of images — signs, signals, window displays, buildings, cars, people, colors, shapes — could be and sometimes is equally confusing. However, the driver tends to filter out much of his confusion and perceive vividly only a small part of it all — the part that demands his reaction.

---

9 June King McFee, **Preparation for Art**, 3d printing, Wadsworth Publishing Company, Inc., San Francisco, 1964, pp. 42–43.

MOTIVATION

That sets can involve and be involved in learning is a commonly known and accepted rule. They control the courses of learning at the start or when they come into action during its course. Motivation may be a factor that lies behind set. Both set and the underlying motivation must be considered as part of the total aggregate of any kind of behavior. However, in perception there are restrictive limits for motivating factors. When a change produced by motivation goes beyond these limits, the percept will result in a distorted view of the environment.

Motivation is the basic operational problem for the teaching of art, whether for the teaching of oneself or of others. By his outward (overt) action man has been able to mold and adopt his environment to his needs. To accomplish this change or adaptation successfully in our perceiving, it is somehow necessary to set up a facsimile of the environment as it is at the start. The amount of tolerance for change and adaptation varies for each individual. If the motive for learning a lesson activity is merely "to perceive," or to find meaning with respect to the environment as it impinges upon our eyes, we are on safe ground; but if the motivation is to perceive the environment in a particular way that is inconsistent with the way it is, and for which the subject is not ready, then difficulties arise.

At the beginning of this chapter a description of an artist looking at his backyard was presented. In attempting to isolate difference between an artist and another person so engaged, it was pointed out that the artist operates with greater facility and his perceptions occur with greater promptness, speed, energy, and magnitude. This is not quite the whole story. His preparation — or set, if you wish — and his motivations included two other factors: *expectancy* and *intention*.

Although in the general course of living the "set to perceive" may be based on nothing more dramatic than familiarity and frequency; in this instance there were strong motivating, emotional, and personality conditions at work. Our artist was prepared for the "looks" of certain structural patterns to emerge from the disordered array of stimuli. His past experiences gave him assurance that these would be forthcoming. He "expected" also to discover new visual patterns because he knew that there was much newness to discover in the varied arsenal of forms and configuration of this world of nature; all that he had previously experienced in his own direct contacts while engaged in similar ventures and from books, photographs and films told him so. He also had one other important motivator to focus his attention; he purposefully set out with the intention to look and to discover. As an outcome he intended to provide a path for others to follow and imitate. This was to be a cutaway view of how one artist looked at one small fragment of his world — an example of how universal qualities of the structure of design in art and nature are to be found if one takes the effort to look for them attentively and with expectancy. If a man or child is led to see the color, form, and order in his natural surroundings, these discoveries will control the world he shapes for himself.

PERCEPTION AS A CREATIVE ACT

In his introduction to *Education of Vision*, Kepes identifies perception as a creative act: [10]

> *Our eyes perceive only the random flow of light stimulation; the light rays that impinge on the retina have no intrinsic order. But our dynamic tendency to create order transforms the basic sense of impressions of light signals into meaningful forms. From the welter of sensation bombarding the retina of our eyes we articulate structures, images; and from the intermingled, interconnecting shifting streams of optical images, we separate persistent patterns, themes, and events. Thus to perceive an image is to participate in a forming process; it is a creative act. In the simplest form of visual orientation and in the most embracing unity of a work of art there is a significant common basis; a sorting and organization of sensory impressions from the visual field.*

The appreciation of art depends upon an open-mindedness on the part of the viewer — that he does not go into the experience with a preset expectation of how the work of art should look or be shaped. This state of openness to a perceptive experience allows one to participate more completely and often brings "effective surprises" for the observer. Also, in the perception of things other than art the absence of a preset state of mind allows us to see objects in a new and different way than would otherwise be the case. An experience with the object pictured in Fig. 2-56 will illustrate perception as a creative act of behavior.

Notable in the account of this experience is the imaginative manipulation of the visual sensory data that was received by the observer. He was not set to perceive a particular kind of object; there was no conscious control from past experience with the object.

One day not long ago while walking through the kitchen, I saw what appeared to be a small piece of metal sculpture on the counter that extends along the wall from the sink. This was of an owl and stood about eight inches high. This was something new to me and I was puzzled about its antecedents. Where had it come from? Who made it? Where had my wife obtained it? It had not yet occurred to me that this object was not a piece of sculpture and all of my associations were in terms of this set of mind. This did not change until I went over to pick up the "sculpture" in order to examine it more closely. Then the mystery was solved. What I had been admiring as a sculptured owl was in reality the head of a Sunbeam Mixmaster (hand), with the mixing blades detached and placed upright to dry. Mixmaster or no Mixmaster, I still perceived it as an owl in sculpture. The two holes and the creased metal at the top formed the eyes and beak; the overall contours suggested the shape of an owl. The total configuration paralleled many art expressions of owls that I had seen in the past. Inadvertently I had become involved in an experience with "found" sculpture. Without any physical manipulation a work of art had been created by my perceptive mechanism (Fig. 2-56).

---

10 From the Introduction by Gyorgy Kepes (ed.) to **Education of Vision**, George Braziller, Inc., New York, 1965; reprinted with the permission of the publisher. Copyright © 1965 by George Braziller, Inc.

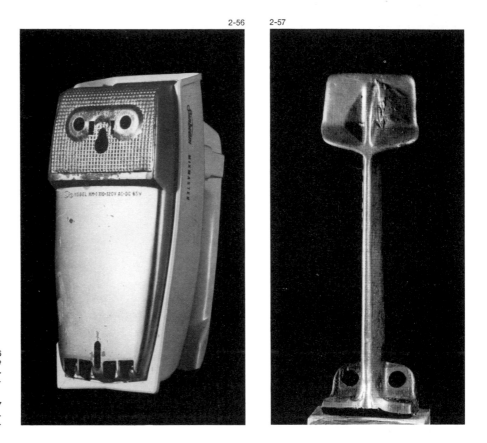

2-56
*Found Sculpture
(Sunbeam Mixmaster).*
Owl.

2-57
*Charles Huntington.
Found Object.*

This is a report of a kind of creative perceiving that is not uncommon; it happens often with children at play and less often with adults. Artists have cultivated this quality as they try to see common objects in contexts that are less common and give strangeness to the familiar. They carry this attribute beyond the stage of perceiving into the action of the creative production of a work of art.

This redefinition of the use of common objects or parts of them — the employment of them in art for purposes other than those that were intended — has been practiced repeatedly in sculpture. Sometimes the found object is kept intact, unchanged and unblemished; it is presented as a work of art by mounting it on a pedestal. This is illustrated by a sculpture by Charles Huntington, to which he has given the title *Found Object* (Fig. 2-57).

Another approach to the redefinition of the object for art purposes involves more manipulation by the sculptor. First the object must be discovered by the sensitive eye of the artist; then it must be placed in a new context both by perceptive associations and by the physical work of the artist. Instead of shaping sheets of uncut metal, the sculptor is arranging preformed shapes and composing his design from them. His attention has been attracted by the aesthetic qualities of the machine parts, household gadgets, and farm implements. He values them as shapes or forms, not for their utility. Later they become symbolic forms and are given meaning as part of his sculptural design. The original machine part

2-58
**An artist's refined perception
of an owl is exemplified
in this bronze.**
*Wine vessel in owl shape.
Yin or Early Chou. Bronze.
Minneapolis Institute of Arts.*

2-59
Charles Huntington.
Sun Disc II.

was used without change or was reshaped and welded to others in order to create figurative, abstract, nonobjective images for the viewer.

Sun Disc II (Fig. 2-59) provides an appropriate illustration of this method for creating sculpture. The artist composed his sculpture from three pick-axe heads, a curved iron plate section of a mold-board of a plowshare, round metal discs from a piece of farm machinery, and a circular casting for the base. Although it might be satisfying for the viewer to identify these units in their original settings, for an appreciation of the sculpture it is necessary to disregard the original purpose of the objects. The artist has redefined their use and has created a sculpture that is independent of the former relationships of shapes. An appreciation of the sculpture takes into account this new relationship of forms without regard to their past as parts of farm machinery.

SCREENING VISUAL SENSATIONS

According to Attneave: [11]

> *As we grow from childhood to adulthood our ways of perceiving have become selective. This has become a necessity which enables us to handle the volume of information which batters at the retinas of our eyes in the normal course of living. We have developed certain processes which work almost automatically to enable us to sort out that which is relevant from that which is not required. In going about our daily existence we employ three processes as identified by the psychologists for screening the visual sensation which our eyes receive.*
>
> *These processes are: (a) classifying homogeneous material or similar things as units; (b) using an averaging mechanism for sensations which vary according to a regular pattern; (c) classifying as wholes or complete units sensations which are only partially complete by a system of "what-goes-with-what?"*

An example of how similar things are classified as a unit is represented by our perception of an animal, a tree, or a field. In these situations we do not focus upon individual leaves, hairs, or blades of grass as separate entities. The object is accepted as a unit named tree, dog, or field.

The averaging mechanism goes to work when a portion of the visual field contains a great quantity of information that varies according to a regular pattern. We average out the nonredundant and essentials in the regular pattern as in the case of looking at an expanse of grass, sand, a building, or a piece of furniture. We give the object a name — beach, house, chair. In these cases a large amount of visual information loss is tolerable. The textured area may be understood by noting the characteristics of the texture and the function and location of its limiting points.

The process referred to as "temporal continuation" comes into play in situations because the individual through experience has learned a

---

[11] Fred Attneave, **Some Informational Aspects of Visual Perception**, *Psychological Review*, vol. 61, no. 3, 1954, pp. 183–193.

great deal about what-goes-with-what from many encounters with similar data. When people are seated in a classroom, many parts of their bodies are hidden from view by the overlapping of parts of the people seated in front of them. From previous experience we can predict that the rest of their anatomy is also present. This prior knowledge of structural relationships present in human beings is important in situations where identity must be determined by a small portion of the total of the visual clues that are available.

Photographic intelligence, or the assembling of critical information from aerial photographs, must often be based upon a relatively small amount of available data. The identification of an industrial complex must be worked out from a few recognizable buildings plus a reference to knowledge of how materials must flow from raw stages to the finished product. Also, attention is given to the special characteristics of the buildings required to house the machines needed for processing the materials. Thus an oil refinery, aircraft assembly plant, or a chemical industry can be identified from a few building units. When this has been established the separate identities of the various structures may be ascertained from the knowledge of the whole complex.

In a similar way, a person seen far off in the distance can be identified as John Smith by one or two characteristics which we have associated with him although a relatively indistinct image is presented to our eyes. A clue might be obtained from the general impression of the way he walks or carries his head, or from something else which gives us the starting point for associating the other things that we have customarily associated with this individual.

These perceptual processes which we use in our normal course of seeing have considerable bearing upon the art that is created and the observation of it by others. Variation is great among the works of individual artists and for different periods and styles of art. A common denominator is the factor that the same perceptive processes used by people in their everyday life are also employed by artists in the work they create. Seldom do artists feel that it is necessary (at least in our contemporary art) to paint all of the leaves on the tree, or blades of grass in the field. Just as in looking at objects, there is far too much detail for the mind and eye to use efficiently. The artist presents a minimum of detail and allows the observer to supplement this in any fashion that is convenient.

We have come to realize that a painting is not intended as a replica of an object. It must be thought of as a painting with all of the inherent qualities of painting rather than those of the object that is depicted. The same is true in the case of sculpture where little or no attempt is made to present all of the hairs upon the animal; concentration is upon its overall form, or shape. There are exceptions here, especially in cases where we are concerned with the pop art or with art products in which ready-made or found objects and collages of material are incorporated. Once again it is appropriate to emphasize that the artist in bringing to the observer his personal image is employing or distorting the same clues that we use for our perceptions of things other than art. Some knowledge of how perceptions are arrived at in general can be of value in understanding how to look at art in particular.

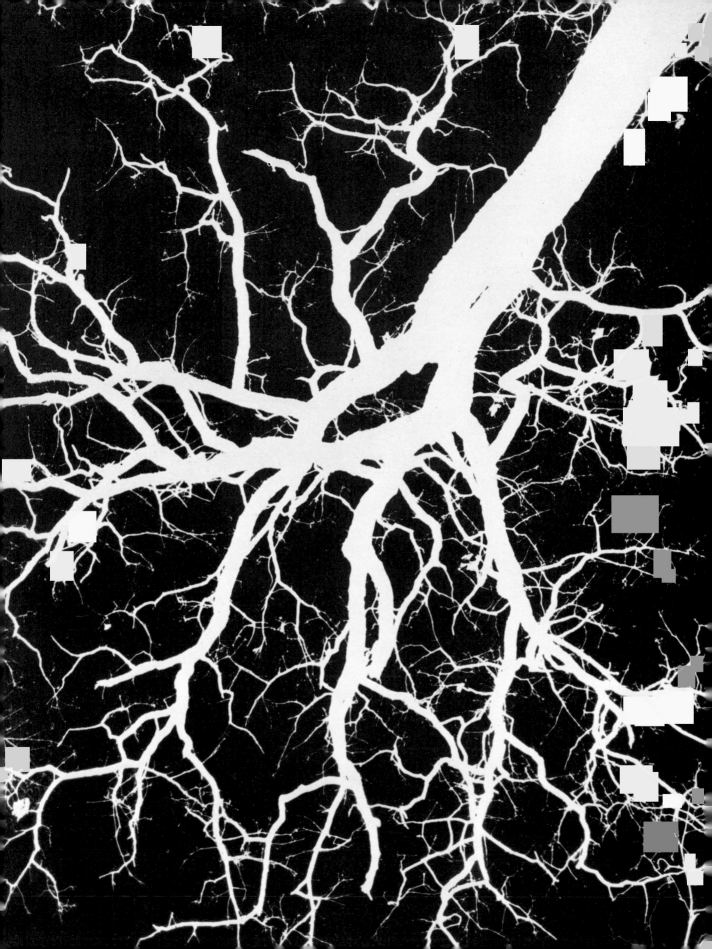

Chapter 3

DEVELOPING VISUAL AWARENESS

The discussion of the aspects of perception in the preceding chapter has focused upon the problem of *how* things appear and to a lesser extent upon *why* they appear as they do. It has been emphasized that clear seeing is a product of accurate sensing and correct perceiving. This "visual literacy" is essential for the artist and for the student and his teacher. It affects the objects created by the artist and the way they are seen and understood by others.

THE NEED FOR PERCEPTUAL TRAINING

"Train the eyes to see and train the hand to put down what the eye has seen": this has been the advice given by artists and teachers to their students during this and past centuries. The painter Rembrandt Peale, in his book *Graphics: The Art of Accurate Delineation*, published in 1845, wrote the following to emphasize the role of art and visual perception in education:

> The art of drawing requires the education of the eye to discriminate forms, before the hand can imitate them with precision. This education of the eye is more to be appreciated than even the skill of drawing, the language of the eye. In early life therefore as it is the first purpose of education to cultivate the ear, by the most correct utterances of sound, it should be esteemed of equal importance to cultivate the eye by the exact analysis and delineation of forms, not only for its own utility in every manufacture and its aid in writing, but also for its constant influence of the public taste, and the variety of occupations it affords.

Since about 1870, when art first became a regular part of the public school curriculum of Massachusetts, we have gone through many changes of teaching methods and goals; however, the development of visual awareness through organized art activity in the schools and colleges has remained an important objective. The results have not always been satisfactory; at times the value of perceptual training has not had a very high rating. Since 1960 many articles and editorials have expressed a concern for what has been called "visual illiteracy" among the graduates from our high schools and colleges and in the population in general.

Visual perceptual training is much broader in its implications than simply being the basis for the production and appreciation of art. It plays a basic role in learning. Much of what we understand about our world and our culture has come to us through visual sensations and the meanings we have given to them. It is an important part of both our formal and informal educational experience as we move from early childhood to our later years. In a world that is so filled with visual stimuli that come to us from all angles the need for better understanding of the visually perceived forms and patterns is apparent.

Today, more than ever before, the individual needs to have efficient methods for discriminating and "selecting out" from the visual stimuli of his day-by-day existence those which are relevant to his survival and moving forward. This is the situation faced by the driver of an automobile as he approaches a busy intersection in the city. He must identify the color of the traffic light — red, green, or amber — against the background of the sound and fury of buses, store signs, holiday decorations, pedestrians, and parked and moving automobiles. On this identification he must act quickly.

We are constantly surrounded by visual situations which provide information far in excess of what we can handle practically. Habits have been developed which allow us to cut through redundant material and center upon that which is in our interest deemed important. However, these same habits may cause us to make presumptions that are not valid because of the omission of important details. When stimuli compete, the items we give our attention to in the visual field and the way they are seen in a particular situation may be affected by many factors, including size, color, repetition, previous experience, familiarity, and the like. Unless we are alert, erroneous habits may be perpetuated and new ones left blocked.

Applications of the knowledge gained from research studies of perception and from informal trial-and-error activities are numerous and extend into all aspects of our lives. Some of this knowledge has been put to widespread use in developing the young child's readiness for learning the essential skills during the early school years. It has also been applied in the private and public programs for children who have been disadvantaged culturally or deprived economically. In these programs special attention is paid to activities that build and train the child's perception of visual and other stimuli, in an effort to provide the same base that comes to other children from their home and community experiences. No longer thought of as a fad or a frill, this is a vital and effective means for helping these children to engage successfully in kindergarten and primary school activities with an equality of opportunity with their classmates. Through special preschool and primary school activities the disadvantaged children have had the chance to experience, through their visual and other senses, things that their classmates may have encountered in their homes and family living. It is sometimes difficult to realize that there are children who have not been exposed to colors, shapes, and patterns, who have not seen books, magazines, and papers, who have not been farther from home than the boundaries of a city block, and who live in homes that are devoid of visual and sensory stimuli which are exciting, colorful, and spacious.

The problem of how to use visual information confronts every teacher regardless of the subject he is presenting; the problem of how to handle visual information exists for every individual regardless of age or occupation. Visual information is used by business, industry, and government to sell their products, to develop the tools which produce them, and to enlighten the individuals who will make the products or benefit from them. Visual statements are the means through which we get the data that will help us to make up our minds about which things and services to purchase, which people to elect for public office, or which vocation to follow and which avocations to select. The use of visual communication is not particularly new, but it is the sheer bulk of the amount and kind of information encountered in the contemporary environment which is the new problem.

With this recognition of the problem and the need for a solution, let us examine some of the informal and formal procedures that can aid us. The camera and its products have real value as a resource tool for the extension of our visual boundaries. The example of how it may be employed imaginatively by the artist and by the observer-appreciator of art will be considered. Then the use of this same tool in other hands will be discussed in order to show how the limits of our knowledge have been expanded. An analysis of a formal procedure related to the education of vision and for perceptual training has been added. Discussion of another practice followed by the artist, that of drawing, is also reviewed as part of the search for methods by which the visual awareness of individuals in our societies can be developed to a level beyond that required for survival in a day-by-day existence.

AIDS FOR SEEING

In addition to the natural capacities of our sense of vision, we have been given other tools which enhance these capacities and allow us to probe deeper into the nature of our universe. One of these is the camera with its photosensitive plate.

Since 1826, in France, when the first photograph was taken by Nicéphore Niepce from his window, the camera has provided us with a record of ourselves and our universe. It speaks of our triumphs, loves, and hatreds; our high points and low points are set down for all to see. It tells us of beauty, ordinary and sublime. We are challenged by its documentation of our past and by its exploration into space and into forces we cannot see without its aid. The camera has assisted and extended our vision with its exploratory powers. It so pushes the boundaries of our knowledge with the precision and complexity of information it can gather that we are hard pressed to take in so much.

The men who make pictures with the camera have become interpreters of the objects and events within their field of focus according to their wisdom and feelings. In this manner, art has been created with the camera. In the hands of a growing number of men photography has achieved a level of excellence in producing images that can stand alone with an intrinsic value as art forms. The works of Edward Weston, Alfred Stieglitz, Alfred Eisenstaedt, Edward Steichen, and others meet this standard.

The camera has furnished a sensitive and precise documentary record of the passing scene of the events of our period in history and of people and the things they have built. Entertainment and knowledge have been brought quickly and abundantly to the many through this medium. Edward Steichen's visual statement *The Family of Man* and the U.S. Department of Agriculture's and Works Progress Administration's documentary photos of the Depression Years, of the Dust Bowl, and of the family migrations from Oklahoma and Kansas to California are well-known examples. The photo essays in *Life*, *Look*, and *Holiday* magazines and the television documentary specials take us to all of the great cities and far corners of the world. They allow us to see events of strife and joy almost concurrently with their happening.

It is our concern at this point to examine, in addition to these attainments, the attributes of the camera as an instrument that serves as an aid for perception — that is, as a tool which helps us to see with meaning.

The camera has provided us with some of the raw-material sources of content, structure, and inspiration out of which art is made; it has helped us to understand the products of art and appreciate them.

AN ARTIST AND HIS CAMERA

The following account describes a man with a camera as he investigates a small segment of the world:

A walk in the woods or field or along a railroad track with a camera and a closeup lens can be a stimulating and absorbing experience. Usually the degree of success is inversely related to the distance traveled. Careful examinations of a six-foot area are likely to produce greater results than a frantic search of six acres. Through the revelation of the lens the green spot of moss is transformed into a teeming forest of spindly trees covered with caps of different hues (Fig. 3-1). The smooth bark of a young linden tree caught in a cross fire of sunlight appears as a somber sky or seascape (Fig. 3-2). A dry and weathered seedpod becomes an eerie cavernous

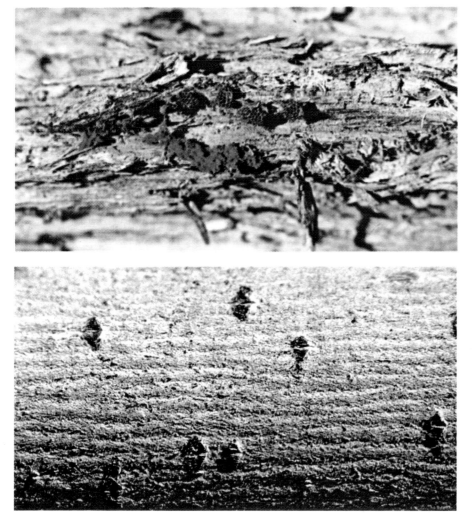

3-1
Lichen.

3-2
Linden tree.

3-3
Wild cucumber.

3-4
Tracery of a bark beetle.

3-5
Silhouette of a dandelion.

3-6
A single dandelion seed.

maze. The skeleton of a leaf bared by decay reveals an intricate network of line and space (Fig. 3-3). Decayed wood is transformed into wind-eroded wasteland, and a wasp's nest becomes a geometrically perfect study in symmetry (Fig. 3-4). Even the ubiquitous dandelion, whose destruction has become a multimillion dollar business, when greatly magnified reveals a breathtaking geometric perfection — a visual explosion of delicate umbrellalike ribs — each rib by itself an elongated parachute with its seed cargo suspended beneath (Figs. 3-5, 3-6).

Through the closeup lens the panorama becomes less important and the seemingly insignificant emerges in all its significant complexity. One ceases merely to identify objects and begins to see them for the first time in all their wonder and mystery. The complex structure, the unique textures, and subtle hues emerge, as if by magic, for the moment. Total reality is narrowed down to the format of the viewfinder, and it seems as though one can physically penetrate into the micro-world. All sense of scale vanishes. The heightened thrill of this visual exploration etches an indelible print upon the mind of the artist. This is the raw image material with which the artist works. This is the preparation of the mind for the insight. This insight is not an unrelated experience, but is prepared for by thought, observation, and experimentation. The emotional stimulus of such experience cannot be overlooked. It is not important whether nature is cognizant or unmindful of the daily drama which occurs between the weak and the strong, the silent and the boisterous, or the adaptable and the perishable, for the artist is free to interpret and anthropomorphize as he wishes.

Through photographic study the artist practices the same disciplines involved in the use of other media, such as selection, rejection, emphasis, and composition. By removing the subject from its relevant surroundings the viewer's entire consciousness is focused upon the visual relationships of line, shape, color, texture, and tone as well as on the harmonious interrelationship of these into the organized structure which we call design (Figs. 3-7, 3-8). It is no longer necessary to know

"what it is." This is the first stage of abstraction! The shallow depth of field inherent in closeup photography literally wipes out all conflicting forms not in the focal plane of the object under examination. A sharply defined image appears to float in a strange background world of subdued color and shadow. The sheer perfection of structural design in nature appeals to the intellect as well as the emotions because these forms are the result of selection for growth and survival or are the results of destruction by time and the elements. In all cases there is an underlying causal factor in action. It is this sense of structure in nature which is so important to the work of the artist. The lessons learned by observing nature's way of construction are a guiding influence whenever materials and techniques allow.

3-7
Lily.

3-8
Lily, closeup.

AN ANALYSIS OF THE CAMERA AS A TOOL FOR THE ARTIST

The above description illustrates some of the unique characteristics of the camera as an aid to seeing. It mentions the discriminatory and the framing qualities of this tool. It also points out how the camera can serve as a means to clarify and magnify the order and pattern of the very small object producing life and excitement in the commonplace. Few of us use our powers of observation for more than mere recognition. We look at the superficial aspects of our surroundings, categorize them, and file them in the dead-letter office of our minds. For some people it requires a trip to distant lands to awaken the sense of wonder and beauty which is present so often in the young child. These are the travelers who never having used a camera for more than photo-album shots of relatives suddenly develop a profound interest in photographing foreign architecture, native costumes, exotic scenes, and sunsets at sea. This is a good beginning. However, the overfamiliarity of daily contact and our search for novelty quite often

3-9
Concrete spiral stairway.

3-10
Tank farm.

cause us to overlook the fact that one's own immediate surroundings may hold equally exciting vistas if we would take the time to explore them more carefully. There is a tendency in our rapidly paced existence to become insensitive to all but the extravaganzas in nature and the bizarre in "man-made happenings." Many of us have become so alienated from the wonder all about us that only phenomena on the scale of the Grand Canyon, Niagara Falls, or a Rose Bowl Parade seem worth investigating.

Perhaps the most unique quality which separates the artist from the layman is his naive childlike sense of curiosity over the commonplace. This is a reward in itself, even if it were to go no further. Par Lagerkvist's Dwarf said of the artist Leonardo, who showed such great interest in and attention to everything about him, "He who finds the simplest stone of value must be forever surrounded by riches." At times it appears that the artist has a special kind of heightened perception, and yet, upon close scrutiny, one finds that most children share this quality. Could it be that instead of acquiring an added gift the artist has for some strange reason failed to lose that which was originally given?

The drama of our transitory systems, the birth-life-death cycle, is found everywhere in nature from the fleeting existence of the insect, which procreates and dies in the same day, to the eternal rock, which ages not an instant in our lifetime. This cycle contains the meaning of life, of which we are but a small part. The story of creation is in evidence all around us and the history of the earth lies at our feet. Nature is inexhaustible as a source of visual excitement and beauty; all one must do is be willing to change his perspective. The group of trees — the forest — is an outdoor cathedral through which we can move. The single tree is a majestic plant whose trunk and branches spurt from large to small to smaller in a preordered pattern as they seek the life-sustaining sunlight. The leaf, with its large stem graduating to ever smaller veins, under close inspection mirrors the structure of the tree in miniature. The bud, a dynamic bursting force of new life, is a virtual explosion in slow motion. The seed has many forms — some lofted on cotton down, some helicoptering to earth, others landing with a thud directly below. The tree grows old and succumbs to ceaseless onslaughts of wind, rain, sun, and frost. Insects attack its aging carcass. The bark peels, baring the tracks of beetle and borer, and the mass of it plays host to countless parasites, which devour it until the once towering tree sinks into the earth from whence it grew. Here it provides the nourishment for the transient seed and thus perpetuates the life cycle.

THE CAMERA AND THE ART PRODUCT

In the same way he has scrutinized nature, the man with his camera can focus upon the landscape of man-made structures. The mass of confusion of the teeming life of the city: the construction site, the supermarket, the secondhand automobile sales row, the filling station, and the sports arena can be framed, isolated, and selectively screened by the camera lens (Fig. 3-9). The surrounding clutter can be eliminated. The center of interest fills up the viewfinder and is all that appears on the printed photograph. Action is stopped. Later on, the viewer of the photo has all the

3-11
Fragment of a city billboard.

time in the world to examine the pattern of light and dark, texture, shape, and line which make up the selected image (Fig. 3-10). This allows us time to go beyond recognition of the object or event and to sense the visual excitement that comes from discovery of the nonobjective formal elements in the design from which our view of reality is constructed (Fig. 3-11).

The regular camera with its standard lens is the door to only a small part of the potential world that is open for investigation. This type of camera can be used skillfully and imaginatively. Although it does not take moving pictures, the person using it can move in closer to his subject and take a sequence of separate exposures which suggest motion when put together. Prints of each exposure in such an orderly arrangement supply a distinctly unique composition of the same subject matter. Because of the change of position of the photographer-viewer (the man with the camera) for the separate exposures, the mood and emphasis received from the prints are often startlingly different.

3-12
*Overall view
of a steam engine
storage yard.*
3-13
An isolated engine.

3-14
Wheel.

3-14

An example of this treatment can be noted in a sequence of photographs taken of a "junkyard." The photos were taken in stages, starting with a rather distant view, which provides a comprehensive look at the subject (Fig. 3-12). This is much the same as the subject might have been seen and painted by the visual realist. More visually oriented students and artists often select such an information-filled conventional arrangement.

Attention (and camera) has been focused progressively upon one machine and then upon one wheel (Figs. 3-13, 3-14). The area of the visual field has been reduced, and some of the unnecessary information has been eliminated; enough remains for an easy and quick identification of the object. As we move in closer with the camera to the hub of the wheel (Figs. 3-15, 3-16), the flanges of metal form a repeated pattern; these images are very much like the selections that a "minimal" sculptor or a "hard-edge" painter would find interesting as the subject matter of his art products.

In order to show a selective eye at work, a few other photos are included. The governor on the top of the engine (Fig. 3-17) has all the qualities that are associated with sculpture; objects very much like this are to be found in art galleries. The end section of boiler plate (Fig. 3-18) and a row of rivets (Fig. 3-19) have obtained beauty and distinction by the effective addition of light and shadow and by weathering of their surfaces. The repetitions of a number of small identical units can create a larger whole that has interest, variety, and vitality under these conditions. By bringing the photographer, the artist, and ultimately the art appreciator into close contact, they are projected into the subject emotionally as well as visually. They are no longer passive, but are actively involved and surrounded by the subject of vision.

3-15

3-16

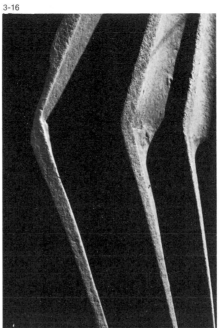

3-17

3-18   3-19

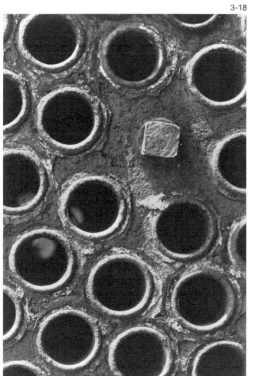

3-15
Hub, detail.

3-16
Wheel tread, detail.

3-17
Governor.

3-18
End of a steam boiler.

3-19
Studded boiler section.

When we look at a good black-and-white photograph or a transparent slide in color, we are quite often reminded of the work of some painter or sculptor. Something about them is reminiscent of the way a particular individual delineated his own perception in a work of art. The selectivity and focus of the camera strengthened our associations and clarified our memory images. The photographer had no intention of simulating a particular work or artist; this is something that happened in the eye and mind of the viewer.

A photograph taken from ground level looking up through the skeleton framework of a water tower showing the black, stark uprights and cross members against the gray-white of the sky is often a reminder of a painting by Franz Kline (Figs. 3-20, 3-21). The upright shell of a slab wall of a building which is being removed for a redevelopment project has the look of a Mondrian painting. The illusion has all of the necessary features: the red-orange rectangle of the wall section of the displaced tenant's living room, with the dirty white of exposed plaster surrounding it, and the whole thing framed in a gridwork of dark horizontal and vertical bars, which were the marks where doors, windows, floors, and ceilings were joined in the original building. From a distance this complex of partially demolished rooms of the apartments lived in by many people has much the same structural pattern of cells that we see when we cut into the hive of community-dwelling insects. The cement blocks in Fig. 3-22 have the horizontal-vertical accents that we associate with the paintings of Mondrian.

Sometimes a photograph has the decorative simplicity of the *Red Barn* by Georgia O'Keeffe, and yet another is reminiscent in subject and viewing angle of works by Charles Sheeler.

A photo of lichen growing on a tree enlarged by the camera lens presents a miniature garden of growing forms with spots of color accent. It has the lush, rich textural qualities that the abstract expressionist has

3-20
Tower against the sky tracing an orderly geometric design.

3-21
Tower against the sky reminiscent of the vitality of a Franz Kline painting.

attempted to present with pigment (Fig. 3-23). The section of weathered wood or asbestos shingle has the same texture and color encrustations that are obtained by the sculptor who welds and brazes his metal with a torch. The action of heat oxidation and of chemistry leaves its mark on the surfaces, which may be kept or removed by the artist depending upon the visual quality he wishes to have in the final product.

THE CAMERA WITH SPECIAL EQUIPMENT

Although most of us have neither the special skill nor the tools to do the work, we do have readily available to us, for our education and enlightenment, the products of photography accomplished with great technical skill and with the aid of very costly equipment. Popular magazines, daily papers, and the photographic sections of the Sunday editions offer many examples. Beginning and advanced textbooks on science and mathematics for the elementary schools, high schools, and colleges contain many photographs which are of interest to the artist, the art teacher, and the student in an art class. A number of books on art and design written or edited by Gyorgy Kepes and others have utilized photographs taken with cameras supplemented by all kinds of attachments for the purpose of clarifying complex theoretical concepts or for dramatic effect. This type of photographic material is published in quantity and has almost become commonplace. It is beyond the resources of most of us to take aerial, time-lapse, or high-speed photos. We are handicapped in dealing with stroboscopic motion studies and X-ray diffractions, and have difficulty with the exploitation of infrared film. Few people have access to an electron microscope or can have photos taken through the telescopes at the Mount Palomar Observatory or have their own photosensitive plates suspended in a satellite orbiting in outer space; yet the results from these sources are all at hand for our inspection.

3-22
Green lichen with flecks of red.

3-23
Concrete blocks.

3-22

3-23

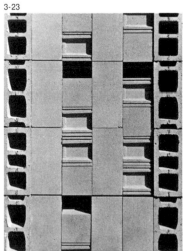

Aerial photography. Viewed from an airplane or on an aerial photograph, the land of trees, farms, and cities appears as an arrangement of textures or as a pattern of colored shapes. Simply by a change of position (point of view), we have come a long way toward abstracting the essentials of a landscape. Extraneous details are removed and we can see the forest instead of the trees. This can be of great help to the artist and the student. Without the aid of the airplane, a great deal of inner concentration would be needed to arrive at the same point, where we could visualize the ordered patterns of our farm landscape, congested cities, and industrial complexes in relationship to the surroundings of hills, waterways, and networks of traffic arteries. Seen from the air, the land and water have a tidy appearance; the pieces fit together into meaningful ordered arrangements. The curved and rectangular chips of color and texture flow together and are cut by sharp diagonals of roads or by curving contours of rivers and hills. On such a large scale, textures and shapes have a habit of repeating themselves with infinite variety. Even when the design of nature is interrupted by man, it can be sensed, perceived, and, to a degree, understood.

The construction of superhighways and freeways, a part of the contemporary way of changing the face of nature, has met with varying degrees of acceptance by the people. The involvement of the individual viewer is less emotional when the results of this activity are viewed from the distance of an aerial vantage point. The examples shown here are taken from a section of a strip photo supplied by the Minnesota Highway Department (Fig. 3-24) and from the "fish-eye" camera view of the California Freeway by J. Eyerman (Fig. 3-25). These show the highly intricate network of the engineering solution to problems of traffic flow with multiple-level interchanges, ramps, and roads in areas of man-made congestion.

When color is used in aerial photography and long continuous strips of land and water are taken on film, the results in positive transparencies are often exciting and dramatic. This is especially true when the subject includes coverage of the exotic-appearing lands and water of the tropics and near tropics. The lush vegetation, coral reefs, and sands seen through the clear translucent waters of the lagoons of atolls and volcanic islands provide a startling pattern of contrasts. The infinite shadings of the changing depth of water and of the clumps of living and dying coral seen from above provide a landscape of swirling, swaying movements of shape, color, and texture. The same is true for other geographical locations: river deltas, glaciated land, rocky coastlands, inland waterways, or cultivated farms, forests, mountains, and deserts.

Aerial photographs taken at night, which show only the patterns of stationary and moving lights coordinated with the movement of the airplane, provide another kind of image for perception. Recognizable and easily identifiable features are no longer visible. The viewer sees only the tracks of light across the photographic plate. These represent the abstracted motion of the plane and the vehicle below to which the lights are fastened.

In a special issue on photography, *Life Magazine* reported on a new aerial reconnaissance system designed by Dr. Edward Yost, which uses color to bring out hidden information. The overall scene was taken with a conventional panoramic camera on color film; this was a horizon-to-

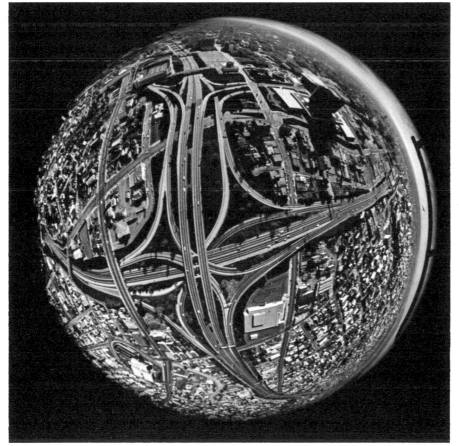

3-24
*Aerial photo of
a freeway interchange. (Courtesy
Minnesota Highway Department.)*

3-25
*California freeway seen
through a fish-eye lens*

horizon view. On the same flight run, closeups of sections of the scene were made. Four separate lenses simultaneously photographed the entire panoramic scene through four different filters. These blue, green, red, and near-infrared filters allowed only narrow bands of the light spectrum through to expose the ordinary black-and-white film. Thus, four somewhat different photos of the subject were produced, each recording how it looked in a different color of light. In the laboratory, using special projectors and dozens of color filters, the differences among the details on the four photo versions were enhanced and exaggerated to give the information which was needed.[1]

Scientific photography. Photography has been widely used as a research tool. Fortunately for artists and laymen, there are very few scientists who look at the microworld of nature through a microscope without receiving a measure of sheer enjoyment from the patterns they see. They wish to share this drama with others. The microstructures of crystals, metal alloys, living cells, and tiny organisms reveal the true internal structure of metal, rock, and living things which results from the physical interactions of the atoms of which they are composed. It is only a small jump in perceptive awareness to an analogy between this basic structural organization in nature to order and design in a work of art, with its interplay of dimensions and shapes. The photomicrograph of a cross section of a living cell or twig or an X-ray diffraction pattern of a seashell shows the interrelationships and the inherent forces within the biologic growth of the living forms. These can be clearly noticed, and the parallel between these forces in nature and the development of the art works may be recognized.

The two microphotos shown here were obtained from a scientist who has employed the electron microscope extensively for his research with animals. One shows a cell fragment, a platelet that is involved in the clotting of blood (Fig. 3-26); the other is of a lymphocyte from the lymph fluid of the cow (Fig. 3-27). These are hardly subjects that would cause a great flurry of excitement and the stimulation of a rash of man-on-the-street interviews, but for both scientists and artists they are objects for perceptive attention. To obtain the photographs, an electron beam was shot through a tiny fragment of matter supported on a screen that has been marked off with 300 lines to an inch. The scientist views the central area of the one three-hundredths of an inch square space between the cross marks and focuses upon all bodies that are clear of the grid lines.

For the scientist the microphoto of the platelet has a great quantity of information within the boundaries exposed to his eyes. He sees the dark areas revealed as hemoglobin and the glycogen granules containing a built-in food supply. He recognizes the springlike microtubules that provide structural stability to the cell and the plasma membranes that surround and define the various parts of the organic whole. He is interested in the contribution that each part makes toward the fulfillment of the function of the platelets in the clotting of blood. This scientific grasp of a "world" of information becomes even more wondrous when we realize that the world we are examining has an actual size of about three microns (a micron is

1 **Life Magazine**, vol. 61, no. 26 (December 23, 1966), pp. 110–111.

one-thousandth of a millimeter) or approximately one ten-thousandths of an inch.

The artist sees this same microworld of the platelet as a designed structure, as a unit without much concern for its bigness or smallness. It is an organized pattern of lights and darks with textured grays in between. He is attracted visually by this pattern defined by strong clean sweeping curves which loop out to the edges of the visual plane; the centrally located, larger and almost circular unit fits in and belongs with the curves that thrust off to the edges at the top and side. The central areas, with their fairly well-ordered repetition of darker spots and wiggly textured groupings around them, provide a focus as a point of interest; the lightest spot, lighter and larger than all the rest, is placed in just the right position to center attention and hold it. The middle-gray textures in the surrounding area, to the right and below the central core, are varied in detail, but hold together as a formed mass that is related, yet a separate part of the whole. The textures, tones, and shapes of this chunk of a living thing are all fitted together like the surfaces of an oil or watercolor painting or of a batik-dyed textile. They are defined into shapes within shapes in the same manner that the artist does when he constructs his work of art.

3-26   3-27

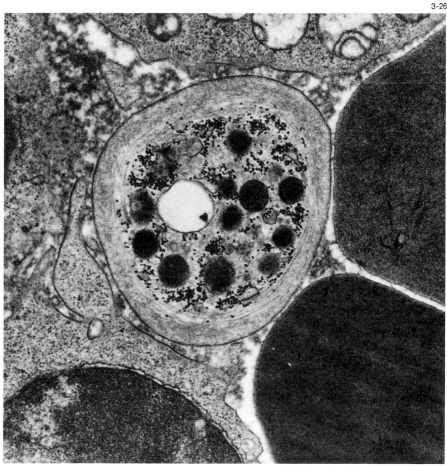

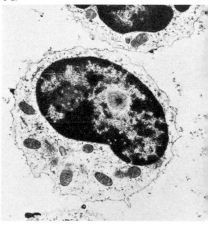

3-26
Platelet, microphoto.

3-27
Lymphocyte, microphoto.

3-28
Photograph of sun corona.
(Courtesy High Altitude Observatory,
Boulder, Colorado.)

We can move from the microworld of a fragment of a cell to the other extreme, the macroworld of the universe, through the products of the camera (Fig. 3-28). Photos taken by satellites orbiting 22,300 miles high show a large area of the earth. They have provided an easy way to view the mass movement of energy-laden air from the tropics into the temperate latitudes. When Mars was photographed by Mariner IV from 7,800 miles away in 1965, it was possible to identify eroded craters as small as 3 miles across. Through photography, astrophysicists have gathered data about the tremendous forces of energy that erupt from our sun to resolve questions that have puzzled man since the time of the primitive people who worshiped it. Balloons equipped with cameras have penetrated the rarefied atmosphere 25 miles above the earth in order to bring us good pictures of sunspots; flares covering enormous areas of the surface of the sun have been recorded for detailed study by the techniques of spectroheliography (Fig. 3-29). The spectrum of visible light with which we normally look at space has been reduced to a very narrow section or band. The sun is scanned and photographed with light from all other wavelengths of the spectrum filtered out. This allows the astrophysicist to detect the activity of such phenomena as sun flares over large areas of its surface; these flares cannot be seen unless such techniques are employed.

This contrast in size requires quite an adjustment in our perceptual frame of reference. In one case, we are dealing with organisms that measure one ten-thousandth of an inch, while with the sun we are referring to something that has a diameter of approximately nine hundred thousand miles. The photographs we look at could be of areas that have the same actual measurements.

The technique of holography produces truly three-dimensional images. The hologram is made with a laser, plus beam splitters, multiples of lenses and mirrors — and a technical knowledge outside the realm of the home photographer. It is a system for viewing a subject in its entirety, from almost any angle. It is now used for research and industrial purposes. With it the microbiologist can see his specimens in the "round," and hopefully it will enable satellites to make contour maps of moons and planets; 3-D movies and television may be developed for viewing without special glasses.

THE CAMERA AS AN EXTENSION OF VISION

As has been noted above, the camera and the results of its work can be a vital and positive tool for clarifying perception in general and artistic perception in particular. Employed as a visual aid, it frames and selects and discriminates; it eliminates peripheral and often confusing stimuli that surround an object upon which we wish to center our attention. When various attachments or mechanical gadgets are incorporated to extend its function, the camera action can be stopped to give more time for examination. The time lapse of things which grow slowly and change minutely can be closed, and happenings which take place over a great span of time can be seen together in a smooth, flowing rhythm. Small things may be made large, large things made smaller, and distant things are brought down to earth. X-ray photos remove the concealing skin or outer shell in order to allow us to see what is and has gone on inside. Familiar things appear strange, and strange things appear familiar (Figs. 3-30, 3-31). Because we are aided in seeing more clearly, preliminary stages of the art process of abstracting are accomplished more readily.

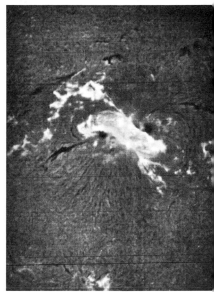

3-29

3-29
Solar flare, spectroheliogram.

3-30
Grain mills on panchromatic film.

3-31
Compare the tonal changes in the areas of foliage and sky with Fig. 3-30. In the infrared photograph the foliage appears lighter and the sky darker.
Grain mills on film sensitive to infrared light.

3-30   3-31

EDUCATION OF VISION

The role of visual perception is known and accepted. It has also been shown that certain visual functions can be improved through instruction or training which develops the ability to observe and to respond selectively to visual stimuli. However, precise training and procedures for the development of specific perceptual skills have not been developed to any great extent.

During most of its existence as a formal subject in elementary and secondary schools, as well as in colleges, one of the aims and outcomes of experience with the arts has been that of the development of awareness or the improvement of one's perceptual skill. It is presumptuous to claim that art experience, even when directed specifically toward perceptual training, can provide all of the visual awareness needed by all individuals in order to apprehend and respond with facility to their environment. Closer within the grasp of preparation in art would come the education of vision for the production of objects that will enhance the environment and for the appreciation of beauty and order in the man-made and natural landscape in which we live.

A wealth of training and experience has contributed to the artist's ability to perceive the subtleties in visual relationships and to abstract that which is important. It also takes training for the artist to transmit this material that has been selected with a sensitive eye into a structural composition — the design of his art product. Perceptual training is also required if the observer is to identify, extract, and receive satisfaction from the emotive meaning which the artist has given to his product.

Programs in art for the elementary and secondary schools, and to some extent for the colleges, are once again reaffirming their aim to include an emphasis on the development of perceptive awareness; however, the development of perceptive awareness has much broader implications than for a school art program and the ability to function within a formal art classroom. They extend to the whole population in an effort to enable all people to function as individuals within a society that places high expectations upon the benefits of a full and enriched life. This means that all people in and out of school have a need for and can derive benefits from a more intensified awareness that will bring them understanding of the things and events in their environment. This also means that people will be able to see with understanding the art in our heritage from the past and will do the same with the art which is being created in their own time and space.

This desire to improve visual awareness has as its goal something broader than the understanding of works of art that are usually classified as painting, sculpture, or architecture. More to the point is the hope that through an increased visual awareness any individual in our society will become sensitive to the visual qualities and the art that exists within his environment in all of the things made by man and by nature. It is hoped that through this sensitivity to beauty and order man will expect and even demand that his living environment will be shaped and organized with beauty and order in mind. Man's interest in and benefit from the environment in which he lives will then go beyond the practical utilization of the resources of nature for his welfare and benefit. Beauty and order will become part of the plan rather than chance by-products; people will expect art to be introduced into every part of their existence. For all of us this will include the shelters we occupy, the furniture and artifacts we use, the graphic design of our visual materials for education, enjoyment, and communication. In fact, all of the content of our everyday life from the planning of our cities to the tools that we will use for work and recreation will be appraised for beauty of design as well as utility.

The "aesthetic" vision, which allows the individual to see an object as having worth for the qualities of beauty it possesses, with all that is practical or utilitarian disconnected from his consideration, is an extension of the "practical" vision — the kind of seeing practiced by all people and necessary for their survival. The following information about perceptual training is examined in order to demonstrate how the practical vision of people can be extended.

FORMAL PERCEPTUAL TRAINING: A LESSON FROM THE BAUHAUS

Quite often when the topic of visual literacy or the lack of it comes under discussion, the Bauhaus will be mentioned as an example of a successful educational program for the training of visual sensitivity. The Bauhaus, an art school, was founded by the architect Walter Gropius at Weimar, Germany, in 1919. The school served as an experimental laboratory in which the new materials and techniques of a machine age and science-oriented culture could be directed toward the aesthetic and functional benefits of man in all his human activities. This was an idea of art for all people and an idea of art in everyday living — a concept that served as the basis for school art programs in the United States in the 1930s and later.

The Bauhaus program attempted to give the artist-designer an understanding of modern living and of the problems of "the basic nature of designs as an integral part of all things used in everyday living." The teachers of this school directed their program with the aim that "education in art should be to help man discover the biological basis of human life and how these needs can best be realized through the synthesizing of design with technological research." To accomplish his program, Gropius assembled a teaching staff which included many of the prominent figures in the world of art. Connected with this school were such people as the architect-designers Marcel Breuer and Mies van der Rohe; the painters Paul Klee, Wassily Kandinsky, Piet Mondrian, Lyonel Feininger, and László Moholy-Nagy, and the sculptor Gerhard Marcks. The influence of the school and its teachers has had a lasting effect upon teaching and production in the areas of art, architecture, city planning, and graphic, industrial, and interior design.

Many of the men connected with the school came to the United States and continued their work and the promotion of their ideas. Gropius came to Harvard University and Moholy-Nagy established a new Bauhaus in Chicago, which later became the Institute of Design and is now part of the Illinois Institute of Technology. The titles and subject matter of books written by men connected with or influenced by the Bauhaus make clear the importance placed upon visual perception by the school and its staff.[2]

THE BASIC COURSE OF THE BAUHAUS

Before we can judge the validity of a program for perceptual training in the United States in our time that is patterned after the courses and teaching at the Bauhaus more than forty years ago, it would be necessary to look more closely at exactly what was done. Fortunately, Johannes Itten, who established the *Basic Course*, which was taken by all students in whatever area of specialization, has published a book which gives details of this part of the program.[3]

According to Itten, the foundation of his design theory was the general idea of contrasts through material and texture studies, form and color theory, and rhythmic and expressive forms. The value of emphasis on the idea of contrast and concentration upon it through a variety of course exercises can be supported by various studies in psychology. Through contrasts in the visual field, the form of an object is identified and its relationship with things and events is perceived. With the tools of art and its processes, we re-create the visual relationships which allow us to see the form of things through contrasts.[4]

A three-stage plan for perceptual training through art featured: (1) the involvement of all of the senses; (2) the combining of thinking and feeling; (3) problem solving through direct experience which gave meaning and substance to exploration.

Although it encouraged personal inventiveness and exploration, the course as a whole was a structured one and required considerable discipline on the part of the student. The course began with a study of light and dark contrasts, and the student worked on a series of exercises to develop a range of tones from black to white and then went on to use these in more or less nonobjective design compositions. Paintings by great artists were analyzed by graphic means to determine their light and dark patterns. Studies from nature and still life followed. Then figure drawing, nature drawing, and free compositions were added.

Color contrasts were the next major unit of study, and then materials and texture contrasts were investigated. It was in this area, dealing with texture contrasts, that the collages and tactile diagrams were developed to heighten the student's sensitivity and to clarify both the tactile and optical intensity of various textures when combined in a visual statement.

2 László Moholy-Nagy, **The New Vision**, and Gyorgy Kepes, **The Language of Vision.** Also Kepes has developed his original ideas further in practice through his work at the Massachusetts Institute of Technology and through his writings, including **The New Landscape** and a series of publications (**Vision and Value**) which he edited. Included in this series are **Structure in Art and in Science**, **The Nature and Art of Motion**, **Education of Vision**, **Module, Proportion, Symmetry, Rhythm**, **The Man-made Object**, and **Sign, Image, Symbol.**
3 Johannes Itten, **Design and Form: The Basic Course of the Bauhaus**, Reinhold Publishing Corp., New York, 1964.
4 When we enumerate the visual contrasts which might aid man in perceiving the things and events of his world, there are the following: large–small, black–white, long–short, broad–narrow, thick–thin, much–little, straight–bent, pointed–blunt, horizontal–vertical, diagonal–circular, high–low, plane–line, plane–volume, line–volume, smooth–rough, hard–soft, still–moving, strong–weak, quiet–loud, as well as the variety of color contrasts.

An important feature of the course was its systematic pattern for integrating the separate units of experience. Each type of contrast was studied, first alone and then in combination with others. In this manner all of the student's experiences were brought together at intervals; each new experience was related to those that went before. A wide range of tools and materials was thoroughly investigated and experimented with in order to discover the full potential. Learning activities also included sense-training exercises, which prepared the student for a heightened sensitivity and full involvement with the art problem. This preparation was very much like that of a "method" actor preparing for a role on the stage, or the setting-up exercises of a dancer or athlete getting ready for a performance.

Toward the end of the Basic Course the student was given units of work with expressive form and problems on subjective form. The latter was an attempt to identify the personal mood and mode of expression of each student that would be consistent with his personality characteristics and his graphic ability. Throughout the whole program, stress was laid upon learning to see intensively and then upon translating this intensive vision into the visual form of art.

INFLUENCE OF THE BAUHAUS

This detailed account of the Basic Course at the Bauhaus provides an illustration of the kind of program that has been successful for the training of industrial designers. The influence of this program went beyond the confines of the limits and objectives which had been set up for it. Directly and indirectly, fragments of the program were introduced into art teaching and programming in many other countries including the United States. This school and its students and the teachers who worked with them have had an effect upon design of products which we are using today. Such widely separated activities as theater design and city planning have been affected by the experimental efforts of the Bauhaus. Traces of its influence are part of the contemporary scene in the design of industrial products such as furniture, automobiles, household appliances, and tools. Graphic design of lettering and type faces for a great deal of our advertising and information media received much which was beneficial from this source. Textiles, woven and printed, ceramics, and other handcrafted products as we know them today show that this school, its students and teachers, had an effect upon the design of products we are using.

GUIDELINES FOR A PROGRAM OF PERCEPTUAL TRAINING

When we consider the far-reaching influences of this single school program, it is little wonder that when people are looking for a model for improving our visual aptitude they look with favor upon the Bauhaus and the example it provided. However, the age and problems are different and a direct translation of something designed specifically for one purpose may not be particularly meaningful in a different context. Nevertheless, it would be senseless to "reinvent the wheel" or to discard without examination something out of the past which might very well be a valuable guide.

By cutting through the specific details of the program and singling out its essential features, it is possible to arrive at concepts or principles which may be valuable guideposts in the training of perception. Basic concepts from an analysis of the Bauhaus program which have implications beyond the training of artist-designers and which relate directly to the improvement of our practical vision are the following:[5]

1. That perceptual training should concentrate first upon how we see things more intensively because of contrasts in our visual field.

2. That clarity and depth in seeing depend not only on the sense of sight but also upon reinforcement and enrichment from information received through the other senses.

3. That a high degree of perceptual awareness can be developed more effectively when an integrated, systematic pattern of experiences is provided for the learner.

4. That perceptive sensitivity is heightened when the thinking mechanism of the learner is brought into the act, so that the individual may classify and otherwise organize the information he has received through the senses. He can then give an objective form to his perceptions through pictorial, structural, or decorative design, or by some other means available to him.

These four points derived from analysis of an art school program have wider application than solely for this field of specialized training. They could be translated into the kind of learning which would aid any individual to progress from the limited practical vision to a more curious, imaginative, or aesthetic response to his environment. In the following sections these four guideposts are explained in greater detail.

VISUAL FIELD CONTRASTS

Much visual information is concentrated at lines formed by abrupt color or value changes or where the contour direction breaks. Also, much can be learned through closer attention to places and points where there are contrasts in size, shape, and direction of elements in the visual field. Perceptual training relevant to these visual cues could provide the ability to see and deal with visual detail in a more selective manner, so that essential cues will not be overlooked and the individual will be more likely to interpret experience for practical and aesthetic purposes more efficiently. In producing works of art and design the artist through his media manipulations establishes a pattern of contrasts which allows the viewer to identify and interpret his subject and message.

"Make your lighter lights lighter and your darker darks darker, and you will have the reason why the world's best pictures are the world's best pictures." This advice was given by an instructor to his students in

---

[5] For comparison, see Appendix 3 for the goals of the Basic Course at the Bauhaus.

an art class many years ago. Although it is hardly comprehensive, it does point up the importance of contrasts established by the artist in order to help the viewer to see more clearly. The artist in any field of endeavor, through his own selective eye and his competence with the tools of his craft, gives the observer of the work of art a form of perceptual focusing which allows him to concentrate upon selected rather than competing images. Even when the art object is reduced to a minimum of visual cues, there are still a number of parts of the composition competing for attention.

Artistically we create or adjust relationships through contrasts. While looking either at nature or at art, we are aided in our process of selecting or separating important elements from a number of other conflicting stimuli which seek attention by the extent or degree of contrasts. There must be a contrast between an art object and its background if we are to see it clearly. Sometimes this figure-ground contrast in nature is minimized for purposes of survival. In the case of protective coloration in nature, the contrast between figure and its background is minimized, so that the animal or insect will merge into its background and become hard to see. This minimization of figure-ground contrast also occurs in art when the architect wishes to have his building blend into a site and designs it with this in mind, as was the case with Frank Lloyd Wright and the Kaufmann house, Falling Water, in Bear Run, Pennsylvania. On the other hand, a setting for a painting or sculpture may be chosen because it provides an extreme contrast which separates the work of art from its surroundings, so that it can be seen clearly and distinctly.

Some research studies have shown that art experience can be directed toward the development of the ability to see and deal with visual detail in a selective manner. Perceptual training relevant to visual cues located in the contour changes of objects and where light and dark value contrasts occur has resulted in a significant increase in the amount of visual information included by children in their drawings.[6]

MULTISENSORY INVOLVEMENT

The systematic involvement of other senses in combination with vision will reinforce and enrich the information obtained. When purchasing a suit or selecting drapery, the fabric is almost automatically tested by the buyer. By touching or squeezing the material in his fingers he obtains tactile as well as visual information. The purchaser of an automobile often walks around a car and kicks the tires to help him make a more confident purchase. The blind and those with impaired vision learn to "see" by hearing and increase their sensitivities by "feeling" objects and obstacles.

When visual and verbal statements are combined (painting to music or illustrating a poem), or when the sense of sight and of touch are united in viewing a single work of art, the empathy for the viewer has added intensity and drama. Many kinetic sculptures combine sound, motion, and even smell to heighten the visual impact on the viewer.

---

6 R. A. Salome, **The Effects of Perceptual Training Upon the Two Dimensional Drawings of Children**, unpublished education dissertation, Stanford University, Stanford, California, 1964. See also R. A. Salome, **Perceptual Training as a Factor in Children's Art**, Art Education, vol. 20, no. 9 (December, 1966), pp. 27–29.

CREATIVE SYNTHESIS

It has been suggested that a higher level of perceptual awareness will be developed when the individual is systematically involved and when his experiences are brought together and unified at intervals. In this way a synthesis of new experiences with old is carried through by plan rather than left to chance. Through a pattern of planned experiences, the individual is more likely to have an attitude or set which allows him to be open and to concentrate upon the visual experience; he has the desire to see more fully and clearly. When this synthesis of experience occurs, it is in effect a new experience which goes beyond a summation of the parts. In science it has resulted in a dramatic breakthrough into new areas of knowledge. When it happened in art, a revolutionary style change was born.

OBJECTIFYING RATIONALLY

Objectifying rationally brings into play the thinking mechanism, which organizes the information received through the senses and gives perceptions objective form. It combines the intellectual with the emotional components of the individual; thinking and feeling have a reciprocal action.

Greater meaning is given to the perceptual experience if the individual attempts to objectify and translate this visual data into an objective form in some manner. In art this is done through pictorial, structural, and decorative design. It may take some other form — charts, graphs, diagrams, or the like — in other kinds of endeavors. Modern technology has enabled us to record visual portraits of all kinds of physical phenomena. Sound waves can be analyzed in visual form; pressure waves can be seen diagrammatically, or as photographic patterns. In one of his paintings Arthur Dove gave us a view of the sound of a foghorn rather than a portrait of the instrument which was making the sound. Modern poets have exploited the visual aspect of words as well as their sounds. The way the words are set in type on the page is very important in resolving the meaning of the poem. The tracks, or lines of force, of the cosmic ray across a photosensitive plate carried into the upper atmosphere by a satellite bring back an objective visual image of something that otherwise might not be seen (Fig. 3-32).

DRAWING AS AN AID TO PERCEPTION

The artist in each of us comes forward when our perceptions of our environment and our experiences with it are objectified in order that they may be seen with greater clarity and depth. Of all the devices or techniques available to the artist or child for this purpose, the preliminary sketch or drawing is most comprehensively used. Although it is only one of the many ways of objectifying visual perception, it is more universally employed as a means of recording, or documenting, what the eye has seen. It is the means by which redundant information is filtered out, leaving only that which is important or critical in the mind of the observer.

In casual conversation the words "sketching" and "drawing" are often used interchangeably without a very precise distinction between them. Perhaps this is because many of the same media are used. They are executed rapidly In a shorter span of time than other art processes. They are probably thought of together because of their function as the artist's means for recording his first impressions directly and quickly. In both, we have something concrete — down on paper, as it were — which serves in many cases as a resource for something of grander scope — a painting, a print, a sculpture, or a building. If, however, distinctions should be made, it is because some drawings have intrinsic value in themselves as works of art. They have distinctive quality as art objects and are valued as such rather than as preparations or incidental but useful notes for something else. For our purposes the term "drawing" will be used inclusively when referring to the quick notations for recording the initial impressions from perceptions and the more thoughtful, imaginatively developed artistic images that are aesthetically satisfying to the observer. In the following discussion of the role of drawing as an aid or record for perception, our interest lies in how the artist uses this process as a research tool in the first stages of abstracting the essence of an idea.

The artist makes sketches or drawings of things, people, and events with varying degrees of care and for many and sundry purposes. During this note-taking he sometimes consciously pays attention to the value of this endeavor as an aid for improving his perception as such. Perhaps the most famous example of this kind of activity can be found in the notebooks of Leonardo da Vinci. Leonardo's sketchbooks included anatomical studies, diagrams of his inventions, and records of his observations of both organic and inorganic phenomena in nature. It was a record of a lifetime devoted to searching for meaning in nature through science and art. These examples of the way an artist looked at his world have been exhibited in museums across the globe; they are reproduced to illustrate many books, films, and magazines, as well as for television shows on subjects of art and science.

Another well known example from a more recent period in time is the "shelter sketchbook" of the British sculptor Henry Moore. These drawings

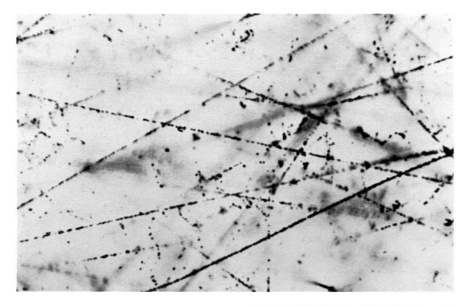

3-32
Tracery of protons from the sun on a photosensitive emulsion (Courtesy of Edward P. Ney.)

were made during the time he spent in the underground air-raid shelters in the subways of London. During the hours when the city was under attack in World War II, he observed and recorded with sensitivity and simplicity his visual experiences with the people and their life together. He made drawings of the rows of huddled, reclining figures wrapped in blankets with contours smoothed out, of family groups camping together, and of the monumentality of separately seated human figures. The people in clothes and wrappings or shawls and blankets for warmth and protection against the chill and dampness filled the pages of his sketchbooks. Later, in his sculptures, we see the reflection of these experiences and a resolution of his perceptions of the simple dignity of humanity under the stress of events beyond their control. The mass and treatment of his sculptures in wood, stone, and metal have a look about them that was first seen in his drawings of his experiences during the war years.

Other artists look upon drawings as separate from their work with other media and processes. The following is an excerpt from a letter written by the sculptor Lynn Chadwick in which he explains the relationship between his drawings and his work in sculpture:[7]

> However, I would say that in the main this paragraph about doing sketches after the sculpture is true in my case. What I have not explained is that apart from one or two "working drawings" which I have made to aid me in the mental requirements of some of my earlier works, I have worked quite directly in iron. Drawings are a separate matter, and are for a purpose — like lithographs to provide another media.
>
> In this respect it is much better to complete the sculpture for me as I find that working out an idea on paper first really does destroy spontaneity. I have recently found that by making a number of maquettes I have difficulty in concentrating on the one chosen to enlarge. There seems to be no excitement of discovery.

AN INTENSIFICATION OF VISION

For both the artist and the student drawing becomes a tool for sharpening their observations. Quick and exploratory notes are made by artists of greater and lesser stature. Many ultimately utilize the vision gained from their jottings and quickly scribbled impressions for compositions in all kinds of materials; as artists they go beyond the act of perception to the delineation of that which has been perceived. Thus when we talk about drawing, we are involved with a complex and compound act of behavior. It is the effect of the experience of drawing upon the individual's ability to perceive that we wish to emphasize at this stage.

Let us look back to what has been said with reference to seeing as "sensing plus selecting plus perceiving" and to perceptions as "sensations to which we have given meaning." Against this background we can understand the importance of drawing as a tool for developing awareness, or

---

[7] Taken from a letter by Lynn Chadwick to a young student who had asked him about some published remarks attributed to the sculptor.

artistic vision, or whatever synonymous label you may wish to give it. While he is drawing, the artist receives a complex array of visual *sensations* from a chunk of the world or from the happenings in it — farmyard, city streets, circus, riot, or whatever has provoked his attention. There are numerous bits and pieces of sensations; many are confusing and many are unnecessary. He *selects* from this mass of sensation and extracts what is necessary in his own interest and judgment. Then he records his selection *with meaning* in the form of a drawing.

The process we call drawing is not mechanical as is a photograph made by the camera, but is much more creatively selective. In accordance with our previous description of seeing as sensing plus selecting plus perceiving, we might describe drawing as sensing plus selecting plus perceiving plus objectifying (delineating).

The mature artist has been made confident by his past experience. He knows what to take in and what to leave out. He is searching for essentials and eliminates the minor and irrelevant details which do not contribute. Patterns, rhythmically repeated movements, and orderly and related elements are selected and emphasized. Dimensional accuracy is not usually the aim. However, these quick shorthand notes often capture more of the fresh living quality and the reality of the subject than can be found in the carefully documented accuracy of a photograph.

The relationship between perceiving and drawing is a two-way street. Falling into the "which came first, the chicken or the egg?" kind of argument is fruitless. This relationship should be thought of as a case of one contributing to the other; one's ability to perceive contributes to more attractive and efficient drawing, and one's ability to make sketches contributes to more sensitive and accurate perception. The mechanical aspects of the act of sketching or drawing — of using the tools with facility and skill to make marks on paper — are our simplest problem. This skill is developed through repetition, drill, or practice. The critical element which distinguishes the master from the novice or the experienced artist from the student is a difference in the degree and quality of their perceptive selectivity rather than their different levels of manipulative coordination.

MEMORY AND ITS RELATIONSHIP TO DRAWING

The factor of memory and its bearing on sketching should also be considered. Because of the personal involvement of the artist and student as they make rapid exploratory drawings, there is a tendency for the memory images to be retained longer and in more detail than is the case with other visual sensations that are received. While making drawings of people in action, of a harbor, or of an arranged still life, the individual closes out all other distractions. He detaches himself and concentrates all his attention on the job at hand. He is not just looking but is also selecting, accenting, and judging the relative importance of one item over another. Added to all of this is the active, rather than passive, participation of the individual in the drawing situation. The delineation of what has been perceived adds another dimension to the experience, reinforcing and strengthening the latent traces of it which are left in our memory of the visual experience; "recall" at some time later on is much easier to accomplish.

3-33
Preliminary sketch.

The short time span usually allowed for completion of a drawing and, sometimes, the brief duration of the subject within our visual field forces an exercise and training of the memory. Quite often the subject moves: a child playing on the floor, animals in a field, men at work, or a rocket launching will not hold still for our convenience and contemplation. The place and condition of observation are sometimes uncomfortable and difficult. In the short period of time, while the subject is in view, it is necessary to record factual impressions quickly. The main lines, shapes, and size relationships must be grasped immediately and put down with facility. In such a situation the memory is stretched and recall is required. Memory training and the ability to recall images develops in very much the same way as it does with the use of the tachistascope, a device used for teaching reading or for aircraft recognition. This device allows an image to be flashed on a screen for a controlled fraction of time, as short as one-fiftieth of a second or less. Practice with the tachistascope has demonstrated that by learning we can reduce the time span needed to grasp and identify a visual image.[8] The individual improves with practice and can transfer his learning to other situations. The conditions under which sketching takes place are hardly as tightly controlled; however, it can be seen that drill or exercise with purpose and attention can improve performance, give accuracy to our perception, and extend the memory of our perceptive experience.

Drawing has been discussed here as a preparation for and a preliminary part of the total comprehensive activity which leads to the creation of a work of art. A drawing is an expression of a perception, often intense and revealing, yet limited in the range and meaning of its imagery. The

[8] The tachistoscope, employed extensively in remedial-reading activities, was an important tool for training airplane pilots, gunners, etc., for aircraft and ship recognition during World War II.

distinction between mere expression and artistic imagery was clarified in the following statement by Kepes:[9]

> The basic characteristic of any artistic expression is the ordering of a visual impression into a coherent complete living form. The difference between a mere expression, however intense and revealing, and an artistic image of that expression lies in the range and structure of its form. This structure is specific. The colors, lines and shapes corresponding to our sense impressions are organized into a balance, a harmony or rhythm that is in an analogous correspondence with feelings, and these feelings are in turn analogous of thoughts and ideas. An artistic image, therefore, is more than a pleasant tickle of the senses and more than a graph of emotions. It has meaning in depth and at each level there is a corresponding level of human response to the world. In this way an artistic form is a symbolic form grasped directly by the senses but reaching beyond them and connecting all the strata of our inner world of sense, feeling and thought.

DRAWING AS THE BEGINNING OF ABSTRACTING

The speed at which a drawing can be accomplished makes it an ideal tool for recording and documenting information directly from visual perceptions; the facility it offers makes it a most satisfactory process for manipulating, adjusting, and reassembling these perceptions. Nevertheless, despite this ease and speed of execution, the person making the drawing cannot record all the information available. As an artist, he does not want to do this anyway; thus, he must make decisions about what to leave in and what to leave out. These decisions are the beginnings of the process of abstracting.

During these early stages, abstracting is a matter of necessity although by his experience the artist takes this opportunity to establish immediately what to him is important and essential. His attention centers on this, and redundant material is cleared away. Even the most realistically rendered research drawing has reduced the three-dimensional world of objects and events to the two-dimensional picture plane of the surface upon which the drawing is made.

The progress from drawings to another art process, painting, is shown in Figs. 3-33 through 3-37. These illustrate a very common procedure employed by many people who take some of the objective facts present in an act of perception and allow their mind to penetrate the form and function of the external objects. They sense some of the organic relationships inherent in the subject and relate to it a feeling of wholeness or atmosphere. Following is an account of this kind of experience:

We had arrived in Medicine Hat late in the afternoon after driving all day across the prairie lands of Canada. Medicine Hat was near the end of the flat country and just

---

9 From the Introduction by Gyorgy Kepes (ed.) to **Education of Vision**, George Braziller, Inc., New York, 1965; reprinted with the permission of the publisher. Copyright © 1965 by George Braziller, Inc.

before the rise of the mountains — a good place to stop. Towns with names like Moose Jaw and Medicine Hat do not seem strange after having accepted Round Bottom in West Virginia, Slippery Rock in Pennsylvania, and Sleepy Eye in Minnesota. But there was still a notion that in Medicine Hat there would be something special. There wasn't if one was looking for the spectacular.

After dinner we drove about in the city, stopping occasionally to make some sketchy notes. At this time the city was quiet. Traffic was sparse and observation was not interrupted by the need for defensive driving. A flash of sunlight — the late sun was strong, low, and bright — reflected off a building ahead. Although the building, actually a church, was not in itself distinctive, the effect of sunlight against deep shadows made it come alive. Somehow it didn't seem real — solid and firmly attached to the ground. It had an indefiniteness, an ethereal romantic quality, as if it were made of shifting blocks of broken light rather than the substance of stone. Nature had transformed a work of man from the ordinary into the extraordinary!

This was the perception, and the artist's tools were clearly inadequate for the task of giving it an objective form. A quick sketch was made of the physical shape of the building (Fig. 3-33). This was done reluctantly because the physical dimensions of the building were quite irrelevant to the total effect of the impression of this experience on the observer. The rough drawing was made because it might act as a cue for recall of the image at a later time. The lapse of time acts as a filter and what is left of the memory of the image is usually the important part. This is abstraction through passage of time and the selectivity of memory.

Months later a decision was made to "take a shot" at putting the idea of this experience into paint. The drawings (Figs. 3-34–3-36) were made quickly. They were trial runs, more or less, to get the form of things fixed in mind and muscle, so that when painting started attention could be given to more important things. The church at Medicine Hat was the springboard for something else and hopefully the townspeople will forgive the liberties taken with their building. The painting in a small way became an expression of the forces of man and of nature working together — shafts of light, disrupting the anchor of fixed boundaries, rising up into an open undetermined space (Fig. 3-37). The painting related to the feelings I have had about a place — an experience which is bound up with many others in other places and other times.

3-34–3-36
Preliminary sketches
in oil pastel.

3-37
The Church of Medicine Hat.
Acrylic.

3-34

3-35   3-36

Chapter 4

THE PROCESS OF
ABSTRACTION

The words "abstract" and "abstraction" in reference to art have been used to describe the kind of products which have been the dominant expressions of painters and sculptors in the United States and much of Europe since World War II. In their broadest and commonest meanings, these words are used to describe almost any kind of product except that which is clearly recognizable as visual realism.

For many laymen and school children the meaning of the term abstraction is often oversimplified as "something that doesn't look like anything!" When schoolchildren are told rather blandly by the teacher, as they often are, "Today, boys and girls, we are going to make abstractions," they most often conclude that the lesson will require them to make something that could loosely be called "designs." More accurately, they think that they are being asked to make decorative patterns which are organizations of colors and shapes with or without any recognizable source in subject matter from their previous experiences with the environment and from events they have observed.

In the following discussion abstracting or abstraction is considered in broad terms as the art process by which the artist proceeds from a perception to the delineation of that perception through his use of art materials and techniques. Through this process the artist, young or old, gives objective form to the meaning he has derived from his experience with nature, man, and man-made things. The artist abstracts, or "takes out," of his world that which is to him important — the essentials of things and events — and sets them down for others to see. Through this process of abstraction he distills and thereby intensifies the character, mood, and spirit of his responses to his environment. For his own purposes and by personal choice he may simplify, distort, accent, fragment, and reassemble, according to his views of the world and reality. In this sense, abstraction has a universal meaning and applies to all artists and even to young children who engage in art activity.

This statement that all art is abstract and that the process of abstracting is involved in the production of every work of art requires further explanation. There are differences in both degree and kind of abstraction that distinguish the products of art and the working methods of artists.

The painter (or, for that matter, the photographer) who puts down on canvas (or on film) the most visually accurate representation of an apple is abstracting, although to a limited degree. He has reduced the three-dimensional actuality of the fruit to the two-dimensional replica on the canvas. He has abstracted and taken away one of its dimensions — which is not an easy task. No matter how realistic the sculpture of a nude woman may be to the viewer, it is still an abstraction. The sculptor has distilled the flesh and bones of the woman and reduced them to the forms of marble, wood, or plaster. George Segal's plaster casts from living models and Rauschenberg's stuffed goat with the automobile tire around its midsection become abstractions because their environment is changed and because the intention of the artist has changed their context and symbolic meaning.

From these examples it can be seen that a certain amount of abstraction is inevitably imposed on the artistic image by the materials and techniques employed and because the subject matter undergoes some changes

as it passes through the eye, mind, and emotions of the artist. Within these extended boundaries lie art forms which are a conscious reflection of the artist's direct experiences with nature. Then there are those art products which are attempts at a synthesis of experience rather than a reflection of individual experience. These reach for the general and universal; the Mississippi River, John Smith, and the Grand Canyon become any and all rivers, people, and eroded places.

Because so many liberties have been taken with the object and with nature, many artists felt that the only reality left for art was the "inner world" of the intellect, imagination, and senses. This has brought into existence a completely nonobjective, or nonrepresentational, art, in which the formal elements making up its imagery are intended to be meaningful in themselves, independent of associations with perceptible reality. However, since the individual is not vacuum packed and sealed off from contact with nature and environment, the formal elements — form, shape, color — have their source in the visual-tactile world.

MODES OF PERCEPTION

Many writers on the subject of the arts have attempted to show that distinctions between works produced by different artists or at different periods may be attributed to differences in the kind of perception employed by artists and that each of these modes of perception was consistent with the thinking in a culture during a period of history. One of these writers on art and artists, Herbert Read, has gone into this subject more extensively. He has developed a theory [1] which connects four distinct modes of perception

---

1 Herbert Read, **Education Through Art**, Faber and Faber, London, 1958.

4-2
*Rogier van der Weyden.
The Deposition. Ca. 1435.
Prado, Madrid.*

which correspond to four types of mental activity (thinking, feeling, sensation, intuition) with four distinct kinds of aesthetic activity expressed in works of art (realism, superrealism, expressionism, and constructivism). Whether one agrees entirely with all of the aspects of this pattern of relationships, his explanation of the different ways people and artists may perceive their world is worthy of examination.

Following are the separate modes of perception identified by Read. References to artists and art expressions are given to indicate that these modes of perception and the kinds of art associated with them are supposed to extend over the length and breadth of the history of art. In his writings Read has also connected parallel categories of child art and personality to make a comprehensive package of types of art, personality, and modes of perception.[2]

---

[2] A graphic analysis of Read's theory is given in Appendix 5.

4-3
*Michelangelo Buonarroti. Pietà.
1501. St. Peter's, Rome.*

REALISM

This occurs when the artist perceives his world and the objects in it in terms of the objective facts present in the act of visual perception. His perception is controlled by the object and the organic relationship between it and other things in his visual field. In his art work, the realist represents, with varying degrees of exactitude, the objective facts he has obtained from his vision. At times he will penetrate the form and the function of the external object with his mind and present it through his skill as a craftsman.

Into this category fit the artists in the Renaissance tradition, such as Michelangelo, Leonardo da Vinci, Raphael, Botticelli, as well as the French impressionists, including Manet, Monet, and Renoir. This category also includes American artists such as John Sloan, Edward Hopper, Charles Sheeler, Ben Shahn, and Andrew Wyeth (Figs. 4-1–4-6).

SUPERREALISM

Painters and sculptors who tend to favor this mode of perception make use of objects of visual origin, but construct of these, in their minds and with the media of art, an independent reality. They put things into new relationships, into "impossible" juxtapositions of materials that somehow still make sense. René Magritte, Chagall, De Chirico, and Dali have brought associative meanings to their subject matter by placing together unrelated and incongruous items as Hieronymous Bosch did almost five centuries before them (Figs. 4-7, 4-8). This kind of organization of images can be noted in the "assemblages" of some pop artists of the middle of the twentieth century, who use this method for arousing the viewer's eidetic and memory images.

4-4

4-4
Pierre-Auguste Renoir.
San Marco (detail).
Minneapolis Institute of Arts.

4-5
Ben Shahn.
The Red Stairway. 1944.
City Art Museum,
St. Louis.

4-6
John Sloan.
South Beach Bathers. 1908.
Walker Art Center,
Minneapolis.

4-5   4-6

4-7
Giorgio de Chirico.
The Anxious Journey.
1913. Museum of Modern Art,
New York.

4-8
Henry Moore.
Sculptural Objects.
1949. Lithograph.
Collection of Ruth Roach.

Also included in this category are those who use images of visual origin, but are primarily concerned with their color and two-dimensional form. Matisse, Georgia O'Keeffe, and others have demonstrated how emphasis on color excitement and shapes arranged in flat, decorative patterns can convey a heightened sense of reality to the viewer. Paintings by Stuart Davis have this same decorative quality; his use of color combinations has brought us a view of the city landscape that is powerful, dynamic, and dramatic as well as decorative (Figs. 4-9–4-11).

4-9
Georgia O'Keeffe.
The White Flowers. *1931.*
Whitney Museum of American Art,
New York.

4-10
Stuart Davis. Colonial Cubism.
1954. Walker Art Center,
Minneapolis.

4-11
Henri Matisse. The Blue Window.
1911. Oil on canvas.
Museum of Modern Art,
New York.

EXPRESSIONISM

This mode of perception involves the imaginative projection of one's own consciousness into the object of perception. The artist of this tendency attempts to find a direct plastic correspondence in method and materials for his immediate sensations and his reaction to the perception or experience. The result in art is personal and subjective; for the viewer there is a vision of intense emotion and at times a feeling that the artist derived considerable satisfaction from his action of shaping the materials of his art. Agony and ecstasy are felt in the flow and twist of the medium and figurative elements used by the artist.

The Crucifixion section of the *Isenheim Altarpiece* by Matthias Grünewald is perhaps the most expressionistic statement of the sixteenth century (Fig. 4-12). Four hundred years later Van Gogh made his landscapes a symbol of rippling, twisting, uneasy beauty in which a touch of unhappiness is mixed with the splendor of movement; this quality is found in his starry nights, rolling clouds, cornfields, and cypress trees. Georges Rouault, Ernst Barlach, Karl Schmidt-Rottluff infuse their works with emotional meaning; Oscar Kokoschka was another who dissolved the material form of figures and objects as he reacted to the emotional and visual possibilities inherent in the subject matter of his art.

4-12
*Matthias Grünewald.
Isenheim Altarpiece.
Ca. 1515. Musée d'Unterlinden,
Colmar.*

Sculptors have also exhibited this expressionistic attitude of perception in their works. Ernst Barlach (*The Avenger*; Fig. 4-13), Wilhelm Lehmbruck, and Seymour Lipton achieve a maximum of feeling, yet control and balance the movement and rhythm of their structures. Germaine Richier in *Don Quichotte* and Theodore Roszak in *Cradle Song* express their deep feelings about their subjects as much by their treatment of the metal as by any symbolic or figurative shape in the composition (Figs. 4-14, 4-15).

CONSTRUCTIVISM

This mode of perception avoids all imitative elements and invites aesthetic response to purely formal relationships of space, mass, color, and sound. There are two courses that can be taken by the artist. The first starts with the artist's observation of the original source material. From this he constructs an original motif — a *rhythmical form.* The repetitions of the measures or quantities he has discovered in his perceptive analysis of his subject matter become the basis for the rhythmical structure that controls his compositon and is to be seen by the observer in the finished work of art. The well-known *Blue Horses* by Franz Marc has this rhythmic pattern in the moving animals that dominate the visual design (Fig. 4-16); the repeated order of the figure groups and soldiers on horseback found in

4-13
Ernst Barlach.
The Avenger. 1923,
Minneapolis Institute of Arts.

4-14
Theodore Roszak.
Cradle Song.
Ca. 1911. Walker Art Center,
Minneapolis.

4-15
Germaine Richier.
Don Quichotte de la Forêt.
1951. Walker Art Center,
Minneapolis.

4-16
Franz Marc. Blue Horses.
Ca. 1911. Walker Art Center,
Minneapolis.

4-13

4-14

4-15

4-16

Paolo Uccello's *Battle of San Romano* represent this conception of rhythmical form (Fig. 4-17).

The other course of action for the constructivist artist begins with the artist's selection of a formal motif — a *structural form.* He then adapts his subject matter to this predecided structure (Fig. 4-18). The analytic cubism of Bracque and Picasso is an example of how the subject is adapted to a predetermined idiom or formal motif; another example is Mondrian's practice of fitting content into a horizontal-vertical format (Fig. 4-19).

Artists in the abstract tradition abandon or deform the appearance of the external world, making it unrecognizable for many viewers. They have perceived — at least in their understanding — that the significance of the external essential aspect of appearance is due to its color and form; thus they have broken away from subject matter of visual realism of the outside world and turned toward what is commonly referred to as abstract art. The two currents of abstract painting, the lyrical abstraction moving from Kandinsky (Fig. 4-20) and the purely intellectual from Mondrian,[3] have much in common with the two-part division of Read's constructivist type of art and its related mode of perception. Hartung, De Staël, Soulages, Kline, Pollack, De Kooning, and Still are among the painters in the United States and Europe who have achieved this lyrical quality in abstraction. The adherents of pure intellectual abstraction include painters such as Albers, Vasarely, Reinhardt, and Noland and sculptors such as Smith, Judd, Anthony Caro, José de Rivera, and Ortman — to name a few. These men follow the concept that there is intrinsic beauty and meaning in pure color and shapes without dependence upon associative resemblances to objects in the environment as seen by people in their daily living.

IMPLICATIONS FROM THEORY

Over a long period of time there have been many serious attempts to discover connections between art and personality. The personality characteristics of the artist and student, or any individual for that matter, have been correlated with characteristics of the "art" work produced by the subject under observation. It is a logical development for researchers to turn to concrete products which can be studied at leisure, measured and classified endlessly as a source of data about what might be going on inside the person which cannot be observed directly. These ventures have had notable limited success, especially where measures of the aesthetic quality of the product were not a consideration.[4]

However, when it has come to more exact and comprehensive parallels and correspondence between personality and art, there has been greater difficulty because our knowledge of personality and of art is far from precise; definition and measurement in terms of art are especially far from exact, thus leaving many areas of disagreement.

Perhaps discussion of the relationship of art and personality diverts

---

[3] See J. E. Miller and Frank Elgar, **One Hundred Years of Modern Painting**, Tudor Publishing Company, New York, 1966, pp. 123–146.
[4] The Goodenough Draw-a-Man Test (for intelligence) and various projective tests of the House-Tree-Person variety.

4-18

some of the reader's attention from the specific purpose for including information about Herbert Read's ideas in this chapter. Although the relationship of personality cannot be excluded, our attention here is focused upon modes of perception which could be identified and associated with particular types of art works and their producers. This also reasserts the concept that when different people (including artists) with normal vision look at an object or event, they are not perceiving the same thing or seeing it the same way, since there are at least four distinct ways in which it may be perceived. This suggests in turn that we should expect the art of one man or one child to be different from that of any other. With this in mind, we should be neither disturbed nor confused, at any period in history, when we find that all of the artistic efforts cannot be brought under one banner.

4-19

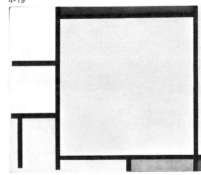

DELINEATION OF PERCEPTION

The preceding section has suggested that there are distinctly different modes of perception employed by people for seeing and for obtaining and communicating an understanding of nature, man, and man-made things. It would be helpful for the critic and those who look at art to have some knowledge of the perceptive impulses that have directed the artist's imagination and motivated or inspired him to shape his materials in a particular way. Teachers will be assisted in their work by knowing about those aspects of visual perception which may be learned and those which are effected by the personality and cultural environments of their students.

To explain or clarify this connection between perception — the receiving of information — and the manner by which the information received is organized into a concrete form for communication with others through an art object, McFee [5] developed the Perception-Delineation Theory.

---

[5] June K. McFee, **Preparation for Art**, Wadsworth Publishing Co., San Francisco, 1963.

4-20
Wassily Kandinsky.
Bright Picture. 1913.
Solomon R. Guggenheim Museum,
New York.

Although this writer was primarily concerned with children's perceptions and art processes, such a theoretical framework has relevance for more mature individuals. Perception delineation is summarized as the process going on within an individual in selecting and responding, mainly through visual perceptions, to stimuli in his environment and communicating his response in a visual arts medium.[6] This is what the artist does; he objectifies his perceptions visually.

This broad and eclectic theory has combined ideas from recent art education thinking and research with insights from the behavioral sciences — cultural anthropology, psychology, sociology — into a single formulation. It provides an analysis of factors affecting the creative art experience of young people. There is little reason to feel that the same combination of factors is not also valid for the adult. The theory indicates the combination of interacting factors and forces that affect the delineation through art media of an individual's responses to his environment. These are also factors that shape the meanings he has given to the sensations he has received. In the Perception-Delineation Theory, attention is focused at four points of the total behavior within and outside the individual. These are not considered separate and progressive stages of a sequential behavior, but are to be thought of as a complex of interrelated actions.

Named in order are the four focal points of the Perception-Delineation Theory, with some discussion of how they might be related to the actions of more mature individuals.

---

[6] *Ibid.*, p. 38.

OVERALL READINESS AND PREPARATION TO PERCEIVE (POINT I)

The manner in which a person interprets and responds to visual and other sensory stimuli may be influenced by response habits previously learned, his attitudes and mental sets which he brings with him to the act of perceiving.

Under this point are included all his previous learnings and his habitual ways of giving meaning to information received through the various senses. His habitual ways for perceiving are affected and conditioned by the forces, attitudes, and responses favored by the cultural or subcultural group to which he belongs and by values held by this group. Other influencing factors are the flexibility-rigidity patterns which have been established. These vary widely from one person to another. Also active at this point is his "orientation to space," which has grown out of experiences received during his early childhood. There are also those perceptual constancies and those "mind sets" which cause the individual to deal with sensory data according to what he "knows" out of his past experience rather than in terms of the color, shape, and size actually presented to the eyes by the visual image at the moment of observation.

Taken together, these factors determine the built-in screen through which a person filters the sensations he receives. In this way he selects that which he is willing to observe and value. When all of these aspects of readiness for perception are taken into account, we can easily understand why there are such varied "individual differences" in the meaning given to stimuli we receive from identical sources in our contact with the same "world."

The conditions of readiness and a preparation to perceive are not things which we outgrow and discard as we grow older. Our reservoir of learning and perceptual development has increased and has been refined. Some of the response sets which have evolved out of this training and experience are well fixed. Our habits of space orientation are different from those we had as young children; they have been adjusted to suit our maturity. The attitudes we have developed and the cultural and other values we hold affect our perceptions of the universe; however, the more a student, a teacher, or an artist knows about the effect of such conditions or agents, the better equipped he is to deal with variables affecting readiness for artistic effort.

PSYCHOLOGICAL AND CULTURAL ENVIRONMENT (POINT II)

Perceptual ability and work in art are influenced by how the individual feels about his environment and by its effects upon him. Much has been written about how the artist Van Gogh was motivated by an overpowering personal desire which drove him to commit certain ideas into the concrete forms of art. There are many such examples in the recorded history of art. We also know the effects of anxiety and fear of failure upon the individual's willingness to undertake or continue with an art activity. In the case of an experienced artist many of the anxieties and fears of failure have been resolved. Such factors can, however, thwart the responses of a young child, or even an older one, in a school art class.

We are motivated through promise of desired rewards. Such motivations are responded to by people of all ages. Approval of his work has a positive effect upon both artist and child, on the contrary, too easy acceptance and purchase of his art products can have a negative effect if the artist allows this to happen. Many have become victims of success to the extent that they have been unwilling to experiment and change directions or procedures. An exception is made for a truly qualified artist, but many not so endowed seek the safety of academic and well-tested solutions because one is assured of their success. Whether he resists or responds to them, all of these things together in their complexity have an effect on and are the conditioners of the individual's manner of response to new situations and to those he may have experienced before. His fears of punishment and anxieties for success, his desire for reward, his satisfaction and pleasure with his achievements, all are part of the psychological environment. They either open or close the doors for individual responsiveness in perceiving and acting upon his perception.

Man's cultural environment and the values of the society or social group to which he belongs place certain limitations upon the individual as an artist. When these factors are too restrictive, it is necessary for the individual artist to adjust inside or outside the frame of reference of his society. Many communities of artists — the Left Bank in Paris, the Lower East Side in New York City, and others — have been sought out by the working artist because the climate and associations are conducive to the cultivation of the kind of values he desires. Other artists prefer to make other choices of working environment. In these group-living environments, ideas can be shared, tested, and expanded; innovations are encouraged, promoted, and refined. The values of living in an environment where members are close enough for easy access to one another's ideas and enthusiasms, yet free to move independently, has been considered beneficial to other than artists and has led to the establishment of the Center for Advanced Study in the Behavioral Sciences at Stanford University in California and the Institute of Advanced Study in Princeton, New Jersey.

Certain themes, media, and styles of working are often given a higher value at a particular time by the artist, his group, or society as a whole. Such value ratings do have an important influence upon the kind of art products produced. Artists, like other people, find it more comfortable to be in style or in step with their times.

INFORMATION HANDLING (POINT III)

With so much information coming to us from the environment through the senses, systematic procedures for organizing, or packaging, this mass of details and separate items of data is essential. Formal and informal kinds of perceptual training can be of assistance in situations where much more information is available to us than we will need or use. Particular patterns of sorting out this data, rejecting or accepting it as we go, are built up consciously and unconsciously by each person. Age, training, and values learned from the culture to which an individual belongs, in terms of intelligence as well as social background, cause individuals or groups of individuals to differ markedly in their facility, manner, and depth of ability to handle visual information. This ability to handle details and to sort out those sensations which have relevance and can be assimilated within the person's frame of reference is important for one in his personal life. It is of the utmost importance to the artist as a producer through creative action.

One of the intermediary devices or procedures used by the artist for sifting visual information is the sketch or drawing. Through this device he makes some of the initial decisions by separating those elements which are important to him from the total area of the visual scene. The sketch or drawing also serves as a document for later study and examination without pressure of urgency. Although the drawing is a form of delineation of intrinsic value, it can be utilized as a technical aid or source for producing a new creation. It also collects information and organizes it into a manageable form for recall at a later time.

DELINEATION (POINT IV)

This is the last of the four points of the theory of how a person's perceptions of his universe are given concrete form. Delineation is the part of the total process that can be seen by others. Creative behavior in art usually results in a concrete product which has been made in order to communicate the individual's responses to his environment. At its finest, art is a highly refined and intensified communication of the mental activity of one human being with the minds of other humans. It ties together the past, present, and future; and it is at once personal and universal. In the creation of their artistic images artists invent or borrow symbols and organize these in a personal fashion. Lines, shapes, textures, tonal values and colors of various media constitute the marks or symbols. These visual symbols have meaning for the creator and hopefully for others.

The ability of the artist to provide a visual image that will communicate his perceptions to others may be affected by all the variables from the three points previously discussed. In addition, his inventiveness, his skill with tools and materials, his past experience with art activities, his vocabulary of visual symbols and such factors as his creativity and motivation will all affect the quality and character of his delineation. Delineation in its broadest and finest sense may be thought of as the creation of an art form which has quality and refinement commensurate with the individual's level of development. It is a creative and expressive act, in which the individual gives physical form to the ideas or concepts that have grown out of his experience with and response to environmental stimuli, both immediate and remembered. At times these responses are made through immediate and direct visual experience, such as drawing from a posed model, a still life, or an outdoor scene; they may, on the other hand, be composed from concepts which come out of the synthesis of the cumulative memory of our past experiences.

In discussing delineation, McFee lists the major art abilities as responding, expressing, designing, and creating. Perceptual skills are necessary for responsiveness; emotion determines what is expressed; and intellect is needed for organizing and arranging in order to create a design. These and other skills are necessary to create an art form of quality and refinement.

VALUES FROM THE PERCEPTION-DELINEATION THEORY

This discussion of the Perception-Delineation Theory has been a condensation of its major points. Here it has been employed to indicate in outline the complexity of behaviors that act upon an individual as he moves from an act of perception to an act of creation through art. The art product which we can see and hang in the home or gallery did not come to look the way it does by chance. It was the result of many direct and indirect forces acting upon the individual who created it. This analysis should give us added respect for the scribblings of a child and some admiration for the products of the artists of our own time and of ages past. Each in its own way represented an attempt by one person or many to communicate what cannot be communicated in any other way; this was done in order that others might experience what they could not experience in any other way. The theory has explanatory value in so far as it brings together a very large number of phenomena and a great amount of information into a completed structure of easily understood relationships. It has a logical consistency relevant to existing knowledge.[7]

ABSTRACTION AS A PROCESS

Earlier in this chapter it was stated that the process of abstracting is basically the same in traditional art and in the most abstract of abstract art. It is a matter of degree; what is labeled abstract art has carried the distillation process further. This process of artistic distillation is like the production of liquor and attar of roses. It takes a lot of original material — grain or flower petals — to obtain a product which bears little physical resemblance to the source material. The result is also more intense than the original raw materials. In the process of abstraction in art an abundance of visual experience is compressed into the product. The physical end product has a different look about it from its original sources, giving the observer a more intensified visual experience.

   The next logical step is to ask the question, "What is the procedure by which abstraction is accomplished?" The following explanation by Georgia O'Keeffe will give us a starting point.[8]

> From experience of one kind or another shapes and colors come to me very clearly. Sometimes I start in a very realistic fashion, and as I go on from one painting onto another of the same kind, it becomes simplified till it can be nothing but abstraction, but for me, it is my reason for painting it, I suppose.

   This statement tells us very little about the details of the abstracting process, but it does point out that for this serious artist it starts with a painting — a visual statement of the perception — and continues through

---

[7] See Appendix 4 for a recommended extension of the Perception-Delineation Theory to include appreciation.
[8] Reported by John I. H. Baur in the text of the exhibition catalogue **Nature in Abstraction**, Whitney Museum of American Art, New York, 1958, p. 6.

a series of paintings, each one becoming simplified by progressive stages until the last ones are less visually recognizable as replicas of the original source material. This artist, like many others, had started and worked for a long time in the representational tradition, but has broken through that tradition to produce work which can be classified as abstract. Artists who have grown up and matured in the abstract tradition or their students who have known no other way of working may automatically bypass many of the intermediary steps and begin somewhere at the midpoint of the progressive stages suggested by Georgia O'Keeffe.

The research type of drawing or painting, which enables the artist to know his subject intimately, is not always necessary for the artist who has had many previous experiences with somewhat similar situations. In these cases the artist-craftsman completes some of the initial stages of abstracting "in his mind." During these mental processes, little outward action in the form of preliminary sketches or paintings is necessary. Also, these preliminary stages may be excluded from the working procedure of sculptors and others who use less flexible materials than the painter. Many people wish to work directly with their final design materials without any intervening stages that might interfere with what they consider vital, fresh, and spontaneous.

The following account is an example of the extended abstraction process, in which an object from nature — an apple — was selected by the artist as his original source material. The illustration is intended to serve as a cutaway diagram or model that can be used as a reference for understanding in detail the comprehensive view of the process of abstracting. Over a long period of time the authors have made careful observations of hundreds of college art students and professional artists while they were engaged in both formal and informal problem-solving situations. In these situations the problem itself concerned direct or indirect abstraction from known source materials. As a result of these studies, we are convinced that the example given here is a good model of the abstracting process in general and not an isolated case.

The artist describes in his own words what he encountered during his adventure into the abstraction of an apple. While reading his account, it might be helpful to keep in mind other works involving this same common object — Oriental brush paintings of three or four apples alone on a large expanse of rice paper or the still lifes with apples by Cézanne. This "stream of consciousness" statement from the artist allows us to get inside the man and follow his process of abstracting from the research drawing to its final results. One can follow the course of its development and note changes in his imagery which came from decisions he made as he went along. We can understand some of the reasons why he changed directions and decided to move in one way or another.

4-21
An apple.

ADVENTURES WITH AN APPLE

As I studied the apple and looked at certain parts carefully, some of them began to hold special interest for me (Fig. 4-21). At first, I merely looked at it from the outside and finding it sort of dull, tried to add elements that really had nothing to do with the way I saw the apple. It was easy to ignore the often subtle, yet vital relationships and qualities of the apple itself. It was good to look at the apple

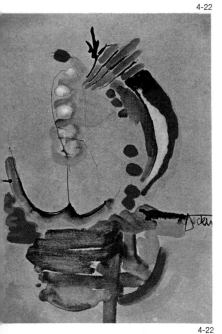

in many different ways from the outside, but I also had to get inside, to the very essence of the apple and its meanings for me.

I soon found myself compelled to use two main approaches to the abstraction of my apple. The first was a very free, spontaneous and exploratory kind of approach; the other involved working in a tighter, more concise, yet analytical manner. Lyrical seems a fitting word to describe the sort of music, sweep and patterns of movement that became so important to my first approach, as I found myself caught in the compelling charm of this free and spontaneous exploration of the mysteries that could be uncovered about my apple. As a supplement, the rational approach helped me to define, clarify and select which of these discoveries should be stressed or evolved into the key elements of the abstraction. Working in both of these ways at more or less the same time helped me to focus on the qualities of the apple that particularly intrigued me. One method seemed to compliment the other and give it greater interest and power.

When the apple became better known, both inside and out, and after it was accepted on its own terms, one could honestly close in on that certain part which had greatest interest. For me the area around the center of the core held a particular fascination. The seeds and their position began to convey a strange life-like quality. This area became my focus for abstraction.

The first illustrations were done with watercolor on pink construction paper and are the initial stages of exploration and experimentation. The apple was viewed from the outside, with my imagination revealing what might be inside. In these first works, I was just "dropping a lot of ideas down the well and checking them for splash!" One thing evolved which would later have special significance. It was the movement in space of a series of red dots, inspired from the apple, but which appeared quite by chance in this and other early probings.

In Fig. 4-22 interest was in the movement away from the somewhat constricting outside shape of the apple; it was obtained by working very spontaneously. New

4-22
Spontaneous red dots.

4-23
Inspired by imagination.

4-24
Two seeds separated by a line.

4-23　4-24

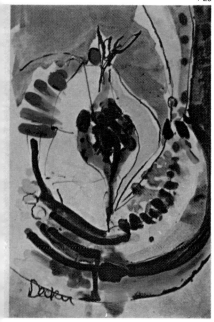

avenues of approach came quicker and the improvements created were more dynamic. Former revelations and ideas such as the red dots were retained, but I began to unite seemingly diverse and unrelated elements to see what could be discovered. Figure 4-23 may have even more elements inspired through imagination rather than by the apple. There seemed to be a need to put down everything that came to mind before picking out points of concentration which might later be perceived as important. In Fig. 4-24 (watercolor on watercolor paper), we have rather an important link with the final product. It was here that I first centralized the idea of two seeds with a separating line, in an overall context of somewhat loosely related elements.

Later, with India ink (Fig. 4-25), I was most interested in complete freedom and spontaneity, now that the qualities of the apple had become inscribed in my memory and mind. Ideas just seemed to flow out, forming shapes and rhythms that apparently had no business being together. They somehow worked to form a more dynamic interest than could have been obtained by planning each part meticulously. The emphasis seemed to be upon those all-pervading seeds, and a center line of the core. I began to be more aware of the organic, almost lifelike quality of this supposedly simple fruit! The good old dots and dashes were still coming through to add to the life and movement. There was still a concern with the internal process and a sort of grouping. Figure 4-26 represented another plunge toward further abstraction. Consciously, I needed to centralize what was becoming more and more the apple's main attraction for me — the two seeds became two eyes and the center core as a sort of rift between them, leading out into some mysterious, undefined and unknown area of blankness. Here a basic black-white contrast, with red added for stress, became the central abstracted element. The basic shape of the apple was of secondary importance.

Figure 4-27 was done with colored tissue paper and India Ink on white paper. Tissue paper is an intriguing material for its color-transparency possibilities. As it

4-25
Rhythmic drawing.

4-26
Seeds and core.

4-27
Tissue I.

4-25

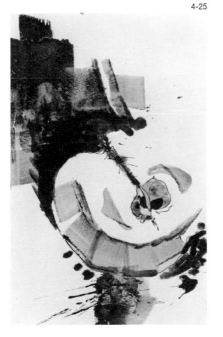

4-26

4-27

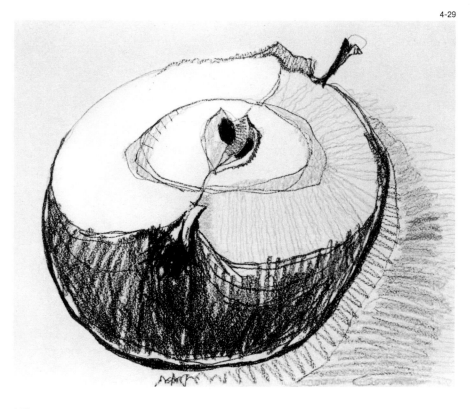

4-28
Tissue II.

4-29
Detailed research drawing.

was applied freely, an attempt was made to represent the central area in a new way — giving it a feeling of pressure and movement in toward the center. This was followed with what turned out to be my final product from the spontaneous phase of my abstraction development (Fig. 4-28). This was also made with tissue paper, but on black background. All of the key elements which had been discovered throughout the abstracting process were integrated into a composition. Once more there is an emphasis on the two dots, with the now completely abstracted core forming a line between them. This helped to give a feeling of the life of the object which started me off on this process. Some supplementary elements such as the series of secondary dots and the basic apple shape were there. To avoid confusion, which can creep in when one is working freely, the dominant vertical direction added unity and set off the circular and horizontal elements.

I could have gone on with this, but I wanted to see what would happen if I held to a more concise analytical and more restrictive orientation. (Figure 4-29 is a detailed drawing in pencil.) Although the two extremes of development — spontaneous and logical — are separated in this description, I didn't really complete one series and then begin another, but worked on them together interchangeably as my feelings led me. The whole thing was an alternating sequence integrated and interrelated in both physical and mental processes. I was still (Fig. 4-30) working toward the apple from the outside, adding from memory my conception of the inner elements to the total.

At this time (Fig. 4-31) I couldn't resist the urge to try an apple tree using this controlled approach. Even here those elements which seemed to pervade many of my other attempts are present, especially the dominance of the vertical direction.

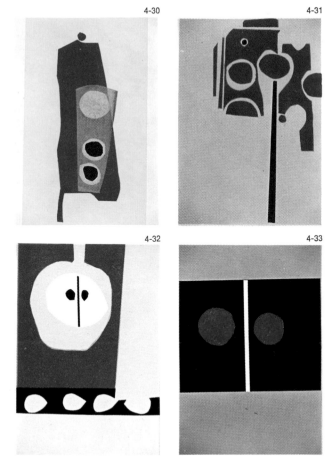

4-30
Working in from the outside.

4-31
Apple tree.

4-32
X-ray view of seeds and core.

4-33
Reduction to essentials.

4-34
The essence of an apple.

There was the process of breaking down and holding to those things which intrigued me — the seeds and center line in this case were viewed from the outside in a sort of X-ray fashion (Fig. 4-32).

Figure 4-33 represented a major step, because it was here that I really began to go to an extreme of reduction. The apple was now down to its very basic essence. Figure 4-34 shows my minimal piece in the abstraction process. It is larger because size has an important affect when something is reduced to its minimal properties. Everything which I abstracted out of the apple seemed to bring me down to this one most basic concept of what the apple meant to me. The two red dots were characteristic not only of the apple's outside shape but also of the seeds and the life-force within the apple. The narrow center space came to represent the core of the apple, but it was also the channel which led out into the larger context of the world in which the apple was a small part. Perhaps the vital life qualities that make up this little apple are characteristic of, and somehow intrinsically tied up with, the qualities of life itself!

Looking back on this experience, I can see that each idea was often connected with the next; very often the negative space in one piece would actually form the positive space of the one to follow. The abstraction process began to integrate and perpetuate itself as I was seemingly carried from one idea to another. I lost myself in the all-pervading concept of apple. Even with something as common as apples, the force, thrust, and dynamic aspects coupled with the static, moody, and endless calm of other areas provided a wealth of inspiration.

REVIEW OF THE PROCESS OF ABSTRACTING

The implications from this account of the discoveries made by an artist about a little thing called an apple are many. In the experience he probably found out as much about himself as he did about the apple. We rarely get such an introspective and detailed diary of an action in art. Seldom do we find that the person involved with the production of a work of art will be particularly conscious of or analytical about his procedure, any more than we are of the physical mechanics of walking from the kitchen to the living room or across the street. Occasionally we have the opportunity to see a sketch or drawing along with the finished painting or piece of sculpture. Although artists seldom keep a file of their preparatory studies, there is enough documentary evidence to indicate that the above example is not an isolated case. In the files available to art historians there are enought materials to suggest that this is a fairly representative example of practice. One fairly well-known example that comes to mind is Theo van Doesburg's *Cow* (Fig. 4-35). The artist's graphic studies of a cow are made available for inspection. The first is a highly representative research-type drawing, a carefully rendered visual representation of the animal; with this, other drawings and a study in paint are shown. In succession, they move away from the representation of the cow as it appears in nature for an observer toward the geometric, rectangular space divisions we associate with this artist's work. A final example in the series is a painting based upon the preliminary studies that would be difficult to separate from Mondrian's paintings in the logical-abstract style, which we have come to recognize immediately as his work.

Picasso is another artist who has kept dozens of developmental studies for separate paintings; in them we can recognize and recall some of his best-known works.

Let us review the developmental procedure found in the example of the artist and his apple, and relate it to other observations and analyses of artistic development in which the artist was working from his observation of objects in nature or from his memory of things and events. We are reminded of the things we have heard or read about the creative process and of the points in the Perception-Delineation Theory reported earlier in this chapter. This is as it should be, because abstracting, as it has been discussed, is a highly creative activity. Also, it is at the same time a fine example of the delineation of the artist's perceptions.

Keep in mind that our example is representative of a process engaged in by a great number of artists and by many students who are seeking experience with the arts. A review of the process by which subject matter is given meaning and visual form could serve to clarify or otherwise explain what happens inside and outside the individual as he creates an art product. There is much to be learned from summarizing the growth of an idea which has started from careful observation of objects or events in nature or in man-made things and environments and has been carried through to a final or nearly final work in an art medium. We are sometimes aided by dividing the total operation into smaller units or phases. Such a separation is sometimes misleading unless we keep in mind that we are dealing with interconnected overlapping phases which do not have precise boundaries and yet will merge into a single, unified action. For purposes of clarification, the total process of abstracting has been divided into three separate phases: (1) preparatory, (2) exploratory, and (3) terminal.

PREPARATORY PHASE

In his own interest the artist or student decides on the object or idea around which he wishes to concentrate his efforts. Sometimes the content is narrowed down precisely to a single object; at other times the content is vaguely defined and very broad, involving a number of symbolic forms.

4-35
Theo van Doesburg. The Cow.
Eight studies, a gouache, and an oil.
Museum of Modern Art, New York.

The content selected to inspire action is often something observed directly from nature, such as a single object or scene, or it can be something out of the apperceptive mass of the accumulated memories to which we have given meaning. For clarity we will assume that the workman starts with a selected object from nature or with a scene that he can observe.

Through careful observation of his subject matter the individual makes a rendering which is a detailed analysis of the subject as he sees it. This is like a research drawing and in a sense serves that purpose. It has been executed with the tools and materials that he uses with the greatest facility. These are also tools and media that allow him to produce an accurate and somewhat documentary analysis of his subject matter. A medium which he can control allows him freedom and confidence, so that he can devote his attention to his subject without concern for technical limitations. This type of drawing forces him to examine his subject carefully and to get to know it completely. It sharpens and focuses his perceptions. These perceptions are embedded within him and become a source of data which can be withdrawn at will.

Once again it should be emphasized that a person's previous experiences and preferred ways of working in art determine to a large extent whether such a preparatory drawing is necessary. This step is quite often eliminated by people who have had many previous experiences in the abstract tradition. However, many artists prefer to start with a graphic analysis and an almost comprehensive rendering in order to feel confident when they begin to take liberties with their subject.

EXPLORATORY PHASE

The artist at this point is searching for a direction or thread of structure which will unify his responses. Exploring by manipulation is an avenue

4-36

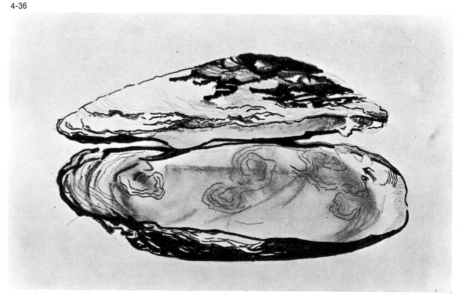

4-36
Detailed research drawing.
Clam, by a high school student.

through which the creative person can find his way toward solutions. In this exploratory phase, selection and rejection are done rapidly as alternative directions are tried out. It is a time of coming to focus upon the "best possible answer." In discussion of the creative process this would be termed the "incubation stage." It tests the flexibility of the workman. These exploratory ventures are carried out through manipulation of the art medium or through a change in the art strategy — in the artist's way of working.

As the result of his actions and his concurrent thinking, the artist begins to discover details, configurations, patterns, and rhythms which intrigue him and around which he prefers to center his attention and subsequent action. It is a time for reducing, distorting, and emphasizing. Graphically, he may pick out salient features or design elements — lines, shapes, textures, and so on — which to him seem important. To accelerate this process he might change his medium from one which emphasizes linear aspects of composition to another which is essentially involved with broad areas or shapes. He could also shift to a medium that gives facility for three-dimensional designing. Changing the medium itself can bring about speed in abstracting. Referring to our example of the young artist and his apple, we can see clearly how his strategy was changed. He gave his reasons for using two distinctly different ways of working.

In observing college and high school art students this switching from one strategy to another is often noted. Figures 4-36 through 4-38 are good examples of this exploration in the work of a high school student. It was a first attempt at a formal set of exercises involving the process of abstracting. There were switches back and forth between a way of working which can be classified as spontaneous-intuitive to one which was more rational in the classic tradition. Throughout art this countermovement of classic and romantic attitudes characterizes the work of artists. Perhaps

4-37   4-38

4-37
Spontaneous abstraction.
Clam, by a high school student.

4-38
Rational abstraction.
Clam, by a high school student.

the student is still searching for the work habits which suit him best; however, in all the examples of the process of abstracting we have shown, this movement between one work procedure and another is indicative of the open-mindedness and flexibility of the persons involved. This is a desirable trait, and it is required for creative action. It can be said, quoting from the Chinese, "Before one begins to paint, one must have the heart, hand, and mind in the tip of the brush." When the mental processes are more dominant, the mind is in the control position; conversely, when the heart takes over, the emotional, lyrical qualities within the individual are more forceful. In any case, it is deemed essential that all three — heart, hand, and mind — work in harmony.

TERMINAL PHASE

Out of his exploratory manipulations the artist has been resolving the direction which his product will take. Speaking pedagogically, he is "establishing a hypothesis" for a solution. In referring to stages in the creative process this is called "illumination followed by verification." With intuitive insight, he has been coming to a decision as to what he wants. His exploration has covered much ground. He has tried and tested alternatives. He may have changed his viewpoint for looking at the subject; he may have combined two or more viewpoints into a single unit. During his action his total matrix of experience — the accumulation of previous experiences to which he has given meaning — has been at work. As these resources have become involved selectively, he has gradually evolved a *creative synthesis*. This creative synthesis, a best solution, will become his abstraction. It includes only those elements from the original content which the craftsman decides are the essentials or the essence of his ideas. Irrelevant details have been eliminated, resulting in a clear and forceful statement of the artist's eye, mind, and hand.

The name "terminal" was given to this phase of the process of abstraction because it describes both the end of the journey and a point of departure for expansion into other areas. When we think of a bus terminal, it is both the stopping place at the end of a journey and a point of embarkation for other adventures. The abstract form which has been arrived at by graphic means can be reaffirmed in more sophisticated pictorial media into a major work of pictorial design or it can just as easily be moved into a structural design application. With the abstraction which he has developed the artist has the raw materials for painting, sculpture, or crafts, depending upon his personal choice. In addition to the design for painting, it can become the design for sculpture in all media, a piece of ceramics, a rug, a woven textile, a piece of jewelry, stained glass or a mosaic, or any of the other forms which art can take.

In our examples there has been an interpretive analysis of an observation. Some art works might take the form of a momentary split-second awareness of a transitory encounter with an object or event. Others might represent a synthesis of a large number of experiences which have affected the artist deeply. In any case, the process of abstracting described in this example could, with some adjustment of detail, serve as a model for the process of abstraction in general.

BACK TO PERCEPTION

It has been said that the artist looks at his world and takes out of it what he feels is important. For the majority of people this world is what can be seen with their own two eyes. Scientific discoveries — the atom, space-time dimensions, forces, and energy — are as yet largely unseeable. When the artist becomes involved with this area of human experience, it is necessary for him to create symbolic equivalents for the unseen forms and forces of the concept of the universe created by science. Since the equivalents in artistic form and shape are derived intuitively, their order and shapes derive from the artist's experience and perceptions of the world as it is seen with his eyes. The works of the artist, whether they are created from logic or from intuition, depend upon his perceptive machinery and experience, which to him is his basic reference point for reality.

Design may be defined as a process by which seemingly unrelated elements are brought together into an aesthetically satisfying unity. In this process of design organization, which is fundamental to art, the artist takes advantage of the same forces and factors that determine groupings and interrelationships in the visual perception of our environment. When we receive a lot of information, both facts and figures, we are more comfortable if we can group them into categories, which makes the process of handling the information much more simple and meaningful.

Knowledge about perception suggests that we tend to classify similar things as a unit. When a number of distinct forms or shapes, colors, or patterns are scattered throughout our visual field, there is this tendency to try to group them so that they are easier to handle. The artist does this in his design composition. The artist searches for a regular pattern in order to classify random, yet distinct, units. Shapes which touch, overlap, or interconnect and have the same directional thrust tend to be grouped together into a unit. Shapes that are alike and forms that are the same or similar in shape, size, and position also tend to be seen as a unit. The artist also uses the knowledge that homogeneous color areas with similar textures are taken in visually as a unit or grouped together. In both art and seeing we tend to have little difficulty in relating items in the visual field when they are related in meaning, association, and symbolism. Here unity is achieved by joining together symbols which have functional, visual, and expressive relationships.

Visually we define form by contrasts; artistically the same end is achieved in the same manner. If one could continue indefinitely to repeat the connection between what the behavioral sciences have discovered about perception with how the artist does what he does, we would have a representative example of perceptual theory put to work.

This discussion on the process of abstracting and the illustrations given have touched upon how the artist's ways of working affect the delineation of his perception. There has been reference to the consistency between the process of abstracting and the outlined stages of the creative process. The following chapters provide a more detailed examination of the creative behavior of an artist at work.

Chapter 5

THE ARTIST AT WORK: CREATIVITY IN ACTION

This chapter will consider the manner in which the artist's vision of his world is given objective form and emotive meaning. It starts with a personal account, which describes with words and illustrations the whole process of creating a piece of jewelry or a small sculpture from its source in the artist's perception to the development of the final product. This single case study of creative action is only intended to establish a "beachhead" or reference base for a more comprehensive analysis of the process of creating a work of art. We feel that a description of how one artist advances from his perception to a finished product provides a good starting point. It will enable us to relate and unite various theories and researches that have concentrated upon artistic creativity as a mental and emotional process. Our example is not so complex as some, but is broadly representative of how many art problems are solved.

5-1
White death cap.

5-2
Morel.

5-1

AN ARTIST-CRAFTSMAN: A CASE STUDY

Before getting into a detailed account of the art process itself, we would like to present a statement of the craftsman's philosophy and manner of working:

I purposely juxtapose unlike materials and intermingle different techniques in order to achieve expression of an idea. While exploring and developing a variety of surface qualities inherent in silver, I found many of these adaptable to natural forms. They suggested seeds, plants, marine life, and insects. The vitality of living things is an inexhaustible source of inspiration to me. I find these forms more vital than pure design or manipulation of design elements without content.

My work evolves slowly and I often do a sequence on the same design idea, developing and refining it through all variations suggested by the materials, tool handling, or technique. I like to exhaust the design possibilities before moving on to another idea.

THE MUSHROOM SERIES

5-2

The following is the artist's account of his perception and creation of a piece of jewelry:

The exciting design possibilities suggested by the visual qualities, structure, and general aura of mystery of the mushroom served as the initial stimuli for the body of work which I refer to as the mushroom series.

Few other growing things have had as unique or persistent a place in our folklore. This fungus has been a topic of conversation from the time elves sat on toadstools to the present day when an occasional misinformed gourmet suffers a gastronomic tragedy.

In terms of sheer beauty and variety, mushrooms could be described as the seashells of the forest. Sizes range from microscopic fungi to the 12-inch-diameter giant puffball. They cover the spectrum from the multihued boletus to the sinister white death cap and vary in texture from the craggy coral fungus to the slick buttery agaric (Figs. 5-1, 5-2).

Since production in art is never an isolated event but is, rather, the result of bringing one's past experience to the solution of a current problem, it seems only proper that in describing one object in a series I should at least discuss the exploratory activity which immediately preceded it.

Mushroom I has utilized the cup-shaped crown and stem of the mushroom. This piece is relatively flat and is frontally oriented. Repetitions of circles within a circle is the basic theme (Fig. 5-3).

Mushroom II differs somewhat from the first in the greater emphasis on the gill structure which constitutes the reverse side of the piece. This particular effect was achieved by cutting radial slots into a charcoal block and forcing molten metal into the depression. The face is built up of many cylindrical pieces of silver (Fig. 5-4).

Mushroom III is a further variation in texture and proportion (Fig. 5-5).

Mushroom IV is primarily based upon the gill structure (Fig. 5-6).

As you can see, the first four pieces in this series were quite flat and front-back oriented, with one side taking precedence in interest and ornamentation over the other. The forms acquired greater volume as different techniques were combined, but beyond a variation in surface techniques and change in proportion, there was no great departure from the original form.

5-3

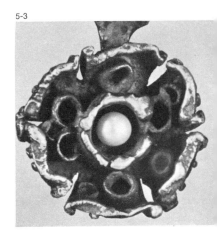

5-3
Mushroom I.

5-4
Mushroom II. *Collection of Mr. and Mrs. David Ward.*

5-4

5-5

5-6

5-7

5-5
Mushroom III. *Collection of Mr. and Mrs. Thomas Blair.*

5-6
Mushroom IV. *Collection of Mr. and Mrs. William K. Smith.*

5-7
Mushroom V.

Suddenly there came the realization that I had been adhering to an unquestioned traditional concept of the form of jewelry and had not been exploiting full use of the third dimension.

Why couldn't a pendant be a totally three-dimensional hanging sculpture? Why shouldn't it have visual and structural coherence when seen from all directions? These questions launched the next pieces in the mushroom series.

Now not only the decorative crown and intricate gill structure were design stimuli, but the volume of the mushroom as well played an important part in my approach.

I began by beating a hemispherical shell out of sheet silver. The shell, filled with asbestos, was placed open side down on a pad and was heated to the flow point with a torch. Silver wire was fused to the shell in a radial pattern. When the wire came in contact with the shell it melted and flowed in rough irregular ridges, and at this great temperature the silver absorbed atmospheric gases, resulting in an exciting pitted and pocked surface. I discovered that whenever the wire was extended beyond the shell it terminated abruptly into smooth globules because of the surface tension of the liquid metal. This unpredicted effect tended to soften the hard outline of the form, so it was utilized around the piece.

When this stage neared completion the shell looked disappointingly heavy. By sawing away the shell from between the ribs a more delicate quality was achieved; the ribs stood out freely like clutching fingers.

Next, I wanted a stemlike form to thrust out of the shell, not only to complete the balance of the piece but to serve as an attachment for the pendant cord as well.

I felt that it needed a plainer surface to contrast with the craggy shell, but one not so refined that the relationship would appear incongruous.

On past pieces I had perfected a method of carving depressions into charcoal blocks and forcing molten metal into these crevices that was much like the cuttlebone casting of ancient times. The advantage over lost-wax casting was its directness of shaping and the speed of completion.

Whenever I get involved in an exciting piece, direct expression is a must. There are times when ideas need immediate fulfillment, and something is lost when substitute materials and processes are used.

A stem was carved (in the negative) into two charcoal blocks. I used a thin rotary saw blade to cut away the charcoal, and this tool produced rather precise longitudinal fluting not unlike growth patterns observed in nature.

After casting silver into the blocks, which were bound together, the casting was removed and I discovered that the reservoir of excess metal at the pouring end of the casting produced an interesting flared termination which had not been planned.

At the moment I had no intention of utilizing this, but began refining the rough casting and shaping it to fit into the shell.

The reservoir, or sprue as it is called by foundrymen, began to look more convincing all the time. It appeared to be the proper termination to the piece although it was a bit heavy. This was quickly remedied by sawing out a large notch, and in so doing I created an unobtrusive means for fastening the cord. Since then I have incorporated the sprues into other pieces.

The assembly of the two units was the final stage of construction. By using gold solder and flushing it generously on the inside surface of the shell, the pieces were not only joined, but a rich gold surface was achieved. This contrasted with the darkened silver surfaces and lent a delicate coloration that enhanced the piece.

This mushroom pendant was the first of the fully three-dimensional pendants (Fig. 5-7). Each subsequent piece became more richly ornamented and structurally complex until the subject no longer held my interest (Figs. 5-8–5-12).

AN OUTSIDE VIEW OF INNER ACTION

What does this one situation tell us? How does it help us to understand what to expect when considering other artists and other media? Is there a pattern or order to this artist's procedure which might apply to strategies adopted by others? To answer these questions, let us first take an objective view from the outside and see what we can state with confidence about what this particular incident has demonstrated. Also we should keep in mind the variations in details of the work process as they are manifested by different individuals who work with techniques and materials other than jewelry and silver.

In our example the artist began his work with a general idea of what he planned to do. The optimum solution was not produced immediately. He had a vague image in his mind from the study of a fragment of nature: a mushroom. This image had a rough shape and dimensions that might be workable in his chosen medium. He took into account the potential and the limitation of his materials and his own skill for shaping the silver. He weighed the alternatives of a variety of shapes and technical processes, and he assessed the potential of each. From his past experience with this object of nature and with the designing of jewelry, he formed some mental picture of what could be done with the metal when one or another tool or process was employed.

After these preliminaries, a decision on a possible direction of working was made, and he began to test his "hypothesis" (Figs. 5-3–5-6). At this early stage the artist had developed certain possible solutions that were of a visual-plastic character, namely pieces of jewelry in silver. These, in

5-8
Mushroom VI
Collection of Dr. Jan Duker.

5-9–5-10
Mushroom IX.

5-11
Mushroom VIII. Collection of
Mr. and Mrs. Elof Wedin.

5-8   5-9   5-10   5-11

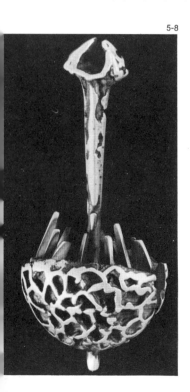

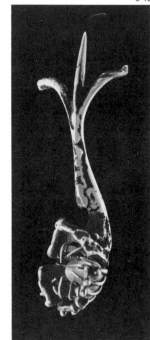
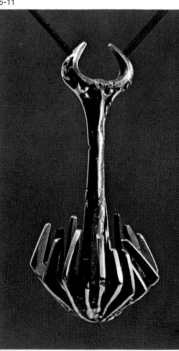

his estimation, had reasonable success but were not the final statement he wished to make about his ideas of the mushroom.

The product (Fig. 5-7) which evolved from the beginning series of tests was in his judgment the best and more nearly represented the goal he had originally set. It was *the mushroom!* Subsequent mushrooms made in silver, although showing considerable refinement, did not equal the quality achieved in "the mushroom" as evaluated by the craftsman. Quite often the artist-craftsman does not know that he has reached the peak of his creative potential unless he goes on to make other products (in our example, other mushrooms). Comparison of these with earlier productions will tell the artist-craftsman that he has reached a plateau — a point of diminishing returns.

Things happened to the metal as a result of the technical process itself. These caused the artist to adjust or temper his original concept — to change his image of the image that should be the solution or end product. Essentially, what we have here is an artist acting upon materials with ideas he has selected. In this case he is acting upon metal; in other instances the artist could be acting upon paint and canvas with selected ideas. In these and in other situations involving art, the artist must have great flexibility in his ability to handle media and open-mindedness in his manipulation of concepts and images. It is only with this flexibility and open-mindedness that he can succeed in achieving visual forms which bring the material and the images from his mind into a harmonious union.

THE CONTINUING PROCESS OF CREATIVE ACTION

Our illustrations have shown the developmental process of an artist working to create an art object in silver from an initiative source of inspiration. The illustrations could have traced the evolution of a painting or a piece of sculpture. Each piece of jewelry marks the limits of a single solution among many — one unit of the total continuum of solutions in which the same initiating cause has served as a starting point. Each succeeding solution owes something to preceding experiences, and together they are considered by the artist as a unified creative action toward one goal.

The examples (Figs. 5-3 – 5-12) point out how the artist has tested the design possibilities of his original source material. In each new piece of jewelry he has modified his original plan, changing elements and areas of emphasis to get many distinct variations of his original theme. The source of inspiration for all was the same; each stands as a valid product in its own right. In this situation, and in many others in art, the creative process can be fully understood only when the whole activity of starting, selecting, modifying, reorganizing, and finalizing is seen as a unit, even when it covers a long span of time.

5-12
Mushroom VII.

THE JEWELRY DESIGNER AND THE PAINTER

Artists — painters, sculptors, jewelers, and all the rest — gain their fame and reputation by the personal and uniquely individual qualities that they bring to their work. Let us see, however, if it is possible to detect certain consistencies in artists' work habits and ways of solving art problems.

Perhaps we can isolate a pattern of similarity between the work habits of our jewelry designer and those of the best-known of our modern artists, Pablo Picasso. We can do this because Picasso seldom destroyed any of his preliminary studies; therefore, the stages in the development of many of his major works are available for inspection. One of his well-known paintings, depicting a young girl with her hair in a ponytail, was the result of a long and continuous filtering process (Fig. 5-13). This development of his ideas can be followed through the first thirty or forty pencil drawings of this girl, which represent a realistic researchlike analysis of the subject; progress and development of the theme can then be traced through more than twenty canvases. Each canvas followed the others in order. In each the artist abstracted a step further from the original, reducing to essentials the image of the young girl. In this way the original inspiration from the

5-13
Pablo Picasso.
Girl with Ponytail.
Museum of Modern Art,
New York.

world around him was transformed by Picasso into a new reality. Only faint traces of the original image remain after his logical step-by-step progression.

GUERNICA: AN EXAMPLE OF CREATIVE ACTION BY A PAINTER

This is not an isolated example of Picasso's way of working as he searched for the right form with which he could adequately express his ideas. An even more complete record was to be found in an exhibition of his work shown in a number of American museums immediately after the World War II. A major portion of this show was devoted to the process the artist had employed in the creation of the large mural *Guernica* (Fig. 5-14). This famous work of art was painted at the request of the Republican government of Spain for its building at the Paris World's Fair. Spain was in a state of civil war. The military group of Francisco Franco, supported by Nazi Germany and Fascist Italy, was attempting to overthrow the Spanish Republican government. Shortly after Picasso accepted this commission, the Basque town of Guernica was bombed and the civilian population was wiped out. This event was selected by Picasso as the subject for his mural.

One of this artist's most renowned and impressive works, the painting stands as a profound expression of man's inhumanity toward his fellowman. As a symbol of revolution and horror, it represents man's deliberate destruction of life and the defenseless.

The material concerned with the painting of Guernica presented in this exhibition included most of the artist's sketches and compositional studies for details of the mural. These are dated and show clearly the time

5-14
Pablo Picasso. Guernica. 1937. On extended loan to the Museum of Modern Art, New York.

sequence in which they were produced. Shown along with these were the preliminary studies of the total design.[1]

Here we have one of those rare cases of complete documentation of an artist at work. From it we can penetrate into some of the mysteries that surround the happenings inside an artist at different stages of his creative effort. When these paintings, drawings, sketches, and final mural were placed in a sequential order on the walls of the gallery, they could be seen as a cutaway diagram which gave a penetrating view of one man's creative activity, thus revealing the anatomy of a work of art.

The exhibition included the artist's first sketch in pencil on a gesso panel. This indicated the general idea for the mural. It established the compositional design for the final work and included many of its main features — the person holding the lamp emerging from the window on the right, the animal form on the left, and the dead figure across the foreground. In orderly sequence were placed the studies for the details of the composition — the horse's head, the woman climbing a ladder holding a dead child, the bull. These were seen in many stages of their evolution as the artist experimented (Figs. 5-15 – 5-17). Also included were subsequent sketches of the total structure of the mural. Taken together they form a clear picture of the overall involvement of an artist in the process of producing a work of art. We can see how he started with a general idea

---

1 Many of the drawings and compositional studies are on extended loan to the Museum of Modern Art in New York.

of what he planned to do, then worked out the details of organization, and created image-symbols and refined parts or units of the composition as he moved progressively toward his final statement.[2]

SIMILARITIES IN WAYS OF WORKING

Making suitable allowances for differences in media and for the magnitude of the concepts involved, there is a general similarity between the work process of the artist using paint and that of the artist using metal, as has been shown above. Both demonstrate an analytical probing, a search for the most effective symbols to convey their ideas to other people.

Unfortunately, it is not often that all the progressive stages of the development of a single work by a proficient artist are available for study. Often changes at each succeeding stage of development are submerged under layers of pigment on the canvas. We can, however, see the same sort of development by looking at a sequence of paintings or sculptures by a single artist on the same theme or idea which may have been spaced over an extended period of time. Artists often go back to or continue with the same general concept in an effort to state their idea more clearly. They also return to a theme because they know more about the subject, see it differently, or are not satisfied with previous efforts. Monet's water lilies,

5-16
Pablo Picasso.
Guernica composition study.
Pencil on gesso. On extended loan to the Museum of Modern Art, New York.

5-17
Pablo Picasso. Guernica study:
Mother with Dead Child on Ladder.
Crayon and pencil on white paper.
On extended loan to the Museum of Modern Art, New York.

---

2 For a comprehensive analysis, see Rudolph Arnheim, **Picasso's Guernica**, University of California Press, Los Angeles, Berkeley, 1962.

Manet's haystacks, Stuart Davis's eggbeater series, De Kooning's women, and Albers' *Homage to the Square* are only a few examples. Mondrian's paintings of trees, spaced over a number of years, when taken together not only demonstrate this artist's development of a symbol but also reveal his way of working as he gradually evolved or developed the kind of imagery we associate with him today.

These examples illustrate one way of working, which is a strategy for attacking and solving art problems followed by many artists of the present and the past. This approach is characteristically rational, logical, and "divergent." It starts with thinking. Thinking is emphasized over action; it proceeds through deliberation toward discovery. It is one of the creative procedures employed by many artists and by students while learning their craft.

CREATIVE WAYS OF WORKING

The study of artistic creativity has taken many directions and emphases in recent years. One of these has been the attempt to identify the working habits and the strategies that creative individuals have employed while going about their work in art.[3]

THE RATIONAL-DIVERGENT STRATEGY

Two artists, one working with metal and the other with paint, have essentially the same approach. In going about their work they use what has been called a *rational-divergent strategy.* The artist or student who attacks and solves an art problem in this manner is concerned with clarity and precision at each stage and with every element in the whole design. He leaves himself free for organizational innovation; he is willing to change the whole plan up to the last moment. His goal is a clear and direct statement. Dramatic impact is obtained through contrasts and opposition.

A theme may be carried over from day to day and elaborated in size, placement, and treatment; the originality of the product is increased through formal organizational invention. This is his road to discovery. This divergent workman pauses at each stage and, after some thought, consciously, attempts to make the next most unexpected, right, feasible connection. He derives satisfaction from and enjoys the surprise of demonstrations of originality and improvisations on a theme. The process itself is under control. This leaves the artist free to seek alternative symbols and metaphoric concepts as well as compositional arrangements which have effective surprise.

This was the creative strategy employed by many of our mature artists during much of history and for most of their important works — the Cézannes, Picassos, and Mondrians of our age and the Michelangelos and Leonardo da Vincis of times past. It was this predominant way of working and the effect it had upon art products which gave consistency and character to certain styles and periods in the historical development of art.

---

[3] Kenneth Beittel and Robert Burkhart, **Strategies of Spontaneous, Divergent and Academic Art Students,** *Studies in Art Education*, vol. 5, no. 1 (Fall, 1963).

It left its mark upon the works of the classical period and the Renaissance and upon the styles of impressionism and social realism. Also, we can see more recent results of this way of working in what has been termed pop, optical, and kinetic art. It is also the creative strategy — a way of learning in art — for many pupils in elementary and secondary schools and for some students in colleges and professional art schools.

THE SPONTANEOUS-INTUITIVE STRATEGY

The discussion of the products of the abstract-expressionist artist and the way he perceives his world [4] has also given an analysis of the critical factors which characterize the *spontaneous-intuitive* strategy of creative action in art. The spontaneous artist-craftsman conceives of painting or sculpture as an intuitive activity demanding automatic responses. This places him in the role of a participant in the act rather than that of a spectator-recorder. The work begins (and it is the beginning stage which is most critical for determining the strategy) with a somewhat centrally located, vaguely defined whole — shape, color spot, or mass-volume. This is followed by placement of related forms or color notations devised immediately and presented directly. The relationships among the parts grow out of the workman's response to his central action and the shapes or colors established moments before.

There is very little reliance upon presketching, contours, and elaboration or rendering of details. The work expands organically, thrusting outward from its starting point; the creator works kinesthetically, seeking freedom as the idea is developed as a unified whole. Works of art in this category show a range of individuality, freedom of movement, directness of statement; unneeded procedures and detail are eliminated.

On the surface, individuals working in a spontaneous manner appear to exert less control over the medium; the work method itself seems to depend more upon trial and error and accidents. Chance happenings and emerging accidents in the course of production are turned to good use, requiring new procedures that often bring new vitality to the whole. The spontaneous craftsman starts with a wholeness or unity; the goal of subsequent action is to maintain this unified concept and to give it interest, vitality, and an extended diversity in which the course of the artist's process is evident. Beittel and Burkhart, in their studies of working processes, have summarized the spontaneous strategy with the statement, "The problem or goal is held constant while the procedure is varied."[5]

A search for the unusual and visual impact is evident in the process; problem solving is the goal of this exploratory and experimental way of working.

The speed of execution, the outpouring of instinctively felt images from a personal inner world which characterizes the work at the extremes of the continuum of spontaneous artists is described by Alexander Liberman in the book *The Artist in His Studio*. Two sections record observations of Hans Hartung and Jean Dubuffet at work. These provide descriptions of

---

[4] See Chapter 1.
[5] Beittel and Burkhart, *op. cit.*, pp. 20–21.

the spontaneous, almost automatic response of these artists along with their predisposition to experiment with traditional tools and procedures.

Liberman wrote the following about Hans Hartung:[6]

> *Hartung is a painter of line as others are painters of color. In Oriental calligraphy a cultivated mind could express itself; in the automatism of Hartung's obsessive sign-making the personality of the artist is absorbed in the anonymity of a moment in time.*
>
> *The white sheet of paper framed in black was ready like a screen for the projection of Hartung's vision. There were minutes of intense quiet suddenly shattered by the piercing hissing sound of his crayon on stretched paper. The violence and speed of his work made it seem like an out-pouring of pent-up urge. Then the drawing was finished, the briefness of execution adding mystery to the intensity of the experience [Fig. 5-18].*

Dubuffet at work is described as follows:[7]

> *It is hard to penetrate Dubuffet's shell of self-protection from everyday life; he knowingly shelters his inner dreams. He looks like a being who could have lived untold years ago. With something of a medium's power Dubuffet links in his art the far-distant past with the unseen — to all but him — future. He has broken more violently with the traditions of conventional easel painting than any painter I have photographed. I watched him throw sand or gravel into amorphous mixtures smeared over a plaster board. With a knife, trowel, rag, or his hand, he shaped the lava-like flows of earth color until he finally brought them to a stop. I marvelled at the amount of stored-up skill he summoned to fix the fleeting images that seemed to well-up like volcanic eruptions [Fig. 5-19].*

To a large degree these are examples of the extremes of spontaneity, as the artists make movement and speed participate in the creation of paintings. In both instances the artists, Hartung and Dubuffet, were involved with a highly personal kind of inner vision which they, to a large extent, were almost unwilling to share with others except in general, almost unintelligible terms.

The spontaneous-intuitive way of working may seem mysterious and remote. In order to open up an intimate recording of this approach to the solution of art problems, the following are taken from a series of rather intensive studies of the work habits of a number of artists living near a large Midwestern university. The studies included interviews with the artists, observations of the artist at work in his studio, discussions of works in progress and on exhibition, and comments from gallery directors and others.[8]

---

[6] Alexander Liberman, **The Artist in His Studio**, The Viking Press, Inc., New York, 1960, p. 71.
[7] *Ibid.*, p. 71.
[8] Josephine Cooke, **Creativity: Its Process, Measurement and Implications for Identification of the Art-Gifted**, unpublished master's thesis. University of Minnesota, Minneapolis, 1961.

5-18

5-18
Hans Hartung. Painting.
1948. Oil on canvas.
Museum of Modern Art,
New York.

5-19

5-19
Jean Dubuffet.
Door with Couch Grass.
1957. Oil on canvas with assemblage.
Solomon R. Guggenheim Museum,
New York.

THE ARTIST AT WORK: CREATIVITY IN ACTION   155

Two of the artists have been selected for inclusion here because they give in their own words descriptions of a work pattern which provides added insight into the creative strategy labeled spontaneous-intuitive. Both artists have achieved a level of success and acclaim; their paintings have been exhibited by prominent museums and galleries.

The first artist stated the following in an interview:

> I do not begin a painting with a preconceived idea. I prefer to keep my mind clear in order to develop my thoughts through the painting. My preference is to get mentally incorporated within the act of painting.
>
> As the painting evolves there are changes — improvisions. Certain parts require alternation — more light. It is as much a process of subtraction as it is of addition. It is inevitable that an image of the finished painting comes into being as the painting is developed. The painting grows and suddenly the image exists.
>
> When people ask me how I know when the painting is finished, I have only one answer. When the painting says to me that it is finished — then I am finished. The painting is completed.

During the process of painting the artist said:

> I have all kinds of emotions — doubt, anxiety, bewilderment. There is also pleasure — and the excitement of being free — to paint without restrictions or the necessity to observe rules or academic regulations.
>
> It is not all "fun"! Sometimes I get stuck. The painting does not tell me what to do — some part of the design is missing, unclear. Then I have to try out many different things. Some work, some don't.

In describing the work of this artist, a gallery director wrote:

> At the beginning of a new picture, he splits up the picture plane in almost any possible order to get it going; it is almost a matter of "establishing chaos" and working from there. He does not start with a set plan and work through methodically to conclusion. Even the most deliberate looking canvases in this exhibition have layers of "incredibile junk" underneath the final surface.

A review of the notes from a series of interviews and discussions with the second artist selected brought out points of similarity of attitudes, work habits, and ideas about what painting is as a process.

Our second artist stated:

> I do not have any preconceived idea of what the painting is going to be before starting to paint. There are no absolutes in approaching a creative work. I start with a spontaneous invention and let the canvas and paint tell me what to do.
>
> The magic of painting is in approaching it with no set ideas. As the strokes are put down on canvas, the ideas begin to

come. Perhaps they come in a bad form — or I might misread them. When this happens, I "get with it," revise the parts and follow the painting to its logical destination.

This artist considered the whole act of painting as one of "hard, grueling work." He said: "Painting is never a pleasure. It is frightening work. There is no guarantee except in the area of failure."

The language of artistic symbols employed by the four artists we have just described is not "all in the public domain." Many viewers cannot read it and are confused, even insulted, because the artist does not make his statement crystal clear for them to take in at a passing glance. Some artists choose to speak in a very complex and personal language, open only to a few who take time to learn it. It remains for the observer of the work to accept or reject the challenge. However, our examples were chosen from near the end of the line of those who work in a manner which can be categorically described as spontaneous-intuitive.

There are others who work spontaneously and produce paintings and sculptures which present images that are clearly understood by the visitor to the art gallery. Their sources and images of subject matter are more objective and universally experienced; their themes are less abstract and less mystically personal. Instead, what is under discussion here is the *work process.* This strategy has been selected by many artists and students with quite different interests in their sources of content, medium, and stylistic idiom. The manner of working is equally evident whether the artist is working directly from a posed still life or a model or is dependent upon his inmost feelings, thoughts, or memory of past experience as his source of direction and content.

We often think of one medium or another as being spontaneous. Watercolor is often thought of as such a medium. But, in the hands of some painters, it has been used as a medium of classical precision. The opposite can be said of stone or metal. It is the person — the artist — who is spontaneous or deliberative rather than the medium with which he is working.

WORK STRATEGIES: A HISTORICAL PERSPECTIVE

This discussion should not be considered as an attempt to reduce all the variables of the artist's work strategy to a two-way, either-or choice. This would be absurd. Rather it establishes two poles between which most of the paths of artists will fluctuate as they move toward creative solutions of their artistic problems.

The history of art shows that one manner of working with its corresponding distinctive product characteristics has dominated the field for a time, only to be replaced by the other as society and the values and thinking of the culture have changed. The two streams of the classical and the romantic, of the rational and the intuitive, or of the spontaneous and deliberative as strategies preferred by artists are interwoven through the fabric of art development from period to period in history. Sometimes the one, sometimes the other, becomes the dominating force.

These styles and ways of working often differentiate the achievements

of one generation of artists from those of another, reoccurring and repeated as art moves from its archaic, formative period of style through its
"golden age" to the time of overindulgence and excesses that make things
ripe for the emergence of a new style. This time of rebellion, revolt, and
reevaluation leans toward the extreme and the new has very little of the
old. We have seen this happen since 1940 in American art. The social realists gave way to the abstract expressionists; these artists were in turn
supplanted by the practitioners of pop, optical, and kinetic art. Regarding
work strategies, the shift was from the rational-divergent approach of the
social realist to the spontaneous-intuitive method of the abstract expressionist; the rebellion of the pop and the optical artists swung the pendulum
back again to the side of craftsmen who work in a manner which can
be regarded as rational-divergent.

In any one period of time, although one way of working and the characteristics which it gives to its products may predominate, there are usually
outstanding examples of work done by artists working in a manner that
runs counter to the prevailing tendency. A very good example of this phenomenon is the concurrent existence on the art scene of the second half
of the twentieth century in the United States of two artists with such contrasting modes of expression and ways of working as Andrew Wyeth and
Willem de Kooning. Thus exponents of the rational-divergent and the spontaneous-intuitive strategies sometimes flourish side by side in the same
place, time, and climate.

When the abstract movement in painting and sculpture of the twentieth
century is examined as a unit, one can sense two somewhat separate
currents, antagonistic for all their insistence upon a nonfigurative idiom
for an expression of reality. One group includes the spontaneous, lyrical

5-21
Philip Guston.
Untitled, 1958.
Minneapolis Institute of Arts.

works that seem to derive inspiration from the tradition established by Kandinsky, while the other group stems from the reasoned and deliberate nonobjective constructions of Mondrian. On the one hand, we have Hartung and Soulages from Europe and Jackson Pollock, Franz Kline, Willem de Kooning, Clifford Still, B. W. Tomlin, Mark Rothko, Phillip Guston, Adolph Gottlieb, and Helen Frankenthaler, all of whom are leaders in the field of "action" painting in the United States (Figs. 5-20, 5-21). The other tendency is represented by Ben Nicholson, Hans Arp, Passmore, Vasarely, and Magnelli from Europe and those artists in the United States who accept a pure, intellectual abstraction, led by Albers, Kelly, Noland, Stella, Young-erman, and other hard-edge painters and joined by the optical artists such as Goodyear, Mieczkowski, Stanczac, and Reinhardt.

Each artist (and hopefully the child as an artist) has the freedom to work out for himself the degree of balance between the intellectual and the emotional (or the rational and the spontaneous) focus which is right and comfortable — compatible with his needs as an artist. This balance of position and his way of working will be determined by his personality pattern, his sensitivity to the culture in which he exists, what he has to say, and the command he has over his chosen materials for shaping them toward the goals he has selected.

THOUGHTS AND QUESTIONS ABOUT THE ARTIST'S WORK PROCESS

Artists and laymen alike are often curious about how a particular work of art was achieved. For those who work with art materials this curiosity has as an extra component the desire to know, so that the knowledge may be put to work for personal improvement. More than curiosity has prodded artists to resort to copying works by others; they have copied selected masterworks in order to learn the secrets of their craft. Many have studied with the "master" in his studio in the hope that they might learn something about his way of working. Thus, knowledge of the ways of working which experienced artists follow is beneficial to other practitioners. The teacher, knowing that artists forge different, distinct, and definable strategies as they solve art problems, will be aided in his work of "getting others to do it." Although often poorly expressed, many people who look at art want to know *how* as well as *why* artists do what they do.

When we stand back and take a long, hard look at the two basic strategies for art action, questions arise. Can all of the individual artists with all their personal uniquenesses be classified according to two distinctive ways of working? Are these explicit enough to be meaningful or useful? Do they apply to the artists we have known? Where do we ourselves fit in?

Depending upon the problem, the medium, and all the other variables, do we not act one way at one time and differently at another time? Probably, but within limits and under special conditions. One of the difficulties encountered here is that of definition and words — not the definition or words in themselves, but the shades of meaning given to them by different people out of their personal experience. It should be stated again that we are talking about an artist's *way of working*, not about his content, style, or medium. We are placing an artist's way of working in an *area*, not at a single *point* along the line extending from the extremes as represented by the spontaneous-intuitive and the rational-divergent strategies. There are probably some limits to the individual's range of fluctuation, especially if he is mature, experienced, and sincere. As the artist moves to maturity, he refines his work procedures and discovers what works best for him — what satisfies his needs and is most compatible, efficient, and effective to serve his own interests.

There are exceptions of course. A student under pressure, real or imagined, often adopts his instructor's bias. There are also those who are changeable, who produce works in painting and sculpture and who can, like the chameleon, take on the coloration of any "new" style and become adherents upon the bandwagon of popular movements. These people can easily accept any change in work habits without pause for examination of conscience. These are superficial manifestations and are less likely to occur when the group structures in which the individual is involved remain stable and secure.

Flexibility is one of the characteristics of creative behavior. The artist should be open to new ideas and ways of working and to explorations of previously untried media and processes. Experimentation is not limited to technical or media aspects of his craft; he also tries out different work strategies for short or long periods of time or for particular problems that are not working out to his satisfaction. Sometimes a variation in his usual work habits is made simply because he wants to try out something different. However, he will gradually assimilate these experiences and experiments into the strategy or work process that he has discovered is best for his purposes.

The sculptor Henry Moore has described his work habits as follows:[9]

> I sometimes begin a drawing with no preconceived problem to solve, with only the desire to use pencil on paper, and make lines, tones and shapes with no conscious aim; but as my mind takes in what is so produced a point arrives where some idea becomes conscious and crystallizes, and then a control and ordering begins to take place.
>
> Or sometimes I start with a set subject; or to solve, in a block of stone of known dimensions, a sculptural problem I've given myself, and then consciously attempt to build an ordered relationship of forms....

From these words we can understand how a mature artist will vary his work strategy with control and confidence.

A TEST OF STRATEGIES

Let us follow through with a more detailed study of the two basic innovative ways of working. As background, we have the artist's statement:

> By introspection and analysis it would seem that my predispositions or my way of working is closer to the rational-divergent strategy. It is certainly more comfortable for me to start by thinking of an idea. However vague and nebulous this might be, it gives me something to hold on to.
>
> As a painter, I know that changes can be made quickly and with very little effort. Quite often I do not work an idea out in detail beforehand. From experience with success and failure, I have learned that certain chances taken and technical maneuvers attempted will bring an exciting and novel solution. I suppose you could call this a kind of deliberate spontaneity—but it hardly changes my basic way of working.
>
> Quite often the final product has very little resemblance to the image in my mind when I started to paint; at other times, it is very close.

This statement points out how certain aspects of spontaneity can be selectively incorporated into a strategy which is fundamentally divergent without changing it. The same will happen with basically spontaneous strategy. During the spontaneous work procedure the shapes and colors will suggest the form of an idea; this in turn is resolved as much by thinking as by emerging accidents while the artist is creating the work of art.

When confronted with descriptions of ways of working, the challenge to test them is very great. This is a positive approach, and one which can suggest answers to such questions as: What happens when one attempts to hold to a particular strategy? How does it feel? Are the results different? How? The alternative is to discard the whole matter with a "so what" remark. The positive challenge approach was accepted! A number of drawings were made. Each was an honest attempt to follow one strategy consistently. The medium (oil pastel) was the same for

---

[9] Brewster Ghiselin (ed.), **The Creative Process: A Symposium**, University of California Press, Los Angeles, Berkeley, 1952, p. 77.

all; the time span alloted for each was approximately the same. As noted earlier, it is at the beginning of the work process that evidences of the different work strategies are most easily identified. It is important to keep in mind that these are the results of two distinct work processes, even if the end products have aspects of visual similarity on superficial examination. The illustrations and the accompanying accounts of the procedure involved are presented in order to offer the reader an experience of how it feels to work in art with a particular strategy.

EXAMPLES OF THE RATIONAL-DIVERGENT STRATEGY

Drawings made in accordance with the rational-divergent strategy are discussed in the following paragraphs.

Gulls in Flight. This drawing (Fig. 5-22) began with a fairly well-set idea — to put down quickly and simply the flying birds, which are so clean and beautiful in motion, quite dull and a bit ugly when they are at rest, and mean, almost vicious, when they search for food. Drawing began by blocking in the rough form and linear thrust of the bottom gull. There was definite reliance upon previous sketching of this and other types of birds that was done as far back as college art classes, where methods of establishing the head-to-body relationships for this type of subject were first encountered. Next, light strokes indicating the general directions of the wings were made. Quickly, the position and contours of the second bird were outlined — head, body, and wings in sequence. Then there was a pause to check the overall arrangement. This was followed by carefully selected heavier strokes to define parts of the drawing and to integrate the gulls with each other in the pictorial space. This was a process of improvisation on a theme previously established like what a jazz musician might do with the melody.

5-22
Gulls in Flight.

HASTE

Downtown. For this drawing (Fig. 5-23), the objective from the beginning was to project an image of a common, uncomplicated encounter with the environment. Why at night? Contrasts of warm lights and cool darkness, shapes softened and indistinctly defined, can increase interest and viewer participation. Perhaps this treatment was selected because I like to see things come into focus slowly as they do when the lens on the slide projector is being adjusted. A few quick strokes established the composition — the rectangle at the top, verticals right and left, and diagonals lower and upper right. Broader vertical strokes with dark blue color were added in the center and on the right-hand side. The whole thing was kept loose, with outlines roughly drawn, but the edge of buildings and streetlight poles were more defined than the rest. Next, the light warm color was added at the right, with edges softened as the light color met the dark; then the figures were drawn in. When this stage was reached, the red was added at the top center and at other points, and the darker heavier spot at the lower left was put in to provide balance.

Pile-up. Artists through the ages have gotten some pleasure from drawings of masses of twisting, interlocked humanity, such as the illustrations for

Dante's *Inferno.* Perhaps in a small way professional football provides some of the same potential interest. This drawing (Fig. 5-24) started with such an intention. The subject could be any teams, any Sunday afternoon in the fall or well into the winter. The placement of the central figures was the first step of this pyramid of bodies. Lighter masses were added next, and the darker accents were put in to give some definition to individuals within the mass. Pains were taken to restrain from "overdrawing" and to hold back on details. The pattern of superimposed lines came last; these came more according to continuance of the rhythm of movement than as outlines of parts of the figures. The result is a fairly decent drawing, but one that leaves out the hardness, impact, and the "blood, sweat and tears" of this activity.

Tracks Across the Land. Having spent some time associated with aerial photography, the artist has been interested in the regular patterns formed by man-made things, such as roads and building complexes seen from above. This drawing (Fig. 5-25) was an attempt to state these impressions in simplified terms. The crossing diagonals came first; then the areas of dark color were added. When the drawing is seen in an upright position, it has an effect of changing things usually observed in a horizontal plane to a vertical plane. The familiar becomes strange, and images unlike the original source material are perceived.

EXAMPLES OF THE SPONTANEOUS-INTUITIVE STRATEGY

The four drawings that illustrate this way of working were started without a preconceived idea in mind. They progressed from strokes of color to ideas. The chalk told the artist what to do. At the start, the picture plane

5-23

5-23
Downtown.

5-24
Pileup.

5-25
Tracks across the Land.

5-24

5-25

was broken up, sometimes with sweeping strokes, at another time with shorter, choppy, repetitive movements. Later these were revised and made into a "logic" according to what they suggested.

Lights and Shadows. This work (Fig. 5-26) began with the broad tracery of a path of light (like trails across a photosensitive plate). At the conclusion, most of the light was gone, submerged under the darker hues. The artist had worked over quite a lot of the page, testing different things, but nothing seemed to fit until something vaguely reminiscent of streets, street lights, and buildings began to push through. When these masses were a little clearer, he stopped work.

The Game. In the short, whipping marks first applied in this drawing (Fig. 5-28) there was the initial suggestion of the rapid movement and the crossing-over of hockey players in combat on the ice. With a few additional strokes these were defined; heads, sticks, legs, and jerseys were indicated roughly. The focus was upon the movement of the bodies, not on people as people.

Movement Up, Down and Across. This is not intended as one of those mysterious titles. It is a straightforward description of what was done

5-26
Lights and Shadows.

5-27
Movement Up, Down and Across.

5-26   5-27

(Fig. 5-27). Applying alternating pressures, the chalk, with its vertical length (long edge) on paper, was pushed up and down to make lines of irregular length and thickness from left to right. Before this became tiresome, the direction was changed to a horizontal movement. With more pressure, darker color was added over the light strokes, but the movement and its direction remained constant. A light, somewhat empty area appeared near the center. In keeping with the improvisation, the chalk was manipulated by putting it down on the paper, exerting varied pressure along the length and pivoting it in an arc very much as a compass is spun around on its point. Five times seemed enough! After examination a few accents were added and work stopped.

River's Edge. This drawing (Fig. 5-29) started with vertical strips of light color, parallel to each other across the page. Looking at these suggested the way industrial buildings pile up from the water level of the river. A strong linear pattern with a vague suggestion of details was superimposed to strengthen the illusion.

The way of working outlined for these four spontaneous drawings follows very closely the reported method used by the German expressionist painter Emil Nolde in his painting in the years just before his death in 1956. It is said that he "usually began a water color by working paint

5-28
The Game.

5-29
River's Edge.

onto a wet piece of paper with a bit of cotton until the colors blended with one another. After the colors dried, he would study the composition to see what unexpected subjects it suggested to him, then outline them." [10] The artist called this practice "passive painting" and felt that his best pictures "always came as a surprise."

USING A KNOWN TECHNIQUE TO REACH A KNOWN GOAL

Thus with evidence from research and support from philosophic inquiry, two work processes stand out as those most characteristic of the methods employed by creative individuals for productions of art.[11] These are strategies of innovation and of original solutions. There are however situations and problems in the broad realm of art which make demands upon the individual for creativity of a lesser order and degree. Even in the arts the levels of creativity attained by individuals are different and have been identified.

The two ways of working toward artistic production, the rational-divergent and the spontaneous-intuitive strategies, are by their nature highly creative. Both encourage innovation, discovery, and inventive improvisation. Perhaps because it is part of the nature of human action, of art, and of the creative process itself to strive toward individualism and to seek out personal differences, we seldom find absolute adherence to a single procedure. As a person matures as an artist he finds that certain ways of working are best for his purposes. He adopts them gradually, fusing them with his personal method for producing art. One or the other becomes his dominating strategy for creative problem solving when the precise goal or the procedure for reaching it is not set at the start.

The artist who follows the working procedure called the "academic" knows from the start, with a fair amount of certainty, what he has to say and how it is to be said. Neither new processes nor new organizational ideas are attempted. He is satisfied with outside approval of his technical mastery. He commits himself early to an idea of what the total product should look like when it is finished and to the technical means for achieving this end. Chances for modification are few; since no vagueness exists at the beginning, variations, transformations, or gradual development of concepts through interaction with the medium are ruled out,

He wants and needs precision; his view of his subject is seldom altered. Characteristically the artist-craftsman who adheres to the academic way begins by blocking out the overall plan for his painting, sculpture, or craft product and holds rigidly to its contours. There is a concept of the whole, but the projected course allows for no adjustments or personal variances. Such a plan allows no distortions for dramatic accent or for the achievement of effective surprise.[12]

---

10 **Time Magazine**, March 17, 1967, p. 76.
11 See Appendix 6 for a brief review of research related to creative strategies.
12 The writers are indebted to the work of Beittel and Burkhart. This description is based on their analysis of type characteristics.

In our discussion of working strategies for the artist and student, the first two — the rational-divergent and the spontaneous-intuitive — were said to be innovative. By innovation it is meant that these ways of working were more likely to produce end products which have qualities of uniqueness and originality. They are open-ended, with final decisions left until the end, as opposed to the academic approach, in which the image of the final product and procedural decisions are made precisely and at the start of the work period. New solutions are expected and sought for in the former instances; the goals are discovery and problem solving. When this is the situation, and with methods that stress flexibility and fluency, it appears more likely that the outcome will have characteristics which can be labeled "truly creative."

The academic way of working as it has been described is in action what the convergent method is in terms of kinds of thinking or cognition. Convergent thinking is the tendency to seek known or predetermined answers by known or predetermined processes; the academic strategy for art activity is evident when a known technique is employed to reach a predetermined goal. The artist who wishes to obtain the visual quality of the intervening physical atmosphere, the flickering character of light falling across the surface of an object, may achieve this end by the broken color technique of the light impressionist painters with modifications to bring this technique up to the 1960s. There are many art problems which may be solved through the academic (convergent) method. However, a dependence upon this strategy has dangers and weaknesses because it discourages innovation and discovery as an approach to art. The artists tend to rely upon a belief that all problems have specific predetermined answers. In this respect the academic approach cultivates a decidedly less creative approach to art activity.

By contrast the two other basic strategies for art action are considered potentially more creative because both encourage *divergent* thinking and action. Both of these strategies (a) stress movement toward novelty, (b) demonstrate flexibility and fluidity in relating forms (shapes, colors, and lines and ideas, (c) combine art qualities and meaning which do not ordinarily go together, and (d) probe into the unknown dimension of art problems. However, experimentation or superficial novelty in itself is not enough to make something creative or art. The highly creative artists have reached beyond sheer novelty and invention to bring about a synthesis of their concepts, artistic forms, and material into an aesthetically satisfying unity.

Chapter 6

THE CREATIVE PROCESS
AND THE ARTIST

In the artist there is something of the maverick — the steer that runs free from the herd. He has to think and act in a free spirit and depart from the well-marked paths. His society has not always understood this and welcomed him with acclaim. This was true in ancient Rome, where the products of the artist's skill were admired as cherished possessions for the home and for the public building; yet, as a person he was not given a place of honor or valued highly as a member of the social order. This has also been true with few exceptions in the affluent society of twentieth century America. Perhaps we can obtain clues to some of the reasons for this from current investigations of creativity and the creative process.

Creativeness as a personal trait is inseparable from success as an artist. It is an integral part of the process through which art is created. Many people who have been closely involved in art possess this trait of creativeness to a high degree or, at least, make maximum use of their endowment. Both artists and teachers were enthusiastic and amused when creativity burst into national prominence as a desirable thing to have. To be associated with it has become popular and the pursuit of it has been approved in the "national interest" as a much respected goal. The artists and art teachers were enthusiastic because, through this general adoption of creativity, more emphasis was being placed upon its cultivation and greater rewards were being given for achieving it. They were amused because they had known of its value for a long time. Now other people were discovering the worth and importance of creativeness. It was like having an old coin tossed in the corner of a drawer suddenly become the object of search by frenzied collectors.

This aroused interest in general and artistic creativity has accelerated scholary inquiry into the analysis of what creativity is as a process. Since about 1950 research on creativity has been conducted on a grand scale and has resulted in some findings which have clear-cut implications for learning and instruction. Research on creativity in art and on individuals who create art has had to overcome many barriers. These obstacles are partly the same as those which faced the researcher in the field of general creativity and creative thinking. The researcher in art has had to face further opposition from the natural suspicion and reluctance of the artist and people associated with art to subject themselves and what they hold dear to analysis, indexing, and rigorous examination by those they have considered unfeeling outsiders. This attitude of suspicion has existed since the time people became interested in the study of creativity in education as an outgrowth of the Progressive Education Movement. It was also present when research on the creative process in art was renewed in the 1950s and still prevails today.

Some teachers of art still feel that the child's expressiveness will be blunted and his freedom blocked if his work process is studied. Many artists and teachers persist in their belief that if the art process is taken apart and analyzed, it will somehow be destroyed and, in any case, nothing of much good will result. The artist has a long history of opposition to the work of the art historian, the art critic, and the museum director for what appears to the artist as an exercise in futility and a concentration on trivia which serves only to depreciate the value and meaning of his products. Fortunately, studies of general and artistic creativity are gradually breaking through these barriers. Positive gains in knowledge have been made without destroying either art or the artist or even any of the benefits that the child might receive from an art experience.

LEVELS OF CREATIVITY

The belief that creativity in art is a mysterious and spontaneous process, impossible to analyze and given only to a very few, is echoed in many remarks which can be overheard daily. In everyday usage, certain products, people, and their behavior are by habit designated as "creative" and others are labeled "not creative." This either-or evaluation on a two-level scale is mirrored in such remarks as "Johnny is creative," "Sammy is not creative," "this painting is creative," or "this one is not creative." Assigning the adjective "creative" to one product or behavior implies that the other is not at all creative. This kind of value judgment is neither correct nor accurate. What we mean is that John has demonstrated more or has a higher measured degree of creativity than Sam.

Our thinking has undergone considerable revision as a result of studies of the creative process. The idea that creativity is a potentiality which all people possess to different degrees is now generally accepted by researchers in the field. They consider creativity as more than the manifestation of a unique talent possessed only by gifted artists who, in spite of circumstances, cannot help but be creatively productive. It is also believed that the individual's potential creativeness can be stimulated and fostered by providing conditions which allow and force it to happen. In the earlier text discussion of the basic working strategies — divergent, spontaneous, and academic — two have been characterized as innovative. These are the divergent-rational and the spontaneous-intuitive ways of working. By innovative, in this case, we mean that these work methods are more likely to produce end products with the qualities of originality and invention. New solutions are expected and sought out in these work processes. Because of the emphasis upon discovery and problem-solving and the demands upon fluency, originality, and flexibility, they are more likely to produce results having characteristics that could be labeled "truly creative." The academic way of working, in which the artist-craftsman selects a predetermined procedure and moves by systematic stages toward the end result, has been described as a *less* creative stategy.

Some of our difficulties in deciding on the relative merits of art works in painting, sculpture, and crafts by both adults and children can be partly reconciled, the apparent differences in opinion concerning creativity can be alleviated, and the difficulties encountered in judging and discussing our evaluations of art can be more precisely communicated if we think of creativity in terms of various levels. In this connection, I. A. Taylor has suggested five levels of creativity [1] in the following order: expressive, productive, inventive, innovative, and emergentive.

These levels are intended to distinguish the creativeness of individuals

---

[1] I. A. Taylor, **The Nature of Creative Process**, in P. Smith (ed.), *Creativity*, Hastings House, Publishers, Inc., New York, 1959, pp. 51–82.

in all lines of endeavor — science, business, and industry, as well as the arts. Persons with special interest in the visual arts and in art education have established similar levels of creativity which encompass the full range of art action.[2] The five levels of creativity with reference to artistic activity are explained in the following paragraphs.

1. *The level of expression.* This is the naïve but profound sensing of the self and the environment. It finds expression in the vivid colors, the freedom, and the subjectivity present in the art work of young children and untutored adults and in the works of artists classified as "primitives."

2. *The level of proficiency* (called "productive creativity" by Taylor). This is the level of the technician and the skilled virtuoso. Most students and artists with academic work patterns are at this level. Their creative products are less free than those of people at "the level of expression," but they are accurate, polished, and usable for the purpose of objective delineation of things and events from the environment. This category also includes artistic products in which there is a tendency to restrict and control spontaneity and free play and to develop techniques for producing "finished" products.

3. *The level of invention.* Individuals at this level use processes, materials, and methods in many different ways and with ingenuity. They see new ways of using old concepts. They have remarkable flexibility and perception and build upon what has already been established. Here we have great variety and ingenuity displayed with materials, methods, and technical processes.

4. *The level of innovation.* Individuals at this level are capable of original interpretations of principles or basic assumptions that are already accepted or known. Through these modifications of a high order they carry basic principles farther forward, as was done by the postimpressionists. In this there is a definite improvement through modification involving high-level conceptualizing skills.

5. *The level of the emergentive type of creativity.* These are the very few who stand out as the discoverers of entirely new principles in art and of new laws in science, such as Picasso and Cézanne for the art of our time and the Einsteins and Newtons of science. They are the founders of schools of painting, sculpture, and architecture. Their vision is recorded for history as that of men who perceived new notions.

As Taylor and others have pointed out, when people talk about creativity they have this fifth level in mind. This, however, is creative behavior which is very rare and in a true sense exceptional. Most of the art products which are studied and the individuals involved in most of the investigations concerning creative behavior are usually somewhere within the first four

[2] Reported by Italo De Francesco, in **New Dimensions for Art Education**, *Art Education*, vol. 12, no. 6 (June, 1959), p. 18.

levels; these people produce most of the art products that are perceived in our common experience.

TYPES OF CREATIVITY

An investigation by Eisner[3] was carried out to determine if it would be possible to identify systematically the types of creativity found in the art products of sixth-grade students. His typology of creative behavior employs four classifications. These types correspond to the levels of creativity suggested by Taylor and De Francesco.

The following are general descriptions of Eisner's types of creativity:

1. *Boundary pushing* in art is the ability to redefine and extend the uses of ordinary objects or ideas.

2. *Inventing* is the ability to use what already exists to create an essentially new object or idea.

3. *Boundary breaking* is the ability to accept or create major new organizing ideas that are later accepted as fact.

4. *Aesthetic organizing* is reserved for those whose products display the ability to organize ideas, qualities, or actions into highly pleasing or harmonious visual realtionships, even though the artists or students did not invent a new artistic style or idiom.

This discussion of types of creativity and levels of creativeness has been presented in order to establish attitudes toward creativity as a general characteristic of many people rather than the few who are exceptionally gifted. This broader conception of creativity allows us to include a wider spectrum of individuals and different sorts of creative behaviors and products when an analysis of art works is undertaken. In this way it is possible to make judgments which differentiate without undue prejudice; it prevents the arbitrary elimination from consideration of works because they do not happen to fit into the rare and very restricted category of creativeness in which boundaries are broken and new styles are developed. Such a broad view of artistic creativeness is required and is certainly appropriate when we consider the whole of our heritage from the arts through the centuries. Many artists who have made enormous contributions to our aesthetic pleasure did not in effect create an entirely new style (Rembrandt, for example). These men did not give much attention to the presentation of either particularly novel ideas or unique subject matter. The vast majority of creative artists work within the limits of art forms and styles which have already been established, but they bring an exciting sense of order, an arrangement and pattern of shapes and colors, which is exciting and aesthetically pleasing to the observer.

Although they still lean heavily on the research of those interested in general creativity, researchers into creative behavior in art have directed

---

[3] Elliot W. Eisner, **The Typology of Creative Behavior in the Visual Arts**, in E. W. Eisner and D. W. Ecker (eds.), *Readings in Art Education*, Blaisdell Publishing Co., Waltham, Mass., 1966, pp. 323–336.

their efforts more extensively in three directions: (1) studies of the characteristics of creative persons involved in art activities; (2) studies of the products of creative action in art; and (3) studies related to the ways people work and solve problems in art.

There have also been some investigations which have attempted to compare and identify the types of instruction and learning experience which seem more productive of art creativity in action. Implications of these investigations are beginning to be considered and applied toward the improvement of self-directed learning and teacher-directed instruction of art. Through better understanding of this process, restrictions on creativity may be identified and eliminated, and a climate for fostering creativeness can be developed. Creative behavior as part of the process of art action can be explained to the degree that will offer a basis for understanding and evaluating the role of art and the artist in any culture.

CREATIVITY AS A NATURAL HUMAN PROCESS

When we accept the idea that creativity is a natural human trait possessed to different degrees by all people, it is then necessary to search for a definition of this natural human process. This definition should be one that, when related to the art aspects of this process, will help us to define for operational purposes the abilities, ways of working and thinking, and the personality characteristics of individuals who reach the various levels of artistic-creative behavior. It should tell us something about the people who can engage most successfully in the art process. Also, it should help us to identify conditions which block or aid its growth. The viewer of art will then have the basis for evaluating and apprehending the kind of products which result or can result from the art process as a creative action.

CREATIVITY DEFINED

Torrance, who has been a leader in the investigation of creative thinking, defines creativity as:[4]

> a process of becoming sensitive to problems, deficiencies, gaps in knowledge, missing elements, disharmonies, etc.; identifying the difficulties; searching for solutions, making guesses and formulating hypotheses about the deficiencies; testing and re-testing these hypotheses and possibly modifying and re-testing them; and finally communicating the results.

This inclusive definition is given because any identification and measurement of the abilities involved in the creative process depend upon an understanding of the nature of the creative process itself. It is equally important that this definition be understood by those attempting to increase

[4] Paul Torrance, **Scientific Views of Creativity and Factors Affecting Its Growth**, *Daedalus* (Journal of the American Academy of Art and Sciences), vol. 94, no. 3 (Summer, 1965), p. 663.

their level of awareness in order to appreciate the products emanating from artists engaged in creative endeavor.

Although, as noted earlier, there is an aspect of creativeness involved in perception and, as will be shown later, in art appreciation, our concern here is creative behavior in relation to the production of works of art. This is the activity in which there is a direct connection between this personality characteristic and its visible expression through the creation of concrete objects. Torrance felt that his definition fitted the creativity of artists and writers as well as that of the creative scientists. This belief grew out of talks with creative artists, writers, and teachers about what happened to them when they were engaged in the creative process and how they guide the creative behavior of their students.

DESCRIPTIONS OF CREATIVE ACTION

Many researchers have tried to describe the creative action of artists and others; these descriptions show remarkable agreement. Most (e.g., Wallas, 1926, and Kirkpatrick, 1955) have identified four steps or stages in the process. Although different investigators have given slightly different names to the various periods in solving a problem creatively, the four stages have usually been identified as preparation, incubation, illumination, and revision or verification.

Allowing for variations arising from special considerations involved In different problems, the process goes forward in something like the following way. First, there is a feeling that something is not quite right, a felt human need to improve, change, or in some fashion modify a situation or product. For the artist this would be a felt need to express his reactions to things and events in his environment — to make a statement different from and an improvement on any that has been made. In this period of preparation one brings together his knowledge, skill, and techniques, plus the elements of experience. This allows one to define or reduce the problem to a manageable entity. Then comes a period of more or less concentrated effort during which, in the case of the artist, sketches, drawings, and memory of past experiences in somewhat similar situations are brought together. These tentative efforts are evaluated for their advantages and disadvantages, and certain possible solutions are formulated. At this time one solution may be selected and carried through in more detail. At least for the moment the problem is solved quickly: everything "goes right." The birth of a new idea comes through insight or illumination and the problem will appear to be solved satisfactorily.

If, however, no single or clear-cut solution appears plausible, the resulting frustration, tension, and discomfort will often cause the individual to move away from the problem itself and "incubate." Intermittently during this period tentative solutions may come to mind, but these are generally rejected as untenable. Eventually, however, out of this period of withdrawal from the problem, by a flash of insight all of the threads are pulled together and a possible solution appears. Finally, to verify the "rightness" of the solution the artist or student elaborates upon the idea, tries it out, evaluates the result, and otherwise perfects the idea he has had. He makes a painting, designs the building, or welds the sculpture.

Those who have rejected the description of the creative process according to four stages of development have offered as a substitute the idea that the creative process for the artist might simply be described as having a beginning, a middle, and an end. This is probably true, but it is not particularly helpful. Beardsley [5] describes creative action for art production as beginning with an "incept," which can be anything that initiates and gets the work under way. Although he rejects the idea of universal stages, he states that there are two clearly marked phases which constantly alternate throughout. These are the "inventive phase," in which new ideas are formed and move from the preconscious to consciousness, and the "selective phase," a kind of critical stage of choosing or rejecting a new idea after perceiving its relationship to that which has been tentatively adopted.

THE ARTIST AS A MODEL FOR CREATIVE BEHAVIOR

Do the models of general creative behavior fit the artist? When one considers the intricacies involved in an art activity, including the range of differences in the art problems and the ways of working that artists have found most convenient for themselves, it would seem hazardous to accept without careful consideration these models of creative behavior as suitable for all people and in all situations in creating art. However, with recognition of the complexity of the problem, our understanding of artistic-creative behavior could be improved by examination of specific situations with the general model as a road map.

A CASE STUDY OF CREATIVE ACTION: METAMORPHOSIS I

When something as individual and personal as a creative activity is described and categorized with the language of the psychologist, it loses some of its flavor. The accuracy of academic terminology has a tendency to extract some of the life and excitement from creative art. In order to give meaning to the words which describe the stages of the creative process — preparation, incubation, illumination, and verification — the following example is given. It is an inside view of some of the things that transpired during the period when a piece of sculpture was created. The reader is taken into the background of the experience that motivated the artist and made it necessary for him to accept the challenge. You can go with him through the preliminaries of coming to grips with the problems he has set himself and follow him through his doubts and frustrations as he seeks a solution. Figures 6-10 through 6-13 show the art product that came out as the "final" answer, at least for the moment; the sculpture is called *Metamorphosis I*.

In order to prepare the reader as the artist was prepared, excited and challenged, we have included a photo essay of a part of the life cycle of the monarch butterfly as it is transformed from a rather non-

5 Monroe C. Beardsley, **On the Creation of Art**, *Journal of Aesthetics and Art Criticism*. vol. 23, no. 3 (Spring, 1965), pp. 291–304.

6-1
Caterpillar attached to a twig.

0-2
Hanging head downward, body arched.

6-3
Chrysalis emerging.

6-4
Glittering gold and black dots.

THE CREATIVE PROCESS AND THE ARTIST   177

6-5

6-6

6-7

6-8

6-5
*Butterfly forced head down
and outward.*

6-6
Swinging precariously.

6-7
Ironing out wrinkles.

6-8
Extending wings to full length.

descript caterpillar into the beautiful winged creature that delights our senses (Figs. 6-1–6-9). The mystery of this metamorphosis and the need and desire to give it artistic form was the sculptor's problem.

Some years back, by persistence, patience, and a great deal of good fortune, I was able to observe and photograph the cycle of transformation of the monarch butterfly. It was a beautiful, mysterious, and fascinating experience, and subsequent reading on the scientific explanations of the process has only served to heighten its meaning.

After thoroughly gorging itself upon milkweed leaves, the caterpillar attached its tail to a twig by spinning a short connection of silk (Fig. 6-1). Releasing its grip, it hung head down, its body arched in a gentle hook (Fig. 6-2).

For the next eight hours it remained in this attitude, digesting its feast, interrupted only by slow undulating contractions. The brilliant bands of yellow, black, and white began to lose their intensity and gradually took on a green cast. It no longer appeared as large as before, but became more elongated as its legs and feelers gradually shriveled.

Suddenly the skin split at the back and a shimmering emerald-green mass emerged. This triggered a response of continuous, almost violent motion. By expanding, contracting, quivering, and swaying, the split extended the length of the caterpillar and the green-yellow tinged chrysalis escaped from its banded transparent skin (Fig. 6-3). Once liberated, its urgent motion subsided as it slowly shrunk to a cylindrical form punctuated with glittering gold and black studs (Fig. 6-4).

During the next twelve days, although remaining motionless, it underwent gradual color changes as the chemistry of nature followed its preordained cycle. The casing became transparent and the black and orange of the developing butterfly could be discerned.

The first indication of emergence was a vertical split that opened slowly like a hinged portal as the butterfly forced its head down and outward (Fig. 6-5). Once its legs were out, it clutched the chrysalis shell — and none too soon, because the heavy abdomen and crumpled wings tumbled out and the creature swung precariously by its delicate feet (Fig. 6-6).

It remained this way while body fluids throbbed into the wing structure, ironing out the wrinkles and extending the wings to their full length (Figs. 6-7, 6-8). After several hours of drying and hardening, it was ready for flight.

Magnification revealed that the horny wing ribs were covered with a dense coat of hair and the pigmented portions of the wing looked not unlike a handwoven rug. Segments taken out of context were like Franz Kline paintings (Fig. 6-9).

The observation of the monarch butterfly cycle has been given in some detail because, even though my involvement was motivated by the immediate fascination with the subject, it was an enriching experience that augmented my visual imagery and posed certain questions on a philosophical level.

Very often the physical aspects of forms in nature are the initial motivating influence on the design of sculpture. Such things as form, color, and structure direct, either consciously or subconsciously, the process, the material, and the physical organization. While many satisfying results may emerge from this procedure, it can also result merely in the production of caricatures of nature or, worse still, academic exercises in the manipulation of recognizable elements.

A greater challenge for the artist is to attempt to capture a quality or essence of nature which goes beyond the physical aspects of an object as seen at any one time. For example, the powerful growth potential of a seed is not apparent by viewing its outer passive shell.

The concept of interdependence of all living things upon each other and their environment is certainly a high order of abstract relationship that can hardly be portrayed in a literal manner.

The process of metamorphosis is an intriguing and challenging subject for the artist to explore and capture in the plastic arts.

Can the essence of metamorphosis be depicted in sculptural form? Taken in terms of the butterfly, can it be done through symbols (patterns, structure, etc.) abstracted and rearranged to become now one, now the other? Or must one resort to a higher level of abstraction by utilizing pure form that is free of association with insects?

Such were the questions which prompted the construction of Metamorphosis I.

With which does the creative process begin — the idea or the action? For me it is a fusing of the two. One feeds upon and stimulates the other.

The problem I set for myself was to create a unified sculpture, complete from all points of view, yet changing character continuously as the viewpoint was changed.

The strong visual kinship of caterpillar, chrysalis, and butterfly was rejected as being too obvious and limiting. Certainly an essence of these forms could be used, but with necessary restraint. A great deal of time was spent pondering the equivocal nature of the subject. How does one depict dynamic change in a static object?

The technique of the mobile occurred to me as being highly appropriate; yet, since I feel that mobiles and Calder are practically synonymous, there was no reason to compound the problem by having to overcome this identity as well.

Should the object be composed of a series of episodes? Could these be combined into one? The magnitude of the problem became more apparent with each new question.

The idea of metamorphosis or transformation encompassing the whole question of the meaning and origin of life has been a challenging subject for artists throughout the history of man.

Agitated by mounting frustration and a gnawing feeling of inadequacy, I took up brush and ink and began sketching in self-defense.

Forms flowed and took shape from remembered images, but they seemed disappointingly similar to past ideas expressed in jewelry or, worse still, like caricatures of the real creature. Other solutions appeared in terms of ink and paper, but when I attempted to translate them into metal, they failed miserably.

Had I been working in a more plastic material I would have begun pushing stuff around, hoping for a direction to occur, but instead I just sat and stewed.

Looking back upon this period of time I see that the intense frustration came as a result of trying to force a new solution on a totally intellectual level and in a substitute medium.

Eventually, I decided to approach the problem by using a cocoonlike form — equivocal in character, in that a single plane defined an intricate series of concave and convex volumes.

This vague idea generated the initial action, and ideas flowed as the metal took shape. I continued to work on an adding and subtracting basis. Additions that at first seemed exciting were pared away or completely removed as I groped along. The lower stem, for example, at one time terminated in large rootlike members. As the work progressed, it became obvious that this area had been given too much emphasis, which defeated the total unity. This particular area was reduced in three separate stages to its final form. Each time one area was changed, it usually affected the overall relationship, so that other areas had to be modified as well.

Sometimes changes seemed vaguely necessary, but the disturbing features were difficult to pinpoint. At such times, one had to stop and look — and look again. It is amazing how certain relationships go unnoticed because of one's concentration on the immediate action. I call this "taking inventory."

On a symbolic level, I was interested in forms which had the dual character of opening and closing depending on one's particular point of view. In addition to

6-9
*Segments taken out of context
resemble a painting
by Franz Kline.*

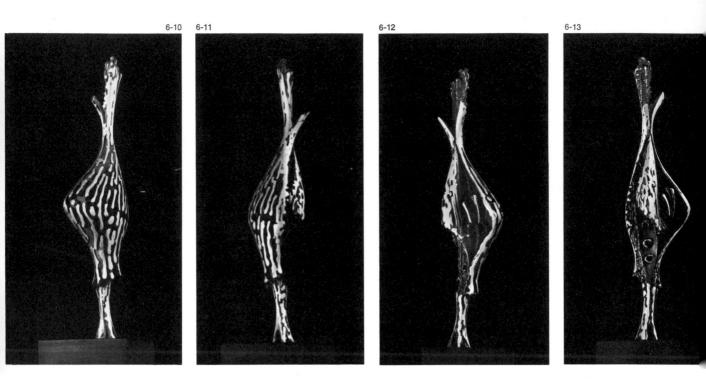

6-10–6-13
Metamorphosis I. *Four views of
the finished sculpture.*

*juxtaposing simple and complex forms in order to set up a visual flow which would
invite further exploration, I attempted to create an ascending form which would not
terminate abruptly but continue on into space.*

*In building up the volume, material was overlayed in striated patterns implying
organic growth and expansion.*

*Many alternative approaches began to occur to me, and work progressed with
great impatience and agitation because of my eagerness to finish and begin another
piece indicated by insights gained through this attempt.*

*The final step was to complete the emerging form within the hollow shell —
the only strong thrusting area in what is otherwise a rather lyrical composition
(Figs. 6-10–6-13).*

*In many ways the finished object is a disappointment in that it has captured
only a small aspect of my intended goal. By doing it, however, I now feel better
prepared for the next try. Every encounter in art is a learning experience for me.*

When this description of a specific series of actions of a person engaged in a creative process is examined with open and broad flexibility,
rather than being restricted to four tight stages that transpire within very
definite time limits, it would seem that most of the situations of creative
problem-solving in art will fit roughly within its confines. There are many
points of contact between our special case and the general stages of the
creative process.

THE FACTOR OF TIME

Some of the studies which have attempted to fit artistic activity into the
four-stage model presented above have had difficulty in harmonizing what
is known about the art process with the model. Perhaps such difficulties

are attributable to lack of a precise definition of when a single creative art process begins and ends. An artist often says that some of his works are never finished — that nothing is final or conclusive, but only representative of a stage in an ongoing process. Also the work in question may have been carried out over an extended period of time, for months or even a year or more. It is also very difficult to establish the precise moment when a particular creative art activity started. The artist quite often comes back to a problem which he has encountered and participated in solving many times in the past.

How does this factor of time, or the duration of the creative act, affect the working procedure? Quite often the interested viewer of a finished work asks how long the artist has taken to complete his work. This factor of time seems to be of considerable importance to the observer, although it is of little concern to the artist. It reflects the notion that the time involved in the production is a consideration in rating the value of the work. In descriptions of purely spontaneous works and workmen, such words as "instantaneous," "automatic," and "rapid" are used. These words refer to speed of execution; but the artist making a painting or a piece of sculpture is not concerned about the time spent at work on the canvas or on the metal. He is seldom aware of the passage of time. Sometimes a great deal of preparation and incubating — an intermittent, semiconscious kicking-around of the idea — has gone on over a long period of time without any active involvement with materials and tools. Those who have worked In the arts, regardless of predispositions and personal work habits, have experienced a time when everything goes right — when the colors, shapes, and masses fall into place almost of their own accord. Artists and students have also experienced times when everything goes wrong — when, for example, the "picture in the mind" won't go down on the canvas or cannot be shaped in the metal. In this situation it becomes a battle of wills and strengths with an "ungraspable adversary."

In our description of the flow of the creative process, mention was made of a situation in which the problem was solved quickly, without much difficulty or delay. An example of the kind of situation in which the painter's solution was arrived at rapidly and almost automatically is to be found in the painting *On the March 1966* (Fig. 6-14). Neither grand nor remarkable, this example had been chosen because its antecedents were known to the authors as recorded below.

The painter grew up in the time when social realism was a major direction in American art. For a long time he was hardly concerned with social commentary in his painting. However, current events — the civil rights marches, student protests, riots in the cities, mass movements, and the surge of peoples in underdeveloped nations — have a way of pressing upon the consciousness of the conscience of individuals. The painter's imagination was caught up by the swell of endless lines of people, personal identities lost in the press of a massive movement. This was all put down in a single short session with paint. It has none of the grandeur of Rivera and Orozco or the other social revolutionary painters. It is a simple statement of an idea, a feeling that wanted to be put down!

One could go into dramatic flights of symbolic meaning — the color contrasts of the black against white, the flashes of red like dark blood in the dirt. These were not In the conscious thoughts of the painter; it is left to the viewer to put them in. This is the way with art and with looking at it.

6-14
On the March 1966.

This illustrates how the single best solution, at least for the moment, was accepted and put down without frustration or discomfort. There was no retreat into seclusion or away from the problem itself. Whatever happened in the way of alternative solutions and evaluation and rejection of those which seemed invalid was done in the period prior to placing the paint upon the canvas. There were no preliminary trials and errors backtracking in this particular instance. It might be said however, that the solution, as presented, did not come out of nowhere, but owes its direction and freshness to a long line of previous paintings on different subjects and to previous problems.

STAGES IN THE CREATIVE PROCESS FOR THE ARCHITECT

This last example indicates how, under favorable conditions, one or more of the stages in the creative process may be left out or become unnecessary for an effective solution.

It is also true that there are no set time limits for the duration of a particular stage or for the whole of the process itself. It is far from a neat and tidy package of clean-cut bundles of time and effort marked off by a ringing bell. There is in a sense overlapping and alternation between stages rather than a direct current of movement from the definition of a problem to the verification of its single solution. Many investigators have found that the four steps of preparation, incubation, illumination, and verification are constantly alternating when poets and artists are at work. However, if this four-stage model is considered as a broadly interpreted set of general guidelines, it becomes a useful tool for understanding artistic behavior.

We can also investigate how the total strategy of the creative process might operate for an architect, who is involved in a creative endeavor which raises problems quite different from those of the painter or sculptor. The building as it is finally constructed represents the final stage of his creative effort and the verification of the solution which has finally been decided upon by the architect. The beginning of the creative activity of the architect can be set at the time he accepts a commission from a client. His period of preparation encompasses the time when he gathers together information about the site, the needs of his client, and the purposes or functions of the building, as well as the limitations of materials, skilled labor, and money. By sorting out all these data surrounding the problem and the limitations in which he must work, the architect will arrive at a very rough definition of the problem he will have to face.

Like other artists, the architect may vary from his colleagues in his general and specific ways of working. There is usually a period of thinking and drawing, during which he formulates many possible solutions. Depending upon his personal preferences, these may take the form of rough drawings or sketches which help him test the advantages or disadvantages of one plan or another against his previous experience. From this emerges a tenable hypothesis for the final solution, which he knows, however, is subject to changes and modifications. He may work from one of two extremes or from a combination of both. In his rough drawings he may attempt to visualize the final look of the building and adjust the design according to the knowledge of the kinds of space units it must contain, or he may start by considering and laying out the interior space blocks and visualizing the exterior forms which these must take. Out of this process comes the formulation of the selected idea which incorporates, in his judgment, the best arrangement, integrating the interior and exterior volumes.

The amount of time spent at this planning stage will depend upon such factors as the magnitude of the project, the novelty of the problem in his experience, and his ability to bring together all of the aspects of the form, function, and material within the limitations placed upon him. His arrival at this solution might be termed the period of insight or illumination in which the problem and its solution come together. Then comes a time for perfecting and adjusting this most promising solution so that others can build it. This plan must be worked out in detail through the architect's drawings, plans, and blueprints — the specifications which must be followed by the constructors and contractors.

In our cities both office and residential buildings clearly show that individual architects can come to quite different solutions to building problems which have many elements in common. In the metropolitan environment of New York City, we have the example of how two distinguished architects worked out distinctly different solutions for the design of buildings which, on the surface, required them to meet highly similar probems. This is the case of the design for the Solomon R. Guggenheim Museum by Frank Lloyd Wright and of the design for the new Whitney Museum by Marcel Breuer. Important buildings by important architects, they were placed in metropolitan New York with all the problems such a setting entails.

As public buildings and more particularly as art museums, their validity must be evaluated against certain criteria. An art museum in a city should stand up boldly on the civic landscape as a symbol and an example of the aspect of life and culture which it represents. Both architects tried in their own way and within the limitations imposed upon them to design buildings which would not look like any other kind of building, but would symbolize the uniquely different position of art in any society. Both buildings are for the purpose of housing collections of art and for presenting the art of our time to public view. The Guggenheim occupies an entire city block, while the Whitney is situated on a street corner in a very restricted space. Yet, in each instance the architect has created a structure which, contrary to standard criteria of good streetscape design, stands out from its surroundings and does not attempt to provide continuity of the existing lines, surfaces, planes, and materials of neighboring buildings. Both buildings have an outward appearance which is uniquely different from that of any other building within the near and far environment. The two buildings have unmistakable identities that make them different from each other as well as from other civic buildings. The Guggenheim (Fig. 6-15) is a gradually ascending spiral of circular forms increasing in size as they move upward; the Whitney (Fig. 6-16) has an upside-down ziggurat profile with each succeeding floor jutting farther out toward the street.

The art museum has fairly common requirements for gallery spaces with excellent lighting and, if possible, flexibility in changing the various sizes of the gallery rooms for different exhibitions. They also need elaborate facilities for storage rooms, offices, auditoriums, restaurants, kitchens, meeting rooms, library, and an art restoration laboratory. These necessary auxiliary spaces usually take up more than one half of the total floor space. The point of this discussion of the two buildings has not been to compare, criticize, or evaluate them, but simply to point out that two men, artists in architecture working with problems of building that had much in common, came up with very different structural solutions. In both buildings the modern vocabulary of building is skillfully and unpredictably used to

6-15
Frank Lloyd Wright.
Solomon R. Guggenheim Museum,
New York.

form novel shapes which at least attract the eye and involve construction techniques that have been adapted by the imaginative vision of the creative person in architecture.

CREATIVITY: PROCESS AND PRODUCT

The works of Frank Lloyd Wright and Marcel Breuer present creativity functioning at a very high level. In our discussion we have stated that creativity is a potentiality which all people possess to different degrees. When creativity is considered in this fashion, it is necessary to demonstrate how a model of the creative process is related to and is, in effect, the model for all human action. In order to make this clear Melvin Tumin [6] formulated a sixfold phasing of the creative process as seen through the eyes of the individual actor.

The whole sequence of six phases should be considered as a unit of interrelated actions. Tumin's model of the creative process is as follows:

1. *Perception of the field* (what the individual knows or thinks). The creative orientation is one in which the individual has scanned a variety of possible goals for the direction of his energy. This is a knowledgeable approach and one which does not accept the goals of others as necessarily correct and legitimate. A goal is judged worthy because it has some promise of making a difference to the individual in terms of his own personal development.

2. *Attitude or readiness to act.* The creative attitude is indicated when a person acts as if he had a set of dominating preferences, such that he prefers (a) novelty over sameness, (b) problem-solving over formula repetition, (c) adventure over security, and (d) individuality over conformity.

3. *Creative action.* The characteristics of creative action are not those of self-consciousness; they require immersion, surrender, involvement, willingness to risk. The person should be ready to give, to try, to yield, and to commit himself to the field of action.

4. *Consequences on self.* Consequences of action upon the actor himself are creative if the experience of acting as he did is meaningful without any necessary regard to the final product. Even if the final product was a failure by some professional or technical standard, the consequences were creative as far as the individual was concerned.

5. *Consequences upon others.* An activity is creative if its consequences for others convey to them the sense of worthwhileness of involved unselfconscious surrendering action, without regard for social acceptance, credibility, or marketability of the final product.

---

[6] Melvin M. Tumin, **Education, Development and the Creative Process**, in *Aesthetic Form and Education*, Syracuse University Press, Syracuse, New York, 1958, pp. 23–38.

6. *The creative product.* The mark of the creative product is that it either reveals a new truth about the nature of man and his universe or it creates a new dimension of experience and meaning.

In his summary of his model for creative behavior the author states that the social consequences of such creative behavior should have a positive effect upon others in the society. At the minimum, the activity must not make it harder for others to find meaning and fulfillment in their lives. At the maximum, truly creative activity has consequences which positively enhance the chance of others to find enrichment and more meaning in their lives.

UNDERSTANDING ARTISTIC BEHAVIOR

When those who are closely associated with the arts encounter any model of creative behavior or of human action in general, their immediate reaction is to test it in order to see if it fits with their knowledge of what the artist is likely to do. When considered at an optimum level, the six phases we have outlined should give a description of artistic behavior which is consistent with our idea of what an artist is like and how he acts.

It is characteristic of the dedicated artist and of those who aspire to this calling to be generally strongly motivated to select goals and directions because they make a difference to the individual in terms of his own personal development. He guards this freedom of choice and even under pressure will maintain his concept of personal integrity. In his attitude and readiness to act he has an inherent distrust for predesigned and preselected procedures. He will seldom adopt procedures and styles because they are popular and will bring him the recognition or acceptance of the public. Certainly this is done by some, but the truly creative artist will resist this temptation and question his colleagues who act in this manner.

The artist does prefer novelty and new or original solutions. He makes a distinction between novelty and originality. Being different or novel in itself is not enough. He describes his approach to art as problem solving and would resist repeating a formula or a previously established pattern. He is certainly adventurous and willing to take risks and to depart from security and conformity because he knows that the latter would limit his freedom of choice, upon which he places a high value.

When describing artists at work, such phrases as total involvement, immersion in his work, surrender, and willingness to take risks are generally used and have become synonymous with creative action in the arts. There is also something about working with art media and upon art problems which brings a return to the individual unlike that from engagement in any other type of activity. When the artist is involved in the act of working with materials and trying to put down his idea in objective form, he receives a satisfaction which for him is often rewarding enough to justify the time and effort. The reward of the experience itself is satisfying to him even when the final product is judged to be less than important by certain technical standards. The history of art and artists is filled with examples of people who have felt so strongly about what they have been doing that they have been willing to disregard the marketability of their products. The pages of our history and literature are filled with images of the artist, living alone in an attic, penniless but proud, because he was driven by something within him to continue with a line of endeavor for which he would receive little or no economic return. Perhaps in our present day this is less often the case. However, we have many examples of artists who take all manner of temporary employment in order to produce paintings and sculptures for which there is no existing market or which might never be marketable. Thus financial reward is not the yardstick by which the creative activity of many people in art can be measured.

When we say that the measure of the creative product is that it reveals a new truth about the nature of man and his universe or creates a new dimension of experience and meaning, perhaps we are raising in the mind of the observer an image which, when taken to its extreme, would exclude all but very few of man's creative efforts in the arts. There are degrees of excellence, and even a modest effort can give an observer a meaningful view of reality.

THE PLACE OF THE ART PRODUCT

In this model of the creative process, only one of the six phases, the final one, refers to the product of creative activity. According to this view the final product represents only one of many phases of a long continuum of creative behavior. The critics and the observers of art are primarily concerned with the product itself and have only incidental interest in other phases that make up the process from which this product has emerged. When we talk about and look at art and make aesthetic judgements of it, we are concerned with those elements which are within the work of art itself — with its materials, formal design, and content or undertones of meaning and how these are interrelated. These are the qualities which we have before us. Our judgments are made upon what we can see now. The traces of other phases of the total creative act represented in this creative product can be perceived only indirectly and faintly. To the individual who produced the work, however, the process and what happened to him in the course of it may be relatively more important than the product itself. This is an idea which is held and supported by most teachers who work with young people in the schools. In these situations, where art is part of the general education of a large part of our population, we must consider that what happens to individuals as they are engaged in the process of expressing their ideas through art has real value beyond that which is placed upon the products resulting from this effort. Here we are making a distinction between art as a process which is important for teachers of schoolchildren and art as a product for evaluation and as a source of aesthetic experience.

PERSONAL TRAITS LINKED WITH CREATIVENESS

At the early stages of our revived interest in the creative process much of the research was directed toward identifying the personal characteristics of individuals who were judged to be highly creative. Guilford and members of his staff at the University of Southern California developed a plan for the study of creativity through experimental and factor-analytic techniques. This study began by hypothesizing distinct abilities which were believed to be involved in creativity.[7] Tests were constructed which measured these abilities. This project was under way in 1950 and the early reports were published two years later.[8]

Guilford's goal was to find measurable criteria which are responsible for creativeness in the sciences. It was based upon people working in the exact and the applied sciences. About this time Viktor Lowenfeld and his associates at Pennsylvania State University were carrying on parallel studies with entirely different experimental groups, ranging from groups of highly sophisticated artists to a "non-art" group. It is significant that these two entirely independent studies with different experimental groups, testing the same phenomena, but for entirely different purposes, arrived at almost exactly the same criteria for distinguishing creative from noncreative or less creative persons. A study was conducted to correlate the two batteries of tests. A multiple correlation between eight measures of the Penn State study and the Guilford study demonstrated that there was a highly significant correlation between the attributes tested in both investigations. As far as the data of these two investigations are concerned, it is possible to conclude that creativeness in the arts and sciences has common attributes.

Later, in his efforts to determine the relationship between creative thinking abilities and other intellectual abilities, Guilford developed a three-dimensional diagram for a model which represented a comprehensive theory of the human intellect. A review of the features of this conception of the entire collection of intellectual factors, or "structure of the intellect," can be helpful and relevant in support of factors that are predicted to be important in the arts.[9]

In art we are concerned with a process or an action. According to the kind of action performed, the thinking factors fall into three groups: (1) cognition factors; (2) production factors; and (3) evaluation factors. The total creative act in art involves all three aspects: cognition as we become aware of things with which we are confronted; production as we produce something of our own in response to that awareness; and evaluation of these products of thought and action.

Since creative performances in art are active, the production factors are the most conspicuous and critical. Among the thinking abilities involved in production, a distinction has been made between convergent and divergent thinking. Convergent thinking is defined as "thinking towards one right answer or toward a relatively uniquely determined answer." Divergent thinking is defined as "a type of thinking in which considerable searching about is done and a number of answers will do." Thus divergent thinking

---

7 These were: (1) sensitivity to problems; (2) fluency of ideas; (3) originality; (4) ideational novelty; (5) flexibility of ideas; (6) synthesizing ability; (7) analyzing ability; (8) ability to reorganize, or redefine; (9) span of ideational structure; (10) evaluative ability.

8 Joy P. Guilford et al., **A Factor Analytic Study of Creative Thinking, II: Administration of Tests and Analysis of Results**, *Reports from the Psychological Laboratory*, no. 8, University of California Press, Los Angeles, 1952.

9 Joy P. Guilford, **The Structure of the Intellect**, *Psychological Bulletin*, vol. 53 (1956), pp. 267–293.

tends to take place when the problem has yet to be discovered and when there is no set way of solving it. Although convergent and divergent thinking may occur together, a divergent-thinking approach tends, at least in an art situation, to be more closely related to the nature and goals of artistic activity. In the arts there is usually no single right answer; some answers are simply considered to be better than others.[10]

Under this general category of divergent thinking have been placed traits and qualities such as fluency, flexibility, and originality, which are very closely linked in art production. Also, many of our tests of creative thinking have been constructed to identify these characteristics of behavior.

TESTS OF CREATIVE ABILITIES

Guilford's elaborate test batteries of creative thinking abilities were originally divised for personnel well advanced on the educational ladder. Torrance and his associates at the University of Minnesota developed alternate batteries of tests for use with subjects from kindergarten through graduate school. The Minnesota Tests of Creative Thinking, although utilizing some of the task dimensions and scoring criteria of Guilford's work, depart from the factor-type test of Guilford by making a deliberate attempt to construct test tasks that would be models of the creative process itself.

Although the work of the artist involves creative thinking, much of his attention is centered on the expression of this creative thought in the form of a product. Thus, some of the tests and tasks which involve nonverbal ability may be more relevant when art behavior and characteristics are being investigated. These nonverbal, or figural, test tasks were designed to tap a somewhat different aspect of creative functioning, closer to that which characterizes the activity of an artist or student at work on the art process. Three of these are the Picture Construction Test, the Figure Completion Test, and the Repeated Closed Figure Test.[11]

The Picture Construction Test. Some idea of the nature of the test problems might be gained from examination of the instructions which accompany the Picture Construction Test.[12] These are as follows:

> At the bottom of this page is a piece of colored paper in the form of a curved shape. Think of a picture or an object in which this form would be an important part. Then lift up the piece of colored paper, and stick it wherever you want it on the next page, just like you would a postage stamp. Then add lines with pencil or crayon to make your picture.
>
> Try to think of a picture that no one else will think of. Keep adding new ideas to your first idea to make it tell as interesting and exciting a story as you can.

---

[10] Joy P. Guilford, **Creative Abilities in the Arts**, *Psychological Review*, vol. 44 (1957), pp. 110–118.

[11] These, renamed the Torrance Tests of Creative Thinking, have been published by Personnel Press, Inc., Princeton, New Jersey, 1966.

[12] Torrance, *op. cit.*, p. 670.

When these instructions are considered in connection with some of the things an artist does and how he does them, a close relationship between the two can be noted. Recall, for example, the work process descriptions of the abstract expressionists. They start by making a mark or shape of color upon the canvas. Then they continue to add new shapes or color patterns, which to their mind have a relationship to the first, and thereafter gradually adjust and integrate these until the canvas is completed.

The whole approach to sculpture based upon the found object is basically similar to the directions for the Picture Construction Test given above. The bicycle seat and handlebars, the child's toy, cans, labels, and any number of man-made and nature-made objects have become the motivational cues for the works of art of adults, just as the piece of colored paper becomes the initiating shape for the test of creative thinking. In itself, the technique of taking an initial shape and adding other forms to it, either in the same or another media, parallels the working procedure of the artist or student when he is composing a collage, a montage, or any other pictorial design.

Final directions given in this test are:

> When you have completed your picture think of a name, or title for it, and write it at the bottom of the page in the space provided. Make your title as clever and unusual as possible, use it to help tie your story together.

Unfortunately, as a part of the current scene in mature art this process of giving a title to a painting sometimes becomes a game between the artist and the viewer, which often challenges the viewer's patience and ingenuity to an extreme.

The Figure Completion Test. This consists of a number of incomplete figures, or lines. The instructions are as follows: [13]

> By adding lines to the figures on this and the next page, you can sketch some interesting objects or pictures. Try to think of some picture or object that no one else will think of, try to make it tell as complete and as interesting a story as you can, by adding to and building up on your first idea. Make up a title for each of your drawings and write it at the bottom of each block next to the number of the figure.

This task forces the individual to control his attention long enough to make the jump necessary to get away from the obvious and commonplace and to fill in the gaps required to complete the visual configuration. This is what the painter and sculptor, and also the architect, must do in order to move through the various stages to the completion of his work. He stands back, or takes a look at what he has accomplished up to that point, and makes decisions for continuing with his problem. At each stage he is confronted with a problem similar to that posed in the incomplete figure task. What he has accomplished up to one point becomes the incomplete figure,

---

[13] *Ibid.*, pp. 670–671.

which stimulates or motivates him in a new direction or causes him to continue his effort along the same course in which he has been moving. Also, in the process of creating a work of art, things sometimes happen by "accident." A slip of the brush, a flow of overheated metal, or an unusual textural pattern may become the starting point (as in the Figure Completion Test) to an entirely different solution. The ability of the artist to take advantage of these so-called "happy accidents" (which are said to be attempts of the unconscious to express itself) and to use them as a springboard for an adjustment of his work is often more exciting and sometimes makes him change his objectives. The result is often a better end product than the original intention. Working in this manner requires openness or flexibility, developed through successful experiences with other similar accidents.

The Repeated Closed Figures Test. This consists of two pages of closed figures, such as circles, squares, and triangles,[14] which force the individual to come back, again and again, to this same stimulus shape and to perceive it in a different way.

The test with circles, triangles, or squares has a parallel in the work of artists as they go back, again and again, to the same idea or theme. Each time, they make a considered attempt to see it in a new way and to improve upon the earlier work. This return to an original starting point is not provoked by lack of confidence. An artist is seldom satisfied and can usually see alternative solutions for any of his productions. This becomes evident if we consider the lifetime production of almost any artist; he will take almost the same art problem and bring forth what for him is a new solution. The amount of change between the old and the new creations will vary among artists, but there is usually enough of the old to identify the point of origin or to make a connection between them.

The parallels that have been drawn for this Repeated Closed Figure Test and the work habits of practicing artists should prevent any arbitrary judgment about the validity of the methods employed in assessment of creative abilities. Perhaps only a few artists have restricted their work to such elementary geometric forms as the triangle, circle, or square, but there are some who have made these primary constructions the basis of their art.

There are many more artists who have made repeated attempts to express the meaning they have discovered in a single theme or subject. In this case the theme replaces the square in the Repeated Closed Figure Test, as demonstrated in Figs. 6-17 through 6-20. The artist, like many before him, has found pleasure and satisfaction in depicting the festivals and celebrations which are part of his culture — the "splashes" of people, lights, decorations, colors, and shapes. The "state fair" is not a very serious or profound subject, but it is colorful, gay, and gaudy and filled with life and excitement for the participants. This annual event, like the harvest festivals of other people in other lands, has become somewhat tarnished by the encroachment of urbanization and commercialism — but it is still alive, lusty, and exuberant. The paintings are an attempt to express some of this joy

---

14 *Ibid.*, p. 671.

6-17
6-18

6-19

6-17
Midway I.

6-18
Midway II.

6-19
Midway II *(detail)*.

6-20
Midway III.

6-20

"for a moment" in living and of being a part of something, even though to some people the "something" isn't very much. In Fig. 6-17 the path of lights and their movement through the night sky becomes the subject matter; Figs. 6-18 and 6-19 present the confusion, movement, and complexity of visual impressions; and in Fig. 6-20 these are treated more abstractly.

This discussion of three nonverbal tests of creative thinking ability is intended to show the connection between what has been studied under the heading of creative thinking and some facets of the complex process of producing works which are classified as art. These two are not quite the same but have many common attributes. Many people associated with the arts have expressed an aversion to testing and measuring. Perhaps this shortsighted view will be modified with the awareness that these nonverbal tests of creative thinking are based on models of the creative process which are so closely related to the way an artist works.

Scoring the tests. Most of the test tasks are scored for three or four attributes which significantly differentiate highly creative from less creative people. These are: (1) *fluency*, or the number of different or relevant ideas; (2) *flexibility*, or the number of shifts in thinking to different categories of response; (3) *originality*, or the number of statistically infrequent responses that show creative intellectual energy; and (4) *elaboration*, or the number of different ideas used in working out the details of an idea. These are aspects of divergent thinking which are deemed essential for successful performance in the visual arts.

When considering creativity inside and outside the arts, it is important to realize that it is a combination of attributes rather than a single commodity. Creative-artistic ability, or "talent," is a complex combination of a number of distinct, although related, traits or abilities. Some known productive thinking factors, such as fluency, flexibility, and originality are the most obviously creative traits necessary for artistic action. If the individual possesses these capabilities to an adequate degree, they may be sufficient even when others are not present to any substantial degree. Also, if any full accounting of the complete creative process in art is to be made, other factors which are not primarily creative (evaluative abilities, visual memory, etc.) must be recognized for their important supporting role in art production.

CREATIVE-ARTISTIC TRAITS

The following personal traits, which are blended within the individual, are separated for the purpose of discussion.

FLUENCY

Fluency is expressed in creative-artistic behavior through an individual's ability to produce many ideas on a subject with paint, clay, or any other medium. Here quantity is important. For this reason, rough ideas for themes in the form of sketches, notes, and drawings, all of which are produced in abundance, can be used to test fluency. All the shades of meaning of the subject are investigated, and many of the symbols inherent in the subject are presented in various combinations and relationships. This is a fluency of ideas, expressions, and associations related to a single subject area.

Outside the art field, research related to the technique of "brainstorming," in which the subjects are encouraged to think up as many ideas about a single subject as they can in a limited time, has suggested that there is a positive relationship between quantity and quality. In these studies those who have thought up twice as many ideas have had twice as many good ideas in the same length of time.[15]

Although we sometimes place great stock in the artist's ability to come up with many decidedly different themes, there are a number of examples of painters and sculptors who have chosen to concentrate in depth on a single theme over a considerable span of time. Albers' series *Homage to the Square*, and De Kooning's series of paintings, *Woman*, are examples. The acceptance of a single initiating stimulus requires an ability to come back to the same idea or theme again and to disrupt it, break it up, and perceive it in different way.[16]

When we think of fluency in relation to the total lifetime output of an artist, we note that there have been many artists of considerable reputation who produced only a few works. The productiveness of artists varies greatly in the recorded history of art; Vermeer and many others produced little in comparison to Picasso. The aesthetic value of the works produced, not the quantity, is important in art. Variations in actual production may be attributed to differences in personality, style, approaches, and materials. We would expect more in terms of number of works from an artist who worked in the style of abstract expressionism than we might from another who was concerned with "precision and magic realism."

FLEXIBILITY

This characteristic allows the individual to adapt quickly to new situations. In the process of working upon an art problem, the situation constantly changes. Each new spot of color added affects the visual interplay of all the other colors and shapes already in place. The addition of a new shape welded to the others or the cutting away of the wood or stone changes the visual impact of what was there before. During the working period, as a product takes shape in the hands of the painter, sculptor, and architect, the overall compositional effect is changing continuously and the mind of the artist must shift constantly to adapt to the ever changing situation of the creative effort.

Flexibility allows the individual to keep his mind open and to make changes and adjustments up to the last moment, when the product is considered completed. Often this means wiping out some part which was "special" in itself but turned out to be inconsistent with the whole.[17]

---

[15] Alex F. Osborn, **Applied Imagination**, Charles Scribner's Sons, New York, 1954 (rev. 1957).
[16] See the earlier discussion of the Repeated Closed Figures Test from the Minnesota Tests of Creative Thinking.
[17] See the description of the work process for *Metamorphosis I* early in this chapter.

The artist is flexible in other ways. He is competent in a number of media and can, with ease, shift or adapt an idea to meet the requirements of a new medium. During the Renaissance era it was common for artists like Michelangelo, Leonardo da Vinci, and others to work with facility in sculptural media, paint, and architecture. Our records are filled instances of men like Daumier, Degas, Matisse, Miró, and Picasso, who were better known for their work in painting but were also successful in sculptural media and print making. Rauschenburg, Johns, Vasarely, Indiana, and others have adapted their ideas from painting to serigraphy, to lithography, and also into the three-dimensional space of sculpture.

Flexibility also helps the artist-craftsman to take advantage of the chance happening which grows out of the medium he is using. Without this flexible willingness to change from a fixed focus on a single way of reaching for a solution, frustration results and many ultimately better solutions will be lost.

Other aspects of flexibility on the part of the artist are evidenced in his ability to move from one way of working to another with ease and competence; he can switch from a spontaneous to a more rational, deliberate approach when this is demanded by the problem he has elected to solve. Also this same flexibility is exemplified by the individual who through a variety of structural devices can express a similar concept with a wide range of artistic solutions. Many people, however, elect, advisedly and after careful consideration, to restrict themselves to a particular arrangement of forms and a limited color selection. Examples are Mondrian, with his structure of horizontal and vertical lines and his restricted palette, and Albers, with his decision to concentrate upon a single geometric shape — the square — for many of his visual statements.

ORIGINALITY

This trait, although exceedingly broad and hard to define, is considered a vital element in the distinction of creative from less creative people. In a democratic society we respect the differences that exist among us. As a creative trait it consists in the capacity to produce unusual ideas. Originality is demanded of the artist and his work. An uncommonness in the arrangement of forms and in the employment of media which creates an effective surprise for the viewer is an attribute that separates one individual from the mass of ordinary practitioners.

In dealing with such a broadly defined trait or characteristic as originality, which includes so many different potentialities in artistic expression, it is perhaps wise to think in terms of levels or degrees. This would be a fairer assessment than saying something or someone is or is not original. By applying such a small yardstick we might find that many art products could be measured and excluded because of a trace of likeness to those previously presented to the world somewhere, sometime. Because the quest for originality in art reaches toward many levels and directions, as does creativity itself, we find that our assessment of a work product becomes a decision between more or less originality.

An "absolute" of originality would be very hard to find. Man (and the artist) is immersed and saturated in his culture. His culture represents, to a large extent, accumulated learnings, gained and remembered, as well as those which have been handed down to him. It is impossible to check the extent to which a creative innovation is influenced by or includes material and meaning from the reservoir of knowledge and experience in the artist-innovator's culture. This needed influence from experiences and culture may be summed up in the remark "Out of nothing, nothing comes." To reject completely any imitation and the influences of the past would deny progress. We would find ourselves continually reinventing the wheel or rediscovering fire. The artist who works in the rich and varied culture of the twentieth century would be in a most impractical position if an uninfluenced originality — total, genuine artistic innovation — were held to be the only criterion for the evaluation of his products.[18]

Where does imitation end and originality begin, is a question which needs some answers for the artist and the viewer of art. This is especially important when artists and art products of the period from 1955 through 1967 are under consideration. There is nothing very original about making plaster casts of the human figure, as can be attested by the collections of plaster casts of Greek sculpture resting in our museums or the shelves filled with casts of parts of the human anatomy in our art schools. Perhaps the originality of the sculptures of George Segal does not rest in the plaster casts of people in everyday costume, but in how these "imitations" have been used as an art form to convey a haunting, ghostly quality of a particular image of man. Although the originality of tying a knot is hard to accept — all the Boy Scouts do this to pass requirements for merit badges — we have pieces of sculpture representing large knots which have been exhibited in art galleries. The soft sculptures of Claes Oldenburg owe much to the masses of stuffed dolls and animals, the playthings and possessions of children and adolescents. The toy model of the steam engine has a lot in common with some of the motor-driven kinetic sculptures; the ready-made materials which are the symbols of collages and sculptured assemblages were made by someone other than the artist who composed them into works of art. Originality was in the new arrangement of the ready-made media and the context, or relationship, into which they had been placed.

It is hardly original, or profound, to say that the artist of any time or place has been influenced by the art and the artists of his own time and by the heritage of art from past centuries. Some of these influences are known to the artist and are either cultivated of resisted by him; of others he is quite unaware and has little consciousness of their effect upon his creative work.

The researchers who have studied the creative process have suggested several ways of measuring originality: (1) the ability to produce ideas that occur infrequently (statistically) among artists; (2) the ability to make indirect, or remote, associations and connections between things and events or among signs, symbols, and meanings; and (3) the cleverness of the response.[19]

---

[18] Ayers Bagley, **The Idea of Imitation**, *Art Education*, vol. 14, no. 4 (April, 1963).
[19] George F. Kneller, **The Art and Science of Creativity**, Holt, Rinehart and Winston, Inc., New York, 1965, p. 64.

ELABORATION AND SIMPLIFICATION

In scoring tests of creative thinking, elaboration was defined as the number of different ideas used in working out details of the problem. Elaboration of visual perception depends upon the embellishment of the stimulus that gives rise to the percept. When we consider an artistic form — the art object which is the stimulus for conveying meaning to the viewer — the creative quality of elaboration must be examined in a somewhat broader way than by totaling the number of details which have been included.

At times in art the basic idea may come from others, but individual uniqueness of expression is evident in the refinement and significant variation (elaboration) made upon the source material. At other times originality of expression consists in the ability to reduce the complexity of another person's idea and to restate it with clarity and directness. Creativity

6-21
An example of the overelaboration of building surfaces.
Minneapolis baroque.

6-22
An example of clean forms and
a simplified purity of
building masses.
*Frank Lloyd Wright,
Kaufmann House (Falling Water),
Bear Run, Pennsylvania.
1937-39.*

through elaboration in art also consists of taking a single idea and carrying it through a large number of improvisations. Each of these is a finished product but is related to the original starting point.

Elaboration or inclusion of a multitude of detail in painting, sculpture, or architecture has been given more or less value as a desirable aspect during different periods of history. At one time it has been held in greater repute than at others. Preference for complexity in artistic production varies according to time and cultural groups. Preferences for perceiving and dealing with complexity or with simplicity have also been investigated in connection with personality assessment and human behavior.[20]

Much of the architecture of the middle of the twentieth century in the United States and Europe stressed clean forms and a simplified purity in the arrangement of building masses; surface and decoration was held to a minimum (Figs. 6-21, 6-22).

Many painters stress simplicity rather than elaboration of form; these men put as little as possible upon the canvas to achieve a "minimal" art. Groups of sculptors followed the same course, presenting a single I beam of metal or an arrangement of flatsided geometric solids as their sculptured products.

This tendency in art, in which emphasis is placed upon reducing to a minimum the elements presented to the viewer, has received much attention in the 1960s through works in both painting and sculpture. The paintings of Ad Reinhardt and Ellsworth Kelly illustrate two approaches to this minimal art. At first glance many of Reinhardt's works appear as canvases totally covered with a single pigmentary hue. On closer examination, the observer becomes aware of extremely subtle variations on this surface. Contrasts of light and dark and of hue have been reduced; the usual suggestions of spatial depth are absent. His square dark, or "black," paintings are compositions of motionless, symmetrical, geometric shapes which

[20] Frank Barron, **Complexity-Simplicity as a Personality Dimension**, *Journal of Abnormal and Social Psychology*, vol. 48, no. 2 (1953), pp. 163–172.

extend to the edges of the canvas. They are compositions with a cold for-mal balance of color bands, textureless and almost undiscernible from their surrounding background. This is an art which searches for the abso-lute, the timeless, and the universal by exclusion of details and incidental symbols.

At the opposite pole is the visibility of painted shapes in the paintings of Ellsworth Kelly. They are as easy to see as those of Reinhardt are dif-ficult to define. Kelly is a "hard-edge" painter; Reinhardt is a master of the "soft-edge" (Fig. 6-23; see Fig. 1-17). In his paintings, Kelly depends on the optical effects of large and contrasting color areas which set up vibrations and create an impression of motion or tension in the viewer's eye. Stark designs, brilliant color contrasts — a few bands of opposing hues or a single curved form which stands out sharply against the background — are remote from visual association. This is geometrical abstraction on a grand scale. Paintings with such titles as *Red, White and Green* and *Blue, Red* are representative of this; they catch and hold the attention. These paintings are flat, precise, and controlled, with no interest in surface articulation or modulation of the sharply delineated edges of the shapes.

The desire for simplicity in sculpture, at least in number and kind of volumes and shapes, can be seen in the later works of David Smith and those of the British sculptor Anthony Caro. Smith's stainless and painted steel sculptures made in the years 1960–1965 included many which are made up of geometrical elements — cubes, shafts, bars, disks, and cylin-ders. These form motifs that do not allude to man and the natural world. These series of works, of monumental simplicity, are impressive for the sculpturally direct relationship of clean volumes, the play of curves against straight lines, in most cases without undue embellishment or interruption. Smith often took a motif and developed it through a series of variations; in some instances, as with the *Cubi*, he made about thirty versions of the arrangement of the steel cubical forms (Fig. 6-24). Other series of sculp-tures made in the 1960s have such titles as *Zig* (from "ziggurat"), *Tank-*

6-23
*Ellsworth Kelly.
Red, Yellow, Blue. 1966.
Sidney Janis Gallery,
New York.*

6-24
*David Smith, Cubi IX.
1961. Walker Art Center.
Minneapolis.*

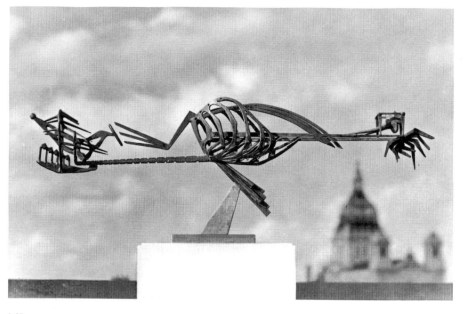

6-25
**Note the change in attitude toward
complexity in the work of David
Smith from 1948 to 1961.**
David Smith, Royal Bird.
*1948. Walker Art Center,
Minneapolis.*

6-26
Anthony Caro. Sculpture Three.
*1962. Walker Art Center,
Minneapolis.*

totem, *Menand* (from the name of a town near Albany, New York), *Voltri-Bolton* and *Becca*. These are large sculptures and their machine-cut shapes seem more impressive against the outdoor background of sky, hills and trees (Fig. 6-25).

The sculptures of David Smith and those of Anthony Caro have a lot in common. Caro presents the viewer a new idea of what sculpture can be — an object in its own right to be accepted for what it is. He does not want his sculpture to be accepted for its abstraction of something out of the environment or for its relationship to other forms in nature, life, and human situations. It is none of these things, but it is an object, a piece of sculpture, and should be accepted as such (Fig. 6-26). His *Horse* does not relate to accepted forms found in abstract sculpture. It is composed of slabs of welded steel which merely sit on the ground. Others of his sculptures — *Strip, Slow Movement* and *Early One Morning* — are to be walked around and present a sequence of "found" situations for the observer, which are independent of association to things and events. Other sculptors have sought to reduce or distill the image to the minimum; perhaps the best-known effort is Brancusi's *Bird in Space* (Fig. 6-27).

The conflict between elaboration as a measurable component or attribute of creativeness and simplicity, a much sought after quality of artistic production, is somewhat difficult to rationalize. In testing for creativeness, elaboration is scored in terms of the number of details that the individual has included. Instead, simplicity as an attainment in art is obtained when the individual organizes complex concepts or shapes materials into a form which has the smallest possible number of structural features. Many artists work to attain this quality. An economy of means is to them a desirable goal. It is their aim to eliminate any unnecessary details which will serve only to confuse the viewer and divert his attention from the main concern of the work of art. Of course, there is a point of diminishing returns. This comes when the image presented by the artist has been simplified or reduced to a point of such purity that it lacks interest and does not stimulate or excite the observer. Thus, it becomes the role of the artist to say what he wishes to say with directness and economy, but with the reservation that he must put in enough to satisfy and command the attentiveness of the viewer.

All degrees and levels of simplicity are exhibited in our art works. Many of the modern abstractionists, some of whom have already been mentioned, such as Kelly, Mondrian, Smith, and Caro, have given sufficient richness to their compositions although they have built them upon a restricted number of geometric elements; however, when these compostions are studied carefully, one can see how even very simple elements may be combined into a very complex pattern. The British artist Ben Nicholson is a case in point. Among his works is a very simple relief, which consists of one regular and complete circle, plus a number of rectangular figures parallel to one other and to the edges of the rectangular frame. An analysis of this composition [21] shows very subtle departures from absolute symmetry in his placement of space divisions. Every part is different from but related

21 For a complete analysis of this composition, see Rudolf Arnheim, **Art and Visual Perception**, University of California Press, Berkeley, Los Angeles, 1954 (paperbound, 1965).

to all others in the composition. No divisions are the same. The close proximity of areas and proportions creates enough attention to cause the observer to sense the subtlety and complexity of the interrelated parts.

REDEFINITION AND ABILITY TO REARRANGE

Guilford refers to this trait as the ability to shift the function of objects and to use them in a new way. This is a fairly common kind of behavior in the creative process of art. As part of the experimentation with materials, something that is designed for one purpose is used in a new way or context in the art action. Artists and schoolchildren constantly redefine the

6-28
Charles Huntington.
Space Station.

6-29
Within a steel frame, iron strips and saw blades support stretched canvas forms ornamented with metal washers and wire.
Lee Bontecou.
Untitled No. 38.
1961. Walker Art Center,
Minneapolis.

6-28

6-29

use of materials — linoleum designed for a floor covering is used for print making; gauze impregnated with plaster, which is used for making casts for broken limbs, serves a new purpose as a medium for sculpture; and a twig or a piece of wood becomes a drawing instrument. Rearranging and redefining manufactured objects and taking them away from their original settings and uses by making them a component element in a piece of sculpture, painting, or craft product are common procedures of the artist (Figs. 6-28, 6-29).

Print making as an area of artistic expression has had more than its share of experimental innovations that have grown out of this human drive to exploit redefinition and the ability to rearrange. The function of numerous objects and materials has often been shifted away from their original purposes and values in order to adapt them for print making. Kitchen gadgets, foods, fragments from nature, odds and ends of discarded trivia have become the tools of the print maker. Prints have been made with bread, cheese, alphabet macaroni, string, glue, twigs, leaves, erasers, paper clips, tubes, lace, and an endless list of unlikely objects and materials. Redefinition in this area has "run wild," almost out of control. One of the first of these to be redefined for print making was the potato. It has been used for so long that there is very little of originality in the making of a potato print. Art quality is incorporated in the arrangement of the shapes, control of their repetition, and the combination of colors.

The examples shown in Figs. 6-30 through 6-32 were only a few of the thirty samples which were made from one potato. The purpose of this activity was to test the range of variations from a limited number of shapes. In our example we have an expression of fluency as well as the artist's ability to redefine and rearrange.

On another level, the artist of one era has taken something out of the tradition of his heritage in art and redirected it, reshaped it, and used it in a new way. Media, solutions, and ideas which are part of the history and tradition of art through the ages have been used by the contemporary artist in a new way, consistent with our time. This is the way solutions are found for the problems which today's artists have accepted; this is meaningful acceptance of tradition and a way of using it to cross new boundaries. There are very few new subjects and completely new ideas.

Creativity can flourish when the artist is openly receptive to new ideas, processes, and products and is not bound by stereotypes and preconceived notions. These deprive us of exciting adventures from the flexible application of the processes and products of science and technology. An artist should employ the products and technical advantages of his own period of history in order to reflect with integrity the culture to which he belongs.

OTHER CONDITIONS OF CREATIVITY

There are many conditions which must be met if true creation is to occur. The artist must be immersed, committed, and at the same time detached He must know when it is appropriate to detach himself from the task at hand long enough to see it from the outside and evaluate it with some neutrality. It is said that creativity consists largely of rearranging what we know in order to find out what we do not know. A certain skepticism and

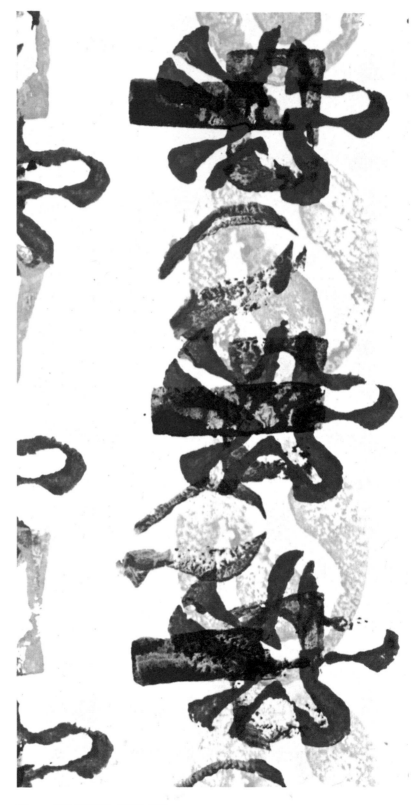

6-30–6-32
Examples of design variations obtained from a single potato print.

ability to take risks and to depart from accepted ideas open the way to new connections between apparently unrelated elements.

Sometimes the connections the artist makes in associating ideas of things and situations symbolically may be remote and indirect. However, the visual statement by the artist may give the viewer the feeling of certainty that everything is right and obviously should have been connected in this way.

The study of the personality of the individuals who have displayed creativeness in many different lines of endeavor has been undertaken by many psychologists. Barron and his colleagues at the University of California's Institute of Personality Assessment and Research engaged in such a study of a large number of individuals in a group including painters, writers, physicians, physicists, biologists, economists, and anthropologists.[22]

He proposed the following as descriptive of creative artists and perhaps also of creative scientists:

1. Creative people are especially observant and value accurate observations more than other people do.

2. They often express part-truths. This they do vividly; the part they express is the generally unrecognized. By displacement of accent and apparent disproportion in statement, they seek to point out the usually unobserved.

3. They see things as others do, but also as others do not. They are independent in their thinking and they also value clear cognition. They will suffer great personal pain to testify correctly. They are motivated to this value and to the exercise of independent, sharp observation. This is done both for reasons of self-preservation and in the interest of human culture and its future.

4. They have more ability to hold many ideas at once and to compare more ideas with one another to make a richer synthesis. They are by constitution more vigorous and have available to them an exceptional fund of psychic and physical energy.

5. Their universe is more complex, and they usually lead more complex lives, seeking tension in the interest of pleasure they obtain upon its discharge.

6. They have more contact than most people do with the life of the unconscious, with fantasy, reverie, and the world of imagination.

7. They have exceptionally broad and flexible awareness of themselves. The self is strongest when it can regress, admit primitive fantasies, naïve ideas, and tabooed impulses into consciousness and behavior, and yet return to a high degree of rationality and self-criticism. The creative person is both more primitive and more cultured, more destructive and more constructive, crazier and saner, than the average person.

6-31

6-32

22 Frank N. Barron, **The Psychology of Imagination**, *Scientific American*, vol. 199, no. 3 (September, 1958), pp. 151–165.

THE CREATIVE STUDENT AND HIS TEACHER:
THE ARTIST AND HIS PUBLIC

It has been reported in the studies of Getzels, Jackson, Torrance, and others that there is apparent divergence between the values of the teacher and those of the creative student. In a report on this in Kneller's *The Art and Science of Creativity*, the description of the creative student in the classroom appears to bear many resemblances to similar descriptions of the artist as he relates to and is looked upon by his society.[23] The description is as follows:

> *The creative student is often difficult to handle. He is more independent and self-absorbed than the conventional child, and hence less friendly and communicative. Often he is less studious and orderly, being more interested in his own ideas and in work per se. Because he sees things differently than others, he tends to get on less well with his peers, which makes him more difficult for the teacher to control. He has a tendency moreover to isolate himself, and to be over-critical of others. In addition he is apt to seek out difficult assignments, often combining different areas of subject matter. He often thinks unconventionally and breaks rules. He is likely to get deeply involved in his task, and to resent having to break the flow of his ideas in order to study another subject merely because a new period has begun. When he is interested he works under greater nervous tension than other pupils, a fact which makes him fractious and irritable. Moreover his tentative and spontaneous ideas are frequently harder to assess than the less original, but also more finished work of less creative students. Often too, he is untidy and slapdash, being interested in ideas rather than presentation and being less concerned to win the teacher's approval.*

Although it is easy to oversimplify the situation, many of the characteristics attributed to the creative students and the teacher's expected attitude toward them have parallels in the artist and much of society's attitude toward him. If we were to substitute "artist" for "creative students" and take the reference situation out of the classroom into the community, the situation and description would be generally the same. The comparison is drawn here to call attention to the relationship between the artist and society and the interaction between the two.

Mental flexibility on the part of the observer is also required to accept the kinds of redefinition of the use of materials and ideas presented by the artist. The observer should be willing to give the artist the same rights to be different and to disagree with him as he would bestow upon his neighbors in their pursuit of everyday living.

Creative discovery in the arts presupposes a willingness to take artistic risks. It is helpful for the observer to be willing to examine new statements of new ideas and to be less trusting of the tried and tested. This does not suggest that something is good just because it is new, but

---

[23] Kneller, *op. cit.*, pp. 70–71.

rather that value decisions should be withheld until more data, more observation, and more contact with the unusual or new has been established. The final choice of acceptance or rejection still remains with the observer. He is not required to accept something merely because it is new or because it is hung on the walls or placed on pedestals in a gallery. The artist can only partially control the perceptions of the observer as he receives an image of a statement which the artist has presented. The connections and associations that will be evoked in the mind of the beholder come out of the perceptive experiences of his past and the meanings he has given to them. Everyone who looks at a work of art sees something different. Thus, looking at art with understanding can also be an experience which might be called creative.

CREATIVITY AND THE ART APPRECIATOR

This discussion of the creative process as it relates to art and the artist has had two purposes. An understanding of what we have discovered about the process, elementary as these discoveries are at the present time, should contribute to any endeavor directed toward production of objects through the processes and materials of art. Also, knowledge of the creative process, even in such general terms as phases, levels, and characteristics of individuals, provides a source of understanding what the artist does and how he does it. This in turn will give the observer some of the keys to open the doors to a more fruitful enjoyment of the works of the artist.

The creative process, its characteristics and conditions, has been discussed in relation to the work of the artist. Many of these same factors apply to the participation of the observer as he looks at a work of art and draws from it some of the emotive meaning put into it by the artist-creator. The observation and appreciation of art requires an open-mindedness on the part of the individual which leaves him open and flexible enough in his thinking to accept the possibility of a connection among objects — ideas and symbols which may not, in his experience, have been associated in this fashion before. This is asking the viewer for divergent thinking, which makes him willing to accept the fact that, although there is no single right answer, many alternative solutions could be satisfactory — an admission that there is no preconceived way for the canvas to be painted, the stone to be carved, or the metal to be welded.

Chapter 7

THE DESIGN PROCESS

Often the scientist will separate one small segment of the whole organism or a fragment from the universe for careful study. The researcher into human behavior will try to segregate some of the variables of the total in order to gain insight into our actions when confronted with a particular condition in the whole of human conditions. These men are aware that their fragment of the total is only a fragment and that the bits of knowledge they have gleaned provide insights or real importance only after they have been related against or into the larger background of the whole of human actions and of the universe. The importance of such an approach to discovery lies in the fact that it is a manageable quantity and gives the researcher time for patient, carefully detailed examination without distractions. For this to have much meaning, however, it is essential that the scientist or researcher have an awareness of the connection between his fragment and the whole organism or between the one response he is studying and the total behavior.

Although our examination of the art process has not been broken down into such small segments as those of the scientists mentioned above, who are often interested in a single cell or a response to a single stimulus, the reader should keep in mind the interrelationship between our discussion of the parts and the total, unified whole of the production of a work of art. This production of art — what the artist does — is one continuous integrated action from its conception with the felt need of the individual to communicate the meaning of his experience with his universe by forming and shaping the chosen material of his craft in such a way that others can see, feel, and respond to the image he has created. Knowing that this is one whole unified experience, we have taken the risk. We have taken key parts of an integrated whole and discussed them in sequence because in this way a carefully detailed study is possible without distraction. It is hoped that the reader will understand the unified complexity of the whole while benefiting from the added clarity given to the separated parts — the looking and the perceiving, the abstracting, and the creative strategies which guide the artist.

As soon as we move from the creative process in general to go deeper into the creative-artistic process in particular, we are then confronted with the term "design," referring to both a process and a product. Much of the vocabulary used in connection with art lacks precise definition. Agreement on a consistent terminology has not been obtained. The same word may have quite different meanings among artists and for the general public. Thus it is important to define this word, which is so widely used for art as well as for other purposes.

We speak of a design for living, of statistical design, of pictorial design, and of architectural, interior, graphic, textile, and other kinds of design. With whatever descriptive identifier the word design is combined, there is one common denominator that fits them all. We are speaking of a plan for something; we are referring to some kind of order or organization. By implication this gives us the idea that design is the planned organization of something. In reference to art, design is the *organization of all the seemingly unrelated elements into a harmonious, aesthetically satisfying unity.* Such a definition is at the same time both broad and specific.

Today, as in the past, many people have restricted their use of the word to describe the decoration of a surface, for example, the decorative pattern of a rug, wallpaper, a dress, or a sofa which makes the fabric more attractive. This limited application refers to only one category: decorative design. Another broad division is pictorial design — the composition for picture making or for painting in all of its extensive applications; this is primarily design in two dimensions. Another category is structural design, which includes sculpture, architecture, and all three-dimensional form creations. With a certain amount of elasticity, this three-way classification of decorative, pictorial, and structural design could serve a useful purpose by helping us to handle the diversity of products and practices of art with a consistent vocabulary (Figs. 7-1–7-3).

Those who like to think of design as a process tried to make distinctions according to the kinds of actions involved. They have thought of design as the creating of new forms or symbols rather than the arranging of borrowed forms or symbols in a new or different way. Whether we think of design as categories of products or as processes or actions, there is an element of consistency in our belief that it is the structural plan for the organizational unification of the parts into the total which we call art.

A VIEW OF DESIGN THEORY

An organized view of design theory is given in many books. In general there is agreement that design means the organization of all elements into a unified whole. However, there is not the same agreement about what these elements are precisely. This same lack of agreement was recognized in the 1920s when the Committee on Terminology in the Arts was established. The design elements were listed in its report as line,

7-1
Structural design: The Tree.
Library of St. John's Abbey,
Collegeville, Minnesota.

7-2
Decorative design: The Tree.

7-3
Pictorial design: The Tree.

7-3

texture, shape, color, and tone.[1] Unfortunately for the student and general reader, most subsequent writers on design either had not read the committee's report or had decided that their own classifications were better. Also, although the original committee made distinctions between the elements and the principles by which these might be manipulated, various authors tended to put these together in diverse relationships and to mix with them newer word concepts that grew out of different attitudes and later needs. For example, there has been a tendency in the experimental forms of art of the 1960s to accept motion and light as essential elements. Previously light had been considered only in relation to color and tone (light and shade) and not as a separate element in itself. Movement was thought of as something which grew out of the way the artist used the five elements of line, texture, shape, color, and tone. The repetitions, undulations, and directional movement of shapes and lines created an illusion of motion. Repetition, overlap, and alternation of tones, colors, and textures could produce the same effect. However, with the air-driven mobile of Calder and the various types of kinetic sculpture (including the sculptures with small motors incorporated in their design), motion itself has come to be considered a design element by many artists, just as color and shape were in times past. Space and volume have also been listed as design elements, although the illusion or actuality of these can be obtained by some arrangement of our original five elements. All of these terms, in one form or another, are used constantly in descriptions of art and the art process. Lack of uniformity in their application to the processes and products of art has given rise to many semantic arguments and difficulties in communication.

DESIGNING AS A PROCESS

There is a vast amount of literature on the subject of design. However, most of these books are concerned with information and the vocabulary required to acquaint the reader with what design is. Seldom, except by implication, do authors get down to the "how of it" because of the individualness which we associate with artistic activity and also because of the variety which we demand in the products of the designer. This is admittedly a difficult task. We would like, however, to make a small scratch on the surface of this complicated process of designing a product which might be regarded as a work of art.

Aesthetic theorists and those who make philosophical inquiry into art provide the background against which our attempt will be made. In their search for basic truths these philosophers have often concerned themselves with the definition of beauty and of art. Their writings are often argumentative and their definitions are difficult to decipher; the language at times becomes vague and general, and those of us who are not versed in the language or its pattern have a difficult time extracting a kernel of meaning from their literary efforts. Yet, the philosophers and others have

---

[1] See Appendix 7 for an outline of design terminology from the committee's report.

traced through the history of art the value that this art has had to peoples and civilizations throughout history.

Aesthetic considerations which have been important sources of creative value for the artist and spectator are identified as *matter*, *form*, and *content*. Matter refers to the materials from which the work is created. Here we are concerned with what Henry Moore termed "truth to materials" — integrity in the use of the materials or their sensuous beauty.

Form is somewhat harder to define because, in reference to art, it seems to connote something more than the common synonym "shape," although the verb "to shape" conveys the creative aspects of this human activity. Form in art has been defined as "the shape imparted to an artifact by human intention and action." [2] Or, in the words of another writer, "The theorists define it thus: a group of elements perceived in their totality, as it were, and not as the product of any chance assemblage." [3]

Another example of the elusiveness of a precise definition follows: [4]

> The world appears to us. It appears to us above all through a form. And thus arises the problem: is there an analogy between these forms? That is to say, is the form of a man, of a cat, of a stone, analogous to the forms produced by the artist? I must confess that for some time now, I no longer set myself problems of this kind in absolute terms, because I no longer believe in the possibility of "demonstrating" what form is. To be capable of this would mean to be capable of demonstrating what life is. Today I am interested only in examining how a form is born, that is how a reality becomes perceivable.

This writer continues with the following statement: [5]

> Form is nothing other than the tangible expression of a reality and when this truly coincides with reality it is in consequence true, it is in consequence beautiful.

As we understand these and other definitions of the meaning of form, it goes beyond the usual idea conveyed by "shape" and is related to the *organized structure* given to the work by the artist as he relates and combines several units of varied size — sections of life — into one organic whole. By this structuring the artist effects an ordered complexity of harmonic proportions in his finished product — a kind of structural legibility which can be read by others.

The third aesthetic factor, content, also needs some definition. By content we mean more than the superficial subject matter. It is hoped that the underlying meaning which has been embodied within the work by the artist will in turn be abstracted by the spectator-observer. There

---

2 Herbert Read, **The Origins of Form in Art,** in Gyorgy Kepes (ed.), *The Man-made Object*, George Braziller, Inc., New York, 1966.
3 François Molnar, **The Unit and the Whole: Fundamental Problem of the Plastic Arts**, in Gyorgy Kepes (ed.), *Module, Proportion, Symmetry, and Rhythm*, George Braziller, Inc., New York, 1966, p. 209.
4 From Leonard Ricci, **The Tangible Expression of a Reality**, in Gyorgy Kepes (ed.), *The Man-made Object*, George Braziller, Inc., New York, 1966; reprinted with the permission of the publisher. Copyright © 1966 by George Braziller, Inc.
5 *Ibid.*, p. 105.

are many writers, including Roger Fry and Clive Bell, who have refused to be concerned with values of subject matter or any allegorical implications of the content. They have concentrated upon the plastic organization of the art work and have tended to exclude content as an important source of creative value for the artist or the spectator. This might, however, be an argument caused by sematic differences rather than fundamental disagreement.

Consciousness of form is received from the natural environment of man; the artist and the observer have, either spontaneously or deliberately, matched this in their artifacts. The products of art of all degrees of excellence include symbolic forms. The purpose of symbolic form is to disclose meaning. The symbols of art are used to signify an unknown or otherwise inexpressible perception or feeling; signs used in art have a closer resemblance to another object and are signs rather than symbols. Through these signs and symbols of the artistic image a content of meaning is translated into something visible or tangible.

When design in art is considered as a process, an action rather than a product, our discussion above brings us to the conclusion that throughout this process we are searching for a harmonious interrelationship of materials, structural form, and emotive meaning.

UNITING MATERIALS, STRUCTURAL FORM, AND CONTENT

To clarify what is meant by harmonious interrelationship of matter, form, and content as it might occur in an art activity, an example is provided. This is only one drop in the stream of artistic behavior, but it should provide some clarification as to what is meant by interaction of aesthetic factors in the act of designing. It can be seen clearly that the process involves a constant movement backward and forward among the three factors and not a straight one-two-three sequence. We have attempted to isolate the factors as they interact with one another. Those aesthetic factors that were the major considration for the artist at a particular stage of his creative activity are noted in parentheses. From these notations it can be seen that the artist moved from one aesthetic element to another. At the end, matter, form, and content were interrelated in the production of his work of art and were never entirely separated during or after the creative experience. The interplay of the constituent parts of the total process continues from the inception of the idea to the concrete form which embodies this idea. For further aid, reference will be made to photographs taken at intervals to coincide with the written statement.

This spurt of artistic activity followed a period of self-initiated observation of insects and insect behavior in the field, as well as delving into technical literature in the realm of entomology. (**Content**)

Since my desire to make jewelry goes beyond the need to make a merely ornamental object, I try to develop ideas based upon interests in and observations of the world about me as well. The fascinating habits and instincts of insects, in addition to their beautiful coloration and magnificent body structure, stimulate a wealth of imagery which compels expression in metal (Figs. 7-4, 7-5).

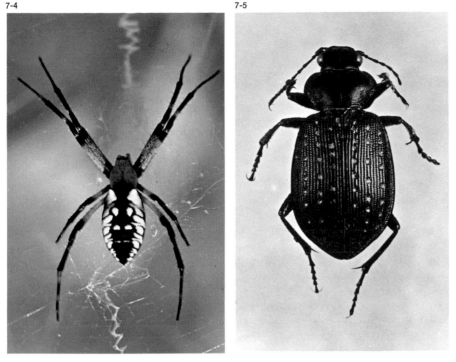

The pendant form of jewelry is most adaptable to this imagery because it can become miniature sculpture in the round; it can be heavier than most other objects of jewelry, it need not have a back or front, nor must it conform closely to parts of the anatomy or wearing apparel.

My current technical interest is the direct fusion of silver pieces by an oxygen-gas torch. It is an exciting technique because it requires speed of decision and great dexterity. Since construction occurs within the elusive margin of temperatures at which silver surfaces flow and attach and the object suddenly disintegrates into a blob of molten metal, one constantly treads the perilous line between creation and destruction. Furthermore, regardless of one's level of control, there are always unpredictable variations that lure the artist down avenues which he would otherwise not have traveled. (**Matter**)

The ability to construct the object directly in a plastic flowing manner rather than resorting to an intermediate material, as in the lost-wax casting process, allows the flow of compelling ideas which might otherwise be lost if completion were delayed. (**Matter**)

The rich textures and qualities of organic flow caused by the surface tensions of the cooling metal are ideally suited to my interpretation of nature. Beginning with exploratory sketching, the general form of the object was indicated. The beetle, with its distinct head-thorax-abdomen relationship, was the initiating form. The geometric relationship seemed to be a firm base for departure. The grasping mandibles and the variety of rich patterns and textures moved through my mind. It occurred to me that the color patterns could be interpreted as structure, thus opening up an entirely new way of looking at these forms. The decision was made to begin with the central or thorax area and continue from there. (**Content**) Knowledge of the tubular structure of insect bodies influenced my choice of silver tubes bundled together. Past experiences indicated that rich structural pattern would result from cutting into such a bundle after it was fused into a mass. (**Content and Matter**)

The piece began with tubing of different diameters, bent from silver strips cut

THE DESIGN PROCESS   217

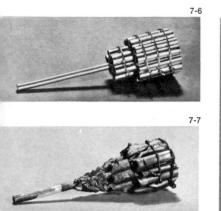

7-6

7-7

7-8

7-9

7-10

7-6
Bundled tubing.

7-7
Fused bundle of tubing.

7-8
Circular openings became ovals
as tubes were penetrated.

7-9
Bent-arm pinwheel.

7-10
Arms twisted together.

7-11
Another insect-motif pendant.

7-11

into two different lengths and bundled around a shaft with silver wire (Fig. 7-6). The bundle of tubing was stood on end with the central shaft of silver protected from heat by a wrap of strip asbestos. Heat was applied with the torch, all the time watching for critical signs of temperature rise. The red glow was observed changing to a fierce red-yellow. The surface began to glisten. The heat was cut back to hold the temperature at this point. The constant play of the torch around the piece equalized the heat flow. A thin fluid line flowed between junctions of tubing — they began to buckle ever so slightly. "Careful! Don't melt completely." The tube ends melted down to form thick walls and some openings closed up entirely. The silver binding wire melted and attached to the tubes, forming regular beaded patterns. I made a mental note that this could be organized and controlled for future use. The junction of shaft to tubing needed thickening — it was too abrupt. Silver wire was carefully fed into this area. By controlling the heat and touching the wire at the right time, the silver flowed like glue being squeezed from a plastic bottle. (**Matter**) The piece was allowed to cool (Fig. 7-7).

I now began shaping it to a long tapered form like an insect's long, probing snout. Shaping began quickly on a grinding wheel. Exciting cross sections of tubing emerged from the fused core. Circular openings became oval and greatly elongated ovals gave way to parallels as tubes were penetrated (Fig. 7-8). As the form approached satisfying proportions, I switched to hand files for more control. (**Form**) At first I felt that this segment should be cut into two units to conform to the original head-thorax idea, but I found that the two different lengths of tubing created a definite visual division. (**Content and Matter**)

The next unit had to be related to this segment. In previous attempts, semiflat segments were used, but they seemed inadequate. Since the form was relatively passive and contained, a more open and dynamic lower form was indicated. More exploratory forms were sketched in relationship to the segment. (**Form**)

I chose a hooked mandible form repeated to produce an inverted cage that was open at the end. (**Content**) How should it be assembled? Although I wanted precision, the vitality of fused forms was needed. By projecting an imagined three dimensional form into a two-dimensional cutout of silver, a bent-armed pinwheel was arrived at (Fig. 7-9). The arms were twisted at the center and bent together until they nearly touched. (**Form and Matter**) It looked too machine-made (Fig. 7-10). So the center was packed with asbestos and attacked with the torch. Silver flowed into junctions of the radial arms and down the rib sides. The ribs being of equal thickness appeared clumsy. They were modulated by filing away excess metal. (Even the most severe forms in nature have modulation of form — the slight taper of the wheat straw, the grass blade, etc. — a quality of growth.) Finally the ribs were cut to different lengths to avoid monotony. (**Form and Matter**)

When attaching it to the first unit, it became apparent that it needed a slender, almost invisible connection like a wasp waist so that the contrast and opposition of forms and surface patterns would be heightened — opposition within unity. The top shaft looked too thin, and the end didn't terminate but seemed to shoot off into space. It had to be thickened by further fusing. (**Content and Form and Matter**)

The final finishing was merely a matter of subtle refinement and craftsmanship. Since jewelry is a form of sculpture, the tactile sense is used for the evaluation and refinement of form as well as for visual appraisal. (**Form**)

The intimate scale of jewelry requires that file marks and other objectional tool marks be removed. On sculpture of greater scale these might not be objectionable; in fact, they might serve as useful surface texture. (**Form and Matter**)

The final step was the patina, an oxide dip to darken all shadow areas to uniform value. All touchable surfaces were rubbed with pumice to give tonal contrast. (**Matter**) The piece was finished (Fig. 7-12). What will grow from this experience? (See Fig. 7-11.)

7-12
The finished piece.

THE DESIGN PROCESS 219

IMPLICATIONS OF THE CASE STUDY

The statement about what happened during the design process was written without foreknowledge of how it was to be used. It is a description of how a craftsman proceeded to create a piece of jewelry. The parenthetical references were added later by someone who was not personally engaged in the process; in this respect it has objectivity. The intention has been to employ this example as a means of demonstrating the continuous interaction in thought and behavior of such nebulous elements as the materials, the organizational structure, and the idea from the thought processes of the participant. Although some details are missing, it should be possible to note how three separate factors were combined in the process and product of design.

Sometimes the content idea and structure were the determinants of a brief phase, and at other times the materials and technical considerations were the forces which controlled the action. In the work process the artist does not say to himself, "This is content at work" or, at another time, "Idea plus structure are making me do this." Frankly, such conscious analysis by the participating individual would be extremely rare and perhaps even nonexistent. However, for the understanding of an onlooker, and even for the artist himself, this "postmortem" examination could be useful.

One of the important by-products of the personal account of this art activity is the illustration it provides of the role of evalution in an art activity. When the artist's statement of his progressive development is reread with the purpose of discovering points at which he was forced into decision making or evaluation, one can understand quite clearly that this is not something done after everything else is finished. It has been continuously involved in his work at all stages. All along the way decision, both temporal and final, must be made, and it is out of this process of constant reevaluation that the final art product receives its form and the visual imagery which will be seen by other people.

The process of designing and the specific example provided here should have some connection in the reader's mind with material about the creative process that was included in earlier chapters. The design process should show a definite resemblance to the creative process because these are in effect the same thing. Creative-artistic behavior is one, and a very important one, of the total kinds of behavior which we classify as creative. The description above does not give any details about the preparatory stages that are noted in any discussion of the evolution of a creative action. Also, very little of what might be classified as incubation has been taken into account. In this example most of our attention has been focused upon what takes place after these stages of the process. We have been more particularly concerned with the artist-craftsman from the point at which he has set his plan for a design solution. We have shown some of the conflict between the demands of his idea and the nature of material as well as how the problems of design structure are resolved as the product advances from its inception to its realization.

Having demonstrated the interaction of materials, structural form, and content in one example of the design process, we can now proceed to study these aesthetic factors in more detail. This can help us to understand the means through which a true work of art may be formulated. As described by Read, the true work of art "works as a bridge between the two worlds of feeling and perception, giving definition to feeling and form to perception."

THE ROLE OF MATERIALS

There have been a number of statements or tenets which summarize and act as guiding principles for the artist with respect to the use of materials; integrity in the use of materials and truth to materials are among those most often heard. These state only one of the main principles in the artist's creed. Material in itself and truth to it do not alone make a work of art. Respect for clarity of form and the need to verify an idea or feeling make demands which must be blended within the course of action.

The British sculptor Henry Moore was deeply conscious of what he called "truth to materials." In his commentary in a movie about the sculptor, James Sweeney gives a very clear description of what is meant by truth to material.[6] He discusses each of the materials used by the sculptor and their characteristic qualities, which must be apprehended and exploited. Wood, for example, has a stringy, fibrous consistency. It can be carved into thin forms without breaking, but it demands to be cut and split. Circular shapes are natural to it because of the cylindrical growth of the tree and the rounded formation of the grain and the natural branching. It is structurally less dense than stone. Because it has seemingly little life of its own, its forms must be strongly accentuated.

Most stones are slightly translucent, their light seems to be within them, and since this light is comparatively even, shapes in stone, unlike those in wood, need not be emphasized. Stone has a structural density that does not invite cutting or splitting. Rubbing is the natural way to shape stone. Sharpness is best given by a thin treatment of the block as a whole. Gradual shapes in stone are most in keeping with its solidity. Metals can be cast into shapes that are difficult to achieve in carving. Modeling permits greater freedom of handling. Extension and tenuousness, quite alien to stone and wood, can be realized from bronze, lead, and other cast metals.

Sweeney's commentary indicates that the workman should be completely aware of the basic qualities inherent in the material and should work within its limits and extend them in the direction which is natural for that material.

With the advance in our technology and the employment of heat, metal has become exceedingly important as a flexible medium for the sculptor. Very large shapes can be formed by adding section to section with the welding torch.

Many sculptors are not content with bronze, wood, and stone; they are investigating the capabilities of industrially produced materials. David

---

6 The film in color, titled *Henry Moore*, with a commentary by James Sweeney, is distributed by Falcon Films.

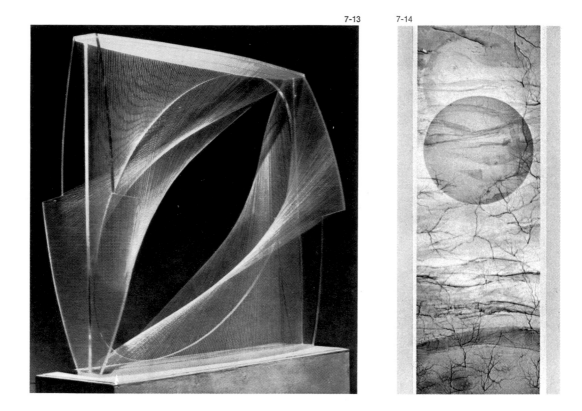

Smith has constructed a series of works, including *Cubi XXV*, from stainless steel; Louise Nevelson's *Atmosphere and Environment* is made of enameled aluminum on a formica-covered plywood base. George Ortman's *Metallurgy 3* is fabricated from aluminum as are other of his wall-hung sculptures. A catalogue of industrial materials — stainless and galvanized steel, Plexiglas, neon tubing, aluminum, plated glass, formica — is sometimes combined, plain or painted, in the sculptural assemblages of Chryssa (*The Gates to Times Square*), Larry Bell, Donald Judd, Michael Bolus, William Tucker, and others (Figs. 7-13–7-15).

In their search for exciting new material, artists are turning to Plexiglas and acrylic plastic. Because it is a thermal plastic, Plexiglas can be readily formed into almost any shape after heating. It has greater permanence and can retain its color and shape indefinitely. Sheets and blocks may be filed, sawed, drilled, scraped and buffed with conventional tools. It can be laminated to itself and other materials. It resists breakage and its light weight makes it easier to bandle. Of interest to any artist are the light-conducting and light-reflecting properties of transparent sheets of Plexiglas. Following the guidelines established by artists working in other materials, the sculptor in Plexiglas has begun to treat it less superficially and rigidly. He is working directly in the material and exploiting its unique characteristics. He has found that Plexiglas need not be thought of as a solid form that requires modulation and light for effect.

Since Naum Gabo, a leader of the constructivist movement, made use of plastics (see his *Linear Construction*, 1940), many artists in the

7-15

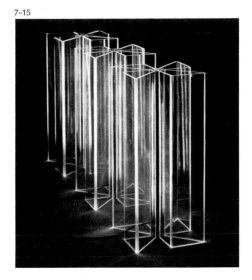

7-13
*Naum Gabo.
Linear Construction Variation.
1942–43. Phillips Collection,
Washington, D.C.*

7-14
*Alyce Simon. Tree of Life.
(Photograph courtesy of
The Rohm and Haas Reporter.)*

7-15
*Preston McClanahan. Cloverleaf.
1964. Walker Art Center,
Minneapolis.*

United States and abroad have explored the potential of Plexiglas and other plastics as an art medium with a variety of techniques, including casting, carving, laminating, and modeling (Fig. 7-15). They have assembled solid blocks of material, trimmed into various forms, together with castings from liquid acrylic monomers.[7]

It has been characteristic of the exploration of all the media used in art that there will be some experiments that reach far out to the extreme limits of its potential. In the second half of the twentieth century, artist have begun to use the tools and techniques of modern technology for the expansion of their efforts in producing objects of art. This has been typical for the fabrication of large-scale sculptures and has also been typical of the exploration of plastics (Fig. 7-14). One of the most interesting of the "far out" combinations of art with technology in plastics is provided by Alyce Simon of New York.

Mrs. Simon developed an "atomic art technique" in cooperation with K. H. Morganstern, whose firm manufactures high-voltage particle accelerators, commonly called "atom smashers." With his assistance, Mrs. Simon exposed many kinds of materials to the laboratory particle accelerator, to see if any would break down to form patterns which she might use for artistic purposes. Through experimentation with the atom smasher the artist was able to produce a controlled crazing and cracking in the acrylic plastic sheets. The sharp linear quality of these forms was worked against flat areas of color that had been added to the Plexiglas after it had been bombarded with radiation. At times, several layers of treated Plexiglas were used to create a strong three-dimensional effect. When these assemblages were given backlight, they could be controlled to change the mood for the viewer. When the molecular structure of the plastic was broken down by radiation forces, the delicate forms that emerged had a

[7] Much of this material was obtained from **The Rhom and Hass Reporter**, vol. 24, no. 2 (March–April, 1966), pp. 4–11.

7-16
A figure into which nails have been driven in order to manipulate powerful magical forces.
Congo Nkonde figure.
Musée Royal de l'Afrique Centrale,
Tervueren, Belgium.

7-17
Richard Randell. Ballast Bed.
1964. Welded steel and rock.
Walker Art Center, Minneapolis.

sharp linear quality. These forms are then placed against flat areas of color. The result is effective and delicate images with much the same quality that is found in Oriental art.[8]

Although the results are expressive and delightful, it is most unlikely that many artists will be able to carry out these unique applications of Plexiglas because it seems hardly possible that the opportunity to use an atom smasher as a tool will become very widespread.

It has always been very easy to be diverted by the novelty and the aura of excitement that is present when an unusual technical innovation is applied to the creation of art. We forget that this in itself does not give assurance that the product will meet the test of quality standards of art; it could be simply a physical exercise with technology, empty of meaning and without artistic form and structure. Before we get carried away by the "sound" of new material, we should pause to consider the cave paintings of Lascaux (Fig. 7-18) or the bushman paintings of the Orange Free State. These were made with the most elemental and primitive materials and processes — earth colors and black soot, or charcoal, mixed with animal fat. These paintings from thousands of years ago stand with the best of today's and stimulate the aesthetic sensitivity of the viewer with the visual impact that comes from the expression of a life and culture that disappeared long ago. This gives added support to the principle that the material or process itself will not make a work of art good or great (Figs. 7-16, 7-17).

The exploration of the new and varied materials of a technological age which characterizes the work of sculptors has been just as much a part of developments in the field of painting, print making, and the crafts. This expanded flexibility has its negative as well as its positive aspects. The danger inherent in the dramatic impact of new media upon the scene is that quite often both artist and viewer have a tendency to equate novelty of technique and materials with quality in art. Media alone do not make art. Nevertheless, availability of new media and appropriate facility in their use are definite assets for an artist of the twentieth century. The utilization of the chemical components of the plastics used for sculpture — acrylics and vinyl, for example — has produced pigments of high quality and stability for the painter. These pigments with binders of different kinds of polymer resins have qualities equal to or better than the traditional oil-based pigments. In addition they have greater stability and act as adhesives for holding all kinds of materials, such as gravel, sand, and crushed rock, on the canvas when they are mixed with the pigment. They also have served as protective coatings on larger objects which make up the constructions or assemblages of the contemporary art of painting.

During the early years of this century the printmakers kept fairly close to the traditional qualities and rules for their products. When one made a lithograph, drypoint, etching, or engraving, the whole print was "pure" to the extent that only a single process was used throughout. As the century progressed, there was a loosening up that allowed the graphic artist to combine a number of traditional techniques such as soft- and

[8] *Ibid.*, pp. 9–10.

7-18
Cave painting. Horse with arrows.
Ca. 15,000–10,000 B.C.
Lascaux, France.

7-19
Robert Hodgell. Crucified.
(Courtesy The Little Gallery, Plainfield, Iowa.)

7-20
Robert Evermon. The Dead.

7-21
Robert Evermon. Earth and Sun.

hard-ground etching, engraving, and aquatint to produce a single print. Since 1960, or starting even earlier, print making has loosened up even more, largely because of the artist's preoccupation with the same freedom and flexibility of techniques and media that had been gained by the painter or sculptor (Figs. 7-19–7-21). Painters who achieved some prominence in the pop art movement turned to print making with the same freedom and vigor displayed in their previous works. Rauschenberg, Lichtenstein, Wesselmann, and Johns are notable among this group. Rauschenberg transferred bits of newspaper and magazines onto a lithography stone; then he inked and printed the image on acetate sheets. He laminated these to Plexiglas and illuminated them with a light bulb. Wesselmann silk-screened the image of a nude onto a plastic, then shaped its contours in relief. Others printed their work on metallic plastic which shimmered in reflected light. At times the print paper was heavily embossed in high relief with the pressure of thick metal objects welded to the plates, to make a print without ink.

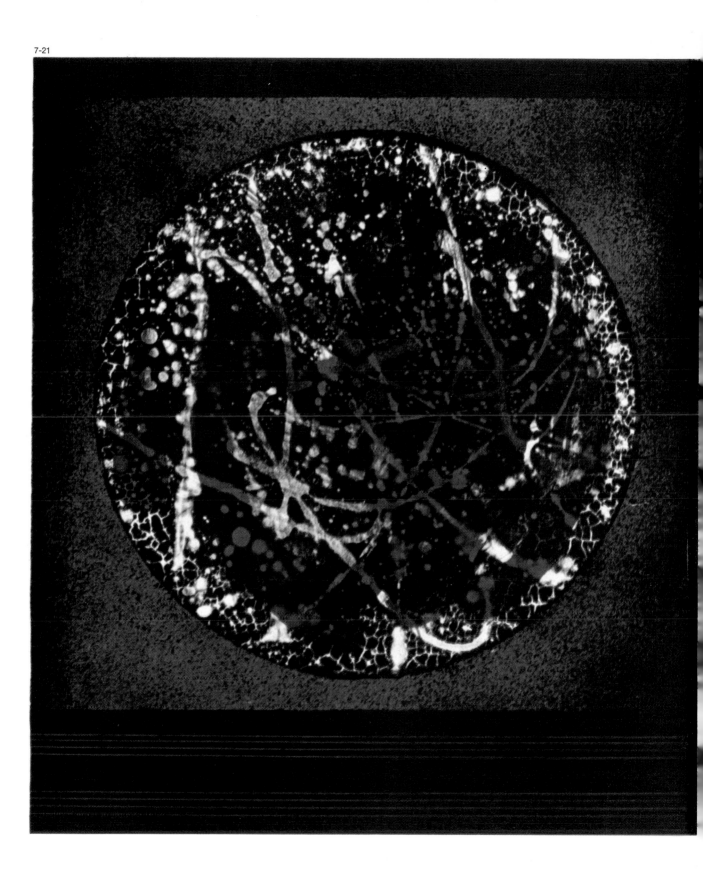

EXPLORING THE POTENTIAL OF MATERIALS

Far back in history the artist has displayed an interest in expanding the potential of the media or the processes through which his art is produced. Leonardo da Vinci and Peter Paul Rubens are classic examples of men who were both willing and able to examine analytically the nature of the material through which they could express their vision on the canvas. In many of his masterworks Leonardo used material in different ways from those which had previously been tried out. Sometimes the results were not favorable and his works have been adversely affected by his experiments. The glazing techniques employed by Rubens have been a subject of much investigation and research. It is quite natural for anyone working in the arts to become involved with exploration and experimentation in the media he will use for his expression. In the twentieth century, with the advent of new technological discoveries, the artist would be somewhat backward if he did not take advantage of up-to-date products and inventions. Also, the materials and processes can be applied and manipulated directly; the results of changes and modifications are directly and easily observed by both the artist and his public. Because they are open to direct physical manipulation, materials are usually the first of the aesthetic factors that are changed and modified by workmen seeking to break conventional boundaries.

Simply by changing his medium the craftsman can often move more quickly to simplification of his symbolism. Also, an excitement is generated in the workman when he encounters a new material for the first time. This excitement can sustain his interest and exploratory efforts over an extended period of time. Out of the raw material itself often comes the motivational cue which moves the artist in a direction not previously attempted and from which he will obtain considerable direct sensory satisfaction.

TESTING A NEW MEDIUM

One of the author's experiences as a consultant with a commercial firm interested in developing and refining materials for the artist and the education market has provided a clear picture of guidelines for effectively and efficiently exploring the potential of an art media. This work as a consultant necessitated a more systematic and comprehensive exploration than is customarily engaged in by the painter or sculptor for his own benefit and purposes. The following is a description of one of many products tested, first to discover its potential for artistic expression and second to determine its possible applications. Selected for this illustration is a surface, ground, or paper upon which paint could be applied.[9]

When the material was left with me, it did not seem particularly different from any of the good quality papers that I had worked with as a painter of watercolors. It had a somewhat different texture when fingered, but otherwise looked like papers previously encountered.

When the time came to give it a trial run, I started off with confidence in the same manner as I would with any other material, according to habits I had de-

---

[9] Art Fabric, a product of the Minnesota Mining and Manufacturing Company.

veloped over a period of time. The paint was the same, the brush was the same, nothing seemed different. Except — nothing seemed to work right. The paint dried too fast and evaporated immediately into the ground. All those nice fluid brushstrokes that I had built up so carefully from years of experience seemed to evaporate. My initial reaction was to tear the stuff up, throw it away, and go back to something that was familiar and with which results were certain. However, one does not like to admit defeat. In addition, it was against my sense of economy to discard the pigment already out on the sheet of glass which I used for a palette. So I kept working and tried my whole repertoire of technical variations. Needless to say, when I finished for the day, things were far from satisfactory.

Because I was more or less committed to give the material a fair trial, time was taken to evaluate the results of the first trial. Only two or three small bits of painting here and there looked particularly good. The rest was a trail of lost effort. Nothing much had really worked right.

Recalling my working procedures, which had resulted in little success and so much failure, suggested that some serious adjustment in technique would be required for satisfactory results. A more fluid approach with the use of more liquid and paint seemed to be indicated. The clean, untouched painting surface looked inviting and so I started again. Corrections were made in the amount of liquid in the pigment. My brush was heavily loaded. This worked somewhat but was far from satisfactory.

This was a problem to be solved rather than something to be discarded without a complete test; it was better to adopt a logical rather than a manipulative course of action. After analyzing the physical characteristics of the medium, certain conclusions were reached. The material was tough and could withstand harsh treatment. It was highly absorbent; yet, when color was applied over areas previously worked on, the result was a clean, fresh appearance to the color. In fact, the color built over another had a visual richness that was quite unexpected because in my previous experience what usually resulted were dull, somewhat dirty colors. Also on the positive side were the textural effects obtained by dragging the brush across the surface of the painting ground. The material did not need stretching and did not curl up when wet. In fact, regardless of the extra abuse which it had undergone, the painting surface had generally remained flat and unwrinkled when allowed to dry.

After this mental assessment of the characteristics of the medium, it occurred to me that my approach to a test situation was perhaps not as sound as it might have been. I had been trying to force a medium to do things that were inconsistent with its unique qualities and was attempting to adapt it in a manner that was more suitable for other traditional painting surfaces. From this evaluation came one basic guideline, not only for this single experience but for any situation in which a new medium is being explored. One should assess the unique qualities inherent in the medium and use these to advantage. This positive advantage could be gained by utilizing these strengths rather than by attempting to transpose the medium into situations and with mannerisms that are intended for something entirely different. Many people fall into this trap and attempt with relatively poor success to force a medium to do something for which it is not intended and which is inconsistent with its unique individual qualities.

The next step (perhaps the one that should have been taken first) was to determine what the unique properties of the new material might be. After this mental effort, I completed a series of four paintings that would provide a basis for evaluating the painting surface. During this period all the conventional painting media (with the exception of oil paint) — watercolor, casein, acrylic, inks, chalk — were involved, alone or in combination. I also used a variety of painting tools, including hard and soft bristle brushes and a palette knife with thick and thin paint on wet and dry surfaces. Each of the four paintings were started with the *intention of composing a painting rather than filling the sheet with a collection of exploratory markings and strokes. This is quite important because a material can only be fully tested in a situation in which the painter or sculptor is involved with the creation of a work of art and is not simply playing around with what might loosely be called "manipulative experiments." Guided by memory of years of observation of other artists and students at work, a wide range of possibilities were exploited.*

This concluded the first stage of exploration. The evaluation of the results gave an entirely different impression than the first random experiment. I had found not only a medium for painting which suited me but also a way to properly explore any new art material. There was the simple satisfaction that comes with the discovery of beautiful bits of color which happened almost in spite of oneself and yet could be repeated because you knew why they happened; there were the areas of texture that had never appeared before but could be made to come again because you knew the reason for their emergence and could control it.

Since these series of trials a great deal more has been learned about this medium. It is manufactured directly from cellulose by a wet method very much like that which is used by the makers of many of the Oriental or Japanese papers. It has been treated to make it receptive to paint. Also, it is structurally composed in such a way that one actually paints into the material rather than on its surface as is customarily the case. This painting in depth produces an extra rich visual effect which is advantageous because the colors have greater intensity of hue and overpainting does not cause a lowering of hue or intensity. The microscopic particles of pigment are suspended separately at different levels in the material. The results parallel the broken-color techniques used by the impressionists, which force the observer to do the color mixing with his eyes. Also, because of its composition and structure, the medium has a translucent quality. This translucence can be used to advantage by artists who wish to experiment with light itself as a design tool and to include backlighting and other such effects in their compositional designs.

After the unique qualities of the material had been established, its potential for art work in areas other than painting was easily tested. Subsequent tests have indicated its use in print making, crafts design, and many other areas.

GUIDELINES FOR TESTING ART MEDIA

The conclusions from this experience and their implications in the exploration of the potential of a medium in general are evident. Exploration is a highly involved physical and mental activity. In the hands of a serious craftsman the activity of exploring the potential of a medium is something more than therapy. Certainly he derives excitement and satisfaction from the physical aspects of manipulating a material, however this is secondary to achieving full mastery of the problem. The exploratory process becomes one in which there is a constant interplay of mental and physical manipulation. The whole process becomes one of constant evaluation and re-evaluation; it is one in which many questions are asked and answers for them are sought.

Spontaneous and chance happenings are part of the exploratory way of working. Beautiful spots of color appear; interesting textures are achieved. One has a godlike, ego-centered feeling when these things happen. The true test of artistic competence comes with the ability to direct "happy accidents" toward a purposeful objective and to use them to do what the artist has set out to accomplish. At the outset one usually has the tendency to test a new medium against experience with the old, to start with known methods and then to expand them. Expansion of a principle or procedure previously established is one level of creative action. Much more to be desired, however, is the discovery of a new principle of procedure — an innovation. Then we can push beyond the boundaries of the established and move into the unknown.

For many people the aspect of novelty, of being different, is enough. Exploration of the potential of a medium must extend beyond simple manipulative experimentation and take into account the full realm of essentials which distinguish the inventive from the superficially novel. In exploring the potential of a medium in art, the final evaluation of its validity rests with measurement of how achievement in the new medium compares with that which is possible with traditional materials and processes. One should ask himself questions; for example, Does this say something that I have to say with more facility and better than with other materials that I have used? The crucial phrase here is "better than," which does not mean just "different from."

In summation, the following are considerations and procedures that could serve as guidelines for a thorough exploration of the potential of a medium for art expression:

1. Obtain information about its unique properties or qualities.

2. Relate these inherent properties to past experience with art expression and to the operational characteristics of media and processes already known.

3. Working from these unique characteristics, try out the new medium in a situation that *has as its objective the solution of an art problem* — the creation of a work of art.

4. Compare results with what has or could be accomplished with conventional media and processes.

Under these conditions, chances for successful exploration are higher, and the conclusions reached will have greater reliability and validity for the direction of art action in the future.

EXPANDING PROCESS LIMITS AND CONTROLS

Up to this point our attention has been focused on understanding the properties of materials as a tool for the artist. The ultimate objective should be the development of a way of thinking about this single aesthetic factor of materials and its interaction with other factors, including design structure and content or meaning, to obtain the utmost from a harmonious interrelationship of the three aesthetic factors. This is the artist's problem. It is imperative that one should never lose sight of the fact that materials alone do not make art. Closely related to the exploration of the potential of a medium is the experimentation with the processes for using the medium. Expanding the limits of a process beyond those which have previously been established suits the artist's disposition. It is natural for him, as a person with qualities of creativeness, to branch out from accustomed pathways and to improvise, modify, and adjust according to his own needs and fancies. After he has learned the fundamentals of a technical process and gained a useful level of proficiency with it, he then begins to stretch its boundaries and adapt the process to his personal demands and artistic needs. This extension of the potential of a process takes different forms, such as: (1) refinement of the technique itself by using it more skillfully and improving the tools and the materials required; (2) redefinition by employing the traditional process to untraditional purposes; and (3) improvisation by moving away from the "proper" or the conventional to increase process flexibility as a tool.

REFINEMENT AND IMPROVISATION

The kinesthetic response to the manipulation of materials and technical processes involving these materials is a strong one; the personal gratification from the action of manipulating inert materials is in itself a powerful motivating force for many people, both children and adults, who engage in an art activity. The manipulation of any media brings satisfactions that support the individual and command his attention and the continuation of his effort. However, it is only a short time before the demands of aesthetic organization and of the evocative expression of meaning are integrated into the total creative-artistic behavior. Consideration must also be given to what is to be said and how can this best be presented through art. Thus the art process goes beyond physical therapy through the manipulation of materials toward the expression of meaning.

The veneer of sophistication is thinner for the student than it is for the mature artist. This allows one to note developmental stages more clearly.

7-22–7-25
Exploration with paint.

7-22 7-23 7-24 7-25

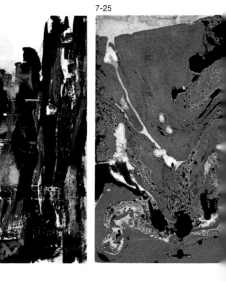

7-28   7-29   7-30

Figures 7-22 through 7-30 were motivated by the goal of exploration of
the potential of an art medium to find out, as an artist, what could be done
with it. Observation of the work process and remarks made by the participants have indicated that concern for design organization was also involved from the beginning of the work sessions. There was a need to make
evaluative choices about the selection and arrangement of color, shape,
and texture although the objective was to expand upon the method for
handling a medium.

    When the selected medium was a conventional one such as a water-
base pigment, experimental improvisations included the use of "resist"
techniques that prevented pigment from being absorbed evenly by treating
areas of the painting surface. Also, a number of textured materials were

7-26–7-27
Resist techniques with wax.

7-28
Paint with gauze added.

7-29–7-30
Cut and torn paper.

THE DESIGN PROCESS   233

attached to selected areas of the painting surface; glues, sand, cloth, and string were combined with pigment for a variety of compositional effects.

Earlier in this chapter an account of the design of a piece of jewelry was presented in order to demonstrate the interaction of material consideration with those of form and content during the creative process. One of those material exploitations involved a technique of bundling several lengths or sections of silver tubing; the bundles of tubes were fused in position and filed. It is interesting to note how this technique was carried through a number of improvisations in subsequent pieces of jewelry design. The basic technique remained the same. Changes were made in the arrangement of the tubes — in number, direction, and location — and produced a variety of visually exciting compositions in metal. In addition textural variations were obtained through control of the fusion process that gave potted, pitted surfaces that contrasted with smooth, plain areas of polished metal. Cutting into the tube clusters with a file, along the longitudinal or the end sections, to different depths revealed quite a variety of visual patterns of sectional structure. Figures 7-31 through 7-35 are closeup photographs of some results of these exploratory procedures with metal.

7-31–7-35
These figures illustrate the variety of visual patterns and sectional structure derived from an exploratory procedure with metal tubes.

7-31

7-32

7-33

7-34

These outcomes of material and technical experimentations, although interesting and sometimes exceedingly beautiful, should be thought of as the means, or the raw materials, from which art is created. This is their value; something else has happened to them as we have composed a work of art. The jewelry designer who worked with the technical device of clustering, fusing, and filing tubes was simultaneously engaged with considerations of content and form. The insect form in nature, which had been the inspirational force that initiated his work with metal tubes, conditioned his response as well as his method for arranging the tubular constructions and for relating them to the other sections of metal. The abstracted insect with its head-thorax-abdomen segmentation found associations and connections with what was happening to the metal. When these were strengthened and refined, the artist was able to fit what was happening to the metal tubes into a unified concept of design — the parts had appropriate and meaningful relationships within the whole.

It should also be apparent that in designing with any medium — be it silver, paint, or plastic — considerations of the medium itself are often pushed into the background (as well as considerations of content, idea,

7-35

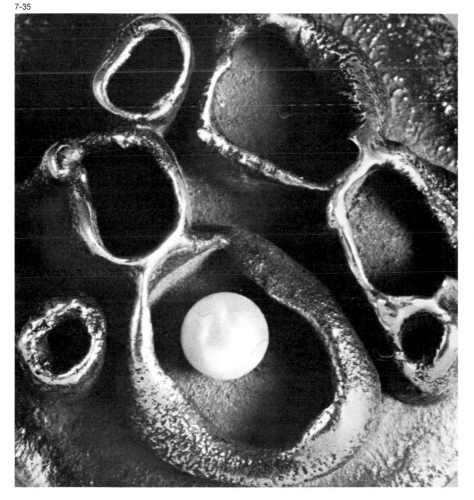

7-31
Tube bundles, longitudinal and filed.

7-32
Pendant detail. Beetle.

7-33
Circular shapes changed to oval by filing.

7-34
Tubes in a subsidiary role.

7-35
Tubes grouped on end. Collection of Mr. and Mrs. Kent van den Berg.

and subject matter), and the artist concentrates upon the "pure" shapes, lines, textures, tones, and colors that evolve from his materials. These latter are accepted as his design tools; the medium is the means to this end. Figure 7-35 illustrates how open and closed curvilinear shapes that emerged from technical handling of the metal tubes were grouped and united to create a design that was dependent upon the abstract relationship of design elements. This design does not depend upon similarity to objects in the environment for its validity as a work of art. All of these are variations from a single material source — the technique of bundling sections of silver tubing.

A SYSTEMATIC APPROACH TO EXPLORATION

Many of the discoveries which bring about improvement in a process emerge as the artist is manipulating his materials. He does not usually have a blueprinted plan for this purpose; however, more efficient and intelligent approaches could come from an analysis of observations of artists and students at work. To illustrate this, we will discuss an analysis of one technical process which could serve as a general model or example: the silk-screen process, or serigraphy. This is a process of twentieth-century origin. Like many technical processes, it came into the art field after having been employed in other areas. Commercial printing establishments used and developed it just as the process of welding with an acetylene torch, widely used by sculptors, was a technological development outside art.

The graphic arts process of serigraphy, or silk-screen printing, is a method by which multiple reproductions of the same design can be obtained. It can be used to reproduce good-quality reproductions of art or nonart works. With the silk-screen process, designs can be printed upon a wide variety of surfaces — paper, glass, metals, fabrics, leather, wood, cardboard, and many others. A serigraph is usually a print made as an art object of intrinsic value, whereas a lithograph is a "fine arts" print made from a lithographic stone or metal plate.

A systematic approach — although such a description is often abhorred by artists — that combines thinking with manipulation can be the most attractive and efficient way of fully expanding any technical process. An understanding of the fundamental character of the process itself lies at the core of any fruitful expansion of its potentialities. Following this guideline, it would seem that the first and important key to opening up a process would be to determine its least, or lowest, common denominator, that is, the vital characteristic upon which the process depends.

Serigraphy, or silk-screen printing, is an advance over the simple and childlike stencil process. We are all acquainted with applications of this process to such rudimentary purposes as stenciling a name or address on a child's wagon or on a packing case for shipment. Traffic signs are stenciled by the crew of the highway department. In schools it is used for printing decorative designs on a piece of cloth or for making posters. Holes are cut in a sheet of protective paper or other material to form the design; inks or other pigments are rubbed, brushed, or sprayed through the openings. This process can be repeated indefinitely to make any number of duplicates of the original design. Then it was discovered that a stencil mounted on a screen of stretched silk on a wooden frame would support the stencil and make it much easier to handle. Thus a thin piece of meshed fabric, silk or rayon, tightly stretched over the wooden frame, became the basic tool for the silk-screen process.

As with the stencil process, the artist creates his design by blocking out some of the holes in the screen mesh and leaving others open. To make a print, ink is pushed through the open screen holes on to the surface of the material placed beneath it, and no ink penetrates the screen holes which have been closed. This is an art tool based on the same operational principle as the computer, a tool of modern science and industry, which works on the basis of a series of yes–no, on–off, zero–one decisions that activate its transistors, resistors, and capacitators. The silk-screen printing process is based on the same kind of decisions over the whole of the surface.

At first, like its prototype the stencil process, screen printing was carried out with paper as the agent to block out selected parts of the screen. The paper stencil is one of the techniques that is still used in the process. Other materials have been employed for closer control of the blocking out of the silk mesh and for obtaining results of varied artistic quality. Stencils have also been applied to the screen with thin sheets of lacquer or with tusche (a lithographic ink or crayon) and glue in order to get textured areas of halftone or design markings like those obtained with a brush. The next development was to cover the screen with a photosensitive emulsion and, using photographic techniques, to stencil directly on this coated screen. The photographic stencil method has endless possibilties, some of which have been employed by artists such as Andy Warhol, who has used this technique for his multiple portraits of celebrities and for his prints using flowers and other objects printed in multicolored patterns.

All of this development is dependent upon the common denominator which supports the whole process — that some holes must be closed and others must be opened to create a pattern or design out of a multitude of tiny pinpoints of color. Once the basic ways of blocking out areas of the screen have been learned and understood, it is only a short step toward beginning to improvise with other materials for this purpose. Stop-out varnishes, lacquers, shellac, water-solvent adhesives, precut gum labels. and many other of the multitudinous products of industry have been used as block-out stencils.

Knowledge of the key characteristics of the process itself gives the craftsman the power to extend it almost endlessly and to harness it according to his objectives and personal ways of working. As the scientist quite often builds upon a principle already established and expands this foundation, the artist or the student can benefit from an understanding of the basic nature of the process as the foundation for his application of this knowledge toward purposes and goals far removed from the original base.

The silk-screen process is only one of hundreds that can be treated in this manner. Resist techniques (crayon and batik), which provide intriguing variation for painting and textile design, all stem from the inherent qualities of wax to melt and to resist the adherence of other substances. Textile designing has broken out of its shell because conventional processes such as embroidery, stitchery, and appliqué have come to be

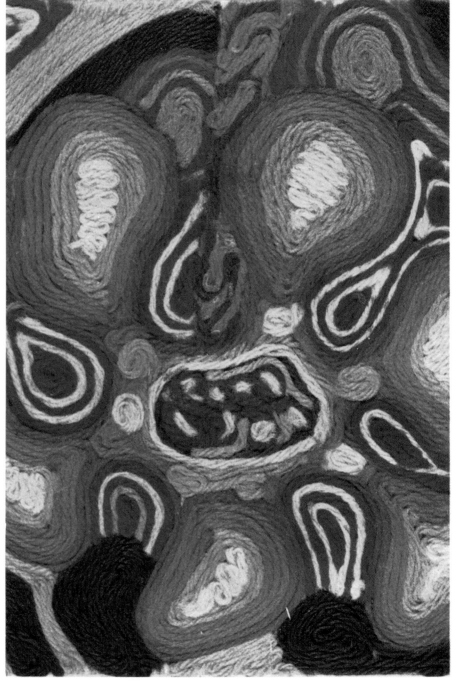

7-36
Gathering Maple Syrup.
Yarn glued to burlap.

7-37
Living Cells.
Yarn glued to wood.

7-38

7-38
Appliqué stitchery.
San Blas Islands.
Collection of Ruth Roach.

thought of as basically painting or drawing with yarn and cloth instead of with chalk and paint (Figs. 7-36–7-38).

CREATIVITY WITH ART MEDIA AND PROCESSES

A very large proportion of what have been characterized as creative developments in art in the last few decades have centered around the aesthetic factor of materials. This is understandable. The second and third levels of creativity include the major part of our population of artists. These are the technicians, the skilled virtuosos, as well as the person who uses processes and materials ingeniously and inventively.

The personality traits of the creative person — fluency, flexibility, originality, and the abilities for elaboration and for redefinition — find a direct outlet for expression in the materials and processes of art. An examination of innovative practices places a large number of them in the redefinition category, in which the adaptations of materials and processes developed for other purposes as means and methods for art expression. Here sculptors have been particularly active with their use of such industrial techniques as welding and such products of technology as plastics, fluorescent tubes, formica, and mechanics of motors and computerized devices. Techniques of collage and assemblage have brought all varieties of man-made objects under the heading of art media. Flexibility is exhibited in the artist's willingness to extend traditional processes and to combine processes without regard for the restrictive conventions. This attitude has given new life to print making and the crafts.

This concentration of attention upon the material aspects of art action has a reasonable explanation. Materials and processes can be attacked directly and call for physically active contact by the participants. There is direct sensory satisfaction from the manipulation of media, and in most cases the basic skills required can be learned without much difficulty.

Creativeness achieved by the artist is dependent upon his willingness to maintain an attitude of "reasonable doubt" toward the traditional and conventional in so far as both materials and methods are concerned. One can ask questions about whether a medium is the right one just because it has always been used for this purpose. Must it be used in a particular way, because this is the way it has always been employed? The individual who asks such questions is open and receptive, and shows a readiness to change. But reasonable doubt has another facet. There should be the responsibility to test and evaluate, before substituting one technique or medium for another when its only qualification is newness.

Curiosity, even childlike curiosity, is a positive force for the treatment of materials creatively. To ask the question that starts with I wonder what would happen if . . .? is a definite asset for any person who is working with art media. There must also be a willingness to take risks, and to depart from academic security. Creativeness with media and processes, however, has its limits in the production of a work of art. There must also be an equal display of creativeness in the artist's ability to identify meaning from his experience in the world and the artistic sensibilities required for giving his perceptions significant form. Competence with materials has value, but the artist must also have "something to say" with his materials.

Chapter 8

FORM: THE STRUCTURAL ORGANIZATION OF A WORK OF ART

"The search for order and structural regularity in the world around us has been a powerful motivation in human evolution." [1]

This search for order and structural form is so much a part of the artist's work that it is almost taken for granted. When we consider form in art as a "group of elements perceived in their totality, not as a product of any chance assemblage," we are suggesting that it is hardly possible to understand the whole of the process by which a work of art is structured by an analysis of the individual or isolated elements that are included in the total composition. In looking at art and in looking at the process through which this art has been created, our ultimate objective must be to understand not only the activities of a single design element, but also the rules and means of their interaction. If we know something about the relation of the parts within a work of art to the visual character of the whole, we can then understand its artistic form.

Different arrangement of the parts can produce clear and distinct visual differences in the product even when these products possess identical parts. Even parts which are not identical or are completely different can produce a similar visual structure. The former statement becomes clear when we think of how many different arrangements are possible in a composition restricted to any given number of identical rectangles; for the second statement, the example would be that a closed circle can be perceived either from a thin line drawn by a compass, a series of dots arranged in circular relationship, or by a series of arched shapes separate, yet arranged in close proximity in a curve which the eye closes to form the desired circle. As we move into our following discussion of the separate areas of structural phenomena keep in mind that proper definition of the nature of artistic order requires us to incorporate both the visual form and what it expresses.

THE OPERATION PROBLEM OF STRUCTURAL ORGANIZATION

In order to achieve his expressions through the arts, man has created original structures, either by rearranging known forms or by creating new ones. He has given original treatment to familiar structures and has created new expressive and structural means. Art movements such as cubism are concerned with the element of original structures; artists as remote in time as Leonardo da Vinci and Picasso illustrate how artists can fulfill their personal intentions through highly individual yet different treatments of a similar structure—the human figure (Figs. 8-1, 8-2). Cézanne's work illustrates how an artist can invent new expressive visual means.

DESIGN ELEMENTS AS TOOLS FOR THE ARTIST

When we look for common attributes, we find that artists since the beginning have employed a small group of design elements. By their personal methods for manipulating them they have given us a diversity of visual

---

[1] Arthur L. Loeb, **The Architecture of Crystals**, in Gyorgy Kepes (ed.), *Module, Proportion, Symmetry and Rhythm*, George Braziller, Inc., New York, 1966, p. 39.

8-1   8-2

images, which when taken together make up our heritage from the arts. These simple elements—line, tone, texture, shape, and color—have been combined and recombined in many different ways through all of the materials that the artist has found useful for his craft. We might not get universal agreement upon our selection of these five as design elements. Others may wish to use other words like light and shade for tone and mass to substitute for shape. They might raise an objection to our omission of space from the list. However, this latter, an extremely important aspect of form in art, may be obtained through arrangement of any one of the elements or by combining them to create an illusion of depth.

Line. With the caveman, art began with the desire to delineate. It begins in the same fashion with the child. Line is one of the most essential elements in the visual arts for sculpture as well as painting and drawing. Its function is more than that of defining the outline on the edge of things. It expresses movement and mass. Line is used to express objects in motion by recording the selective observations of the eye during a split second of the movement when the object is in a precarious state of balance as the action progresses. Also, lines and repetitions of line build up a quality of motion which is intrinsic in the line itself rather than in the motion of the object or thing represented (Fig. 8-3). Some of our best examples of this are to be found in Japanese and Chinese art—the paintings, drawings, and woodcuts—or in the drawings of William Blake.

Through carefully chosen interruptions in the continuous outline—directional changes and the variations in weight and pressure—artists can suggest converging planes and three-dimensional volume, or mass, by line alone. Artists have for a long time recognized the importance of line drawing in connection with work in sculpture or in any of the rest of the art processes. A list of the works of expert draftsmen would represent man's proficiency in many kinds of art and from all historic periods. It would include Giotto, Botticelli, the great Renaissance painters from Masaccio to Tiepolo, sculptors Michelangelo and Rodin, and modern masters like Picasso and Matisse. It would be difficult to single out one or two men from

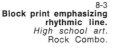

8-3
Block print emphasizing rhythmic line.
High school art.
Rock Combo.

the total group of printmakers because this art form required authority with drawing for its processes of etching, drypoint, and engraving, which emphasize linear techniques.

We usually think of the whole field of drawing as consisting of three basic types—contour, calligraphic, and tonal. In contour and calligraphic drawing, line is the dominant element, while in the last, light and shade have been incorporated to achieve the formal and expressive possibilities of the art. In developing contour drawing the artists works by careful selection and deliberate omission in an effort to both clarify and define his subject matter. In this kind of drawing there is a tendency to idealize the subject, as can be noted in the drawings of Ingres. Calligraphy embodies the power of the line to capture the expressive gesture. It suggests the feelings and temperament in a more emotional sense. There is an intensity of concentration on the part of the participant (Fig. 8-4). Drawings done in this manner express a quality of life and energy; the interest is on characterization and upon capturing the pose and pause of the subject (Fig. 8-5). Tonal drawing

8-4
Richard Koppe. Head. St. Paul Art Center.

8-5
Calligraphic line drawing in child art.

8-4   8-5

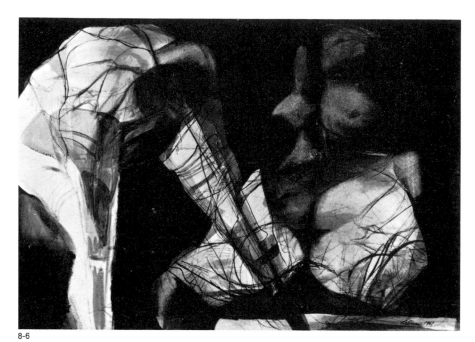

8-6
Rico Lebrun.
The Peach and the Cripple.
St. Paul Art Center.

8-7
Albert Sangiamo. Lobster.
St. Paul Art Center.

8-8
Jiro. Drawing No. 2.
1963. St. Paul Art Center.

8-6

8-7   8-8

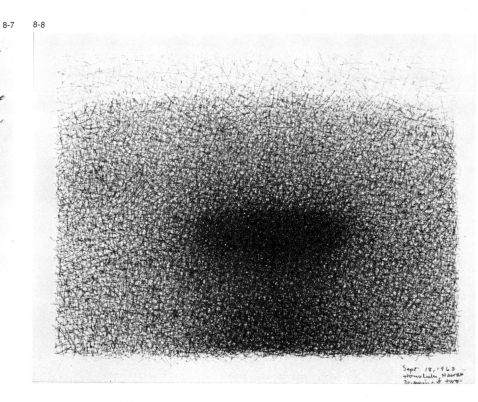

8-9
Douris.
Women putting away their clothes.
Painting on a terracotta kylix.
Ca. 470 B.C.
Metropolitan Museum of Art,
New York.

8-10
Contour drawing in child art.

with its use of gradations of shading with accents of line tends to place attention upon surface quality rather than outline. Also incorporated in this way of drawing is the suggestion of the textural quality of the subject to provide a sensation of light, space, and atmosphere (Figs. 8-6–8-8).

The wall paintings from ancient Egypt show an expertness and mastery of the contour line in conjunction with flat color areas of "local" tone; the paintings on Greek vases are excellent examples of the ideal purity of the "classic" line at its best (Fig. 8-9). The drawings of Delacroix, Daumier, and Van Gogh are among the finer examples of the calligraphic line. The tonal mode of drawings was well suited to the interests of the romantic realists, impressionists, and postimpressionists; the drawings of Millet, Renoir, Toulouse-Lautrec, Seurat, Cézanne, and Gauguin made effective use of line.[2]

In order to achieve a vitality of line as well as a training of perceptional skills, the technique of "contour" drawing has been employed by artists and teachers. In this procedure the drawing instrument is placed on the paper and the eyes of the student are focused upon the subject to be rendered. The eyes carefully search out and follow the outline edge of the subject as the drawing instrument follows along without being observed. Drawings done in this manner require little practice and have a dynamic vital quality, although there are deviations from accurate measurements and proportions (Fig. 8-10).

---

[2] For a full discussion of basic ways of drawing with precise references to artists and their works, see Lorenz Eitner, **Nineteenth Century Drawings**, in the catalogue for the loan exhibition *The Nineteenth Century: One Hundred Twenty-five Master Drawings*. This exhibition was organized at the Solomon R. Guggenheim Museum, New York, 1962.

When line is employed as a sculptural medium, it often takes on the quality of drawing with wire instead of another tool; it becomes essentially a line drawing in the three dimensions of space rather than on a flat surface. Many sculptors have used thin metal rods, wire, and tough nylon string in their work. In his sculpture *The Bride*, Henry Moore obtained a contrast of the brittle, sharp flicker of light from the strands of wire seen against the surface dullness of the central form—the sharpness of the wire line acted as accents for the molded curves of the solid heavier material (Fig. 8-11). *The Fountain by* Leonard Lye is made up of a 7-foot-high bundle of stainless steel rods. It was intended as a model for a larger sculpture which would be activated by powerful jets of water. The flows of water would make the construction rotate and at the same time the rods of the fountain would sway and oscillate. Another of Lye's tangible-motion sculptures, *Rotating Harmonic*, is composed of a rod one-eighth of an inch in diameter which goes into a whipping, sideways action as energy is imparted to it. A sculpture made by Jose De Rivera for the Smithsonian Institution's Museum of History and Technology was an 8-foot-high stainless steel piece called *Infinity*. The stainless steel band (or line) based on the Mobius strip principle is a loop twisted on itself so that it contains one continuing edge and one plane (Fig. 8-12).

The majority of sculptors of the twentieth century have the line represented in their contours or edges. With the adaptation of new materials the line as an element in sculptural design often becomes important with intrinsic interest as a thing in itself as well as an edge of a heavier mass.

8-12

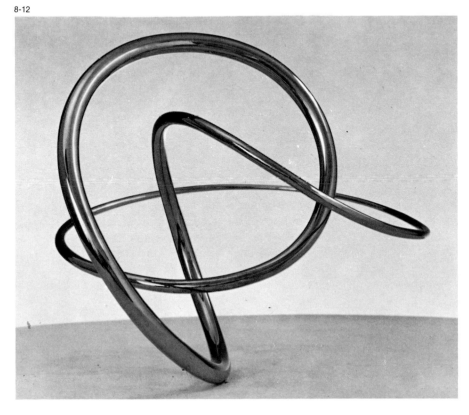

8-11
Henry Moore. The Bride.
1940. Cast lead and copper wire.
Museum of Modern Art, New York.

8-12
Sculpture with line enclosing space.
José de Rivera. Construction No. 35.
Hirshorn Collection. (Photo courtesy of O. E. Nelson, New York.)

8-13
Jan Vermeer.
Young Woman with a Water Jug.
Ca. 1663.
Metropolitan Museum of Art,
New York.

Tone (light and shade). In drawing and painting the shifting variable qualities of light—the objective reality of its presence, changes of intensity, and the direction of its flow—have been represented through this element named tone. Especially in painting, tone has been employed to indicate the passage from light to deep shadow upon a surface of one predominant color. Marked tonal values provide the viewer with knowledge of the nature of this mass or surface with its indications of the three-dimensional volume of the object. When the artist used monochrome (a single color) for his work, the tonal gradations suggested the relative intensity of the different colors present in the subject matter. Tones from light to dark in a painting were also indicators of how different objects and areas within the composition were affected relatively by its main source of light.

The elaboration of tonal qualities has progressed through different phases in the history of art. The early Italian painters during the Renaissance studied the effect of light and obtained their spatial qualities by isolating it or focusing it upon each object represented. This gave the objects a quality of low relief as the light was depicted evenly across the sur-

8-14
Rembrandt van Rijn.
Night Watch.
1642. Rijksmuseum, Amsterdam.

face of the canvas. The North European painters from Van Eyck to Vermeer through their control of tone achieved the full illusion of a uniform spatial atmosphere (Fig. 8-13). Later, painters like Rembrandt used light and shade dramatically and for staging purposes, rather than to effect gradual changes from light to dark, as the light went around a volume (Fig. 8-14). In this way the visual structure of the objects was almost eliminated through the free play and emphatic pattern of contrasting lights and shadows. In much of Oriental art where line is the dominating element, the local tone of objects is indicated by colored pigment spread lightly over the area. In some cases the local tone is flat and even, but in others there are gradations of this local tone across the surface as well as the addition of deeper tone to accent edges of the subjects depicted.

Color. In painting, the element of color has been used naturally in accordance with the real or visual appearance of objects or events as seen by the eyes of the observer. Also color has been used symbolically, as was the case in European painting under the rules of religious symbolism laid down by the Church. In the art work of children we find this symbolic selection of color, but it is chosen according to personal preference rather than because of some outside regulation. The sky is painted blue, the grass green, and the trees brown by preference, even when the sky is gray and stormy, the grass withered and brown, and when the trees may vary from black to a brilliant red-orange, according to the season (Figs. 8-15, 8-16).

Seurat and the impressionists before him had used color to depict sunlight and atmosphere. They broke up the light and color into short strokes and dots of pigment sometimes in contrasting colors to heighten the effect of vibrating, dancing light. The colors are mixed in the viewer's retina. Matisse used color in a decorative way; the Fauves and the German expressionists depended upon the strength, vigor, and emotional impact of their color. Cézanne created an illusion of three-dimensional form which was conveyed directly by color irrespective of light and shade. Practitioners of optical art have carried on experimentation with color to an extreme where color is the key element with which they work to excite or

8-15
Color usage in child art. Firebird.

8-16
Color usage in child art. Charlie.

8-15   8-16

bring pain to the eyes of the viewer. In the attempt to use color for its own sake, artists have been able to eliminate restrictions determined by associations with things and events of daily life and can concentrate upon the inherent properties of color and the ability of a single color to change in terms of value, hue and intensity when related to another color.

Following is a statement which illustrates the attitude and thoughts of a person who is seriously interested in using color independent of associations with nature and the visual environment: [3]

> As a painter my concern has been with the modes of appearance of color, defined broadly as surface, film and volume. In terms of illusion, surface color is to look at; film color is to look through; volume color is to look into. My earliest work dealt with the surface aspects—for example, the juxtaposition of colors to achieve simultaneous contrast. But film color soon became my principle field of exploration... Film color in painting produces the illusion of transparency. If it can be suggested that Renaissance painting dematerialized space and Cubism dematerialized form, my objective in working with film color might be described as the dematerialization of color.

Although color was a part of sculpture in the polychrome applied to their carved objects by primitive peoples and others in the earlier periods of art, not much interest on the part of sculptors in color is noted until the middle of the twentieth century. In addition to the utilization of the materials of modern technology, the sculptor has recently become highly involved with the application of color on the surfaces of his work and often depends upon the applied pigment to obtain the effect he desires.

Shape. After careful consideration, the word "shape" has been selected to identify this particular element. One alternative, "form," has had a much wider usage. However, it has been used elsewhere in this text to describe the fundamental quality that characterizes a work of art. Form is the end result of the interaction of all the numerous yet hard to define characteristics and elements that have gone into the creation of the work. In this writing, shape is intended to represent an easily recognizable element on the same level with all of the others mentioned (line, color, tone, etc.).

The artist, whether painter, sculptor, architect, or designer, has available to him the shapes made by man and those made by nature. The geometric man-made shapes have more regular and precise outlines. The organic free-form shapes of the natural world vary in and out at their boundaries presenting the artist with a vocabulary of dynamic flowing and undulating imagery. Upon the canvas the shape has a two-dimensional actuality but also can give illusion of thickness and volume. In architecture and sculpture the materials and methods of construction are such that when the plane-surface shapes are joined they create the actuality of depth and three dimensions.

---

3 Ben Cunningham, in **Art in America**, vol. 54, no. 4 (July–August, 1966), p. 32.

Through the course of the history of art, the creative individual's attitude toward and employment of shapes as an element of his expression have varied from the precise to the indefinite. The hard-edge painters have presented precision and definiteness in the boundaries of shape; also the cubists gave definiteness to the shapes presented and a clarity to their contours. Other artists have employed the softness of the edges of the shapes in painting to cause indecision on the part of the observer, giving him through this uncertainty an illusion of the indefiniteness of the shape. Where one mass begins or ends could not be determined. One flowed into another, and there was an ambiguous quality to the whole composition.

Each shape contributed to the direction of visual flow of eye movement within the work of art. This movement was accented and assisted through the placement and direction of the shape as perceived by the observer. The eye tended to build relationships between objects in a composition, both because of their shape and their direction. In the composition a rhythm or movement can be created through the repetition of similar shapes, usually in diminishing sequence, just as it may be obtained by the repetition of lines.

In painting, architecture, and sculpture, individual shapes are grouped and related to give the total composition a basic structure which may be quite different from the unit shapes from which it is composed. The geodesic domes designed by Buckminster Fuller illustrate this in architecture. With a basic building unit, the tetrahedron, this architect has developed the curved dome-shape of many of his buildings. An example was the United States exhibit hall at the Canadian World's Fair, Expo-67. This arrangement of precisely shaped modular units to form a unified structure happens often in nature.

The overall structure of a work of art is composed from a balance of regular and irregular spaced units or shapes. These are so disposed that they combine to form other structural schemes that bind the parts or individual shapes into a unified whole, found quite often in painting and in sculpture. The architect has also made this the method by which the various unit blocks or shapes in his total structural complex are visually unified. Perhaps the best-known example for this in painting is to be found in the preference of many artists for the pyramidal composition. This compositional design has often been chosen because it provided a sense of stability with its broad base, and forced the eyes of the observer along the directional slant upward to a culmination at the apex. Here we have a logical placement for the center of interest with dramatic impact. This may be seen in a great many of the religious paintings with the Madonna and Child at the central focal point, flanked by single figures or by groups of angels or saints on each side.

In the last forty years there has been a growing number of artists who have emphasized geometric shapes as the basic units of their composition in painting and sculpture. Two good examples of this tendency are Charles Biederman and George Ortman. Biederman has remained apart from developments in American art, yet has been in the forefront at the development of much that is now acclaimed as "modern." Since 1937, geometry has become the major structural agent in his work and organic shapes are

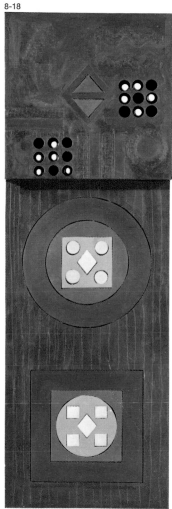

seldom present. With his constructions, usually titled simply as *Structurist Relief* (with the date added), he has managed to bridge the context of painting, sculpture, and architecture (Fig. 8-17); structurist reliefs contain properties associated with all three of these art forms. These relief constructions usually consist of a flat rectangular plane with an ingeniously organized array of smaller planes attached to the background and to one another. Within the limitations of the painted geometric shapes and their parallel and perpendicular positions, these planes create a unique stratification of form and space. This artist claims that he has studied nature's building methods and has translated these into abstract art of pure geometric form.

About 1958 George Ortman began to isolate geometry and to use it as the discipline and content of his work. His construction form is a flatly painted relief with geometric elements built out from or recessed into the surface. His *Journey of a Young Man*, in 1957, is a large horizontal construction which contains a single major element in each of seven panels

8-17
Charles Biederman.
Structurist Relief: Red Wing No. 6.
1957–63. Walker Art Center,
Minneapolis.

8-18
George Ortman. Rites of Love.
1961. Walker Art Center,
Minneapolis.

to describe the seven stages of life. Each element is a plaster relief of overlaying circles, squares, or hexagons in different combinations and sizes. Each houses a symbolic form (Fig. 8-18). Geometry tends to be his major concern, and overlapping geometric elements—triangle, square, diamond, cross, circle, and star—become the visual vocabulary for the expression of his ideas.

Texture. The element of texture as a tool used by the artist can be actual or illusionary. Texture can also be used as a term to describe areas of the composition which have been treated in a decorative manner, as in cases where the area or shape is covered by a formal arrangement of linear patterns or decorative symbols. These cover the surface area and separate it from other parts of the composition. Painters like Matisse have adopted this aspect of texture to great advantage.

At times, to achieve a particular desired texture, the artist has incorporated "real" materials into his painting or sculpture. This happens in the making of a collage and in the form of art which has been called "assemblage." In these techniques the composition is often dependent upon the interplay and arrangement of various materials chosen for their surface textural qualities.

Long before the Renaissance the work of the artist was applauded and he received acclaim for his ability to reproduce with exactitude the texture of the various objects included in his composition. A section of the viewing public has tended to give approval to artists and art works in which objects looked real because of the artist's skill in rendering a replica of the surface texture of his subject matter. Through the history of art there are many examples of textural rendering which was so exact that the viewer felt that if he touched it or picked it up it would be the "real thing." Textures of silk, fur, and fabrics, as well as the skin of the subjects, were precisely rendered in their appropriate textural quality by portrait painters with great technical skill (Fig. 8-19).

As art and artists have moved away from realism, the element of texture has taken on a different character. There is a greater interest in the texture of the actual materials which have been used by the artist and in those aspects of texture which result from the technical processes by which they have been treated. The technical processes involved in working with metal leave their mark upon the final product; the same is true in the shaping of wood and stone and the newer materials like plastic. Heat treatment or the abrasion of a tool can mark the surface just as the tracks of an animal are imprinted on the sand or snow. These traces of the artist's judgment often play a role in the final character of his work.

Painters, especially those who have worked in the styles of expressionism, abstract expressionism, and cubism, as well as the current tendencies in art, have made paintings in which thick overlays of paint were applied so generously that the marks of the knife or brush were thickly

8-19
Peter Paul Rubens.
Self-portrait with Isabella Brant.
Ca. 1609. Alte Pinakothek,
Munich.

imprinted upon the surface (Figs. 8-20, 8-21). This created a texture important to the visual image desired by the creator. Also, to obtain textures of variety and richness, many kinds of materials—sand, marble chips, and gravel—have been mixed with pigment. The "accidental" textures obtained in the process of experimentation with materials are often cherished and incorporated into the final work to give it vitality and uniqueness. The phrase "interesting texture, isn't it?" is often heard in reference to a creative effort when other more explicit descriptions are not available.

OTHER ELEMENTS SUGGESTED

With changing times the artist has been given new tools and materials. He has also raised questions about what should be classified as the art elements. Two new ones have been singled out as appropriate; these are *light* and *motion.* We have already discussed how the illusion of light was created by the painter and how the illusion of movement was suggested by artists of the past through their use of the elements of tone, line, etc. However, it is not the illusions of motion and light which are under discussion, but rather we are talking about light itself and motion itself as design elements—actual and not illusionary.

It has been said that Alexander Calder established motion as a design element for the artist when he originated his mobiles because motion in these sculptures was an integral part of the design. The artist was designing with motion! This motion was a designer's tool on the same level with

8-20
Elof Wedin.
Svolvaer Fishing Port.

the other elements previously identified (line, shape, color, texture, and tone). Lye with his rotating forms and other artists who have been interested in kinetics have designed works in which motion was essential—the motion was achieved either by natural means of wind and water or by the incorporation of motors and springs into the work.

When we speak of light as an element, our attention is carried to the experiments beginning with the Bauhaus—Moholy-Nagy in his design classes, Oskar Schlemmer in the theater workshop, and Herbert Bayer in typography. These men and their students were actively engaged in research with the use of light as a creative force. During the last few years, individuals and groups in the United States and Europe have made art products with light as a medium (Figs. 8-22, 8-23). The production of light murals, mobiles, and sculptures has become a highly involved technical development for which the producer needs all of the skills of the scientist-engineer, as well as those of the artist. Included in these light and luminal explorations are works which incorporate fluorescent tubes, incandescent light, stroboscopic lights, polaroid screens, and diffraction gratings. Constructions and canvases are illuminated by backlighting or with attached incandescent light bulbs. Transparent and translucent plastic reflecting metal cones, spheres, disks and mirrors, as well as projected shadow plays and animated films, have become part of the "hardware" from which art objects that either receive or give out light are constructed. Chryssa's *Fragments for the Gates to Time Square II* is a programmed neon and Plexiglas complex; Lucio Fontana's *Spatial Ambiance* includes nine hun-

8-21
Elof Wedin.
Svolvaer Fishing Port.
Detail showing thick impasto.

8-22
Otto Piene. Electric Flower.
1967. Walker Art Center,
Minneapolis.

8-21

8-22

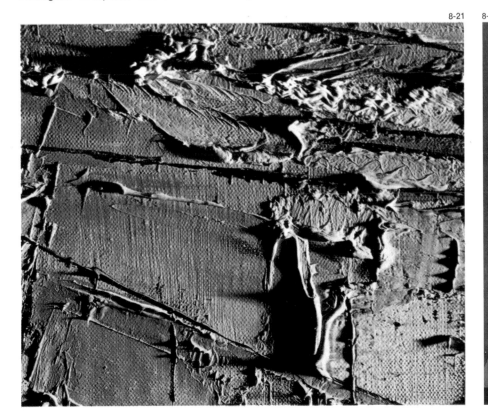

FORM: THE STRUCTURAL ORGANIZATION OF A WORK OF ART   259

8-23
Ben Berns. Untitled, 1966.
Walker Art Center, Minneapolis.

dred feet of neon piping; *Light Rain* by Gunther Vecker is fabricated of suspended aluminum rods containing fluorescent tubes, programmed to go on and off in cycles; and *Lux II* by Nicholas Schöffer is a spotlit, motorized, polished metal construction which revolves behind the translucent screen of a prism-shaped and mirrored enclosure.

These have been discussions of motion in art achieved by machinery and of light in art obtained by sundry photomechanical means. It has become apparent that what we are talking about is a medium for the artist. These are raw materials, which have been employed in much the same way that paint, metal, stone, plastic, and inks have been as the materials out of which an art object has been created. The artist who has elected to work with the media and tools of light and motion, like any other artist working with his selected media, must filter his view of the world through his imagination and express it with the elements of shape, color, line, tone, and texture.

UNITY OF DESIGN ELEMENTS

The basic operational problem for the artist is to bring all the design elements together into a satisfying unity. There is an essential quality involved in the creation of a work of art which cannot be accounted for by simply adding together lines, shapes, colors, textures, and tones. This has suggested that the interrelatedness of these elements is the important factor. We have a parallel to this in the more mundane arena of team sports, where the all-star team composed of the best individual players from a number of teams is often overwhelmed by a team that has only a few stars but has learned how to interact cooperatively in a well-designed, systematic manner. In order to produce art objects of quality and refinement, attention should be centered upon the principles through which these elements are caused to interact with each other — the action through which a harmonious interrelationship of elements can be obtained. For this we turn our attention to principles of balance, proportion, rhythm, emphasis, and to those other principles which bring the parts together and which give our visual images of both art and nature a quality that we call beauty.

The argument for the consideration of design elements in a unified, correlated fashion rather than as separate and distinct entities is reinforced by the following experience.

Many films and books on art and design include pictorial examples of things found in nature and art which have been chosen to illustrate each of the design elements singly. When line is under discussion, a number of these visual aids are shown; the same applies for each of the other art elements. We have long been curious to find out if the learner-observer understands these examples in the manner intended. When an example chosen by the teacher or author to illustrate line is shown, does the viewer or reader identify it as line? Is it possible to separate one element from the others in vision, or does the viewer identify the example as something other than what it is intended to represent?

In a number of informal experiments and test situations the subjects, college art students, were asked to identify the dominant design element illustrated by a series of selected visual examples. Examination of the responses has indicated very little consistency or agreement among our subjects when they were asked to identify the particular design element represented. The results show that, even for samples which seemed obvious to teachers and experienced artists, the responses of the students were scattered over the entire range of alternatives.

The conclusions from this are hardly world-shaking, but they do suggest that any design element can be seen or identified as more than one element. For example, when is a line only a line? If it is brought around until it nearly closes, it becomes shape. When there are more than two parallel lines, we have texture and not just line. A range of tones or shading is often obtained with a carefully placed gridwork of lines, which take the direction of the contour of the surface over which they fall and give an illusion of tone and texture. When we place a brushload of color on canvas, it may become a shape and at the same time a texture, although it was placed upon the canvas with one horizontal or vertical motion.

This discussion supports the consideration of design element in a unified, correlated fashion, rather than as separate, distinct entities. The machinery needed for handling information quite often encourages us to break down complex interrelationships into small, compact, easily handled packages. However, as students and teachers, artist and laymen, we must constantly be aware of the fact that in the visual world of art and reality the situation is complex and interracting, never simple and separate.

STRUCTURAL ORGANIZATION: FUSING THE PARTS INTO A UNIFIED WHOLE

Among those who write and talk about art there has been a substantial amount of agreement to the effect that the quality or value given to a work of art depends upon the final cohesion of its parts in the mind of the spectator. The process by which this fusion is achieved, first by the artist and then by the spectator, happens quickly and to a large extent instinctively or intuitively. It takes place much more smoothly than a clumsy explanation of it in words. The artist is motivated by a strong desire to give form to his perception. He takes the material of his choice, provided by the productivity of his age, as the physical material for giving an objective shape to the images of his eye and mind. With these materials he combines and relates several units of various sizes and sections into a single organic whole. This end product is what the spectator sees. To achieve the final unity, the single unified whole of his design for sculpture, painting, or achitecture, the creative artist must not only knit together the formal elements of design, but must also bring into harmony with these the functional requirements of his medium and the expressive relationships of the meaning which he intends to impart through his finished work. In the visual organization of the design, its formal visual character, the artist's ability to utilize certain principles which discipline the connected interdependent functioning of the design elements becomes the controlling factor. Among the controlling factors which establish the formal relationships within his work are balance, unity (within variety) and spatial order, and movement.

To achieve the formal compositional relationships, the artist depends more upon his intuitive judgment and sensibility than upon consciously applied rules or knowledge of the psychological findings on how people perceive relationships in the visual field. Only in rare instances does a creative individual consciously apply information about the perception of space, balance, movement, and so on. His decision on the arrangement and grouping of shapes is directed more by his judgment of what "feels right" than by direct application of his knowledge that shapes which touch, overlap, and interconnect are seen as units. From readings in psychology we are aware of certain factors—nearness, similarity, direction, and clo-

sure—that help the observer to obtain a unified visual organization. Spots or lines seem to go together when they are close, but appear as separate and different units when isolated. Equal sizes, similar shapes, and shapes that have the same direction or corresponding colors and textures are unified as "similarity groups." A straight line tends to continue in its path, and a curving line or shape tends to continue in a curving movement. This kinetic inertia, or tendency toward closure, serves to bind objects and shapes together. However, while this knowledge may be available to the working artist, only in special cases does he apply it directly or consciously as he makes decisions.

BALANCE

While watching children at work in an art class or after examining hundreds of their paintings, one is often impressed by their determination to achieve balance in their compositions. This felt need for balance or equilibrium is often satisfied at the expense of what to an adult is pictorially illogical; for example, a second sun is placed at the opposite side of the picture. The order and balancing of people, trees, and flowers happens too often and in just the right places to be a random choice (Figs. 8-24, 8-25).

The mature artist achieves a balanced composition systematically or through intuitive judgment when he vaguely feels that something is not quite right in balance. An equilibrium is established by counterbalancing the different thrusts, visual directions, or patterns in his work. It is a process of continuous adjustment by counterbalancing different visual weights in the composition. The visual weight of an area is derived from a combination of shape, direction, size, and color (value and intensity), and from its position in the total composition. A large dull shape of

8-25
Example of formal balance in child art.
Sunlit Landscape.

neutral intensity near the visual center of the composition can be counterbalanced by a small area of intense color placed farther out from the center.

Opposing attractions in a composition are controlled by an explicit central axis (axial balance) and are combined by rotation around a central point (radical balance) or by felt equality between parts of the visual field (occult balance). In axial balance, the first type mentioned, we have symmetry when both sides are exactly the same, but more often we have more of an approximate symmetry when the two sides are similar enough to make the axis positively felt. Occult balance (Figs. 8-26, 8-27), which is more subjectively apprehended, offers more freedom and surprise for viewer and artist alike, because it is less static and more dynamic in its visual effect.

UNITY AND VARIETY

Parallel with the requirement of obtaining unity of visual organization in his design, the artist is also required to remove monotony from the image he presents to the spectator. Artists have at different times moved backward and forward between the static and the dynamic, between the simple and the complex. Each unit in his work affects every other unit in some fashion. The artist's operational problem is to bring them into unity and yet to control the visual flow from one unit to another with a variety of emphasis which strikes a point of balance between harmony and confusion. This is not an easy task, but it is a problem which must be solved for the satisfaction of the artist and the spectator.

The repetition of similar forms and directions can result in unity, but judgment must make him stop at just the right moment and insert something not quite similar to prevent a dulling of the interest of the observer.

8-26
Example of occult balance in child art.
Decorative Landscape.

8-27
Example of occult balance in child art.
Blue House.

8-26   8-27

Unity may be obtained through (1) a closed pattern of movement, subtle yet decisive; (2) a balance, either symmetrical or occult; (3) proportional relationships of units, with size, number, and degree held in control; or (4) a rhythmic movement of repeated or alternating lines, colors, shapes, or textural patterns. A decision must be made at just the right point of equilibrium between the confusion of overcomplexity and the "silence" of oversimplicity, according to the expressive meaning the artist wishes to give to his work for the viewer.

THE SEARCH FOR BASIC PURITY

Abstraction as it was discussed earlier in the text was limited to the kind in which the artist's goal was simplification of his chosen subject to its essence. There is another kind of art process that is also called abstraction. By his own choice the painter or sculptor removes consideration of any naturalistic imagery and everything personal and accidental from the subject matter or content of his creative effort. This is a situation in which circle, square, and free form are substituted for reliance upon house, tree, person. It is purely intellectual and nonobjective and is geometric and schematic in character.

In his attempt to achieve what he considers basic and pure, the painter or sculptor concentrates on the structural elements—line, form, tone, color, and texture—and considers these alone as his subject matter. With the elements themselves and without adding associative references to nature and things in the environment, he endeavors to create what he considers a "new reality." An explanation of how this is carried out may be obtained from the statement of an artist who has felt and worked in this manner: [4]

> My concern is with the width and beauty of plastic organization. Each picture is ordered, deliberate and calculated, then moves as far as I can take it away from accident, anarchy and chaos. In the beginning, one key unit spawns the picture, one particular move begets another, each shape demanding its own color, depth of relief and juxtaposition with its counterpart. Finally, if it succeeds, the work becomes its own non-objective world of shape, color, texture, light and shadow; exact, yet fluid in movement; precise, but not frozen; organic, but not rooted in any constricting dogma.

There has been a tendency for artists who work in this manner to exert a rigid control over the number and kinds of units to be included in any particular work. It is their goal to reduce expression to its most essential terms, subscribing to the belief that this reduction means that there are fewer decisions to be made and that each decision is then more important in relation to the others. Around this ideal a kind of "minimal" sculpture and painting has grown up during the 1960s (Figs. 8-28, 8-29).

It should also be remembered that many of the artists who have pro-

---

[4] *Ibid.*, p. 53.

duced nonrepresentational art claim they have studied nature, are motivated by nature, and are creating images that establish what nature really is, rather than representations of its surface aspects. They claim to have studied how things in nature are built up and the process that underlies all forms in nature. They have in turn developed a vocabulary of symbols for representing natural qualities and experiences. This vocabulary is reduced to simplest terms in geometric shapes with an occasional free form for variety. In order to understand fully the degree to which this minimal nonrepresentational art can be extended, it is essential that we consider the concept of modularity as it relates to artistic expression.

8-28
Nicholas Krushenick.
Battle of Candy Stripe.
1964. Walker Art Center,
Minneapolis.

8-29
Tony Smith. Amaryllis.
1965. (Photo courtesy of
Fischback Gallery,
New York.)

THE MODULE: THE BASIC BUILDING UNIT

The desire to reduce expression to the most essential terms is a goal of many artists regardless of their personal preferences for style and content. Differences among them arise in their interpretation of what is essential. There are also differences in the degree to which any artist wishes to limit himself and adhere strictly to a preordained, preset systematic procedure.

WHAT IS A MODULE?

Something more than a desire for security and confidence is involved in this quest for fundamentals. The scientists have been looking for nature's basic building blocks and for the modularity that is the natural order; the architects of our historical building styles have given their works unity and proportion through modular concepts that have allowed variety within a coordinated and regulated frame. The painter and sculptor have also sought the ideal proportions, the "golden rules," and the basic sets of building blocks that would ensure orderliness and at the same time provide flexibility and the richness of variety. The builder with bricks, the weaver with threads, start with a small number of alternatives from which to choose; yet, by combining and recombining the parts, all the diverse patterns of woven textiles and brick walls have resulted.

We have been shown many examples of how the rather small number of basic units in nature in combination follow regular rules. Crystals, snowflakes, honeycombs, sunflower seeds and seashells are among our examples (Figs. 8-30–8-34). Chemists have shown us that all matter on earth—solids, liquids, and gases—is made up of various combinations of about one hundred elements. There is reason to believe that the same basic materials—these elements—make up the entire universe. Scientists have worked with the atom, the smallest part of an element, and have shown that an atom of one element can be united with an atom of another element to develop a compound with properties that are not shared by either of the elements which have gone into its construction. Further, they have discovered that organic compounds contain carbon which unites with a wide variety of elements to form the long chains that are the basic structure of polymers, the giant molecules of which everything that lives and grows is made up. The next step has been to create giant molecules from small ones by applying the theories of structure, that is, of how the arms or points of the stem link up with others to form a chain. With this knowledge of structure, chemists have developed means of controlling the linking together of various arrangements of small molecules. From this has come the synthesis of substances upon which are based many of the conveniences and "necessities" of everyday living in our society, ranging from nylon to gunpowder and from medicine to protective coatings for space age vehicles.

Combinations of similar elements are arranged in sequences of alternations to form units of our man-made environment, such as mosaic floors, geodesic domes, the grid of city blocks formed by intersecting cross streets, the vaulted interiors of cathedrals, and the precast concrete panels

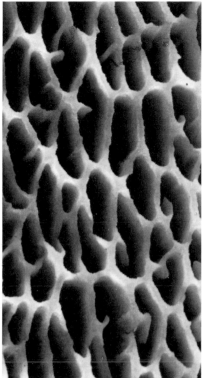

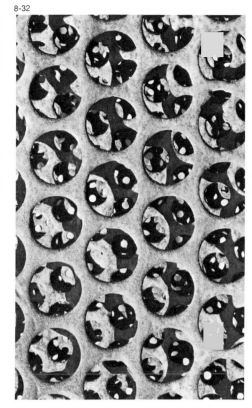

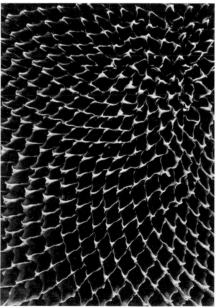

8-30
Bismuth crystal.

8-31
Fungus.

8-32
Hammermill screen.

8-33
Corn.

8-34
Sunflower.

FORM: THE STRUCTURAL ORGANIZATION OF A WORK OF ART   269

used in the construction of manufacturing plants, sports palaces, and college dormitories.

As was the case with the earlier public attitudes toward synthetics, there is a kind of prejudice against prefabricated units in architecture. Nevertheless, as we learn how to take advantage of the durability, economy, and facility gained in the organization of prefabricated basic units, without accepting the conclusion that their use means dullness and an endless pattern of sameness, the attitude toward utilizing the strengths of a basic unit structure without its disadvantages can only lead to further modifications of public attitudes.

Perhaps because one of the simplest ways to obtain unity and cohesion in the art product is by repeated use of similar or identical units, there have been movements toward the systematic conception of structure, that is, toward making plastic elements uniform and, in a manner, standardized. There have also been just as many vigorous protests against standardization and systematization. Our discussion of abstraction demonstrated how the artist has attempted to identify basic building blocks in nature through simplification and distillation of objects in the visual world as they are seen by the eye. This is one way to recognize a modular unit. With this knowledge it seems reasonable to rebuild or combine the units which have been discovered to create a new and personal artistic expression.

Another approach to developing an art form that is sometimes chosen begins with the selection of a single unit shape and then proceeds with controlled repetition of this unit according to a systematic procedure based on the logical application of regular rules. These rules are found in the growth of nature or are mathematical sequences of proportion, rhythm, and symmetry. Acceptance of these rules will establish a built-in order in the structure created by the artist. This method is to be found in all the arts, including music, theater, literature, as well as the category of art which is our special interest (painting, sculpture, and architecture).

MODULAR PRINCIPLES IN ARCHITECTURAL DESIGN

Clear-cut and easily understood examples of the principles involved in modular concepts can be found in all the ages of architecture. Although the architect is concerned with a functional art, in which the building is usually erected to fulfill some practical purpose, he has largely attempted to give his structure qualities of visual attractiveness from an outside and inside viewpoint. One of the earliest and most prevalent units of construction was the post and lintel. Examples of this are to be found in Greek and Egyptian temples dating back to the centuries before the birth of Christ. The basic structural unit of this type of construction is composed of two vertical posts or walls bridged by the horizontal element, or lintel. Many architectural styles depend upon systematic repetitions of these structural units. The Parthenon in Athens, the cabins of Colonial America, and many of our homes at the present time adhere to this method of construction.

The arch and the vault of stone or fireproof materials are also among these elementary structural units or modules (Fig. 8-35). The repetitions and combinations of the arch and the variations applied to this structural unit from the art of Rome until the present day attests to the flexibility that is possible even when there is strict adherence to a simple modular plan. Wood-frame ("ballon") construction, cast-iron construction, and steel-frame construction of multistory buildings are very familiar to us (Fig. 8-36). Ferroconcrete construction has created its own freedom of design and has extended the range of architecture and removed some of its limitations (Fig. 8-37).

Although the methods developed in the twentieth century have given the architect new freedom, he has nevertheless tended to search out those unifying visual elements which have become the modular basis for his design. The buildings of the Italian architect Pier Luigi Nervi, who uses a repeated sunflower-seedlike motif inside his domes and repetitive Y's as exterior columns, tend to bring us back to control with variety, which can be obtained by imaginative use of a repeated basic unit. Perhaps the most easily recognized and dramatic examples of architecture based upon a precise structural unit are the geodesic structures of Buckminster Fuller, as well as the highly publicized Habitat at Expo-67.

8-35
Cathedral of St-Pierre, Angoulême. 1105–30.

8-36
Hood, Godley, and Fouilhoux. McGraw-Hill Building, New York. 1931.

8-37
*Eero Saarinen. T.W.A. Flight Center,
John F. Kennedy Airport,
New York. 1956–61.*

8-38
*Buckminster Fuller. U.S. Pavilion,
Expo-67, Montreal.*

The geodesic domes are essentially based upon combinations of tetrahedrons, figures constructed of four triangles that are joined into complex groupings in order to extend and form parts of spheres. These small modular elements are joined together in a weblike form that can enclose rather large areas of space as either permanent or temporary structures. The basic units are made of cardboard or of plastic, cloth, aluminum, or steel sheets.

The United States Pavilion at the international exhibition of 1967 in Montreal has been applauded for its beauty under varied lighting conditions and because of its functional flexibility (Fig. 8-38). A huge geodesic dome, 187 feet high and 250 feet across, it was constructed of a lightweight metal frame covered with plastic and glass sheets. This provides adequate proof of the validity of Fuller's choice of the triangle or tetrahedron as his basic building unit, because he has found that with this structural system he can cover areas of vast dimension with lightweight materials without the necessity of internal columns or heavy supports. The construction principle is such that the stress of the forces of compression and tension are distributed by the system of triangles and the architect's materials can serve to their greatest advantage.

Habitat 67, also included in the Montreal exhibition, was created by the architects Moshe Safdie and David Barott of Boulva Associated Architects (Figs. 8-39, 8-40). The project is a proposed model which attempts "to meet the need for more intensive use of land and to develop and utilize new building methods to meet the challenges of expanding urban population, traffic congestion and urban sprawl." It demonstrates how prebuilt quality units may be assembled like children's blocks into many structural arrangements that would provide maximum privacy as well as comfort and living space without presenting a stereotyped, monotonous façade to the observer. The basic elements are prefabricated concrete

8-39–8-40
*Moshe Safdie and David Barott,
Boulva Associated Architects.
Habitat, Expo-67,
Montreal.*

boxes, 17 feet 6 inches by 38 feet 6 inches by 10 feet, hoisted into place by a crane. The housing units vary in size from 600 square feet (one bedroom) to 1,700 square feet (four bedrooms), and each has its own terrace on the roof of the unit below.

MODULAR PLANNING FOR PAINTING

Many have searched for an ideal modular conception which would satisfy the conflicting demands of unity and diversity when applied to the task of painting. They have also been interested in discovering some way of working which would combine a liberal amount of freedom with the security of intelligible standards by which they might proceed with assurance of an outcome that would be beautiful and harmonious. These painters have decided that unity in their products can be ensured by a combination of two factors: (1) by repetition of a few identical or similar units and (2) by systematic control of the repetition of these units according to a preset formula based upon a mathematical proportional order. As a result, we have an approach or tendency in painting which is dependent upon logic and cognitive power intead of feelings and emotions.

Work done in this manner would fall at the extreme of the rational-divergent range of the continuum, directly opposite from art works produced in a spontaneous fashion, and it attempts to achieve variety within seemingly severe limitations. Adherence and discipline, according to the organizational scheme of systematic structure determined for the work at its beginning, are demanded of the painter. These demands in discipline are so strict that many of the works of Mondrian might be criticized because he did not develop the logic of his constructions far enough and because the different-sized components in his composition—their placement and position—were determined emotionally and were not systematized. When we view the works of such men as Mondrian in our visual fashion, this is perhaps the last criticism that can be leveled against him.

In this abstract nonobjective and nonrepresentational type of painting, a sequence of components are arranged in rhythmic progression according to a proportional, systematic conception. By this controlled arrangement the units or component parts have a precise relationship to one another and to the total picture. Everything that is placed on the picture plane is regular and regulated to give a visual consistency to all these elements. The development of systematic composition of uniform structures has taken several decades and has its roots in cubism and the conscious aims of the de Stijl painters.[5]

Among the artists, besides Mondrian, whose works are within the classic traditions of this tendency toward uniformity and structural consistency in painting are Theo van Doesburg (*Rhythm of a Dance*, 1918; *Simultaneous Composition*, 1929), Albers (*City*, 1928), Georges Vantongerloo (*Function of Lines*, 1937), and Richard Lohse (*Twelve Vertical and Twelve Horizontal Progressions*, 1943–44; *Ten Similar Scenes in Five Colors*, 1946–47; *Thirty Systematic Series of Shades*, 1950–55). The constructivist reliefs by Anthony Hill, for example, show careful adherence to modular principles in sculpture.

Systematic composition employs various organizing influences from mathematics which give a basic geometric progression (the golden number) and the proportional system based on a mathematical series discovered in the sixteenth century by Filius Bonacci. In the Bonacci series the two previous terms are added to give a third term: 1 plus 2 equals 3; 2 plus 3 equals 5; 3 plus 5 equals 8; etc. The ratio between any two consecutive numbers is 1.618.

The pictorial structure is developed through adherence to logical rules by which all units are connected because of (1) the ratios of their dimen-

---

5 Richard P. Lohse, **Standards, Theories, Module: New Problems and Tasks of Painting**, in Gyorgy Kepes (ed.), *op. cit.*, pp. 128–162.

sions; (2) the direction in which they point; and (3) the relationship of the elements to the expanse of the pictorial surface. Appreciation of the pictorial structure rest upon an understanding of the place of the modular unit within the total complex. The artist usually starts with the division of his pictorial surface into a network of units — squares or rectangles. This lattice of modular units serves as a guide for facilitating the placement of his pictorial elements. By additive accumulation and multiplication of the units (squares or rectangles) or by proportionate subdivision, a variation in the size and shape of the individual parts is obtained. The artist has confidence that each new subdivision or unit created will have an orderly relationship with others in the composition. When the standardized modular units are combined into groups in this fashion, a logical pictorial relationship is ensured, for each subdivision will have both a mathematical and visual order of relationship to all other units involved. In more than a casual

8-41

8-42

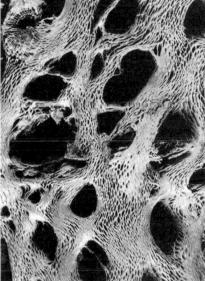

8-41
The artist achieved this pure abstraction by distilling his observation of a weathered cactus.
Gary Wedin. Relief Sculpture.

8-42
Cactus.

way we are here involved with "painting with numbers"; it is not intended as a derogatory simile of the commercial painting-with-numbers kits, because a very serious intellectual exercise is required, and those who work in this fashion are very serious indeed. Restrictions which to some artists might be unbearable are to these men a welcome test of their ingenuity.

MODULARITY WITH FLEXIBILITY

This discussion of modularity in connection with painting has attempted to make a fair presentation of the concepts and logic that support this viewpoint. There are reasonable men in the arts who question the assump-

8-43
Modular arrangement: culverts.

8-44
The flexible modularity of this natural form suggested the validity of a less rigid approach to design. *Modular arrangement: cross section of a dandelion plant.*

8-43   8-44

tion that a severe preliminary systematization of the elements of the pictorial or sculptural product is a significant accomplishment. They resent the implication that such an art form is expressive of and consistent with the thinking of our age except in a superficial way. They also feel that the problem of creating such art forms could and should be resolved by the computer. There is recognition of the fact that science and scientific systems are an acceptable feature of the nature and thinking of society in the last half of the twentieth centry; but (and this is a big "but") this is only one characteristic of a most complicated period of history. These men in the arts think that art and the arts should find more human and expressive symbols and methods for the representative visual equivalents of this time and culture.

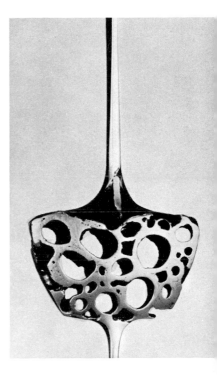

8-45
Holy pendant.

Artists have sometimes reached quite similar conclusions even though they have started from very different sources and have proceeded along courses that were far from parallel. After all, the painters of northern Europe developed perspective as a device for representing three-dimensional space on a two-dimensional surface through careful observation of the environment and through a process of trial and correction. Meanwhile, their counterparts in Italy were reaching very much the same technical conclusions by methods that depended upon the use of intellectual and logical analysis for solution of identical problems.

Some artists, such as Ortman and Biederman, have developed a "pure" abstraction by distilling their observations of nature rather than by exercising logic and establishing rational rules (Figs. 8-41, 8-42). The visual impact of their paintings and sculptural reliefs have a close affinity with those of Anthony Hill, Ben Nicholson, Albers, Theo Van Doesburg, and others who have based their work upon strict adherence to mathematical disciplines.

The dissatisfaction with the modular system as applied to design for art production is not provoked by the idea that a cohesive structure can be obtained through the orderly repetition of a number of small, simplified basic units. Much of the disagreement arises from the rigid application of rules and the machinelike adherence to preset formulas for decision making — that is, not from the idea but from the manner of its application.

An artist can achieve a creative synthesis of basic principles derived from observation of nature with the logical system obtained from analysis of the principles of modularity and structural regularity. A very good example of how this is done is explained in the following account. In the example the coherent structure of his designs is obtained by the artist through the repetition of similar small units (modules); flexibility and variability are provided, like growth and change in nature, by the effect of the conditions of environment, in this case by the conditions of tools, processes, and the sensitivity of the artist.

THE CYLINDRICAL SERIES: AN EXAMPLE OF FLEXIBLE MODULARITY

There are times when one's fascination with material and it's manipulation can result in a productive adventure in art. The repetition of a simple unit in the creation of a complex form is a device used by artists from antiquity to the contemporary scene.

Composers have used simple melodic themes or rhythmic patterns in endless repetitions and variations as building blocks for monumental compositions. The

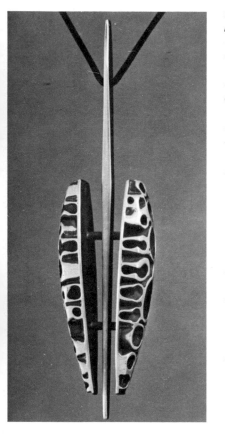

four note rhythmic pattern used by Beethoven in the first movement of his Symphony No. 5 in C Minor is a case in point. The musical form of the fugue, a many-layered overlapping . in time of a single theme, has been employed by composers for centuries.

I decided to explore a variety of ways in which cylindrical forms could be combined by fusion. The most obvious manner prompted by observation of piles of corrugated culverts was the cluster (Figs. 8-43, 8-44).

Cylinders of various diameters were placed on end and fused into a mass on a charcoal block. Attention was directed toward the arrangement of sixes, so that some semblance of balance would result. The irregular surfaces of the mass were filed to create a smooth plane and a vertical stem was added to complete the pendant form in a crosslike structure. The object had a great feeling of depth when held up to the light because of its open perforated structure (Fig. 8-45).

In the next experiment I chose to oppose two similar units against each other. This time the cylinders were fused onto supporting plates of metal. Cylinders which extended beyond the edge of the plates were filed off and an unexpected pattern emerged as the result of seeing some in cross-section. These two units were assembled in a formal construction by using a supporting shaft between them. Although there was a great deal of variation in the pattern formed by the cylindrical ends, the rigid formal character of the completed composition was not satisfactory (Figs. 8-46, 8-47).

The next attempt began by arranging cylinders of various heights and diameters, including some which were not completely closed, on a charcoal block. These arc-shaped modules thrust into the surrounding space, and the composition appeared less contained than its predecessors. To accentuate this dynamic tendency, an angular leg was added to terminate the piece. The surfaces of the cylinders were left rough instead of being refined as in earlier pieces. In order to create a subtle color contrast and a focal point for the asymmetrical design, a small opal was inserted into the central opening (Fig. 8-48).

The next variation began with the intention of constructing a multiaxial cluster of different-sized cylinders. These were fused together several at a time over a sphere of asbestos until the entire sphere was covered. The asbestos was soaked in water and was removed through the cylindrical openings. A thrusting hollow cluster resulted which reminded me of a meteor. This form was pierced with a shaft of forged silver and was allowed to retain all of its rich rough fused surface (Figs. 8-49, 8-50).

Influenced by the contrast of the forged termination of Meteor and the asymmetrical balance of the pendant with opal, I decided to place greater emphasis upon linear quality as opposed to mass.

This time I began by fusing a row of cylinders (graduating in size) onto a supporting plate of metal to form a rather heavy angular arm. A series of bent ribs were fused to the arm in a radial pattern generating the feeling of great motion. To complete the growing feeling in my mind that this piece had taken on certain characteristics of the crustacean family, a pearl was set at this junction (Figs. 8-51, 8-52).

Subsequent pieces began accentuating the rib structure and playing down the cylindrical involvement until later constructions utilized no cylinders at all. A new direction had furtively taken over and my quest for form was off again into unexplored areas (Fig. 8-53).

In studying my work I discovered that unlike previous series, which were abstractions of form in nature and were visually related to each other because of content, this series had a greater variety of form even though each was based upon the same structural module.

Of course, my own subjective preference manifested itself as the cylinders grew into abstract insects, prehistoric fossils, meteors, and fantastic plant forms.

8-46
Pendant with Shaft.

8-47
A side view showing the complex pattern achieved by the repetition of a similar unit.
Pendant with Shaft, *detail*.

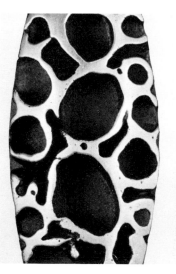

8-48

8-49

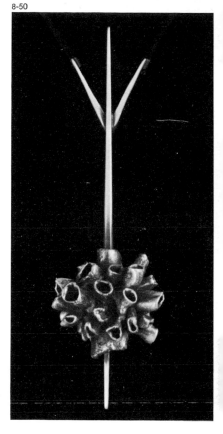

8-50

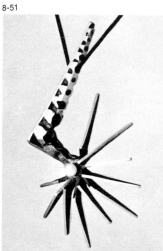

8-51

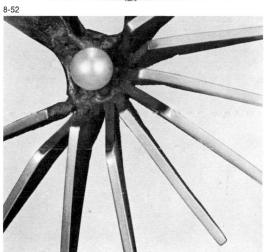

8-52

8-53

8-48
Pendant with Opal.

8-49
A bursting quality is achieved by the radial clustering of tubes.
Pendant detail. Meteor.

8-50
Pendant. Meteor.

8-51
Pendant. Spliney.

8-52
The design emphasis has shifted from cylinders to ribs.
Spliney, *detail.*

8-53
Pin. Crawler.

Chapter 9

CONTENT: COMMUNICATION THROUGH ART

Art is communication. The artist often thinks of his work as a visual statement of an idea. More often he is concerned with the communication of his emotional reaction of that idea. While looking at a work of art, we react to the *form* of the work, which is the relationship of the formal elements in its structure as the artist has organized them for our satisfaction. Expression is embedded in and derived from the visual features of the composition and the order of their arrangement. Pottery, the most elemental and abstract of the art forms, has very little of what we describe as content in the customary sense. We respond to the concepts of form given to his work by the potter. When we consider other kinds of art and the whole of our art heritage, form is not necessarily all there is to a work of art for either artist or spectator. Much of what we think of as art is about something and has meaning. This "something" is often more than simply an arrangement of shapes and colors; meaning, though often obscured, is there.

Although many philosophers — Susanne Langer, Clive Bell, and others — have not considered content a key factor for aesthetic consideration, the widely used phrase "expressive form" suggests that something is expressed and that meaning for the spectator lies in the structural arrangement of the art product. According to Langer, "The work of art becomes the physical embodiment of the artist's resolution of his intuitive feelings and conceptions; it enables the viewer to apprehend this resolution as experience rather than as discursive language."

Meaning is projected into the work of art by the artist through the incorporation of signs, symbols, and images and is derived from the work by the viewer. The meaning incorporated by the producer and derived by the viewer is based on personal identifications and feelings associated with (1) previous experiences, (2) general knowledge, and (3) literary and historical events and personalities as well as an acquaintance with (4) traditional symbols and (5) cultural influences.

Throughout time people have come to art for those values which could be called "psychological." These evolve from the common human interests, desires, and aspirations of our conscious and even our subconscious life. We go beyond formal values and are affected by the emotive meaning that the artist through his sensitivity has inserted into the physical structure of his work.

For mankind art has been an expression of the "eternal verities" and of truths that are not so eternal. Man has expressed through art his hopes and fears, his frailties, his triumphs, his pessimism and optimism, and the ecstasy, exaltation, and depression that have been his lot. It has reflected the fragments of his discovery and the beauty of his world; it has been a pathway into the mysteries of the unknown. Because art is a product of his hands, mind, and heart — of his own making and therefore a personal thing — it has all the variety and differences which distinguish one individual from others.

9-1
Joseph Stella.
American Landscape.
*1924. Walker Art Center,
Minneapolis.*

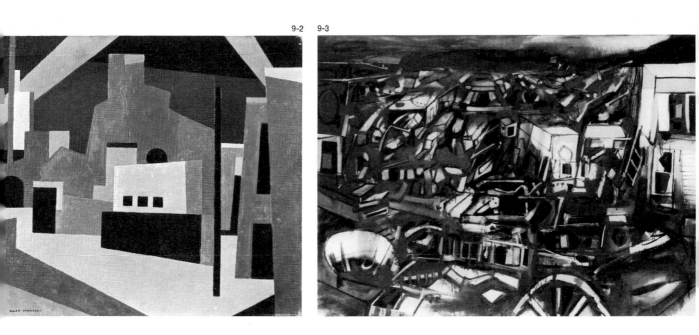

9-2
Niles Spencer.
Wake of the Hurricane.
*1951. Walker Art Center,
Minneapolis.*

9-3
John Hultberg.
City by Searchlight.
*1961. Walker Art Center,
Minneapolis.*

ART AS COMMUNICATION

Many men have attempted to define art. The following is a clear, straight-forward description of a work of art: [1]

> *A product of man which has a defined form or order and com-municated human experience. It is affected by the skilled con-trol of the materials used in its construction to project the for-mal and communicative concepts that the artist wishes to present.*

Now that the majority of the "family of man" has chosen to live in cities, the urban community has become a rich source of inspiration, structural form, and content for the painters and sculptors who live in it. It is the near-environment and the locus for much of their experience which they have to communicate. This has also been true in former times. In an industrial society, like that of the United States, we have had many artists who had strong feeling about the city. The members of the "Ashcan school" portrayed one aspect of the city; Sheeler, Hopper, Bohrod, Shahn, and Marsh have presented their own feelings about it; Joseph Stella, John Marin, and Stuart Davis have presented its vitality with different images (Figs. 9-1; see also Figs. 9-2, 9-3).

Examples of how artists have skillfully ordered the materials of art to communicate a human experience or a response to their environment are presented below. The environment with which the artist was concerned in each of these cases was the city.

---

[1] Nathan Knobler, **The Visual Dialogue**, Holt, Rinehart and Winston, Inc., New York, 1967, p. 26.

THE CITY

The intention of these young artists was to transfer their feeling of what was essential in the community — its essence — through the language of art into a visual statement. These two young artists have selected what, in their own interests, was important. The experience of one of our subjects, Richard Kriebel, is described in his own words.

I found the billboards around the city to be both interesting and varied. To me, they became the subject of my study and the interpretation of my city. My interpretation of the city was worked out directly from the billboards and gave my feeling about these advertisements with their strong, forceful messages which suggested bright colors, strong lines, and simplified shapes. They had no subtlety, but had everything on the surface for immediate interpretation. This strength and directness were my main concern.

The subject matter of billboards became both content and media for my work. Actual billboard paper, anything I could find that had the right quality of a quick, direct message, became more directly involved because everything seemed so right and was the right material to use. By lifting the ink from sections of the magazine pages and billboard sheets, I was able to make compositions in which the type and its message were held constant. In the final study, I used three large blocks of wood painted pure colors of red, white and blue in a simple sculptural composition. These were not "artistic" materials, but neither were the billboards around me. The paper, the ink process, and the blocks of wood had within them the flat direct feeling that I got from the billboards. These were not ornate with intricate textures and indefinite lines, but were just simple strong statements of my impressions of the city.

Although many people have strong negative feelings about the signboards, billboards, and masses of commercial signs, posters, and banners

9-4   9-5   9-6

which clutter the cityscape, the painter Stuart Davis found in these an ordered expression of the vitality, the life and gaiety, of the city scene. Our first young artist has also chosen to concentrate upon the posters which are a part of everyday life in the city environment. He was interested in the forms of letters and words that appear in such profusion. He used them to represent his idea of the essence of the city. The letter forms were employed not as words for direct communication but as a subject matter of shapes and colors for creating his designs. The shapes and colors of the letters themselves were the design tools for his expression of his feelings about the city. Technically his process involved the separation of the ink from the paper with a solvent. The film of colored ink was adhered to a new surface for his designs. In his compositions the letter forms were arranged in a collage technique, without reference to word meanings, as pure shapes and colors that made up his abstraction of a feeling he had about his environment. These are shown in Figs. 9-4 through 9-8; in the last of these we can see how he changed his technical process to print making but held his visual statement within the same boundaries of his earlier efforts. Mood and design structure are held constant throughout the series of products.

Our second artist, Carleen Olson, saw the same city at the same time. The following diary description of her procedure for arriving at her visual statement of the essence of her city provides an excellent view of an extended period of creative action (Figs. 9-9–9-13).

In my search for the essential character of the city, I concentrated upon the alleyways, or the back-door entrance through which the lifeblood of the city flows. These traffic arteries are often forgotten as we promote the façade of the city that we would like others to see. There are many different types of alleys; these scenes

9-7   9-8

9-4
Richard Kriebel. Scream.

9-5
Richard Kriebel. Schizoid.

9-6
Richard Kriebel. Quiet City.

9-7
Richard Kriebel. Night.

9-8
Richard Kriebel. Impact.

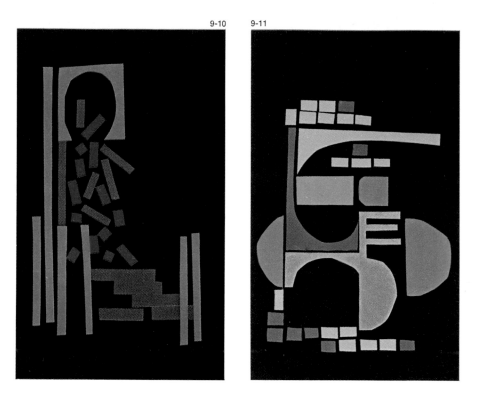

9-9

9-9
Carleen Olson. Charcoal Alley.

9-10
Carleen Olson.
Alleys: Accents on Shapes
and Color No. 1.

9-11
Carleen Olson.
Alleys: Accents on Shapes
and Color No. 2.

can be handled with great variety and have a life of their own. To me there are many small areas of subject matter which can be observed for detailed concentrated study.

In the first phase I sketched three alleys in charcoal. The sketches were fairly detailed, and in doing this I became aware of the character of old brick walls, garbage cans, signs, fences, and various discarded junk items — broken ladders, planks, bottles, and cans. I used charcoal because it allowed me more freedom in getting the contrast which was needed in defining specific shapes and objects (Fig. 9-9).

The second phase was an abstract analysis of shapes which I observed and had rendered representationally in the sketches. Now I wanted to develop my ideas using the technical process of a collage of cut-paper forms.

In one collage I concentrated upon the vertical ribbing of one garbage can — representing it by using cut pieces of modulated gray paper. Diagonal lines which were observed behind the garbage can were added. In another collage I emphasized the vertical shafts of a fence combined with an open square designating a window. As I worked with the cut paper, I began to sense the overall feeling of shapes and spaces which was especially obvious in one sketch; in another collage I cut small rectangles of paper and combined these with other shapes to create a design with more of the feeling of texture. Several collages were made in this technique. In these I selected areas from the alleys and then broke these areas down into a geometrically patterned design. Certain forms were selected and rearranged in different combinations; still, their basic structure was maintained.

For the final collage (Fig. 9-13) I used a long vertical rectangular fiberboard, covered it with black construction paper and with cut paper created an alley in tones of gray shading with a city scene above it. To add color to the collage

I depicted the city in tones of blue, blue-green and purple. I was now more con-cerned with color and shape than with exact representation.

In the final phase I printed a piece of textile as dress material, concentrating on the textures that were so evident in the brick walls and the planks of the buildings in the alleys. In the wood block I concentrated on the design of vertical nonobjective shapes. Using black ink the wood block was then printed on a gray linen material to carry through the feeling of overall roughness and continuity in pattern. This was the end result of textures and shapes which had become the dominant element of the alleys in my observation. For me it expressed the essence of my city!

9-12
Carleen Olson.
Alleys: Accents on Shapes and Colors No. 3.

9-13
Carleen Olson.
Alleys: Accents on Shapes and Colors No. 4.

Two very young artists were chosen for our examples of the process through which the artist's feelings about his environment could be com-municated. In these instances the process was more direct and perhaps less complicated than it would have been if a fully established painter, sculptor or designer had been our example. Here we have less subtlety and greater clarity. Through a number of experiences and attempts to find the right visual imagery for his feelings about the city, the more mature artist has already tried out a number of different possibilities for his expres-sion. Usually the painting or sculpture we see in the exhibit halls and museums is the final distillation of a number of previous attempts. Because our young artists are more at the beginning stages, we can see the fresh-ness and honesty of their endeavors without the gaps or an overlay of previous contacts with the same artistic problem of which we as viewers are unaware.

THE PROBLEM OF COMMUNICATION

Communication through art refers to the transfer of information, ideas, or feelings from the producer to the spectator. The language used in this dialogue is one in which the artist combines separate design elements to construct pictorial symbols. The degree of communication depends upon the artist's skill in forming and arranging these pictorial symbols and upon the viewer's familiarity with the symbols employed by the artist. There is often confusion and even inadequacy in communication between the transmitter and receiver when the language of art is used just as there are breakdowns when we communicate with words of our common language in our daily activities.

The artist is a person for whom visual sights, sounds, and emotional experiences refer symbolically to marks on his canvas or shapes in his sculpture. The observers of works of art must translate the visual forms employed by the artist and give to them meaning or symbolic reference to the emotions that the artist wished to evoke. Thus in the visual language of art there is a two-way symbolic reference — from things to visual forms on the part of the artist and from visual forms to things on the part of the observer. When symbolic references are present in an act of human experience there are two sets of components, symbols and meanings, with some objective relationship between them. This relationship will vary greatly in different instances. The total constitution of the percipient has to effect the reference from the symbols to their meaning.[2]

Communication through the language of art starts from the common experiences that the participants have had with the immediate world and with the development of the equivalents of symbols for an object of information about it. There must also be a procedure (as with written language) for combining these symbols which has a common meaning for both artist and observer. With the visual language of art, however, there may be many equivalents for the same object in nature. The appearance of the symbol for house, tree, or woman, for example, varies from time to time and from one artist to another. Also, an artist changes and refines his symbols for an object or group of objects as his art progresses toward maturity. This has been the case with the sculptor Henry Moore and the symbols which have been used in the prevailing themes of his works: the mother and child and the reclining woman.

The symbols used for the human figure by the Egyptians in their wall painting, by the Renaissance artists, and by more contemporary painters such as Gauguin, Picasso, and De Kooning are certainly visually different from one another, as examples of the contemporary artist's approach to the subject of woman (Figs. 9-14–9-16). It is difficult to see their common aspects without concentration. Thus the appearance of an equivalent, or symbol, is often affected by factors that have nothing to do with the subject matter. The artist is immersed in a culture and is subject to the traditions and demands of that culture.

---

2 Alfred North Whitehead, **Symbolism, Its Meaning and Effect**, Capricorn Books, G. P. Putnam's Sons, New York, 1959, pp. 12–13.

9-14

9-14
Pablo Picasso.
La Femme au Fauteuil. *1927.*
Minneapolis Institute of Arts.

9-15
Fernand Léger.
Plongeurs sur Fond Noir.
1941. Walker Art Center,
Minneapolis.

9-16
Grace Hartigan. Greek Girl.
Walker Art Center,
Minneapolis.

9-15   9-16

CONTENT: COMMUNICATION THROUGH ART   **289**

9-17
Child art. Summertime.

Also, there are many ways of looking at things and events in nature. Objects in the picture and experience with them may be understood and seen in different ways. At the same time there are many different means in art for communicating what has been experienced. Thus the artist must be and is selective when confronted with the impossibility of expressing simultaneously all the potential meanings in his subject matter.

Going back to our examples of the essence of a city as presented by two young artists, we can see and understand how this process of selection figures in the decisions they made about what was to be represented and how it was to be represented. The immediate urban environment was the same for both. Each of the young artists wanted to make their statements more universal, so that they would refer to any or all cities, not to Minneapolis, San Francisco, Columbus, or Denver. Their own and other cities are a complex of many objects and happenings. As it was certainly impossible to express all the meanings inherent in even a small fraction of their general subject matter, they were selective according to their own judgments and interests. From the general omnibus environment one artist selected alleys, the other billboard posters as areas of focus.

Carleen Olson employed a systematic procedure for abstracting essentials from the specific subject matter. She found certain shapes, colors, and textures to her liking for the meaning she wished to communicate. Her visual experience was communicated at the beginning in a manner which might be described as perceptual representation; the representation of what she saw was then modified or supplemented by inclusion of what she knew about her subject (conceptual representation). As her technical process and medium changed, the content was treated in a more decorative fashion; colors and shapes became the dominant vehicle in her imagery.

Then her personal reactions become more personal. In her final adaptation of the subject matter to a design for textile, there was another change toward a more abstract concept, in which she dealt with material common to the experience of many people in society. In her last effort she reduced and eliminated most of the recognizable features, leaving only a pattern of linear textures which had been suggested to her by her subject, the city.

Our first artist, Richard Kriebel, made no attempts from the beginning to parallel the experience of an observer; although he used the symbols of the written language, there was no attempt to employ them as tools of communication, as words with their customary meanings. His interest lay in letter forms, shapes, and color patterns, but his dominant emphasis was upon the orderly arrangement of these into a nonobjective composition. The letters were taken out of their normal setting, and no reference to word meaning was involved. His intention was to make them recognizable as part of a formal structural arrangement with only slight reference to the familiar physical reality of the city.

For discussion of what the artist wishes to communicate, it has been suggested from an examination of the work of artists throughout history that subject matter might be broken down into three categories: (1) the world of perceptual reality; (2) the personal response to experience; and (3) a communication of order.[3]

From the examples we have given and from a look at our art heritage it becomes apparent that these three areas are not mutually exclusive; In works of art they are quite often combined. Also there are many examples in which one is emphasized and the others are excluded, as may be the case with our series of examples (Figs. 9-4–9-13) in which the communication of order was a major concern. In the art expressions of young children the world of perceptual reality (and conceptual reality) and the emphasis upon a personal response to experience are almost universally accepted. There is sometimes an overt expression of the desire to communicate order, but seldom at the expense of perceptual reality and the expression of a personal response. Children generally use art as a means of refining their perception of their world and expressing their feelings about experiences they have had (Fig. 9-17).

THE MOTIVATIONAL CUE: SOURCES FOR CONTENT, STRUCTURAL FORM, AND INSPIRATION

Almost any sort of thing can act as the motivational cue, or the initiating force, for getting a work of art under way. This and the two preceding chapters have discussed the aesthetic factors of matter, form, and content. Depending upon his personal choice, the artist may at different times embark upon his creative adventure with one of these elements as his starting point. As work progresses, however, there is a harmonious interrelationship of all three elements and a movement backward and forward

---

3 Nathan Knobler, *op. cit.*, p. 50.

among them, with changing emphasis; there is a strong interplay among the aesthetic factors whereby they promote each other for the ultimate goals of harmony and unity.

There is much that goes on during the process of making a work of art, from the time of its inception until the work has been finished. But it does have to get started, and quite humble and mundane causes often motivate the action. It is these motivating causes that we wish to consider at this point. There have been many reports about what has started creative efforts. These initial causes range far and wide and include such things as a remembered momentary glimpse of a sunlit landscape, an accidental configuration of twisted metal, a colored postcard of a Paris street scene, a weathered fragment of bone, a bicycle seat, the memory of a line of poetry, a composition from a museum exhibit of the masterworks of a great artist, a wave-swept rock, or the flight of a gull. These sources of inspiration are many; content comes from all human experience. Careful observation of nature and man-made rules of logic are the sources of the artist's structural organization and order. Sometimes the incept which starts the process comes in a flash of insight; at other times it grows out of the longer period of exploratory deliberation. The following is an examination in some detail of the major sources which have set the artist to work and have sustained him in other ways.

SOURCES AND RESOURCES

When we say that the artist's source material is all human experience, we are only indicating part of the reason for the great diversity in the works of art. It should also be kept in mind that there is diversity in the ways different artists choose to use the same source material. The different ways of treating source material can be illustrated by reference to one subject among the many obtained by the artist from one of his sources — the natural environment; this is the portrait, a subject for art over many centuries.

Frequently we hear of differences of opinion about a portrait of a prominent public figure. That the President, the Governor, or the Chairman of the Board did not like his portrait has sometimes become a matter of public record. This should be understandable in view of the disagreements that arise among relatives over the choice of the high school graduation photograph. As the proofs are examined and discussed, we hear such remarks as "That doesn't look like you," even though we know that all the proofs were taken of the same individual by a machine under the same lighting conditions. A portrait is made by an artist and not by a machine; there are differences in the lighting conditions. This accounts for only a small part of the variations in portraiture; nor are these variations just a matter of skill. Much more can be accounted for if we understand the intention of the artist and what he wanted to do with his source material.

Some artists wish to document or describe their subject; others wish to idealize or refine and otherwise improve upon the features presented to their eyes. For others the portrait of one person is intended to represent more universal than personal characteristics. The portrait of a young girl,

Jane Smith, might exemplify the characteristics associated with adolescents in general; that of a patriarch or rabbi which incorporated all the important characteristics of a religious group could be entitled *Israel*. Some artists who paint portraits are interested not in the physical likeness but in shape, color, and texture; their portrait of Jane Smith would be treated in a manner which we call "decorative." Then there is the artist who is not interested in the physical features and the objective reality of the subject; he paints his feelings about his subject. Some artists break down their subject and then reassemble the planes and shapes in a manner that interests them. They might strip away facial detail and redesign or rearrange the subject emphasizing continuity of rhythm and shape and essential forms and absolute beauty.

These are only a few of the treatments of the portrait by artists through time, but they illustrate how a single source material — the human head — in the hands of the artist finds its objective form in art in many quite different kinds of imagery. This should be kept in mind when examining the following major categories of source material for artistic expression. These broad categories of resource materials for art are treated from the standpoint of the artist and vary according to his intentions.

THE ARTIST AND THE NATURAL ENVIRONMENT

Nature as a source of inspiration, motivation, and subject matter, as well as a reference for the structural order of the artist, needs little further amplification. Almost all of the illustrations of the process of creating art employed throughout this text relate to the natural environment as the source for the artist. The series of examples of sculpture and jewelry used to illustrate the art and creative processes, ways of working, and so forth, all had their source in nature. The series of mushrooms and the one of insects and sculpture inspired by the concept of metamorphosis, for example, are clearly related to life and growth in the natural world. (See Figs. 9-18–9-21 for additional examples.)

It has been interesting to note that even those who are responsible for art products which appear to have very little physical resemblance to natural objects and form have constantly referred to their indebtedness to nature as the source for their work. From the time of the caveman to the present nature has been the major source and resource for artistic expression. The scope of man's interest in his natural environment has been so broad that it would take only a little effort to trace all, or nearly all, art back to this source, either directly or indirectly (Fig. 9-22).

The artist's reliance upon nature has been summarized as follows: "Cézanne's series of apples, his series of the Mont Sainte-Victoire, Monet's water lilies, cathedrals and haystacks are the images of man's creative motion flowing around a fixed point of interest, nature. That fixed point rallies the scattered senses, intensifies the creative urge by channeling its drive." [4]

9-20

9-18
Gall.

9-19
Pendant. Gall. *Collection of Mr. and Mrs. David C. Johnson.*

9-20
Pendant. Beetle IV.

9-21
The design of this and the preceding pendant was motivated by the structure and decorative qualities of insects. *Pendant.* Priest Bug.

9-21

---

[4] Alexander Liberman, **The Artist in His Studio**, The Viking Press, New York, 1960, p. 17.

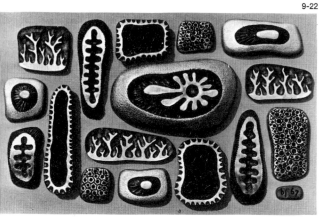
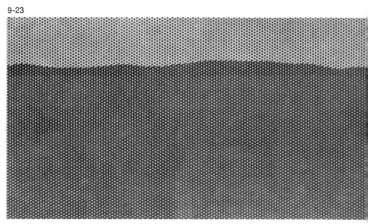

THE ARTIST AND THE TOOLS OF HIS CRAFT

9-22
William Lockhart.
Environmental Forms.
Cast aluminum. Collection of
Mr. and Mrs. Jim Steele.

9-23
Roy Lichtenstein. Littoral.
1965. Walker Art Center,
Minneapolis.

What is meant here by tools are media and processes and the elements and principles of design. Reference is made to the influence of media and processes in themselves on artistic expression. Design elements and the focus upon them and their manipulation as a unique resource, separate from other factors that affect the production of art works, are considered under this heading.

Media and processes. It is not uncommon for anyone who works with art materials to follow for a short period of time a course of action which has grown out of an accidental happening that was the result of a technical process. This is a common occurrence with a rapid free medium such as watercolor, and it happens with many other processes.

On occasion. with considerable self-discipline, craftsmen develop a facet of a technical process in depth, and this alone becomes the major force around which his design is developed. Process becomes the subject matter and substance of his composition, and other considerations are intermingled. Design elements and structural principles are, as they should be, instrumental to a change in his direction; meaning and content ideas have given the artist a reason for taking a particular course of action. However, the process of manipulation of the medium has dominated and controlled the artist during the whole period of his creative activity.

Elements and principles of design. Reference has been made to works of art in which there is no dependence upon subject matter of any sort. These art objects represent attempts of the producer to exploit the potential of the design elements — color, form, texture, and so on — as the subject matter without direct reference to nature and objects. This kind of thing has appeared periodically in art history whenever men have rejected for philosophical or aesthetic reasons any reference to the illusion of nature and the physical environment as a meaningful objective. This has been discussed in some detail elsewhere in this text in connection with "pure" abstraction and the principles of modularity. These men sought the ultimate in the purity and simplicity of abstract symbolism. This emphasis upon the elements of art for both content and structural organization has attracted many artists of the twentieth century. It depends upon the precision of geometrical and mathematical rhythms for proportions, patterns, and movements. Painters and sculptors who rely heavily on shape, color, line, and texture and who exclude any reference to things and events in the environment are associated with such contemporary tendencies as minimal and optical art or with the artists called "primary structuralists" (Fig. 9-23).

THE MAN-MADE OBJECT AND ENVIRONMENT

Man has adapted his natural environment to his own needs and purposes, or he has adapted himself to live more comfortably within it. Man, the artist, has been sensitive to these changes and his feelings about them are to be found in his paintings, sculpture, and architecture. The artist-craftsman has designed tools and products for others to use and to wear. These man-made and industrially produced objects, large and small — buildings, tractors, bridges, pots, bottles, cars, and nuts and bolts — have all been employed for artistic purposes as well as for their intended practical purposes. In art we find either the object itself or a representation of it.

Throughout history man has built many associations around the objects he has made and has employed them for symbolic purposes. The creation of the object itself evolved from the discovery of its functional form as a tool that had utility; the making of the tool was then refined until it reached a point of maximum efficiency. Next came the stage where refinement went beyond efficiency and the object was cherished as a free symbolic form. The form itself becomes significant beyond practicality as a source of harmonic proportions or for ritual and ceremonial purposes.

The painted object. For the painter the objects that man has created and placed in an environment for living have been of interest as subject-matter content. His attitude toward objects as content has varied. At one extreme he has had the desire to depict them with absolute fidelity. This has been done with such acute accuracy that the three-dimensional volume of the object was rendered so convincingly on the two-dimensional canvas as to cause the representation to be mistaken for the actual object.

The Romans, in their paintings and mosaics, achieved naturalistic renderings of ordinary objects and made them the whole subject matter in works of art. This was forgotten during the early centuries of Western art, when objects in art served a secondary role as symbols or accessories in connection with a religious imagery. Later artists, more concerned with secular matters than with religious ones, employed objects in their still-life paintings for their storytelling qualities or for their associations and also used them as the whole subject matter. Objects were also included as accessories in portrait painting when they had a special reference to the persons portrayed.

In the fifteenth, sixteenth, and seventeenth centuries, in France and in Holland, the still-life became an art form of aesthetic significance which recorded an overwhelming interest in material possessions; these paintings gave inanimate objects a quality of stability and permanence in carefully

9-24
Pieter Claesz. Still Life.
1643. Minneapolis Institute of Arts.

9-25
Juan Gris. Still Life.
Minneapolis Institute of Arts.

organized compositions (Fig. 9-24). This, the supreme illusion of the actuality of objects, was modified by such painters as Rembrandt, Chardin, and, later, Monet, who preserved some of the illusion of objects, but their work also evidences painterly qualities, for which they can be enjoyed as paintings instead of for their faithful illusions of the object itself.

In the twentieth century this tendency to draw attention to the physical aspects of the artistic creation — the process of painting and the pigment itself — has been carried forward. Although the artist employs an arrangement of objects as the content of his composition, he feels no obligation to imitate the shapes, textures, and colors of the actual objects. He reserves the right to destroy the autonomy of the objects and to disassemble and rebuild them according to the demands of compositional design and of paint and canvas. Subject matter is secondary to the integrity of the object itself evolves from the discovery of its functional form as a *painted* object. His color is not confined within the contours and his brushstrokes are independent of the objects. He has sought to organize an original subject matter according to directions, textures, and visual patterns that are essential to the painting structure (Figs. 9-25, 9-26). Other artists, such as De Chirico, Dali, Roy, and Magritte, have painted objects that can be identified and counted. They have created with these perceptions of the real world but have made of them an independent reality by the juxtaposition of objects in a manner different from any existing arrangement and combination in the everyday world. Familiar objects were placed in unfamiliar situations!

With the acceptance of the collage technique (pasted paper), flat pieces of objects — cardboard, labels, newspaper — are incorporated with the paint to make a composite artistic image. At first, the materials used in the collages had a readily identifiable connection with the world of familiar activities. Then the Dadaists and surrealists manipulated and assembled the actual objects to serve as works of art in themselves. These objects were valued by the artists and their public for their semantic connotations and associations. Works of painting and sculpture were made from the materials and objects taken from the mass production of modern technology; mechanical objects or their fragments were incorporated to create plastic images typical of our culture. In the "combine" paintings of Rauschenberg, Johns, and Rivers, "artistic objects" are incorporated and transformed as the new media for their constructions. In these paintings objects which might otherwise have been destroyed or scrapped are preserved. In this new context, the objects have acquired a value symbolic of the world from which they were taken.

In his book *Purposes of Art*, Elsen has summarized the range of performance of the artist as a painter of objects as follows: [5]

> From imitator to creator, to selector of objects; from fabricator of illusionistic familiar surroundings to inventor of new environments. He has ranged from playful deception through story telling personification, moralizing, and philosophizing metaphor and emblem making, aesthetic contemplation and meaningless-

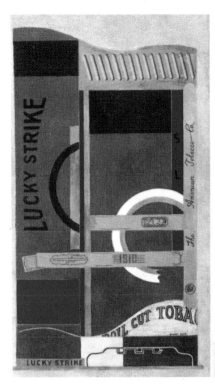

9-26
Stuart Davis. Lucky Strike. 1921. Museum of Modern Art, New York.

5 Albert W. Elsen, **Purposes of Art**, 2d ed., Holt, Rinehart and Winston, Inc., 1967, p. 336.

ness. Painting of objects reflects great changes, not only in style, but in man's attitude toward his environment — whether it be one of fear, reverence, wonder, curiosity, pride, dependence, distaste or pleasure.

The found object. Collages of printed objects — cut, torn, and pasted — have been incorporated as a valid extension of the media for picture making; the found object or selected parts of it provided the motivational spark that expanded the art of sculpture. Fleeting references have been made to this practice earlier in this text, and it seems appropriate to clarify here its proper position as a useful tool for artistic expression.

Students and laymen tend to become intrigued by the employment of a familiar object from their common experience for a new purpose as part of a work of art. A child's toy, a section of machine parts, or some neon tubing welded into the composition of a piece of sculpture has provided a point of recognition for them; often they are "carried away" by the surface association and are distracted from the undertones of meaning intended for the work and the reasons which had prompted the artist's incorporation of the familiar object into his design. The following discussion concerns a sculptor who has expressed with sincerity a clear view of the why and how of the work of art that depends upon discarded objects, tools, and possessions from our daily experiences for its visual insight into an image of man — where he came from and where he is going.

Perhaps the artist's philosophic statement can help us to appreciate his work and, with a broader understanding of the powerful motivating force that has driven him (and some other sculptors), change the context in which familiar objects are seen anew. Charles Huntington is his name, and here is his statement:

In order to make sense out of my environment and to function in a hostile world, I must have something of a personal philosophy, a system by which I can understand, and through which, to a degree, manipulate my scene.

Basically, the only thing, or things, that can truly be changed is a relationship, or relationships. Man neither creates nor destroys matter or things, but he can rearrange and set up new or different relationships among them. Thus, the difference between the creatively aware person and one who is not is simply that the aware individual realizes that every action or word produces a revised association between objects, people, or events.

Therefore, visual "creation" depends upon the artist's ability to see and judge relationships; the measure of success of a visually creative individual is the extent to which he is able to see and judge these relationships that he has produced. Evaluation is not made on the ideal of "good" and "bad" so much as on whether it is useful, harmful, or irrelevant to the intended message.

The use of the found object or "junk" seems natural for me since any medium can be valid. The exercised taste in execution is of greater importance than the object itself. By my training and acquired aptitude the workability of metal seems attractive. Even more, the material that has already served one function, that of utilitarian usefulness, can be re-used to set up a different kind of relationship, an aesthetic association, a new function. In this way, for me, a true metamorphosis has taken place.

I make sculpture as statements of relationships. Relationships within — part to part, positive to negative space, texture to texture, plane to plane. These are within the work of art itself. Then, on the outside are others, the whole, to the maker and the viewer; the communicator to the recipient, and thus to the total perceived environment.

With this sense of the sculptor's purpose the products of his craft can be examined more sensitively. It should be remembered that for him the objects themselves have only a secondary position in his hierarchy of values. He has utilized the prefabricated forms as he might clean untouched sheets of metal as his medium of expression. Fabrication of a new concept, or — as the artist described his problem — a new relationship, is not an easy task. It is not an unmixed "blessing" to work with parts that have already been shaped, especially when these shapes have firmly fixed associations. The artist must break down these associations at the outset and keep them from rebounding into his new set of conceptions. The ax head, gear segment, or steel wheel hub, must be disassociated from its relationship with its former employment and purpose. It has to be considered as a chunk of metal, a shaped slab tapered to points, a crescent-curved form with an orderly patterned row of cuts, or a circle with radiating bars of lines.

9-27
Charles Huntington.
Trophy.

There is also a risk with the spectator. The recollection of former associations could insert itself so strongly upon the perceptions of the viewer that the new relationships could be obscured and even missed entirely. There is a tendency to become enamored of the piece of furnace grating or engine manifold and to stop at this point. The artist knows this, but he feels that it is part of his function to open up the awareness of the viewer for the discovery of new forms and associations to replace the old ones.

When the prongs of a hand cultivator, portions of furnace grate, and miscellaneous castings had been redefined by the artist, the title *Trophy* (Fig. 9-27) suggested the panorama of images that could come forward for the viewer. This carefully structured and organized selection of fragments that have meanings out of past experience projects a fresh set of associations when their context and relationship to each other has been transformed; now we receive an image of the proud "hunter" and his mounted trophies. Depending upon our personal attitudes and inclinations, a commentary on values can be identified – the collection of discarded "junk" could be a revealing view of trophy collection in general and much that goes with this activity.

The sculptor's perception of an agricultural implement, a rotary hoe, is intensified by combining it with segments of a steel wheel and a steel grating for a base. The observer receives an abstracted expression of *Aggression* (Fig. 9-28). The rotary blades have a quality of frozen motion. We known that, if it were released, the mechanism would be able to cut, tear, and rip its vengeful way through any obstacle.

9-28
Charles Huntington.
Aggression.

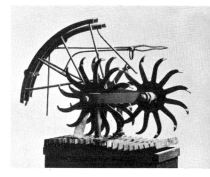

Prisoner (Fig. 9-29), *Zen Tree* (Fig. 9-30), and *Archangel* (Fig. 9-31) consist of seemingly unrelated units that bring us subtle, yet recognizable, symbols that have no connection with the former association we have had with the source material. The works have a quiet dignity; the inanimate object-parts out of which they have been created have been given a spirit that is alive and growing.

Winged, Plumed Serpent (Fig. 9-32) has the power to evoke memory images and recollections from mythology. Although we are far removed

9-29
Charles Huntington.
The Prisoner.

9-30
Charles Huntington.
Zen Tree.

9-31
Charles Huntington.
Archangel.

from the ancient Aztecs, they still stir us to imagine and dream and even to make up our own explanations for things that we cannot explain in terms of our own experience. It does not matter that our imagination has been triggered by the juxtaposition of a piece of a corn planter, a grate, or a harness for a horse. The sculptor with "found" materials, when successful, touches them with a special kind of magic that transforms the ordinary into the extraordinary.

HISTORY AND HERITAGE IN THE ARTS

The heritage of art products, materials, and methods serves each new generation of artists and prepares them to take a place in the vocation which they have selected. This resource from the past is employed by the artist selectively according to his interests and for purposes which he feels are valid. He may reinvestigate themes that have been explored by others; he may adapt a compositional arrangement established by an earlier master and bring it up to date with the symbolic trappings of his own time. The artist takes principles and styles that are already established and extends them beyond their original limits; neoclassicism, Neodadaism and postimpressionism owe a great deal to the old which preceded the new. Older techniques and processes, such as the lost-wax process, are rediscovered after being lost for many years.

In Chinese and Japanese painting, copying the works of revered artists of the past was traditionally an accepted practice. This was done not for literal imitations, but in order to gain true insight, as well as an aesthetic experience, by understanding nature through the work of art.

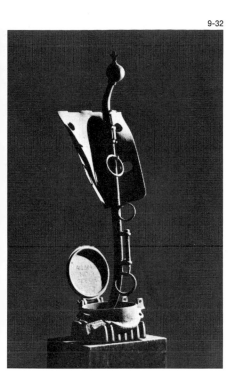

9-32

9-33

9-32
Charles Huntington.
Winged, Plumed Serpent.

9-33
Saul Baizerman. Nike.
1949–52. Walker Art Center,
Minneapolis.

The painter learned the various ways of rendering the principal features of landscape art — the typical strokes for mountains, trees, and water; however, the test of artistry and quality lay in the painter's ability to transmit a unique personal reaction to a given subject.

In Western art, where the students were trained in the studios of the masters, much was learned from copying the works of the master and from studying the drawings of earlier craftsmen. Established themes growing out of religion and mythology were repeated again and again by new generations of painters and sculptors. Although the methods of art training have changed and the master-apprentice system is no longer used to bring a number of students together in a studio or workshop, there nevertheless has been a persistence to learn by copying and studying masterworks. Now it is necessary to go to the museum or exhibition hall in order to find materials for study.

There are numerous examples of how sources from the history of art have been employed by the artist to act as a positive influence upon his personal expression. The acquaintance of young painters in France with the wood blocks and prints from Japan affected the styles they developed; observations of primitive sculptures and those from the classical period of Greece are clearly discernible influences in the work of Picasso and in the painting and sculpture of the first part of the twentieth century; Henry Moore has admitted the value and influence of pre-Columbian art and other historic periods in his own work. Many other examples can be found of solutions made by artists of the past and their influence upon artists of our time in a manner that is sensible, sensitive, and uniquely personal when applied in the new situation (Fig. 9-33).

SOCIAL INTERACTION

The artist, in his work and the manner of its production, is affected by the culture to which he belongs. When we are classifying activities as "cultural," it is not by accident that art is placed at the head of the list. Art provides a record of how men have responded to their environment and interacted with their fellowmen. In this cultural context, from the beginning of civilization to the present, art has been created for many social purposes and has been a visual statement of social customs, traditions, and values.

During the past century and a half there has been a dramatic change with regard to the kind of social commentary many artists have wished to make. This is seen in the subject matter they have selected and in the intentions of their work. These men have dealt with mass catastrophe, man's inhumanity to man, poverty, and strife and have sought to make socially significant statements in hopes that action would be taken to remedy flaws in their society. Their statements have been direct and emotional. They were offered with a sensitivity that they hoped would carry over to the observers of their work. Goya, Daumier, and Manet pointed out the conditions of their times (Figs. 9-34, 9-35). The Mexican revolutionary painters Rivera, Orozco, and Siqueiros employed their art for protest and social reform. Social realists on the American art scene before World War II covered the panorama of life in a time of stress in a manner that could be recognized clearly by their audience.

9-35
Edouard Manet.
The Execution of Maximilian.
Städtische Kunsthalle, Mannheim.

9-36
Gustave Courbet.
The Stone Breakers. 1849.
Formerly, Dresden Gemäldegalerie
(destroyed in 1945).

9-37
Henri de Toulouse-Lautrec.
At the Moulin Rouge.
Art Institute of Chicago.

9-38
Pierre-Auguste Renoir.
Luncheon of the Boating Party.
Phillips Collection, Washington, D.C.

Other artists of this same period saw the activities of their fellow-men in a gay, joyful mood with less intensity and insistence upon reform. From them we have a record of men at work and play which is descriptive of their time and social conditions. (Figs. 9-36–9-38). In recent years artists have held up for inspection the objects of mass production, the possessions we seem to value. This visual panorama of our times is presented in a fashion which is direct and bigger than life and serves as a mirror in which we can examine ourselves and judge the worth of our system of values (Figs. 9-39, 9-40).

THE ARTIST LOOKS WITHIN HIMSELF

In the twentieth century psychology has made us aware of the "inner world" of the unconscious and subconscious. For some who paint, the internal workings of the mind have replaced the external forces of the physical environment as a source of subject matter. Their methods have tested the comprehension of those who look at their art products. The viewer has reservations about whether inkblots, torn bits of paper, or paint dropped on surfaces to form random or chance combinations should be taken seriously as art even when the artists hoped that these configurations would suggest images from the deep recesses of their own minds.

Because of this extreme of spontaneity, chance, and automatic painting of uncontrolled images, the surrealists have changed their techniques. They put their images down on the canvas surface with photographic

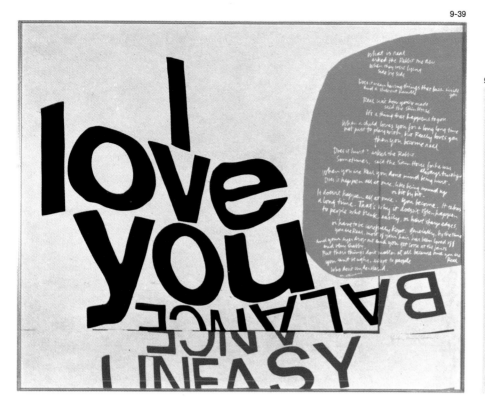

"EXTREMISM IN DEFENSE OF LIBERTY, IS NO VICE"

clarity and precision. This method is not revolutionary, but it is claimed that the images come spontaneously and are related to unconscious experience. The surrealists claim that their representations on paper and canvas are photographs of their thoughts, desires, dreams, and memories of childhood.[6] In the process, ambiguous and, at times, fantastic worlds are created; although the scene may appear to be conventional, there are often some details which have no logical connection with others.

Artists who have emphasized this principle of automatism have resorted to this method for the purpose of bringing forth what has been described as "the real working of the mind." The images are dictated by the unconscious In the absence of any control exercised by reason and free from aesthetic or moral preoccupations. The images presented by the surrealists are quite different from those of the abstract expressionists, who also work by automatic responses.

Automatism seems quite mysterious until it is related to jazz improvisation, stream of consciousness in fiction, the doodling of the layman, and the psychological tests in which the subject responds on cue by stating the first thing that comes into his mind. When the artist engages in this activity, his previous training and focus upon composition and organization, as well as his commitment to good taste, will control and play a part in what eventually comes through.

9-39
Sister Mary Corita. I Love You. *Serigraph. Collection of Mr. and Mrs. Jay Roach.*

9-40
Robert Hodgell. Extremism in Defense of Liberty is No Vice. *(Courtesy The Little Gallery, Plainfield, Iowa.)*

---

[6] Alfred H. Barr, Jr., **Fantastic Art, Dada, Surrealism**, Museum of Modern Art, New York, 1936.

Many artists state that they begin their work without an image or plan in mind and just draw or paint according to impulse. What is important is that the marks they make help them to see figures of objects, and on seeing them they are encouraged and strengthened, so that they work consciously to give order to their compositions. It often happens that what might have started as uncontrolled exercises takes on the character of a structurally controlled composition. The images may remain abstract, or they may be refined to become more descriptive of objects and events of visual perception.

The painting *Ships and Rocks* (Fig. 9-41) is a good example of how what started as a series of intuitively placed chunks of color was given the recognizable order of a familiar piece of scenery. The painter had, according to impulse, placed a number of strokes of color across a clean surface of heavy watercolor paper with a palette knife. Then the definition of the composition was established with a brush; the painter had no intention of doing a harbor scene until the marks on the paper suggested such a subject. The person who looks at the finished painting has no reason to think that the painter did not start out to render a view of Monterey, Vancouver, or the New England coastline with water, rocks, and boats. Imaginative art without recognizable subject matter, whether pleasant or unpleasant, familiar or unfamiliar, is highly subjective and therefore somewhat more difficult for the outside viewer to understand or accept.

When the artist sets out to present his feeling about his subject, rather than the perceptual features of it, the result will incorporate a great deal from his inner personal world. A stage beyond this is the kind of art in which the producer chooses to render his expressive images in non-representational form. For the spectator the customary and direct frame of reference is absent; he has been given in its place a visual equivalent of the emotional experience itself. For the artist, the process is one of complete personal contact and involvement in the act and action of creating by changing, destroying, and rebuilding. The formation of his images eventually came through. The creator stopped when he felt his was "right."

9-41
Ships and Rocks.

9-42
Milltown.

9-41   9-42

Many artists — Paul Klee, Joan Miró, and Marc Chagall, to name a few — have employed recollections of their childhood years as the content of their art expressions (Fig. 9-43). Sometimes these memories of things long past consciously or unconsciously take the form of symbols in the mature expressions of the painter or sculptor. The past seeps into the present for the artist as it does for others and influences his expression in a manner of which he is quite unaware. The painting *Milltown* (Fig. 9-42) demonstrates this. The painter started with quite modest aspirations — to make a direct statement of the structural complexity inherent in the industrial development of the Midwest. The grain mills — Pillsbury, General Mills, and all the rest — were once the symbols of progress in that area of the country. Looking now at the finished works, it seems clear, at least to the painter, that the grain mills of the Midwest have taken on the "look" of other mills and industrial complexes he has known. The predominant color and the repeated cylindrical forms have as much to do with the memories of childhood as the general local environment of the present. The painter had no overt intention of giving his work the color and pattern of blast furnaces and open-hearth furnaces lighting up the night skies of his childhood memories, but somehow they are there.

9-43
Marc Chagall. I and My Village.
Museum of Modern Art, New York.

TOWARD THE UNKNOWN

Through his art man sought to explain the unexplainable as his emotional attitude toward the universe evolved from magic and animism. His art has reflected his humanness as he sought an agent for controlling those natural phenomena over which his control was limited — birth, life, and death. The form of his art was designed to express the artist's own personality, and it gave a visible presence, which served as a visual reminder to his people, of celestial authority and the intelligible nature of their deities. It satisfied his need to come to terms with things he did not understand; it helped to make the strange familiar and to bring him closer to his "gods."

The art of primitive man existed as a function of worship and ritual. It helped him to appease the unseen spirits and his fears of things he did not understand in the external world. He hoped that in this way he could affect the course of his existence. There was very little essential difference in this respect between primitive men in the societies of East and West. Questions of birth and death were expressed in his art up to the time these cultures started to become quite sophisticated. Beginning with the fertility images of Stone Age man, the mystery of birth was the subject of the sculptured objects of the Aztec and of tribal groups of Guinea, Ghana, and the remote Pacific islands. Ceremonial masks were used by tribal societies in Africa, by the Northwest Indians of the United States, and by the peoples of the South Pacific (Figs. 9-44—9-46). Art connected with ceremonies for the dead has given us the wall paintings of the tombs at Thebes and Chinese ceremonial vessels, and it can be traced in artifacts from the Zapotec culture of North America to the African cultures of the Ivory Coast.

9-44   9-45

9-44
Mask worn by master of initiation ritual during circumcision rites.
Suku Kakunga mask.
Musée Royal de l'Afrique Centrale,
Tervueren, Belgium.

9-45
Used in protective magic.
Songye male figure.
Musée Royal de l'Afrique Centrale,
Tervueren, Belgium.

9-46
Ancestor figure
from Admiralty Islands, Melanesia.
Early twentieth century.
Museum für Völkerkunde,
Munich.

9-47
Buddha,
Tam Yang,
Korea.

CONTENT: COMMUNICATION THROUGH ART   309

We are impressed by the images of Apollo, Buddha, and Christ as the artist has created these images as a gesture honoring his gods (Fig. 9-47). The highest attainments of classic art, Christian art, and the art of the Middle Ages and beyond have been dependent upon man's search for meaning in his religion. These images depicted how the scale of transcendental values reflected the beliefs of his culture. Religious architecture has provided lasting monuments that have brought to us aesthetic satisfaction and some understanding of how works of art can transcend time and the boundaries of religious beliefs. The ethic which man has used to control the conduct of his life is expressed in buildings that are separated from one another in space and time — the Parthenon, the monastic churches on the pilgrimage route, and the cathedrals of France and Italy (Fig. 9-48). Although for the last four or five hundred years art and religion have not been so closely related, there are still examples of how spiritual sensibilities can affect the work of an artist. Matisse's murals (1951) for the Rosary Chapel in France and Le Corbusier's Notre-Dame-du-Haut (1950–1955) at Ronchamp, France, are examples of how inspired artists can meaningfully symbolize their beliefs (Fig. 9-49).

It has been said that good science and good art are dedicated to the exploration of the unknown. Discoveries and scientific developments in the twentieth century include man's exploration into the unknown reaches of space and his investigations of the small world of the atom, as well as his search for the components of living cells. The artist by intuition has attempted to supply visual equivalents for the forces and forms that cannot be seen directly through our sensory perceptions. Related to either science or religion, the artist's search for and vision of the unknown continues to occupy a place of importance in the artistic expressions of the age and the culture to which he belongs.

SUMMARY OF THE VIEW OF CONTENT

This analysis from the viewpoint of the artist about the content of art — what art has been about — has been treated under the various headings for the convenience of the reader. Taken together, they give a comprehensive view of the different categories of the artist's response to his environment and are not mutually exclusive divisions, as any particular work of a given artist might conceivably overlap from one area into another. The purpose has been to demonstrate how the artist's concern for content and meanings will often initiate his action and, to a degree, determine the final emphasis in his work. The source of the feelings and ideas of the artist has centered around: (1) his interests in nature; (2) the tools of his craft; (3) the man-made objects in his environment; and (4) a review of the heritage which has come to him from other artists in the history that is available for him. Other sources are (5) what the artist gains from his interactions with his fellowmen in the social order which they have built and (6) the resources to be found when he looks within himself or extends the boundaries of his vision into the unknown. From these sources he draws inspiration and help for the preparation of a visual statement which represents his response to his environment.

9-48
Cologne Cathedral, west façade.
1248.

9-49
Le Corbusier.
Notre-Dame-du-Haut,
Ronchamp. 1955.

Chapter 10

FROM THE ARTIST TO HIS AUDIENCE

A famous definition of the process of art by Tolstoy provides a good description of the exchange that takes place between the artist and the spectator. It is given in the following:

> *To evoke in oneself a feeling one has experienced, and having evoked it in oneself, then by means of movement, line, color, sounds or forms expressed in words, so to transmit that feeling that others experience the same feeling — this is the activity of art.*
>
> *Art is a human activity consisting in this, that one man consciously, by means of certain external signs, hands on to others feelings he has lived through and that others are infected by these feelings and also experience them.*

CREATING THE WORK OF ART

The three preceding chapters were introduced with a case study of the creative action (Metamorphosis I), which showed how three aesthetic factors — matter, form, and meaning — had been interrelated at stages of the art process from its inception to the tentative conclusion of the artist's work. Each of these three elements involved in the creation of a work of art, which when combined would elicit an aesthetic response from the people who look at the end product, were discussed in detail. It is now our objective to make a transition from the artist to his audience — from what is involved in the production of a work of art to what is involved in looking at it and experiencing the feelings and meanings the artist put into it.

We have stated that the incept for the creation of art can come from anything; it may be exceptional or very ordinary. There are differences of opinion about whether (1) the incept holds and acts as a control, directing the artist's effort until the work has been terminated; or (2) the controlling agent is something that exists prior to the process; or (3) it is the final goal toward which the process aims. Also, the matter of how the artist knows when to stop can be summarized by stating that the artist generally knows when he is finished, but this does not mean that the work itself is finished.[1]

With this demarcation of a beginning and an end we are left with a lot that goes on in the middle. The work has gotten under way by the motivational spark of a tentative commitment to some initiating force. The process moves by stages through a series of evaluations and decisions. There are reevaluations and decisions based on weighing what has been done against what might have been done. Each addition that is made changes the set of alternatives for decision making. Whenever a new stroke, color, or chunk of metal is added, or when some of the original mass is deleted, the artist is provided with a whole set of circumstances in which he must make decisions. He must decide what is not satisfying, or satisfactory, and what does not fit in with the rest of his composition at each stage of the unfinished work.

---

[1] Monroe C. Beardsley, **On the Creation of Art**, *Journal of Aesthetics and Art Criticism*, vol. 23, no. 3 (Spring, 1965), pp. 291 304.

Such a process of trial and test, or trial and adjustment, makes it all sound very chancy and very complex. For the person engaged in the action it does not seem very complicated or mysterious. In fact, he does not mark off each decision, but follows a rhythmic action which "feels right." Periods of frustration are taken in stride and often accepted as normal encounters. They are "part of it all" — troublesome, yet necessary — as an idea takes an objective form out of materials. From their personal experience with painting, sculpture, and jewelry design, the authors feel that those achievements which have been judged their most successful were, with few exceptions, carried through from start to finish in a fairly straight-line progression. Although adjustments were made along the way and the decisions made contributed to the work, there was steady progress directly toward a satisfactory final product. In these cases the process was intuitive and swift; the finished product had qualities of decisiveness and the sureness of its execution was evident.

SKILL OF EXECUTION

There is general acceptance of the fact that a necessary attribute of quality in works of art is the skill displayed in their execution. Unfortunately, the concept of skill has often been limited to the artist's ability to manipulate his materials and to control his technical processes. Certainly, this is exceedingly important, even essential. But time and again we have seen that technical virtuosity alone "gets one nowhere."

There are factors that contribute to the confusions that occur with reference to skill as an ingredient of artistic excellence. The display of technical skill is more easily recognizable to the general observer than other factors when he looks at a finished work. He understands what technical skill is and has enough references from his past experiences to make it familiar for him, even if other aspects of the art product are strange. He feels confident in his judgment and is disturbed when an art product does not display skill as measured on his own yardstick. He thinks of "skill" as a single item — one thing — rather than as a combination of separate and different skills. This technical, manipulative skill is only a small part of the roster of abilities and competencies which unite to form what we refer to as the artist's skill of execution. From the previous discussion of artistic behavior it is evident that at least four broad areas of skills, abilities, or competencies are required for the skillful execution of a work of art. There are: (1) technical skill; (2) structuring abilities or the ability to organize; (3) evaluative competencies; and (4) the ability to express meaning. It should also be noted that perceptual ability makes a contribution to each of these.

TECHNICAL SKILL

For the working artist skill in handling his chosen media is an unquestionable essential. It allows him to act with confidence, surety, and speed; this confidence in his own technical skill enables him to devote his attention to other things. When he is in technical command, he has the basis for developing variations from routine practices. He can do the kind of exploration that is essential for him to get the most from his medium for his expressive needs. We know from psychologists that there are efficient methods for learning skills. In learning skills, repetition and practice are important. Learning the skill as a whole is more effective than breaking it down into component parts and learning these part by part. Spaced practice sessions over a longer period of time are more effective than long sessions crammed into a short time span. These skill learnings are based upon drill and spaced repetition and usually move from simple to complex in an orderly fashion. In this area experience has a direct bearing upon one's improvement as a practitioner.

Intimate knowledge of the medium or the technical process in which it is employed places the artist in command. He can make judgments about his own strengths and weaknesses. Also, he can decide what medium and what method of technical manipulation of the medium will best serve his purpose. This eliminates much waste effort; he can make it an efficient tool for the accomplishment of his particular goals. He knows when process and media have been extended to their limits and that movement beyond this point will result in diminishing returns. Judgment of this is important and will make him both efficient and effective. Frustrations are avoided. He is not placed in the position of frustration that is experienced by many children when they reach the point where their technical abilities are judged insufficient for presenting their ideas and feelings in the form of art.

Must all of the technical aspects of the creative production be done by the artist personally if the product is to bear his signature? Can he entrust some parts of it to skilled technicians and still claim it as his own work? Historically there have been many different attitudes toward what should be done by the artist with his own hands and energy.

We have many examples of creative artists who have entrusted certain parts of their art production to technicians. We know that in many cases the final bronze casting of many pieces of sculpture has been made in a foundry by someone other than the artist from his model in wax or plaster. Lithographs by quite famous artists have been printed by others without detracting from their value to collectors. We also know of cases in which the wood blocks and plates are not prepared by the artist himself. Many professional artists prefer to do all of the work themselves. They feel that there is a personal and creative quality that might be obtained in the casting and printing processes. When these are performed by the artist himself, the result has more personal integrity and a greater degree of personal creative expression.

There have also been instances in which the parts for a sculpture have been ordered to specifications from a metal supplier and then assembled by the artist; tapestries have been woven and glass has been engraved from the artist's sketches. These examples are not intended to cast doubts on the importance of the artist or on his integrity. They point out the variations in our attitude toward certain aspects of technical skill and process as absolute essentials in the creation of a work of art.

Individuals were once acclaimed for certain technical capacities, such as the ability to draw a straight line perfectly or to make a precise circle with pen or brush. For many, the training required seemed wasted and redundant since there were tools available for obtaining a perfect straight line or an exact circle with speed and accuracy. A straightedge or tape, carefully applied and then removed, is used to obtain clean-cut edges when spraying paint on an automobile. The same procedures can provide straight lines in a painting. A compass or round object can be used in the delineation of a true circle. The hard edge of the circle itself is not as important as knowing where to place it and what color and texture it should have.

STRUCTURING ABILITIES

The ability for organizing or structuring as part of the total skillful execution of an art product is a complex or composite of related skilled actions. Unlike the manipulative skill, it is not a process of development from the simple to the complex. Rather, it involves the individual's ability to take in a complicated assortment of perceptual data and to reduce and simplify this into the kind of image we call art by careful placement of the subsidiary forms he has selected. When the artist works in the opposite direction — starting with the basic shape or form and then, by an additive process, building related forms around his initial starting point — the process might be said to go from the simple to the complex. But this is a complexity of intricate relationships of simple forms rather than a complexity based on the elaboration of one shape by making its contour more uneven or its surface more textured.

This organizing or composing ability distinguishes the quality of one man's effort from that of another. It requires the ability to apply previously experienced structural plans derived from nature or from the individual's heritage of experience with art and the works of other artists.

From his inspection of natural forms the artist can be guided by the example of how quite complex final structures are held together by the repetition of very simple units according to a systematic plan. In nature the overall plan could be radiation from a central core, a branching out from a vertical or horizontal axis, a spiral of biologic growth, or the addition almost indefinitely of units having the same basic shape. This organizational plan found in nature can be applied to composition in art.

In other times an awareness of compositional plans used by other artists served in a similar fashion as a reference base in the organization of painting, sculpture, and architecture. This should assist rather than hinder the individual from developing creatively with a personal uniqueness of expression. Basic compositional plans or motifs — pyramidal, elliptical, spiral, vertical, and horizontal repetition — have been employed in different centuries for quite different expressive purposes. Sometimes the structure of the work is not obvious to the spectator; at other times, an easily identifiable scheme is presented boldly to the viewer. The pyramidal scheme gives a solid base and leads the eye to the apex for a focus upon the center of emphasis. The cohesion of the radial plan, with spokes moving outward, or of the spiral or axial plan provides rhythmic movements of action. These organizational plans have a visual vitality consistent with the needs of the artist and typical of the period in which they evolved.

During certain historic periods a structural motive was sometimes followed by preference and expressed the dominating spirit of the time. For example, the stability of the pyramid and the repetition of triangles has been related to the earlier Renaissance tradition and often appeared in the religious art of the time (Fig. 10-1). The spiral form, characteristic of Rubens, produced a more dynamic rhythm that was expressive of the time when there was a desire to break away from the more static compositions in painting and architecture of the Renaissance artists and builders. The works of many artists have been analyzed in detail by art historians and others to show the structural plan of their compositions. This has been done with the idea of aiding the understanding and appreciation of the spectator. The composition and painting of some artists, such as Cézanne, Picasso, and Matisse, have been the subject of analysis to a point where "too much is more than enough" and the visual qualities of their artistic expression have become submerged in academic exercises.

Composition for the artist requires: (1) the careful selection of key units; (2) the placement of these in appropriate relationships to each other and to the total picture-plane space or the three dimensional space of sculpture; and then (3) the adjustment of the secondary elements for emphasis, directional movement, and unity. The final unity in the composition had to be consistent with the kind of rhythmic pattern that meets the needs of the idea or feeling to be communicated. These are skills of a high order that demand of the artist subtlety and readiness to make judgments. This is where a background of design-oriented experiences is required, including a working knowledge of "what goes with what," not only in perception but also in terms of artistic organization, plus disciplined judgments of "what is primary and what is secondary." Training in the act of perception plus knowledge of and experience with the ways of artistic order are essential. In this action the individual is able to bring together the best of his past experiences of looking at art and nature for a particular purpose identified with the special problem under consideration.

COMPETENCIES FOR EVALUATING

It has been remarked previously that the person engaged in art activity is involved from the outset with a continuous evaluation of his best course of action. As each new color or form is added, a decision must be made on the relative merits of the new choice and its appropriateness in terms of the relationships the artist has already established. The decisions are many. For example: What color works best for this purpose? Should a shape be placed here or there? Does it need to be larger or smaller, textured or untextured? After making one decision, he is then forced to evaluate the alternative courses of action for the next appropriate step.

In this ever-changing situation the artist must be able to stand up to the fact that there are many alternative courses of action in his search for the optimum, not only for the moment, but of the predictable eventuality of his product. When ambiguous choices of this nature are present, he must be able to work within this system of ambiguity. He must accept the knowledge that one choice might or might not be overwhelmingly better than another. He must know that the decision made at any one

10-1
Raphael. Sistine Madonna.
1513. Gemäldegalerie, Dresden.

point could lead to the validation or failure of his art activity. He must also be able to accept a decision that means the restructuring or readjustment of parts that he has already accomplished. This could mean the destruction of some "special" part of the composition that he "loved dearly" — that looked very good to him, but did not fit in with the rest. These are hard decisions to make, but quite often they have to be made rapidly if progress is to be made.

The artist's ability to evaluate is based largely on his previous experience and on that of others whom he has observed. He needs this frame of reference against which a decisive change can be made with confidence in the outcome.

This backlog of experience and knowledge provides the frame of reference against which any separate decision during the course of the work can be made with assurance. It is hardly a formal system, in which the positive features are lined up on one side and the negative features lined up on the other. Only on rare occasions is there a slow intellectual weighing of alternatives. During the work process one generally employs an intuitive rather than a highly logical analysis. The work proceeds fairly smoothly, although at intervals there must be a pause to survey the whole work as it has progressed. This is a time of careful assessments and of weighing alternatives more carefully. This is done by stepping back and becoming somewhat removed from involvement; a look is taken from outside, more or less as the spectator would. Sometimes the work in progress is approached in a more contemplative way; its weaknesses are assessed and its strengths are noted. Through this process the work develops in progressive stages and moves according to evaluation.

In the following precise description by a practicing artist of his own painting procedure, Matisse [2] explained how each succeeding addition of elements to his canvas prompted a new set of decisions and an entirely different set of relationships upon which his decisions had to be made.

> If on a clean canvas, I put at intervals patches of blue, green and red, with every touch that I lay on, each of those put there previously loses in importance. Say I have to paint an interior; I see before me a wardrobe; it gives me very vividly a sensation of red, and so I put on a red which satisfies me. A relation is established between this red and the white of the canvas. When I put on besides a green, when I represent the floor by a yellow, between this green and this yellow and the canvas there will be still further relations. But these different tones mutually diminish each other. It is necessary that the various tones which I use should be balanced in such a way that they do not destroy one another. To secure that I have to put my ideas into order; the relationship between the tones will establish itself in such a way that it builds them up instead of knocking them down. A new combination of colors will succeed to the first one and will give the wholeness of my conception. I am obliged to transpose, so it will look as though my picture has totally changed if, after successive modification, the green in it has replaced the red as the dominant tone.

COMPETENCIES RELATED TO EXPRESSION OF MEANING

This area of competency is also a composite of individual skills and abilities. The meaning of his work concerns the producer even before a mark is placed on canvas or one piece of metal is welded to another. Eventually this meaning will be achieved through the artist's ability to coordinate the demands of his process and its materials with the structural devices which he has selected as he directs materials and structural form toward the idea he wishes to convey. This idea sometimes maintains the form of its original inception and at other times changes as the work progresses.

From the sources available to him, the artist either borrows symbols or is in the process of inventing new ones. Judgment and selectivity are required in order to discover which are best for his purpose. The symbols

---

2 From *Notes d'un Peintre* contributed by Matisse to a French review in 1908. These were reported in Herbert Read, **The Meaning of Art**, Pitman Publishing Corporation, New York, 1931, pp. 193–194.

10-3

10-2
Henry Moore.
Reclining Mother and Child.
1960–61. Walker Art Center,
Minneapolis.

10-3
Henry Moore.
Mother and Child with Apple.
Collection of Ruth and Edward Weiss.

10-4
Toltec culture. Chacmool.
Minneapolis Institute of Arts.

10-4

used by the artist may not be particularly new or original, as is the case with Henry Moore's use of the symbolic theme of the mother and child or, in other works, of the reclining figure (Figs. 10-2, 10-3). Examination of his works indicates that in each new one he maintains the basic theme, yet endeavors to express a somewhat different meaning through each. He has also borrowed liberally from sources of his own selection. He owed a great deal to pre-Columbian sculpture, particularly the Chacmool (Rain Spirit), from Chichén Itzá of the Mayan New Empire (Fig. 10-4). This

10-5
*Pablo Picasso.
Monkey and Her Baby.
Minneapolis Institute
of Arts*

previously established symbol provided the direction for his work and the ideas and feelings he wished to convey.

The mother and child combination is an established theme that has tempted artists for hundreds of years, from the time of primitive man until the present. However, each new artist has brought his own particular brand of experience and meaning to this age-old theme. The problem is not to draw a woman holding a child but to embody in this symbolism the expressive meaning desired. Many have succeeded in giving this imagery a quality of mood and passion or by their treatment of it have achieved classic simplicity, weight, and strength. The result has been a series of personal variations which were dependent upon the artist's ability to evoke meaning through the particular way he has interrelated his process and materials, structural devices, and the meaning that he wished to evoke (Figs. 10-5–10-7).

One of the artist's problems in regard to the expression of meaning arises from the fact that quite often the same superficial subject matter or content can be treated at different times in such a way that it has quite different symbolic meaning for the observer. This is the artist's choice. Meaning is derived not so much from the symbol itself as from the context and treatment which it is given by the artist. Let us take again the example of the theme of the mother and child. It is a theme which has occurred for thousands of years. It has been used to exemplify fertility, love, protectionism, defense of the home, despair, defiance, independence, and dependence, to name only a few. Primitive man used this theme as a fertility symbol to beg favors from his god; in Western religious art it became the expression of man's adoration and love.

For the artist who wishes to use this theme there are many alternatives. Some artists have wished only to describe or put down a portrait of a particular mother and a particular child. Others have used the same subject matter to characterize all mothers and all children as an ideal standard of behavior. Some have not been interested in describing or characterizing, but have been intent upon treating the subject in a decorative manner, accenting the shapes and colors of their subject. It has sometimes been treated more in terms of the artist's feelings (as in the case of the expressionists) instead of as it might appear in direct observation. To this end the paint was applied and the colors were selected according to their impact upon the emotions of the artist and for their effect upon the emotions of the observer. Pain and passion, love and serenity, were felt and shown. Other artists have become interested in the rhythmical curving and enfolding movement and have stressed this; others have chosen to explode their subject matter, to take the volumes and planes apart and rearrange them into what the artist considered a meaningful and expressive construction; our best examples of this method are the analytical cubism of Bracque and Picasso (see Fig. 8-1).

In each instance, the meaning to be expressed and the artist's skill in obtaining it were directing forces which determined how the materials would be manipulated and their structural arrangement on the canvas or in the finished work of the sculptor. For some artists, expression is not to be found in a violent gesture or the inner life which radiates from a face. Their expressive meaning lies in the total composition of their picture or

10-6
Mbala female figure carrying child. Musée Royal de l'Afrique Centrale, Tervueren, Belgium.

10-7
Jacob Epstein. Madonna and Child. 1953. Convent of the Holy Child Jesus, Cavendish Square, London.

sculpture. Everything is important — the space occupied by the figures, the empty spaces around them, and in some cases the apertures, or holes, penetrating the figural space of painting or sculpture. Many artists have found expressive meaning in proportions of their figures, as in the case of El Greco or in the dynamic distortions of the physical proportions of figures and objects employed by some of our contemporary artists. Everything plays a part and helps bring to the spectator some of the qualities that the artist has hoped to evoke.

Expressive meaning is communicated to the observer through stylistic features and through the manner in which the creative artist has focused all of the means available to him upon the single unified concept of form. Depending upon the meaning he wishes to insert, the artist can emphasize those elements that are most appropriate. He can accomplish this objective by employing his knowledge of how other people are affected by the set of perceptual cues which he has incorporated into his imagery. He has an awareness, at least to some extent, of how certain configurations, colors, and rhythmical patterns can affect the spectator. He understands how moods may be communicated or emotions may be heightened by an accent that will give some parts of the design added strength or emphasis; by blending the familiar with the unexpected he can achieve a higher level of response and emotional involvement from the spectator.

Child art has this capacity for surprise. The adult observer who looks at the art products of young children with the expectancy of finding graphic portrayals that agree with his knowledge of objects and events as they occur according to his frame of reference is open for many surprises (Figs. 10-8–10-11). The artist, like the child, takes liberties with the observer's accustomed way of perceiving his world. This is accomplished through many channels — abstraction by simplification, distortion for emphasis, unexpected juxtapositions, unusual art treatment, and many more.

10-8–10-11
*Illustrations of
"effective surprise"
as found in child art.*

PERCEPTUAL ABILITIES

Within each of these areas of competence that have been enumerated — heightened technical skill, structuring ability, evaluation, and the ability to evoke a meaningful response — must be placed the artist's perceptual ability and training. Skillfulness of perception is required at every stage of the creative act from prior to its inception until the process has been culminated. Initially, the artist's perceptive skill helps him select and identify key units which are characteristic of his idea from the total of his perceptual data. His focusing and framing arrangements are brought into play, and he concentrates upon that which to him seems important. He also notes evidence of repetition of similar shapes or the concentration of directional movement toward a center of interest. He senses where accent or emphasis could work to the best advantage. In effect, what he is doing is similar to the procedures all of us use in practical vision in everyday living, but with more refinement and greater intensification. Part of his task was confined to taking advantage of the attention-getting factors of this practical vision and stressing these in order to reach the objective he had set for his product.

When work starts, the subject matter of perception changes for the artist from observation of the world to observation of the various resemblances in the constructed reality that make up the painting or sculpture. When this happens, perceptual ability and its refinement is of utmost importance for the artist. At this point it can help him to make the decision necessary in his construction of an equivalent of reality that will render his end product more effective for the spectator. The configural patterns observed in his original subject will now be simplified and emphasized and, in effect, reconstructed in his art product. The source may be recognized only to a minor degree. Nevertheless, without the data and clues from his initial perception of the real world the man-made structural arrangement of art would not have been possible.

In his perception of his work and in its progress, constant references are made to these original sources, and he is constantly engaged in making decisions or evaluations at progressive stages of production. Perceptive awareness allows him to make these decisions with greater confidence; references to his original source materials are balanced against the meaning which he hopes to project through his work. It thus becomes apparent that perceptual skill is an attribute that has an effect upon the artist's control and manipulation of his technical processes and materials, including (1) what he selects as important, shapes, colors, and textures; (2) how these are arranged and structured; and (3) which symbols and images are most expressive of the meaning that he has decided upon and has hoped to carry across to the spectator.

In summary, skill of execution should be considered as a composite of skills, abilities, and competences which have been directed toward the expression of feeling and the bringing forth of understanding for the observer. It has been emphasized that these are interlocked at different stages throughout the development of a work of art. Each separate aspect of skill, however important it may be for one artist at one time, is simply one of many within the complex. A display of usual technical skill might excite wonder and admiration, but unless this is combined with all of the other displays of skillfulness expected from the artist the purposes of art will not be fulfilled.

THE AUDIENCE FOR ART

Up to this point we have been concerned to a large extent with the process of art as experienced by the artist-producer. Attention has been directed toward how the artist looks at or perceives his world, and how he takes out of that perception those things which are important to him. We have then gone on to discuss how the artist has found a visual equivalent for his perception — how he has abstracted that which is important to him and in effect given it a distinct symbolic form. In this process he has employed his creative energies to build a design — an orderly structured arrangement of the art elements of line, tone, shape, color, and texture — that will convey his feelings and meaning to an observer. One might say that we have been observing the various forms of interaction between the artist and the art object that take place in the course of production as the work progresses. An interaction somewhat parallel to that between artist and art object takes place upon a different level when the product is seen by others not involved with its production.

When the work of art exists as a completed physical entity and is presented for the response of the viewer, its meaning and the feelings which it will evoke are dependent upon the receptive attitude of the viewer. His ability to perceive and understand the formal and expressive aspects of the object produced by the artist are fundamental to appreciation.

The artist works better when he has a sense of an audience. His work reaches its final level of value and purpose when it is in the presence of other people and is seen by them. For the producer there is a sense of value from the creative act; a great deal of personal satisfaction is felt by the artist during the process of creating the art object. The ultimate value of the work comes when others look at it and derive satisfaction from it, especially when they experience some of the emotive meaning given to the work by the artist.

Sensitivity to art — aesthetic appreciation — is present in most people and not restricted to a chosen few. This sensitivity to art is not dependent upon intellectual standing; previous experience with examining art is helpful, but the lack of it does not prevent a person from obtaining pleasure or satisfaction from an experience with art. Aesthetic satisfaction can be obtained when the spectator's attention is directed toward the object, when he gives it his full and undistracted attention. There should be a willingness on the part of this spectator to take the work of art at its face value with an open mind and without predetermined expectations of what it should look like or of how it should have been done.

The responsibilities of the artist in terms of the spectator are summarized by Matisse in the following:

> The thing is to direct the attention of the spectator in such a manner that he concentrates on the picture but thinks of anything

but the particular object which we have wished to paint, to detain him without embarassing him, to lead him to experience the quality of the sensation expressed.

And he goes on to say about the spectator:[3]

It is not necessary for the spectator to analyze — that would be to arrest his attention and not release it — and there is a risk of setting up analysis by a transposition that is carried too far. Ideally the spectator allows himself, without knowing it, to be engaged by the mechanism of the picture. One should guard against a movement of surprise on his part, even that which escapes his notice; one must hide the artifice as much as possible.

Throughout time the artist and his work have served various roles in the cultures to which they belong. Art visually represents the era in which it was produced. Thus art products have been a valuable source of information about cultures into the distant past. At the same time, knowledge of the cultural setting from which they came is a valuable source for a full understanding of the objects created by the artists.

THE ROLE OF THE ARTIST IN HIS CULTURE

The artist has served his tribe and its chiefs, his church and its priests, his people and their leaders — dukes, kings, merchants, and commissars. Finally, today, with certain exceptions, he has become more or less a free agent with only a token obligation to create his work for the public welfare or under restrictions from someone besides himself. As is true of scientists, there are probably more artists living and working today than there have been in all the rest of historic time.

The artist in primitive societies and in early civilizations probably received training as an apprentice in the skills and traditions of his craft from a master craftsman. The products by his hand were seen and used by his fellows for everyday pursuits and for ritual and ceremonial purposes. In Egypt and Greece the work done for palaces and temples was distinguished from the handicrafts, and the best artists were in the service of the state and its religion and government; many of the projects were intended for public display and had a large audience. Art required hand labor which was not held in high esteem in many ancient societies; the artists were not given much honor, although their work was appreciated. This attitude toward the artist who worked with his hands did not begin to change until the Middle Ages when religious art was executed by monks, whose religious orders included many noblemen.

The monasteries were great production centers for art. In them, books were written and decorated. In addition to manuscript illumination, both monks and skilled laymen produced works in metal, sculpture, and weaving, as well as church buildings and other architecture throughout Europe.

---

3 *Ibid.*, p. 194.

By the fifteenth century, as the artist began to concern himself with liberal and theoretical knowledge, he and his work were given greater dignity; the artist was raised above the artisan category and his work ranked with the scholarly pursuits of the liberal arts.

After the twelfth century there was the gradual transition from the making of art by monks in monasteries to production by artists outside the church in the city workshops. The support for art was broadened to include the middle class of merchants and tradesmen. There was an increased demand by people in urban centers for both religious and secular art. Guilds, or lodges, of artists were established, which gave the artist an amount of collective security. The guild set standards for membership and for craftsmanship. Members were given a measure of respectability, their welfare was protected, and they shared technical knowledge and the advantage of quality in tools and materials. Only a few of the most distinguished artists, such as Leonardo da Vinci, Michelangelo, Raphael, Titian, and Dürer, were able to break away and work independently. They achieved great success for themselves and recognition for their scholarly learning as well as their artistry.

Academies or clubs founded by outstanding artists provided organizations or schools in which younger members were given a definite educational program. This consisted in drawing from life and from plaster casts of sculpture and architectural fragments from antiquity, and in the study and copying of masterworks in the museum collections. The academies established in France, Italy, Holland, and England persisted through the nineteenth century. Although they had released the artist from guild domination, the academies were conservative in outlook and in their control of exhibitions and selling policies of works of art. The trend toward independence for the artist continued until it is now the accepted way.

Artists in Europe and North America now receive their training in professional art schools, in colleges and university art departments, or through self-teaching; they are to a large extent self-sufficient and not obligated to present a view of the world as others would have it. They are not expected to work for the satisfaction of a patron or for the intellectual pleasure of a few connoisseurs. The choice rests with the artist. The market for art products is extensive; it has been diversified to include a large part of the public. As long as he can withstand pressure from art dealers and critics, the artist has great personal freedom. He has the opportunity to make a significant contribution to his culture through the record of his personal search as he has been engaged with the values and experiences of modern life.

LOOKING AT THE WORK OF ART

Such a neutral sounding heading as "Looking at the Work of Art" brings to mind a number of questions which are quite difficult to answer in simple language and to the satisfaction of the reader. How and why does one look at a work of art? What should we obtain from this experience? These are only two of many questions which have been raised. Unfortunately, many strange misconceptions and a great deal of folklore have grown up about this very human activity. Consequently, there has often been the feeling that it is something reserved for a few special initiates who understand its mysteries rather than something that is open for all people.

There is agreement that one can obtain an aesthetic experience from looking at art. We can receive a kind of satisfaction from that experience which will affect us emotionally and sensitively. The aesthetic experience depends upon the perception of an object. The artist has made the object (and in this a painting may also be thought of as an object, just as we think of a work of sculpture, crafts, or architecture as objects). It is a situation in which someone looks as a spectator at what the artist has made. This is very much like any other act of perception, with the exception perhaps that the object was created for the purpose of having people look at it and derive a full measure of satisfaction from the experience.

The person who made the object, call him an artist, had looked at his environment and had reacted to the physical qualities he found in it by sensing the color, shape, surface, and mass of things. He selected what to him was important and arranged these into pleasing forms and patterns. This artist was at his best when he made his pattern or arrangement correspond with the state of feelings or emotions he had about his experience with his environment.

FREEDOM FOR THE VIEWER

Just as the artist had freedom to look at his world and take out what he felt was important, the viewer looking at the object which has been created has freedom to take out of it what is important for him. In this manner he can derive satisfaction from his sensitivity to what has been put in it by the artist. It has been said that an object or work of art is perceived by the spectator. "Perceived" is the crucial word in this statement. Do all people perceive the same thing when they look at a work of art? The answer is unquestionably in the negative. Taking our definition of perception as a sensation to which *we have given meaning*, the reasons for differences become apparent.

The viewer of art receives certain sensations of color, value, texture, shape, and mass. He then gives some meaning to these sensations. The meaning given is to a large extent dependent upon his past experiences and the meanings he has given to them. The past experiences or sensations of one person, as well as the meanings he gives them, are certainly different from those of another; neither their past experiences nor their interpretations of them have been the same. Thus the perceptions are colored by the associations the person makes with the total of his past experience when receiving visual sensations from looking at the art object. Although the visual sensation received from the work of art by many people may be the same or nearly so, the associations out of their past experiences can be expected to differ. In effect, they *do not see* the same thing at all. On this basis it is quite understandable that many divergent opinions are expressed about a single work of art. The creator (the artist) has control over the shape of his object, but has no control over how

10-12
Edgar Degas.
Portrait of Mlle. Valpinçon.
Minneapolis Institute of Arts.

others will see it. All art is not controversial. Quite often the differences among observers are slight, and there is a close similarity between what they have seen and the meanings they have given to it.

THE COMMUNICATION GAP

Art is a visual language and communication depends upon the speaker (artist) and the listener (viewer) having a common language composed of symbols and their arrangement. Even when people speak the same language, misunderstandings do occur. There is usually more agreement between what the artist has intended and what the spectators have received when there are enough common elements of association in the artist's work and experience with that of his audience. This is the case when the artist has chosen to make his work consistent with the expectations and values of his cultural group and when he has depicted images that are common to his own and his viewer's experience. The range of agreement is closer when the artist employs symbols or a mode of structural organization which is familiar to his viewers. A painting done in the style of "visual realism" has this familiarity because it presents symbols as they are seen by people in their daily contacts with the world.

A gap between the artist's intentions and the spectator's understanding occurs when strange symbols are employed and the way of organizing them by the artist is unfamiliar or open to ambiguous interpretations by the observer. In these situations the image making differs from the usual conceptual realities of the observer. Objects and shapes are made to exist in ways which are not clearly defined. They are formed into shapes, positions, and relationships that do not communicate experiences of the physical world which are common to both the producer and his audience.

10-13
Paul Cézanne.
Chestnut Trees at Jas De Bouffan.
Minneapolis Institute of Arts.

10-14
Paul Gauguin.
Under the Pandanus.
Minneapolis Institute of Arts.

The following excerpts from reviews of art exhibitions written by critics and journalists illustrate the gap that sometimes separates artist and audience: [4]

"This painting, at once vague and brutal, appears to us to be at the same time the affirmation of ignorance and the negation of the beautiful as well as the true."
"The impression produced by these men is that of a cat walking on a keyboard of a piano, or of a monkey which has run off with a paintbox."

The following excerpt describes the reactions of visitors to the gallery:

"There are some people who burst into laughter at the sight of these things — these self-styled artists take canvas, color and brushes, fling on a few tones at hazard and sign it. In the same way mental deficients pick up pebbles on the high road and think they are diamonds."

The work was described as follows:

"These must be seen to be imagined. They excite laughter, but should rather provoke grief. They denote ignorance of design, of composition, and of color. When children play with paper and paints, they do better than this."

These comparisons to work by monkeys who paint and to the art of children have a familiar and contemporary flavor; yet they do not refer to paintings and sculpture of the last twenty years by abstract expressionist or pop artists. These statements were made ninety years ago (1874–77) about works by Monet, Manet, Degas, Renoir, Cézanne, Pissarro, Sisley, and others (Figs. 10-12–10-14). The people who went to the exhibits were

10-15
Constant Troyon. Cattle.
Minneapolis Institute of Arts.

10-16
Frederick Edwin Church.
Scene in the Catskill Mountains.
1852. Walker Art Center,
Minneapolis.

---

[4] Reported in George Edward Slocombe, **Rebels of Art: Manet to Matisse**, R. M. McBride and Company, New York, 1939, pp. 59-63.

familiar with the spectacle of nature in the greatest works of the Renaissance and of the Dutch and French masters (Figs. 10-15, 10-16). They were accustomed to its representation in the precise green and brown of trees and rocks and in the exact shade of blue, green, and brown for water. With the impressionists the visual language of symbols and colors changed, and temporarily there was a communication gap between the artist and his viewers. The same paintings are now accepted and appreciated, and they give pleasure to most people who look at them today; in fact, with familiarity they have become the reference symbols of reality in art against which many of the innovations of the last twenty-five years are measured (Figs. 10-17–10-19).

The artist has made a statement that is embodied in his work, but it is the observer who interprets the statement for his own purposes. The communications received by the viewer are dependent to a large extent upon what he chooses to see of what the artist has put down. An example of how the viewer can respond in his own way, quite different from the meaning of the actual symbols put down by the artist, is to be found in reports of playgoers on what they heard while attending a performance of Edward Albee's *Who's Afraid of Virginia Woolf?* A number of members of the audience reported, with surety and conviction, to have heard lines of dialogue that were quite different from anything that the author would have written if he possessed any sense of decency (which he did); nor were they words that would have been spoken by any member of the cast, even one who was willing to take extreme liberties with the playwright's dialogue (which did not happen). This is an extreme case, but one in which the audience heard what they wanted to hear.

In a painting, in a sculpture, or in print the artist has committed his ideas to symbols which are a visual equivalent for an experience he has had with his world. This was important to the artist. The viewer must find

10-17
Yasuo Kuniyoshi.
Lay Figure.
Walker Art Center, Minneapolis.

10-18
Stanton MacDonald-Wright.
Synchromy in Green and Orange.
Walker Art Center,
Minneapolis.

in these symbols something which has a visual equivalent in his own experiences in this same world. The artist has the need and desire to represent certain objects and events which he has experienced in the real world in an artistic style and arrangement that he feels will fulfill the objective of what he wishes to say.

At times there is a discrepancy between the artist's selection of pictorial equivalents (symbols) and his manner of presenting them and that which the viewer holds valid and, in fact, expects the artistic image to satisfy. In this situation, when the form of visual language contains nothing in common to artist and spectator, then a lack of communication is inevitable. It is not necessary that all of us see and receive exactly the same meaning from any one work of art, or that this meaning be exactly the same as the artist had intended. Sometimes, except in general terms, the artist is not too sure. Also, he often makes his image with the consideration that different people will find somewhat different things as they look at it. It is very difficult to devise a form of visual language which can appeal simultaneously to the whole mass of the population.

Sometimes the view of an object and its form gives us a sense of pleasure — we say it has beauty. There are however art objects that do not give pleasure in the usual meaning of the word. They are not for us things of beauty. The word "beauty" has not been adequately defined even by the philosopher who deals with definitions and meanings. Art often deals with subjects that for us have meanings of sadness, misery, pathos and horror. Are these considered terms of beauty, or must beauty always have the connotation of delight and enjoyment? Sometimes for various reasons a work of art may outrage our sense of decency, so that we feel displeasure or indifference. Since art deals with all human experience, it is understandable that some facets of this experience may be unpleasant and annoying to some observers. Nevertheless, by extending our concept of the satisfying end of beauty, we can take in a wider range of visual statements and find beauty in them. This would include the work of many artists whose products are the basis from which we derive a visual experience which has a very immediate influence upon our very human emotions and which has a contagiousness that can be said to affect us. We can receive from a very wide range of contacts with art some of the emotive meaning the artist has placed in his work.

THE PROBLEM OF TERMINOLOGY

Many of the words and phrases which we use to describe and explain the inner action between the art object and the observer are enveloped in a kind of mystic. These terms have been subject to very arbitrary and loose definitions. We often use words synonymously that have quite distinct meanings, such as the substitution of "art history" for "art appreciation." "Art preference" and "art judgment" are often used in writing and discussion as if they were identical in meaning. The art preference of any person is a much different matter from his art judgment, which involves an ability to evaluate and make distinctions between objects of art.

Preference indicates one's personal emotional attitude of liking or disliking a work. Some evaluation is included in the way one arrives at his preferences; but it is not the decisive factor. There is a tendency for us to prefer what we feel is superior among the alternatives. When one is asked to state his preference, what he says it is will be the right answer for *him*. It does not need to be defended. If, on the other hand, one makes a judgment as to which art product is better or best, some support or reason as basis for the decision may be expected.

Art appreciation is often confused with art evaluation. The goal of art appreciation is to achieve an aesthetic experience and response while looking at a work of art; the goal of art evaluation is to make a value judgment which distinguishes one work of art from another on the basis of certain valid criteria. It is a judgment of which one is better or best in its field. Also connected with art appreciation and art judgment is the matter of whether or not we "like" the particular art object. Our personal likes and dislikes affect our actions and judgments. It is hardly to be expected that we will like all of the art that has been created; some work

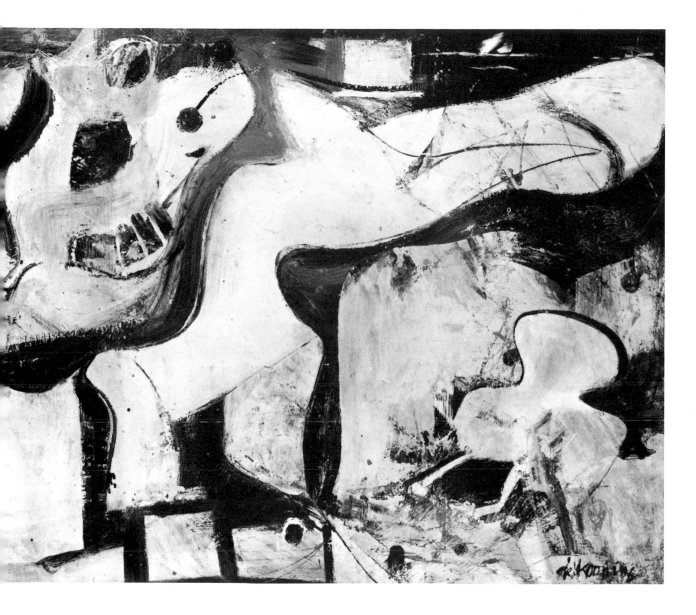

10-19
Willem de Kooning. Night.
Minneapolis Institute of Arts.

and periods, styles and tendencies, will leave us cool and somewhat indifferent, while others will excite and interest us. The qualities of an art object can be appreciated even when we do not particularly like it. We can find satisfaction and meaning in the masterworks of the Renaissance even when we do not like them and would rather look at contemporary works which we do like. In making art judgments, the personal bias of "like" and "dislike" should be excluded. Objective rather than subjective measures should be applied.

The following chapter attempts to clarify the factors which have a bearing upon the appreciation of art as it might be achieved by any and all people who are willing to open their minds and eyes to the experience.

Chapter 11

ART APPRECIATION: REACTING TO A WORK OF ART

As an introduction to the subject of looking at a work of art in order to obtain a measure of aesthetic satisfaction, it seems appropriate to review what has gone before in this book. Then we can expand upon what is known from research and philosophical inquiry about the complex activity which we call the appreciation of art. We will concern ourselves with the who, why, what, and how of it. Our discussion includes: (1) the person who can and does engage in the process; (2) what it is that takes place; and (3) how a person can achieve satisfaction from the encounter with a work of art. References will be made to material from previous chapters, but it will be related to appreciating rather than creating an art product.

Aesthetics has been defined by the philosopher and the psychologist as the study of what constitutes the beautiful. Although beauty may be found in many places, we are concerned specifically with the beauty found in the work of men who are called artists and the physical objects they have made with their hands, minds, and hearts.

ART APPRECIATION DESCRIBED

The appreciation of art as an aesthetic experience involves in its simplest terms a person looking at a work of art in order to derive satisfaction through his apprehension of the beauty and meaning that have been given to it by another person who created it. It is an experience which depends upon the perception of an object. It cannot be fully understood by analyzing the object which is perceived or by studying separately its units of sensation — color, shape, and so on. To understand appreciation it is necessary to become involved with the characteristics of the person doing the perceiving and the *interaction* of these with the properties of the work of art which is being perceived.

The art historian can give us much information about the art object. He has collected data about who made it and when it was made. He has analyzed the materials from which it was constructed and can give its measurements. He has described it and analyzed its compositional features. This information is thorough and descriptive, but it is peripheral and does not tell us anything about the spectator — the person doing the perceiving. When we consider the spectator, our information consists of less that is exact and more that is variable. There are many spectators and each one has characteristics that are hard to measure precisely. But even if we knew all these things about them, it would not be enough because the perceptive experience in the appreciation of art must be studied in the relationship of the person to the object with its involved interaction of the characteristics of the perceiver with the properties of the object. Complicated as this might be, a start can be made by reviewing what we know from research about appreciation and aesthetic awareness.

THE CAPACITY FOR AESTHETIC AWARENESS

For a long time people have had the notion that creativity — thinking and action — has been in the possession of only a few rare men, or "geniuses." This common notion is wholly mistaken. Likewise there has been the belief that special artistic "talent" was something held only by the monumental figures in the world of art, such as Leonardo da Vinci, El Greco, or Rembrandt. These men were placed on a pedestal as they should be. When, however, all others are excluded from this select company and the art produced by them is put aside as having little or no merit because they lacked a "birthright," we are acting in ignorance. We have changed our notions of creativeness and have come to think of it as something that is within the capacities of all people with the reservation that differences among them are a matter of degree. Some may have more or may endeavor to utilize their capacity more effectively. Everyone has the capacity for art production and also the capacity for aesthetic appreciation, but they are left for the most part untrained, unemployed, and underdeveloped. For many years there has been a false assumption that a few cultured, or intellectually oriented individuals, the connoisseurs, made up an aristocratic segment of the population and that they were the only ones who could appreciate and provide support for the arts through patronage. We would like to dispel this notion by stating that the latent capacity for aesthetic appreciation is inherited by everyone.

Evidence to support this comes from tests of aesthetic appreciation applied to schoolchildren and adults: "Tests indicate that here as elsewhere every grade of variation is to be found and that the distribution is approximately normal: an average amount is most common and minimal and maximal grades are rare." [1]

It has been shown that the different forms of appreciation are positively correlated with each other, which suggests that a general factor underlies them all. This general factor for art appreciation is probably due to the still more general factor of intelligence, innate all-around ability. Even when the influence of intelligence has been partially eliminated a separate general factor for aesthetic appreciation still remains. This holds true not only for appreciation but also for artistic creativity.

Now that we conceive of aesthetic appreciation as something that is within the capacity of many people, rather than just a few, some of the barriers to its development are removed. What is this then that is within the capacity of everyone? What does it involve?

PSYCHOLOGICAL DIMENSIONS OF AESTHETIC EXPERIENCE

In looking at a work of art and becoming sensitive to its quality, we say that we "feel" something. We experience it emotionally and it affects us and causes us to react to it. But there is also another aspect of the experience. When going through the actions of looking and feeling, there is an element of making preferences, comparing, and judging. What we see now is compared with other things in art and nature. Ideas are formed about what is being experienced and these ideas are related to the mass of our organized knowledge which has been obtained through all of our past experience. Against this background we are going through mental ac-

---

[1] Cyril Burt, **The Psychological Aspects of Aesthetic Education,** *Art Education*, vol. 20, no. 3, (March, 1967), p. 26.

tivities which involve recognizing, organizing, judging, and reasoning. In other words, we are thinking and knowing.

In summary, we can say that our experience of looking at the work of art had two dimensions. One aspect involved our emotions and feelings and perhaps something called "empathy." At the same time, it has also been cognitive — that is, an intellectual activity in which meanings and associations that are being reasoned, judged, classified, and recognized. When looking at the work of art, we know as well as feel.[2]

This is not an awkward attempt to make something out of looking at art which will make it an acceptable "status" activity for the academic intellectual community. It only suggests that the activity leading to aesthetic awareness, like most things people do, does not use only one human capacity to the exclusion of all others.

We expect a certain personal element in the work of art — individual sensitivity from the artist and an individual response from the spectator. Assuming the work is a good one, it will have a direct and instinctive appeal. The source of this cannot be reduced to a simple formula. The appeal is to the emotions; intellectual analysis, if called for, comes later. This expressive value put into the work by the producer appeals to the *feelings* of the viewer. Emotions felt by the producer are conducted and controlled by the form and materials of his craft; the sensitivity of the person who looks at the work is affected, and he feels what has been expressed and is moved by it.

There is an instantaneous aspect, often overlooked, in the workings of the mind and emotions in a situation when we are looking at art. A person even with modest sensitivity does not go through a long period of involved analysis of the situation before he admits that he is pleased or displeased. The impact of the work usually "hits" us quickly. Only on some occasions, under some conditions of viewing, is it not possible to receive almost instantaneous impressions. To grasp a work of art properly it must be isolated in some way, and we must be in a position to grasp it in its entirety. There is an intuitive feeling of the "rightness" of it.

In some situations we establish a relationship between ourselves and the experience — in other words, "we feel ourselves into it." We feel it so strongly that in a sense we are projecting our own personality into the thing or object. By doing this we obtain a better understanding of the feelings the artists has given his images. In some situations we almost feel ourselves being involuntarily thrust into the rhythmic, swirling movement of the wave or the sky, as with the Japanese print, the Van Gogh painting, or the Brancusi sculptured form (Figs. 11-1, 11-2). In other situations we feel the oppressive weight or the precarious balance of sculptured or painted form, almost as if we, the spectators, were trying to hold up fragments of the world in suspended balance. This empathy, or "feeling into," brings us as onlookers closer and more able to release our feelings in a manner that heightens them. The two psychological dimensions, affective and cognitive, are in some form of balance in both the

---

2 Dale Harris, **Aesthetic Awareness: A Psychologist's View**, *Art Education*, vol. 19, no. 5, (May, 1966), pp. 17–23.

production and the observation of art. Balance of thinking and the feeling of emotion and knowledge do not mean that in every situation there is the same amount, an equal quantity of both. In the aesthetic experience, "the essential thing is rather the harmonious blend of feelings and a certain attitude of mind." [3]

From the point of view of the psychologist there is no special kind of thinking involved in the aesthetic experience. The cognitive part is performed by the person looking at art, very much as he does with any information he receives while acting or being engaged in any other activity. In the art situation he comprehends and classifies the information as he does any other kind of information. The data he receives is visual for the most part — of visual forms that have not been reduced to the verbal symbols of a written or spoken language. In some cases we must add to this tactile and kinesthetic sensation. While looking at the experimental art forms of the twentieth century, we have the smells and sounds of the environments created for the spectator. The viewer's own language structure and his accumulated verbal knowledge are the tools involved. These can help him in relating the sensations he receives with previously accumulated knowledge. The visual experience can then be adjusted to the patterns of his thinking and his total cultural environment.

---

[3] C. W. Valentine, **The Experimental Psychology of Beauty**. 1962, p. 9, as quoted in *ibid.*, p. 18.

CHARACTERISTICS OF AESTHETIC SENSITIVITY

Aesthetic sensitivity, a product of development and learning, is grounded in perception. It is not a unique or special case that is separate, in conditions and kind, from the general way of perceiving required for our practical existence. When we are engaged in looking at a work of art, there is a heightening of our visual faculties to bring about the condition of awareness and sensitivity to the experience. The earlier discussion of awareness in Chapter 2, which dealt with levels of vision, also applies here. It was pointed out that the vision used by people falls into four categories — practical, curious, imaginative, and aesthetic vision, or awareness. These manners of seeing have characteristics which are often mentioned as essential for art appreciation: (1) curiosity; (2) an open-mindedness, or willingness to manipulate or change aspects of the direct sensations; and (3) a definite concentration of attention. These contribute to the viewer's attitude, or set, which makes him ready for an aesthetic experience.

CURIOSITY

There is unanimous agreement that a full appreciation of art demands open-mindedness from the observer. This is the willingness to become involved and to free oneself from previous notions or expectations of what the art object should be like. Being more open and curious about what the artist has done and how he has done it sets the stage for a fruitful encounter. The observer is not locked out because of his preset limits for "how and what" the art object should express. Boundaries are not placed upon the sort of symbols that the artist may use. We often speak of the sense of wonder and the unlimited curiosity found in young children; perhaps if the adult could recapture a bit of his lost youth, he would in this respect derive a fuller satisfaction from looking at art. The sense of appreciation would be free to function, and he would take in stride the moments of unexpected surprise that are part of art.

WILLINGNESS TO PARTICIPATE AND OPEN-MINDEDNESS

Sometimes the images presented for the spectator are at variance with his prior experience and, as such, are not easy to accept or assimilate. Readiness to accept the unexpected from art provides the climate for appreciation. This is not a surrender to novelty for its own sake or an acceptance of the arbitrary whim in the name of art. However, it does mean that time is allowed for a more contemplative consideration of the intention of the artist. It also means that flexibility on the part of the spectator will involve him directly in the experience as he manipulates the imagery by mentally adjusting and rearranging the symbols and meanings into new relationships. In this manner the viewer finds that his role is a creative one. When the viewer participates fully in relating the elements of the art object (when he unifies them with meaning), we have a parallel to the creative synthesis that is so important for the producer.

CONCENTRATION OF ATTENTION

Another characteristic in the aesthetic experience is this very definite concentration of attention. This means that attention should be focused upon the art object and that all peripheral conflicting stimulation should be erased. This is what the artist has done in his productive effort. He has abstracted and to a degree magnified what he felt to be important. At the same time he has cut out any and all things that do not contribute to his idea. This concentration upon essentials should not be very difficult to accomplish because we already exercise a filtering out of conflicting sensory data in the normal course of everyday life. Even in common pursuits and in practical vision we screen out surrounding stimuli from the object of our interest; by doing this we are able to concentrate our attention and to be efficient and to survive. While looking at art, the observer often becomes detached from his surroundings, and it is at this time that there is a distinct feeling of satisfaction and excitement aroused by the art experience.

Paintings, sculptures, and other works of art usually have a degree of interest as well as complexity. There is sufficient complexity to give the observer enough stimulation to hold his attention and interest. A degree of complexity in the art object can keep him busy, absorbing its visual symbolism. When the work of art is a good one and the observer is attentive, the experience has a quality of isolation from other kinds of conflicting stimulation. The observer feels detached and almost separate from his surroundings — hardly conscious of things going on around him.

CHARACTERISTICS OF THE OBJECT AS A WORK OF ART

The object or work of art of which the individual is becoming aware of as he looks at it should have certain identifiable characteristics that separate it from others which he looks at in his general environment. Psychologists and philosophers are in agreement to the effect that the art object has above all a sense of wholeness; there must be order and unity which pervades the whole of the work. This is what is meant when we speak about significant "form." People must get something from art that makes them willing to devote purposely a large part of their leisure time toward the end of obtaining aesthetic enjoyment or satisfaction. If the observer derives something of that from this experience, then we must describe a measure of value to the structure or form of the object that is responsible for it. He is aware of and has apprehended the special kind of order or organization in the object of his perception. This order is a systematic pattern in which a number of parts are organized according to the meaning involved into a unitary whole.

The artist in his work has created a physical object which (when taken to its lowest common denominator) consists of an arrangement in space of certain molecules capable of reflecting a specific pattern of visible light waves. This physical description does not tell the whole story by any means. What is important is that the creative artist has taken these physical components and given them life and meaning for the observer through the specific form of his arrangement, which carries meaning beyond an arrangement of molecules. In his aesthetic system the constituent parts and their relationships to each other are so ordered that they can be grasped implicitly by an observer. The observer is aided in his aesthetic sensing by a background of experience with art and by his way of thinking about things and events in the world. His past experiences with art have at least two functions in any new situation. These other experiences tend to make the new situation familiar and comfortable. Also, the cumulative total of past experiences provides the reference base or background to which new ones can be compared, recognized, related, classified, and evaluated. Those cognitive habits and ways of thinking about things and events in the world which are customary for the spectator come into play as he looks at art. The subject matter might be in a different package, but his thinking process is much the same.

In the object experienced as beautiful there must be this unity in complexity. Simplicity for its own sake when presented to the observer will leave him empty. A degree of complexity in the arrangement and design created by the artist is required by the spectator; its absence will leave him indifferent and he will move on to something else.

In describing the function of composition it has been said that the structural design of his composition as arranged by the artist should be such that the eye of the spectator will be carried through to all parts of the composition and finally come to rest at the center of interest. The spectator's eyes should not be permitted to wander out of the edges of the composition and should be held inside its boundaries. This statement adds another criterion for aesthetic satisfaction. In addition to some degree of complexity in the work of art — crafts, architecture, painting, or sculpture — at the same time the work must have a focal point for attention. This adds to its coherence and unity. These three aspects — unity, complexity and center of attention or focus — are felt to be identifiable and objective characteristics that can be applied to formal art criticism and judgment. They are regarded as objective when judgments as to the amount of complexity, unity, and centering of interest vary with the variation in the art object being judged, not according to variations in the persons making the judgments.

PERSONAL QUALITIES LINKED WITH AESTHETIC SENSITIVITY

It has been stated that aesthetic sensitivity is inherent in all people. It is a product of development and learning. When people became interested in the creative process, a method of inquiry was adopted to discover why some people could perform more efficiently and effectively than others. Study began by asking what kinds of people were able to perform in a manner characterized as creative. Professor Child of Yale University and his staff conducted their investigations of aesthetic sensitivity by the same avenue of approach. Their research depended upon determining which persons were sensitive to aesthetic values and which were not; they next attempted to discover some significant relationships between measures of aesthetic judgment and several measures of personality characteristics. Child[4] summarized these findings as follows:

> The aesthetically sensitive person is a person of actively inquiring mind, seeking out experiences that may be challenging because of complexity, or novelty, ever alert to the potential of experience offered by stimuli not already in the focus of attention, interested in understanding each experience thoroughly for its own sake rather than contemplating it superficially and promptly filing it away in a category, and able to do this with respect to the world inside himself and as well as the world outside.

This research included Yale undergraduates and was later extended to all seventh to twelfth-grade students in the secondary schools of a suburban town. The following personality traits were found to correlate with aesthetic sensitivity:

1. *Independence of judgment.* One maintains his own perceptual judgments despite contrary judgments by their fellows and does not yield or modify judgments to conform or adapt to what they have heard others express.

2. *Tolerance of complexity.* This requires a tolerance for the complex ways of looking at experience. This implies no need to understand in simple terms or to look to others for evaluative labels or to reduce experience to an elementary structure or explanation. It is a willingness to investigate works of art in ways leading to complete understanding and genuine appreciation.

3. *Playfulness.* This requires an ability to relax temporarily the restraints of adult life and to fall back into ways of thinking associated with childhood. It allows one to draw upon richer and more complex ways of thinking than those of the person who tightly and rigidly holds himself to act always as a mature adult.

In addition appreciation of art seems to require consideration of conflicting emotions or attitudes. Also, it means acceptance of ambiguity and of ill-defined and unresolved meaning.

Of interest is the close consistency between these personality characteristics correlated with art appreciation and the same characteristics, or personal qualities, which have been attributed to creative persons. This conclusion is supported by the results of research by many people who have studied the creative process as well as aesthetic sensitivity. Common to both are: (1) independence of judgment; (2) tolerance of complexity and the willingness to tolerate ambiguity; and (3) a tendency toward playfulness and willingness to use analogies which help to make the familiar strange and the strange familiar.

From these sources it has become clear, as expected, that judgments

---

[4] Irvin L. Child and Rosaline S. Swartz, **Personality and the Appreciation of Art**, *Art Education*, vol. 20, no. 1 (January, 1967), pp. 33–55.

of beauty are related to the personal characteristics of the judge. We know that it is hard to remove all of our personal bias in a situation when judging art. There are many personal attributes which are worthy of cultivation for purposes other than looking at art. These include curiosity, intellectual outreach, interest in complexity and novelty, and sensitivity to the possible significance of the seemingly trivial in art and in life. It is also desirable in other actions to have a willingness to examine an experience in its own right without making an immediate classification of it without fair consideration. This could eliminate dependence upon labels, slogans, clichés, and "pigeonholes." Obtaining aesthetic sensitivity from looking at art does not consists in naming the work pop, op, or kinetic and then conveniently forgetting it.

AN EXPERIENCE WITH APPRECIATION

Although there are individual differences of temperament and sensitivity which are not entirely eliminated by experience and training, psychologists believe that there is a strong learning component in aesthetic awareness. That there are an infinite variety of attitudes among men and women to things commonly thought beautiful must also be accepted. There are however many research findings which testify to the educability of tastes. Many studies with school children who were exposed to a variety of works of art over a period of time indicate that their ratings of works changed significantly. "Better" works replaced the more sentimental, representative, and conventional portrayals. Judgments of laymen and less educated adults resembled more closely the judgments of children and their color, design, and composition preferences than do those of specially trained or even well-educated adults.

Many people in educational and social situations express an interest in suggestions for developing taste and aesthetic sensitivity. One remembered plan is worthy of repetition; it is for self-education of appreciation. It was outlined in a talk given to a group of art teachers by a man whose major area of interest was not art appreciation, art history, or art teaching, but semantics.[5]

The procedure is an exceedingly simple one. Anyone interested could follow it by expending a very small amount of energy. Its simplicity is deceptive, and analysis will uncover the many characteristics of aesthetics sensitivity which have been incorporated. The process starts with the assumption that you wish to develop an appreciation for the works of a particular artist. The artist selected in our description which follows is the painter Hans Hofmann. Anyone might have been selected, but he has been chosen because many people would like to know how to distinguish a good abstract painting from a bad one. This is what might happen once the decision has been made.

---

5 From a speech by S. I. Hayakawa given at a meeting of the Indiana Art Education Association, Richmond, Indiana, 1958.

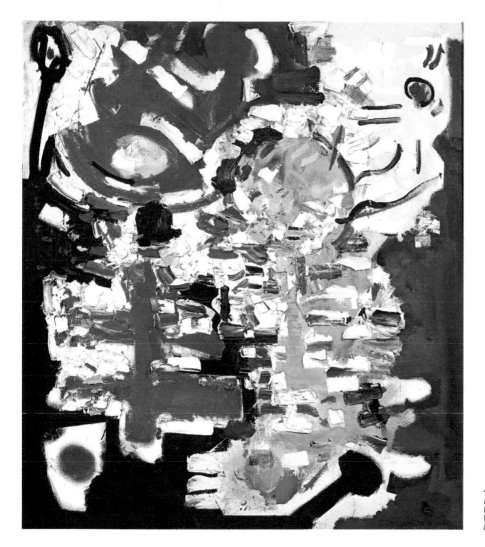

11-3
Hans Hofmann.
Fantasia in Blue. 1954.
Whitney Museum of American Art,
New York.

The first step is to get a fairly large and good reproduction of one of Hofmann's paintings. This is neither difficult nor expensive. Good quality reproductions are now available at a modest cost. Also many public libraries have good reproductions on loan. At this stage, any of the artist's paintings that interest you a little will suffice (Fig. 11-3).

Put this painting up somewhere in your sphere of living, in some place where you will be able to see it often — a room or part of the house where you spend a great deal of your time, even the kitchen or bathroom. The main thing is to have the chance to see it quite often at your leisure or when engaged in routine tasks that do not require much of your attention. The main thing is to have it as part of your environment. Incidentally, this is a good way to make up your mind when you are thinking about purchasing a painting for the home. The added familiarity helps to reveal the strengths and weaknesses of the work as far as your own attitudes are concerned.

After a week or two has gone by, go to the public library and get a book about Hans Hofmann and his work. Read it and look at any other illustrations of

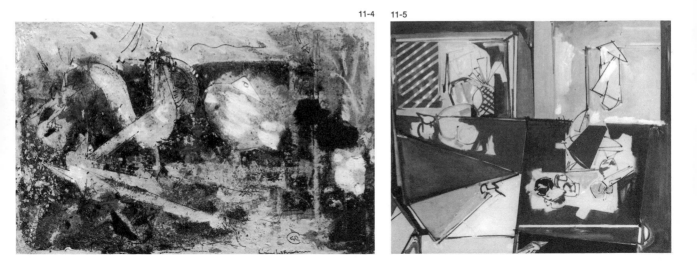

11-4   11-5

11-4
Hans Hofmann. Elegy.
Walker Art Center,
Minneapolis.

11-5
Hans Hofmann.
Magenta and Blue. 1950.
Whitney Museum of American Art,
New York.

his paintings that are included (Figs. 11-4–11-7). It could be very helpful if the books included some personal remarks by the artist about his beliefs and work habits. Information about Hofmann would tell you that this artist has a fine reputation as a teacher as well as a painter in Germany and the United States and has been one of the leading spirits of the abstract-expressionist movement. His aim in paintings (he has said) is "to create pulsating luminous surfaces that emanate a mystic light determined exclusively through painterly development, and in accordance with my deepest insight into the experience with life and nature." [6]

Klee and Kandinsky helped him to understand the idea of color as an expressive force in itself (see Fig. 4-20). This is a characteristic of his work. Also he did not feel that nature is limited to the objects we see, and believed "that everything in nature offers the possibility of creative transformation, depending, of course, on the sensibility of the artist." He has described his way of working as follows: "My work is not accidental and is not planned. The first red spot on a white canvas may at once suggest to me the meaning of morning redness and from there on I dream further with my color." [7]

Now might be a good time to move the reproduction from its original location to some place that you feel is more important as far as your living space is concerned. Usually this is somewhere in the living room where it can be seen by other people who visit your home. In the meantime, read more books about your chosen artist and look at as many other reproductions of his work as you can find. When a visitor makes a remark about the painting in your living room (as they will), answering their questions should be quite easy because from your reading and observations you have become considerably more aware of the artist and his work than the person asking the questions. As you answer their remarks, either critically or by supporting your selection, you will personally be acting in a critical capacity. You will be forced to clarify and to support your reasons for choice. In a limited sense you will have become a critic with foundation rather than one who acts out of arbitrary judgments of initial "like or dislike." This is a critical stage because inadvertently you are becoming an "authority" on the art of at least one painter.

---

[6] Katherine Kuh, **The Artist's Voice**, Harper and Row, Publishers., Inc., New York, 1960, pp. 118–129.
[7] See his painting *Rising Sun*, 1958.

350   **ENCOUNTER WITH ART**

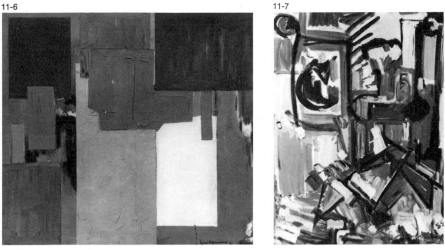

11-6

11-7

11-6
Hans Hofmann. Radiant Enclosure.
1961. Andre Emmerich Gallery,
New York.

11-7
Hans Hofmann. Exuberance.
1955. Albright-Knox Art Gallery,
Buffalo, New York.

The next thing that might happen comes as something of a surprise. While walking or driving through the city or country, there might come a time when you see the sun come up and with it the "morning redness," and you say to yourself, "That's the way Hans Hofmann might have seen it."

ANALYSIS OF AN EXPERIENCE WITH APPRECIATION

At this point you have moved to personal involvement in his painting and have begun to perceive In somewhat the same manner that the painter sees his world.

In this account nothing much seems to have happened, but in its simplicity it involves many of the principles around which the development of taste and appreciation are summarized. First of all, you have made a commitment. You have placed yourself in a position that took some action, and "put your foot forward." The position you have placed yourself in is one of "readiness to appreciate." You have also started with the first requirement of appreciation, which is open-mindedness.

Next, the situation, however simple, did provide for concentration of your attention upon the work to be appreciated. The informal arrangement and the intimacy of the setting, for the most part, originally allowed you to examine the painting with detachment, without the conflict of other people and other things going on. In a way there was isolation if even for a moment you examined the work alone.

About the middle of your experiment something else was happening. The visual experience was being supplemented by other resources — books and writing, the comments of others, historical data, and so on. The visual experience was being tempered by adding another dimension to looking at art — adding to your associations and references that which would help you to find meaning in the experience. At the same time it was possible for your experiences in looking at one example of an artist's work to be compared with what other people said about it and about what they felt the artist was attempting to accomplish. Your position was changed from the act of an observer to that of a person who is attempting to

11-8
Morris Graves.
Bird in the Spirit. *1940–41.*
Whitney Museum of American Art,
New York.

11-9
Franz Kline. Mahoning.
1956. Whitney Museum of American Art,
New York.

communicate his ideas and feelings with others. Your responsibilities had changed. It was now necessary to defend and support statements and, at the same time become broadly aware of how other people might be seeing a painting. You are making art judgments, supporting them, and at the same time placing yourself in a position where recognition of another point of view was expected of you.

At the end, when you saw something in the environment that suggested how the artist might have seen it, there was an indication of awareness and a kind of vision which might be called aesthetic. A change in vision was indicated. Along the way your visual habits were changing from the casual, practical vision to a more curious kind. Then there was adjustment to a reflective imaginative vision, in which you were manipulating the shapes and colors seen in the painting in some way, so that these made sense to you. Another thing in this hypothetical experience is that a period of time seems necessary to provide the familiarity that is essential.

GENERAL APPLICATIONS OF THE PROCEDURE FOR APPRECIATION

Does this procedure for the personal development of aesthetic sensitivity have applications to other artist and their work? The answer is yes, it works for most artists and their work. Carrying our example a step farther, we can apply it to Morris Graves and Franz Kline. The procedure will be the same except for an adjustment of what you are looking for in the significance of the artist's work and of your attitude during the experience according to the knowledge you have gained of the artist's intentions. Graves, in his paintings, conveys the influences of his early contacts with nature in the Far West and the aesthetic-spiritual attitudes from Japanese art and thought that were impressed upon him in his youth. He has employed known symbols and has discovered very personal symbols, which after a while were accepted by others and became general. He wanted others to see in his paintings something that they would come to recognize as their own experience (Figs. 11-8, 11-9).

Kline takes a slightly different kind of mental adjustment on the part of the viewer. Information about Franz Kline tells us that he had an academic background, which means he studied and drew from models. By his own description he does not paint objectively — bridge construction, tables, or skyscrapers; he paints an organization that booomoo a painting. If it sometimes happens to look like something, this does not bother him; but he did not use real objects as models. Sometimes he makes preliminary drawings; if he begins this way, he does not enlarge the drawings, but combines a number of them, and each small one becomes a separate area of the large work — a process of combining and adding or subtracting from the original sketches. He works mainly in black and white, but wants to feel free to introduce color where and when he feels it is necessary. His paintings are named after the work is finished; they might refer to places he had been. The painting entitled *1960 New Years Wall, Night* (Fig. 11-10), for example, was painted on a studio wall around New Year's of 1960. Many of his paintings have night forms.[8]

11-10
Franz Kline.
1960 New Years Wall, Night.
Sidney Janis Gallery, New York.

---

[8] Katherine Kuh, *op. cit.*, pp. 145–154.

11-11
*Alberto Giacometti.
Head of Diego.
Walker Art Center,
Minneapolis.*

11-12
*Henri Matisse. White Plumes.
1919. Minneapolis Institute of Arts.*

Should the artist be one like Gabo, Albers, or Mondrian, who were interested in the purity of the formal elements of art and an intellectual approach to art, another sort of mental adjustment is required of the viewer. It is necessary to accept the concept that these formal elements — line, shape, color, tone, and texture — are in themselves the subject matter and content. This admission removes the necessity to seek out recognizable objects in nature and the environment; attention can be given to the form and arrangement of the structure of the canvas. These men considered themselves *realists* (they wanted to realize themselves). For them, abstraction was real — more real than nature (see Figs. 1-15, 4-19, 7-13). Others have expressed a more conventional view of reality in their art (Figs. 11-11–11-13).

FACTORS WHICH CONTRIBUTE TO AESTHETIC SENSITIVITY

When we endeavor to participate in the basic aesthetic experience of looking at a work of art we are influenced by many factors; the effects of these vary greatly from one person to another. Perhaps it will be easier to recognize these factors if we group them under two categories — those which are within the work of art itself and those which are outside its boundaries and which can assist or inhibit our sensitivity in the experience with art.

FACTORS INSIDE THE WORK OF ART

In his description of essential features of a work of art leading to a basic aesthetic experience, Beardsley states that "the essential feature of such a work — I am tempted to say, but recognizing that I am likely to sound dogmatic — the essential feature is not merely that certain visual elements (lines, shapes, colors) are assembled together, but that as we concentrate on their natures and relations, we become aware, suddenly or gradually, of what they add up to as a whole. For what they add up to is not an addition at all, but the projection of a new pattern, a new quality of grace or power." [9]

This emphasizes the "wholeness" of the arrangement of the visual elements in a work of art, which gives it its form as apprehended by the observer. It suggests that of primary value to the experience of art are the observer's abilities to become aware of the fashion by which the artist has shaped his materials, organized them, and composed them. A pattern emerges in the mind and eye of the viewer which is no longer pieces of color and pieces of shape, but a unified coherent structure. The complexity of individual parts and elaborations on them are brought into a center of focus whenever the artist's arrangement of parts is seen related to each other. This is a relationship which happens when the artist's materials are formed according to design and plan in such a way that they have meaning for the viewer.

Some knowledge of what these plastic elements of the artist are individually could be helpful. Since they are segregated neither in nature nor in art, a conception of them as they work together would be of greater value.

FACTORS OUTSIDE YET RELATED TO THE ART PRODUCT

Because an aesthetic experience depends upon the perceptual relationships between an individual and an art object, there are many things that are brought through association to the experience by the viewer. These can hardly be discounted because they are a part of him — his knowledge, attitudes, frame of reference — and as such will affect his ability to perceive and apprehend the physical features and artistry displayed in the object.

The art process. One of the major leisure-time activities of the public is that of being a spectator at a sporting event, either at the game or watching it on television or the movie screen. The avid viewer who understands all the niceties of strategy and skill seems to get a great deal more from the experience than the casual viewer who appears indifferent or apathetic

---

[9] Monroe C. Beardsley, **On the Creation of Art**, *Journal of Aesthetics and Art Criticism*, vol. 23, no. 3 (Spring, 1965), pp. 291–304. Reprinted in Ralph A. Smith (ed.), *Aesthetics and Criticism in Art Education*, Rand McNally and Company, Chicago, 1966, p. 169.

because "nothing is happening." For him, without the home run or the spectacular touchdown, nothing much is happening. His background of experience and associations does not allow him to sense the details of skill and the ways of working employed by the participants as they maneuver against one another. Certainly looking at art is different from going to a ball game, but some knowledge of the "how and why" of what the artist has done could stimulate the viewer's attentiveness.

In this book we have attempted to give the reader an intimate picture of the process of art — what the artist does and how he does it. Certainly art can be looked at and appreciated without this knowledge. There are many who feel that it makes no difference at all — that knowledge of creativity is irrelevant to participation in a basic aesthetic experience. The latter can be accomplished without knowledge of how the artist produced his art. The authors disagree with this view, at least in the matter of degree. We are saying that, for many people who look at art, this knowledge will provide a frame of reference for their focus upon the work itself. Knowledge of creative-artistic behavior is more than just interesting knowledge to have; it can also contribute to the involvement of the observer in the process of observing. It helps to make the strange familiar and to bring the observer inside the operation and its product.

Historical frame of reference. Just as knowledge of the artist's way of working can supplement and assist the spectator toward familiarity and participation, some broad knowledge of our heritage from the arts through the study of the history of art can also make a contribution to art appreciation and art judgment. In learning about the history of the field, it is necessary for a person to look at many different kinds of art from many different times and cultures. The study of art history has been systematized and thoroughly documented. Through courses or by reading one begins to establish certain generalized concepts which connect the kinds of art being produced with happenings in the cultures which produced them. Acquaintance with a considerable number of examples selected (according to merit) can serve as a yardstick for measuring or identifying artistic qualities of a new work which has not been seen before. One also obtains information and descriptive statements about works of art from reading and instruction, which help him to connect or correlate the verbal language with the visual one.

The student of art history becomes acquainted with the verbal language, vocabulary, and different methods of organizing information about art. For the cognitive aspects of aesthetic appreciation this can be of help because thinking is facilitated by our ability to place or group miscellaneous scattered facts into manageable categories. There is also an acquaintance with the kinds of symbolic forms which artists have used and some speculation about the intentions the artist has had in using these symbols.

Such knowledge about (1) the purposes of art, (2) the symbolic forms — borrowed, modified, and invented — and (3) the intentions artists have had in the past can at the minimum broaden the individual and also make him broad-minded in his encounter with a work of art from any period of history.

We assume that if one can learn to look at art by looking at a quantity of it, the study of the history of art is at least a beginning. When coupled with understanding of the creative process through which the work was created, the individual should have at least a base of confidence and reference which can set the stage for a full and beneficial aesthetic experience. This assumption holds even when we admit that it is possible for someone to have aesthetic sensitivity to beauty in the work of art without this previous contact and knowledge. All our findings from research and observation strongly suggest that education can make a difference in one's sensitivity and will at least provide the climate for this sensitivity to flourish.

NONAESTHETIC FACTORS OUTSIDE THE WORK OF ART

There are also many factors outside the work of art which influence the observer and have a bearing upon the infinite varieties of attitudes among men and women to things that are commonly thought to be beautiful. These individual differences of temperament and sensitivity are often affected by something which has very little direct bearing upon the art work being observed. We know that standards of beauty may and do vary among groups whose cultural learning contexts differ. Previously, relationships of the aesthetic sensitivity to personality characteristics were developed; aesthetic sensitivity was shown to be related to and affected by differences of external cultural stimulation. The history of art is a record of the different ways of thinking and seeing in different human societies and of how art takes its character from the culture it expresses. The sensitivities and preferences of people who look at art are also subject to these same cultural influences.

Aesthetic sensitivity and awareness have their roots in an act of perception, and anything that has an influence on visual perception also has a corresponding effect upon the people who do the perceiving.

It is true that art work reflects the different ways of seeing and thinking which are characteristic of different human societies. Those social ideals, concepts, habits, and attitudes which are part of the culture and tradition of the observer will have an affect upon his way of looking at art and the values he will derive from it. An exhaustive study [10] of the influences of culture on visual perception concludes as follows:

> *Perception is an aspect of human behavior and as such it is subject to many of the same influences that shape other aspects of behavior. In particular, each individual's experiences combine in a complex fashion to determine his reaction to a given stim-*

---

[10] Marshall H. Segall, Donald T. Campbell, and Melville J. Herskovits, **The Influence of Culture on Visual Perception**, The Bobbs-Merrill Company, Inc., Indianapolis, 1966, p. 213.

ulus situation. To the extent that certain classes of experience are more likely to occur in some cultures than others, differences in behavior across cultures, including differences in perceptional tendencies, can be great enough even to surpass the ever-present individual differences within cultural groupings.

Concepts of "good" and "bad" vary from one culture to another. Group attitudes and values tend to exert an almost unnoticed effect on behavior of persons of the group. Generally, group members have a tendency to modify their own judgments and to act in accordance with group judgment. Research has also shown that perception of color and perception of size and shape are affected by aspects of cultural life. Sensing the relationships among the separate symbolic parts of the art object is an important part of aesthetic sensitivity; relationships are commonly established on the basis of perceptual concepts, unique to the culture. The economic endowments of a particular culture distort not only the way we perceive things, but also their relative values.

The effect of outside influences upon the person looking at art becomes quite apparent when one is repeatedly exposed to individuals and groups during tours of art galleries. One is impressed by their attitudes and the rise of the level of expectation that is evident when the price tag placed on a work by an artist is in the five- or six-figure bracket. There is a tendency to feel that anything so highly valued will provide a richer viewing experience and that it should be appreciated because of its price tag. The same attitude of reverence was present as an important force affecting the aesthetic sensitivity of long lines of spectators who in close-order file, separated by ropes and guards from the exhibits, marched past paintings taken from the salt mines after World War II. The publicity in news media about their monetary value, rarity, and aesthetic significance influenced many people. Although labels, price tags, and even the artist's signature are not aesthetic in character, it is not possible to remove entirely the effects of these from judgment of the merits of the art object.

Influences from cultural and other sources upon the individual who is looking at art are extremely difficult to eliminate. In the twentieth-century Western world the mass media's interest in publicizing news reports about works of art has had a strong influence upon the spectator who has had only a limited exposure to art. Add to this the popularizing of a particular style or tendency by the art dealers. This gives us some idea of the forces at work in the cultural environment. A work of art obtains its validity as an object for aesthetic satisfaction because of its "expressive form." It does not acquire merit because it happens to be done in a popular current style or because its subject matter is recognizable or popular. But these factors do influence many who look at art and have an effect on their viewing habits which is almost impossible to eradicate.

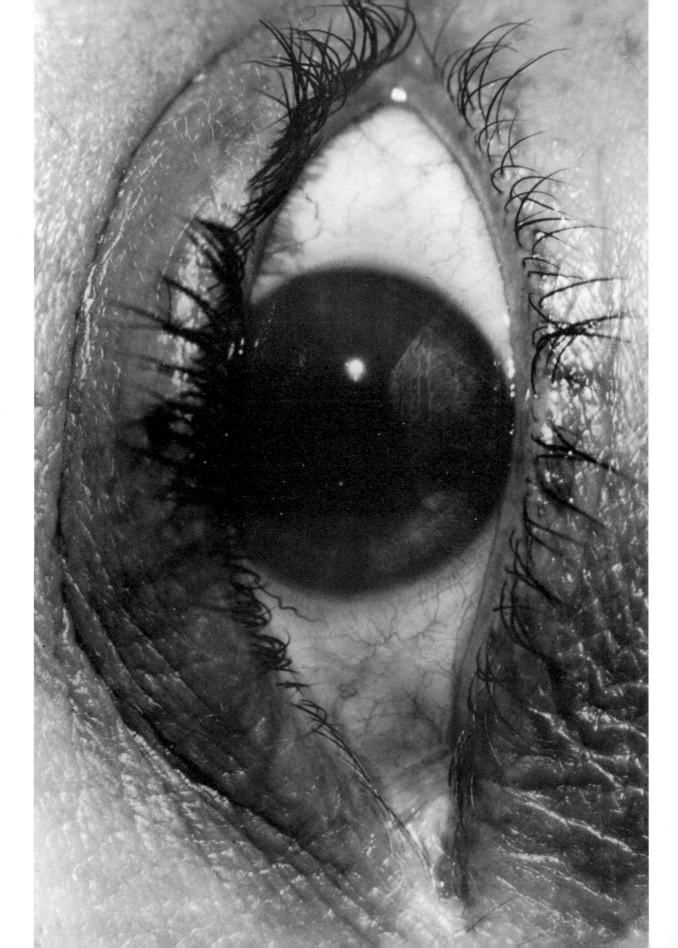

Chapter 12

DEVELOPING AESTHETIC AWARENESS

Aesthetic awareness for the artist-producer has been outlined as a flow of action — of seeing, selecting, forming and presenting; for the spectator it includes seeing, identifying, and appreciating. Appreciation has been described as a combination of feeling and thinking.

A number of people think that "awareness" would be a more suitable term than "appreciation" to identify the quality of experience that may be derived as people look at art in order to obtain something of satisfaction for the enrichment of their lives. In any case, we are convinced that a level of awareness or appreciation of art is within the province of all human beings. Just as the artist explores and creates, the spectator can examine the works of man, the artist, for the personal satisfaction and enrichment that comes from the experience of seeing.

At this stage in history the work of art can be appreciated for its qualities of condensation and distillation, even if we fail to grasp any of its other qualities. In a worthy effort the creative craftsman has brought a broad spectrum of experiences together, weighed their relative importance, or value, and distilled out of the mass the few drops of critical essence. This is what he has repackaged into his visual statement for the viewer's contemplation and appraisal. It is a "visual digest" to outdo the digests and capsule summaries which are so popular in our fast-running twentieth-century civilization.

When art has been done properly and the appreciator meets it at least halfway, the abstraction presented by the artist can be expanded beyond its former limits. The experiences of the viewer are added to those of the producer. The work of art serves as a catalyst to bring to the surface a chain reaction of residual thoughts, meanings, and feelings that have been lying dormant within the person who looks at it. This is the "enrichment and satisfaction" that a work of art brings forth — a different and very personal encounter with the special kind of ordering of the visual equivalent that one man has composed for the universal reactions of all men to their environment of objects and events.

After this discussion of awareness, a logical question can be inserted: Where does one find all this art that is to be appreciated?

THE MUSEUM AND THE ART GALLERY

In recent history the museum-art gallery has served as the central collecting agency for housing and preserving current and, especially, historic examples of our art heritage. These institutions, under public and private control and support, have amassed quantities of artifacts and have displayed them in an appropriate setting for the public. In the course of time many have become famous for great collections. Some possess art that traces the mainstream of artistic development over long periods of time; others are noted for their special concentration upon art from a particular period or cultural group. Some have specialized in one or more kinds of artistic expression, such as manuscripts, prints, tapestries, sculpture, crafts, or paintings. Many were started with the endowments of kings and princes, and others have grown out of generous gifts made by wealthy patrons of the arts.

For the general public and for scholars with specialized interests, the art museum is usually the place where one goes to find examples of art to appreciate and study. Throughout Europe, the United States, Latin America, and other countries with some cultural drive which makes them aware of the importance of preserving and presenting the arts of their own people or from other sources, the museum has been the agency responsible for collecting, preserving, and presenting this record of man's artistic development. Governments such as those of Mexico, Egypt, and Israel, following in the path of others before them, have made a national goal of preserving the art monuments of the past centuries that are connected with the nation and its culture. These are a source of national pride; the people, through the art of the past, can understand the fullness of their heritage and gain a sense of their destiny.

In the United States the refined art of collecting and presenting art through the museum is a fairly young venture compared with older countries. The geographic spread of land and population has made it necessary to disperse museum locations across the nation. Most large urban centers and even some of modest size have established museums in order to make art available without traveling long distances. New York and the East Coast, however, have a greater number of museums and collections with the largest quantity of art products; they are still considered by many as the "only" places to go and look at art. This attitude is hard to change, although all logic and the quality of collections in other places have suggested that art objects of quality are to be found not too far from the majority of our population.

The past half century has seen the increase in the number and quality of private collections which have been opened to the public. Also, there has been an increase in the number of smaller galleries supported by the art dealers and of local exhibit centers in both large and small communities. Art has become a valuable and costly item, and a fairly substantial fund and income are required to start or continue building a good collection. This does handicap new institutions and makes it necessary for them to specialize along lines that will receive support from a smaller and perhaps less sophisticated segment of the population.

Usually when one wishes to go somewhere to look at art, the city museum or the gallery in the nearest urban center is the place most likely to satisfy this desire. The increase in museum attendance testifies to the interest of many people in this activity; the selection of the art museum as a place to visit during a vacation trip confirms it.

When considering sources available for looking at art, it should be noted that the mass media — television and movies to a lesser extent and the publishing industry to a large extent — have devoted some of their resources to enhancing judgment and taste. Although they are not quite the "real" thing, the abundance of excellent color reproductions produced by the printing industry and the large number of well-illustrated books on art subjects and portfolios of reproductions have brought examples of art within financial reach of many. Reproductions in color are framed and used to brighten homes; they serve also as an excellent background of acquaintanceship with art, which is very helpful whenever there arises the opportunity to view the actual work in the museum collections.

AN EXPANDED VIEW OF OUR ART RESOURCES

In our discussion of art we have taken a broad view of what should be included and have been attempting to draw attention to the human control of form and space and color no matter where it occurs. When art is mentioned, although many of our examples have of necessity been limited to painting, sculpture, and architecture, the reader should understand that this reference has included all that goes under the label of art. What has been discussed about the creative process for the painter or sculptor has equal validity when applied to the potter, weaver, graphics designer, jeweler, city planner, and interior designer. With this broader view of what can be included in a discussion of art, the reader's opportunity to look at art is greatly increased.

Many years ago a very thoughtful man, while riding on a train, voiced the thoughts that many people have had about the panorama of sights that meets the eyes. He was especially disturbed by the apparent lack of visual sensitivity expressed by the public's unconcern for the environment of the small towns and of the outskirts of our great cities. He wondered about the apparent lack of application of all the art that was being taught to children in the schools and about the inconsistencies between what people said was desirable and what their actions indicated. This was in the 1930s, not a particularly optimistic time to start a crusade focused upon the solutions to art problems in everyday life. Melvin Haggerty decided that something should be done about helping people to become more aware of the existing art in their environment and about the use of education to help them solve the art problems they face in everyday life.

Owing to his initial leadership, the emphasis of art education in the public school was changed from a limited focus on painting and sculpture to a broader concept of art as a part of all human endeavors. The emphasis in education was organized around functional areas, including art in the home, business and industry, recreation, religion, school, and community as well as art and the individual. It was in effect an art for the consumer, which here means more than "purchaser." Perhaps the most lasting effect of this idea was that it gave new dignity to the crafts. It also helped to make teachers and people in general more aware of the breadth of artistic expression from which personal satisfaction might be derived.[1]

At intervals there have been drives for city beautification, highway beautification, city planning, for a city center, a mall, or parkway, and there have been crusades to remove visual illiteracy, to clean up billboard advertising, and to establish community art centers, cultural complexes, and centers for the performing arts. These are all indicators, however slight, of a renewed public interest and demand for something that will build the felt need for satisfactions with an aesthetic component. Despite all the indexes pointing toward an interest in art and aesthetics, many obstacles remain in the road ahead.

---

[1] Melvin Haggerty, Dean of the College of Education, University of Minnesota, supported by the Carnegie Foundation, organized the research project around the idea *Art in Everyday Life*, which influenced curriculum planning in art education throughout the United States, starting about 1936 and extending, with changes, to the present.

Because of the prolific amount of news about art developments thrown out to the public, there is both caution and misunderstanding about the outpourings of creative zest and energy of the artists of our time. There is so much going on that is experimental. This so bewilders the spectator that he wonders if art and artistry are stable and safe. They, the artists, seem interested in strange things and have a peculiar way of showing what interests them. Whatever the reason, there is still a persistent feeling that art is something far off in space and far back in time. This view is not only held by the layman and the person less educated in art; there have been collectors, highly educated and sophisticated people, who have been unwilling to admit that any art of quality has been created since about 1870. One collector and patron of the arts sold all the works in his collection that were made after this date; as a result, many less restricted museum collections have benefited by procuring some of their finest works. Although the general audience for art is not so specific about time limits, there is still a tendency to consider art from periods in the past and by the "old masters" as the only art worthy of consideration. This unsupportable concept will have to be adjusted if the spectator wishes to fully appreciate the art in his environment.

ART APPRECIATION: A BROAD EXPERIENCE

Chapter 2 of this book included an example of how the artist looks at his world which gave the reader an account of how an artist sees his backyard. It was purposely limited to the kind of adventure in seeing that was within the frame of reference and potential of most people. We wish to introduce the reader to how he might see and look at the art in his immediate environment with a parallel illustration.

For this purpose we have selected a relatively small suburban community; one can find many like it surrounding most large and medium-large urban communities. A certain amount of selectivity was necessary in order to be sure that the art to be found was of fairly good quality and represented the broad spectrum of situations and small environments in which art might be found. The chosen example is a good one, fairly representative but not quite "average." Any small town would not quite serve our purpose, although, if one looks carefully, it is possible to discover "gems" of art, notable monuments that have been generally overlooked and unappreciated by local inhabitants and the world at large. For example, there are two small towns on the border between Minnesota and Iowa, both of which have banks that were designed by the very famous architect Louis Sullivan. They are small banks in small towns; yet they are visual statements of a qualified and respected artist and bear the marks of his expressive abilities. In one's own backyard there are often quality expressions of artists to be seen and appreciated. By becoming sensitive to the art close to home, one can have a springboard for an expanding awareness of and sensitivity to aesthetic experience in the world at large.

Our example is a residential community with very few residents who work within the village limits. Established early around the fringe of the inner city, it has become the home of many of the city's middle- and higher-income business people. It is a community of nine thousand good single-family homes; there are about one thousand multiple-dwelling units within its borders. There are two country clubs, above-average schools, sixteen churches, and many acres of park and playground space. About eighty percent of its high school graduates attend college. Almost all of the parents graduated from high school and more than half had education beyond high school. Its residents are mainly in the professions, business, office work, sales, and skilled trades. As reported, this is not strictly "typical," but it is a hardworking, striving community of relatively young families with strong social drives. It is interesting to note that with all their advantages of funds and location very few of the parents subscribed to cultural activities, attended concerts, or went to art galleries with any degree of regularity.

EXPLORATION OF THE RESOURCES OF THE COMMUNITY

A preliminary review has suggested that one of the most likely places to find art would be in architecture — in residential, educational, religious, business, and recreational buildings.[2]

Selections were made with a view to our interest in calling attention to likely sources for the discovery of an experience with art that might be open to a fairly large segment of people across the country. We eliminated the central cities that were more likely to have a formal art center, museum, or gallery with the collection and exhibition of art as its function. This then is art outside the formal museum setting and in the best example we could find of the small town as a living art museum. The illustrations for this section represent only a small part of the total.

Using this small town as our example, we would like to indicate a few of its features that have broad applications to other towns and give a sense of how the artist has brought unexpected pleasures to those who wish to look for them.

This is not a comprehensive selection, but it demonstrates what can be found in a smaller community that is so often overlooked. There is not the dramatic contrast of the magnificent cathedral rising above the village or out of the cluster of shops and houses; what there is of noteworthy artistic expression has human scale and, having been woven into the fabric of daily existence, is somewhat harder to isolate because the examples of good design have been integrated into our other purposeful actions.

ART IN YOUR TOWN

Certainly, if we had adopted the customary procedure of other writers on modern art and architecture, our examples might have been more breathtaking, but taking them all in would necessitate a world cruise, plus

2 The authors are indebted to Beryl Christesen, an art teacher in the Edina, Minnesota, public schools, for her preliminary investigation on this project. She wished to develop a program for the junior high school students that would help them become aware of the aesthetic aspects of their community. From her efforts a visual statement, with slides and taped remarks by the students, was created for presentation to other junior high school students in art classes.

carefully annotated directions and unlimited time and patience. The selections of many authors have been spread sparsely over the globe. Our problem was to locate a large number of good quality examples within narrow geographic limits as proof that there are *resources for art appreciation* — "acres of diamonds" — near at hand for all of us.

The architecture within the narrow geographic limits of the community we have selected, as in many other communities, includes some representative examples of the broader scope of twentieth-century architecture. Its characteristics are an emphasis on technology, rational and functional, with surface decoration kept to a minimum. The dominant elements of this modern architectural style have spread throughout the world. The examples included here, although not world famous, are of good quality. Perhaps if we had all the world to choose from, our selections might have included Le Corbusier's chapel at Ronchamp, Mies van der Rohe's buildings in New York and Illinois; Robert Mailart's bridges of reinforced concrete, and Juan O'Gorman's library for the University of Mexico. There would also have been some of Frank Lloyd Wright's houses and buildings, Oscar Niemeyer's Cathedral of Brasilia, the new capital of Brazil, as well as Joan Miró's ceramic mural for the UNESCO building in Paris, or Naum Gabo's steel construction outside a department store in Rotterdam, and even Wallace K. Harrison's First Presbyterian Church in Stamford, Connecticut.[3]

Since we are concerned here with one town that could be like other towns, our choices were somewhat limited but, nevertheless, have beauty and excitement.

The home. In the mass of residential and other types of buildings it is often quite difficult to find a few homes that are significant as art and architecture. This is especially true in relatively new areas without a long tradition. Nevertheless, it is possible to find a few homes that have a special place in history and make comparisons with those representing our present ideals of prestige and building. In this community, as in many others, there is an example of the older type of home with its simplicity and ideals of decoration and construction according to the materials and skills of its era. It provides a convenient and acceptable comparison with new, larger dwellings with characteristics expressing the values and expectations of the second half of the twentieth century. The home representing the present time is built "into" the land with materials selected to provide visual satisfaction and to serve the needs and expectations of its owner for convenience, prestige, and even luxury.

The church. When the long tradition of art in relation to religion is considered, it is logical that one should look at the church architecture of the community. Here, as in residential edifices, there is usually a wide range of styles and ideals, so there should be very little difficulty in discovering good examples. In some cases it is the overall impression of the architecture; in others it may be a special feature that has a particularly strong

---

[3] The authors are indebted to a summary article by Allen Temko, **The Dawn of High Modern**, *Horizon*, vol. 11, no. 1 (August–September, 1959), pp. 4–22.

12-1–12-2
Hills, Gilbertson, and Hayes.
Lutheran Church of the Good Shepherd,
Edina, Minnesota.

12-3
Paul Granlund. Crucifixion.
Lutheran Church of the Good Shepherd.

12-4
Paul Granlund. Resurrection.
Lutheran Church of the Good Shepherd.

effect on vision. We have taken two examples out of many. One is illustrative of how styles of historical importance have been adapted or adjusted with spirit and in accordance with the aesthetic as well as deep religious ideals of the congregation (Fig. 12-1). The other, for comparison, respects the qualities of our age and time but is nevertheless adjusted to religious purposes that are significant to the people who use it.

The central church and its related buildings in many communities provides one of the best sources for observing a variety of satisfying art works that are not purely architectural. Sculptures and examples of handicrafts in metal, wood, and other materials are likely to be part of the total church complex. Also with the broadening of church-related activities, one is likely to find sections of the church complex which are designed for and dependent upon the use and exhibition of art to provide an atmosphere or mood consistent with the purpose of the structure. Paintings, tapestries, ceramics, and a wide range of other such materials are placed in the meeting rooms and work centers, which are open to observation even when there are no church services.

Two of the community's sixteen churches were chosen for our study: St. Peter's Lutheran Church and the Lutheran Church of the Good Shepherd. They contrast architecturally and show how different viewpoints have been accommodated within the form of the church building. The examples of sculpture have been given to show the continuation of a demand for art connected with the expression of religious ideas and ideals that goes back into the distant past. It is a bond with tradition, a heritage that has been carried forward. The photographs of the Lutheran Church of the Good Shepherd show the outside view (Fig. 12-1), the interior of the church (Fig. 12-2), and closeups of sculptures by Paul Granlund (Figs. 12-3, 12-4). The illustrations of St. Peter's Lutheran Church include an exterior and an interior view, plus the altar and a detail of the ceiling construction (Figs. 12-5–12-8).

Art and business. The design of buildings for industry, business, and commerce has given us some of the finest examples of architecture in the twentieth century. These examples indicate how a building can be beautiful to look at even though it has been designed for functional efficiency. Notable examples range from the Johnson Wax Company buildings at Racine, Wisconsin, to the T.W.A. Flight Center at Kennedy International Airport, New York, with skyscraper office buildings of insurance, publishing, and industrial corporations in between.

Many businessmen have discovered that aesthetics does not interfere with efficiency. A building can be attractive to the viewer and still have excellent functional efficiency. They have discovered that sound architecture and art can give them the kinds of space arrangement required for the manufacture and distribution of their products; at the same time, good design can provide the climate and atmosphere that helps their employees to work effectively and still enjoy the environment in which they work. Many business concerns have taken the initiative in supporting art beyond the architectural space. They have placed sculptures, paintings, mosaics, murals, prints, and other art objects in the offices, lounges, entrance halls,

12-5–12-8
Ralph Rapson.
St. Peter's Lutheran Church,
Edina, Minnesota.

12-5   12-6

12-7   12-8

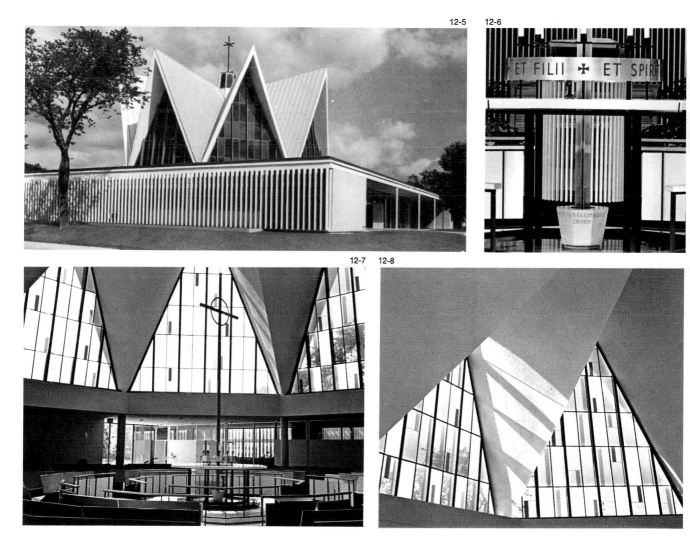

and dining rooms. These examples of art have been contemporary in style rather than conservative in taste. This initiative has done a great deal to acquaint the public with various art forms and to give people a chance to discuss and make up their minds about the art of their time.

In our selected community one of the best examples of the connection between business and art is Southdale Shopping Center. For our purposes this has advantages because from the original concept there was a plan and a desire to incorporate art objects into the total environment. Sculptures and mosaics were commissioned for the central court and for other areas outside the sales spaces. Murals were installed in the dining spaces and paintings were placed in the bank and in the complex of business buildings included in the center.

Prominent and well-qualified national and regional artists were commissioned to create works especially for this shopping center. The *Golden Tree* by Harry Bertoia is perhaps the best-known contribution, but there are other works that are consistently strong (Fig. 12-9). The sculptured trees placed in the Garden Court stand about 50 feet high; they consist of 250 rectangular panels of steel coated with welding bronze and are lacquered to keep their gold color.

12-9
Harry Bertoia. Golden Tree *(detail).*

12-10
Renee Sintenas. Burro.

Among the other sculptures in the center is a small bronze donkey designed by a Berlin sculptor, Renee Sintenas. This is something that greatly attracts young people, who can climb on it, so it is seldom without a rider (Fig. 12-10). As a result we can see how the rubbing of little bodies has given the bronze a patina that can only be obtained after years of hand rubbing and polishing by human contact. This is an art that people can get close to and use.

12-9   12-10

In keeping with the mood of the center are two other sculptures, *Three Clowns on a Unicycle* by Dorothy Berge and *Boys on Stilts* by Louise Kruger (Figs. 12-11, 12-12). The first is a vertical construction representing clown figures on a unicycle made of welded and brazed copper and bronze rod; the other consists of two figures carved out of laminated walnut which stand on 8-foot-high rods of welded brass. Another sculptor, Daniel Soderlind, created a 25-foot-long and 7-foot-high work of abstract sculptural relief that has been placed on one of the exterior retaining walls (Fig. 12-13). This is composed of small pieces of copper welded together and given a bronze-covered surface.

12-11
Louise Kruger. Boys on Stilts.

12-12
Dorothy Berge.
Three Clowns on a Unicycle *(detail).*

12-13
Daniel Soderlind.
Sculpture on retaining wall.

12-11

12-12

12-13

12-14
Cyrus Running.
Harbor, Evening 1960.
First Southdale National Bank.

12-15
Cameron Booth.
July 25th 1960.
First Southdale National Bank.

12-16
William Saltzman.
The Bridge Between. 1956.
First Southdale National Bank.

Paintings have been used effectively within the business establishments of the Southdale Shopping Center. In addition to creating a pleasant atmosphere, the management of the First Southdale National Bank has acted as a patron by collecting works of prominent regional artists. Other businesses in the center have followed its example (Figs. 12-14–12-16). Taken together, the works of art shown in this shopping center could not be labeled "provincial" and should be taken seriously as examples of the art of our time.

Nearby are other buildings, not in the shopping center, which add to the spectator's concept of art in business. The Modern Medicine Publications Building has an exterior which follows the curvature of the pond in front of it. It has a bold, clear design with glass walls and stone as the building materials.

Another, the Fairview-Southdale Hospital building, has made a defi-

12-17–12-19
Ellerbe Architects.
Fairview-Southdale Hospital.

12-17
Entrance.

12-18
Foyer.

12-19
Foyer rug, detail.

12-18   12-19

nIte attempt to dispel many of our aversions and unpleasant feelings about entering it. The entranceway and lobby are made attractive with sculpture and paintings; the selective use of color is evident in handmade rugs. Special consideration was given to make the children's section cheerful with color and symbols (Figs. 12-17–12-19).

Other examples. This identification of some of the uses of art objects and of design to improve an environment that will serve as a starting point for our personal development of aesthetic sensitivity is far from complete even in the narrow geographic limit we have selected. There is a children's playground in which the usual structures for sliding, swinging, climbing, and crawling have been designed imaginatively and look more like pieces of abstract sculpture than playground equipment (Fig. 12-20). The schools have kept up with educational innovations. Community meetings are held

in these buildings, providing for many people a contact with design in architecture.

The implications should be clear; although fragmentary and scattered, representative examples of art are to be found within a community and the process of art appreciation does not need to be delayed until one goes on a trip to distant cities and faraway lands.

There is art of quality within the reach of most of us. Learning to see and look at art can start from very modest beginnings. Our example also implies that the individual has to do something about it. Art appreciation is not something that is injected or taken in capsule form. We have illustrated how a public school art program might beneficially devote some of its efforts to taking an honest look at the whole community and identifying for the learner some examples of how art functions within the environment.

This has been essentially a rather broad approach to the development of aesthetic awareness. We would like to follow this up with another experience which illustrates awareness in depth.

12-20
Sculptural playground forms.

APPRECIATION: AN IN-DEPTH APPROACH

This illustration parallels a kind of experience that many people have and will have with looking at art. Our art object is a reputable work of architecture. Except for its location in a small community in Minnesota, it will give the spectator much the same experience as looking at the noted art monuments in France of Italy, for example, during a trip to Europe. With our example we hope to identify a procedure that can aid the viewer to center his attention upon the artistic order found in the overall composition of the building and then to move on to the unique features of interest that are seen separately. The parts within the whole can then be brought together more meaningfully and seen in relationship to the total compositional design. It is very much like our first illustration of the artist looking at his backyard. The individual starts with the whole church or yard, moves to some part of the total, which in turn becomes a new whole with an orderly relationship of the subunits making up its structure.

Our subject is St. John's Abbey Church located at Collegeville, Minnesota; the major architect was Marcel Breuer.

ST. JOHN'S ABBEY CHURCH

The church of St. John's Abbey with its majestic bell tower dominates the surrounding landscape and creates a magnetic aura to which few observers can fail to respond. There are countless structures of greater mass and physical dimension, but few can surpass the excitement generated by this edifice (Fig. 12-21).

Here is an architectural statement rooted in a liturgical tradition reexamined by the forward-looking Benedictine Order and implemented by the methods and materials of contemporary technology at the hand of a master artist.

The towering banner stands as a proclamation of faith; it is a guardian sheltering those who pass beneath its crossed vaults, but at the same time serves as a stern reminder that here is a building to be approached with reverence (Fig. 12-22). In addition to being a monumental sculpture in its own right, it serves as a standard for the cross, the sign of salvation, and as a tower housing the five bells which order the monastic day (Fig. 12-23). The great vertical slab reflects the sun on the north wall of the church (Figs. 12-24–12-26).

A journey into this church is an adventure into ever-changing space. Moving under the upward-thrusting bell tower, one enters the church through a low, narrow sheltering baptistry. Space has been compressed to a nearly human scale — the ceiling slopes gently upward and one enters the sanctuary proper under the increased height of the freestanding balcony supported on four massive cantilevered piers (Fig. 12-27). As one moves from beneath the balcony, space soars (Fig. 12-28). The folded concrete walls surge upward and across to form the pleated ceiling vaults; these in turn march forward as all space now seems to impinge upon the

12-21–12-24
Marcel Breuer.
St. John's Abbey Church,
Collegeville, Minnesota.

12-21
Façade.

12-22
Bell tower.

12-23
Cross in tower.

12-24
Crossed vaults.

12-22

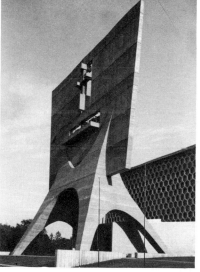

12-21

12-23   12-24

12-25–12-28
Marcel Breuer.
St. John's Abbey Church,
Collegeville, Minnesota.

12-25
Vertical view of tower.

freestanding altar — the primary purpose of the church. This emphasis is heightened by the semicircular choir stalls surrounding the altar and by the white baldachin floating from the ceiling on nearly invisible cables (Fig. 12-29).

The psychological impact of the space varies with one's particular vantage point. At times one feels an intimacy with his surroundings, and at others one experiences an awesome feeling of his own insignificance.

For example, the stairs to the balcony are narrow and of a comfortable human scale. Continuing up a ramp, the rear pews can be seen through openings in the cantilevered piers a short distance below. As the ramp rises, one becomes conscious of the powerful upward sweep of the massive folded walls, which arouses an uncontrollable feeling of exhilaration and awe (Figs. 12-30, 12-31).

Since the sidewalls are raised clear of the ground and are supported by concrete buttress piers, the space does not end within the confines of the sanctuary but extends through large window areas on both sides of the church. This creates a feeling of lightness that counteracts the massive structure of the enclosure. Screen-walls of glazed tile enclose cloister gardens on either side of the church and control the outer limits of the visual environment.

Although nothing is pretentious, the attention to detail of ordinary materials and the simplicity of form born of the structural process has resulted in a unified structure of subdued elegance. Throughout, richness of surface and detail has been achieved without the addition of superficial ornamentation. The ferroconcrete interior surface reveals all the carefully planned structural parts. The surfaces of the form boards have been imparted to the concrete and the thin relief ridges where concrete was forced between the boards creates a rich surface in the ever-changing light. Large areas of concrete have been articulated by shadow lines, produced

12-26

12-26
Spiral stairs ascending to bells.

12-27
Balcony against window wall.

12-28
Note the dramatic cantilever construction.
Balcony.

12-27   12-28

12-29
Church interior.

12-30
Openings in piers.

by strips of wood fastened to the inside of the forms. These serve to provide a finished joint between the various pourings of the concrete and serve to hide any separation which might have occurred in the curing. Even the air bubbles in the concrete are a part of the beauty and honesty of the construction.

Large floor areas of red paving blocks are accentuated by different methods of coursing. Aisle areas are laid in herringbone pattern, while other areas are laid in parallel rows.

In the crypt the ceilings reveal the deep concrete coffers which are the structural form of the floor above. Careful consideration was given to relating the scale of the coffers to the diverse volumes of the crypt areas (Fig. 12-32). One deviation from the direct use of material and simplicity of treatment is the granite-block facing on the exterior walls of the church. The busy character of the small module which exists nowhere else seems out of character (Figs. 12-33, 12-34).

Consistent with the creative use of ferroconcrete are the lectern and communion stations, which are simple, classic concrete volumes with a bushhammered finish that sets them apart from the texture of the general structure (Fig. 12-35). This process is used elsewhere in the crypt as well.

Wood is used throughout in a simple, strong, tasteful manner. The pews and choir stalls are of laminated oak stained nearly black. The pews, a simple L shape in cross section, have no legs, but are supported by three dark marble blocks (Fig. 12-36). The choir stalls are somewhat more complex because of their function. The rows terminate in stark treelike shapes which loom like silent guardians in the reflected light (Fig. 12-37).

The direct use of wood is continued in the confessionals where pierced rectangular patterns are not only decorative but allow for the passage of light and air. Simplicity of detail continues down to the plain wooden door pulls.

12-31

12-32

12-31
Folded wall.

12-32
Assumption Chapel in the crypt.

12-33
Exterior view of folded wall.

12-34
Detail of small granite blocks.

12-33   12-34

12-35–12-40
*Marcel Breuer.
St. John's Abbey Church,
Collegeville, Minnesota.*

12-35
Lectern.

12-36
Pews under the balcony.

A simple definition of architecture is "the manipulation of mass, space, and light." It is light which breathes life into this structure. The daily movement of the sun throughout the changing seasons produces an infinite variation of light and shadow.

The tremendous vertical concrete slab of the bell tower reflects the southern sun onto the north wall, which is a self-supporting concrete honeycomb inset with stained glass. The ever-changing flood of colored light warms the gray concrete walls and gives rise to an atmosphere of mystery and joy (Fig. 12-38).

Piercing the roof directly over the white granite altar, a lantern of amber glass allows a shaft of golden sunlight to scribe a profoundly symbolic and richly aesthetic arc across the sanctuary (Fig. 12-39).

The reflections of cloister walls and church interior on the clear fenestration at ground level create the illusion of transparency, adding another dimension to the existing space (Fig. 12-40).

The artificial lighting of the building has been studied just as carefully. Nearly all fixtures are either hidden or set into deep perforations in the ceiling construction. Along the walls, lights hidden in the edge beam shine upward, heightening the dramatic sculptural quality of the folded concrete construction. The sanctuary becomes illuminated without an obvious source of illumination.

Consistent with the strength and simplicity of the architecture is the discreet use of religious artifacts; very often their indiscriminate use tends to obscure the significance of major sacramental elements.

A twelfth-century Madonna adorns a small chapel niche at the rear of the church, and in its setting of contemporary ferroconcrete and glazed tile, it creates an unmistakable bond with the rich religious tradition of the past (Figs. 12-41, 12-42).

The subterranean corridors are lined with thirty-four individual chapels to serve the many priests of the monastic community. Each has its own

12-39

12-37
Choir stalls.

12-38
Stained glass, detail.

12-39
Stained-glass wall as seen from behind the altar.

12-40
Reflections.

12-40

12-41–12-44
*St. John's Abbey Church,
Collegeville, Minnesota.*

12-41–12-42
*A twelfth-century Madonna in
a contemporary setting*

simple granite altar composed of various geometric solids supporting a rectangular slab. Many are adorned with a sculpture of the saint after whom the chapel is named, and each has its own unique crucifix (Figs. 12-43, 12-44). The ceilings are faced with solid dark cork, which acts as a sound barrier and creates the solitude and sheltered atmosphere conducive to personal worship.

Much can be said about the liturgical symbolism inherent in the design, such as the bell-shaped plan, the entrance leading through the baptistery, and the central altar, to mention but a few. As in the great religious architecture of the past, however, the structural logic of the enclosure becomes one with the spiritual function which directed its form.

IMPLICATIONS OF THE BROAD AND IN-DEPTH EXPERIENCES

When we have identified the unique aspects of looking at and appreciating art, one thing stands out — that we are sensing a special kind of order. The description of St. John's Abbey Church reinforces this belief. Theory is taken out of the abstractions of words and placed in a context of tangible, visible reality. Here we have and can see how every part of a struc-

12-43   12-44

12-43
Roger Majorowitz. St. Louis.

12-44
Gerhard Marcks. St. Boniface

ture has been welded together for one purpose. The architect knew and felt this unity, and we can see and feel this same thing.

In our narrative we have, from a more prosaic point of view, incorporated a number of architectural precepts, such as "truth to materials," "fitness to purpose," "movement in space." Above all, we have attempted to illustrate the functioning of unity in complexity and to show that despite a lavishing of interest and concern upon all the small details of construction, there can be an overriding concentration upon the whole. It is one building and must be seen and remembered for its oneness; the parts, however intriguing they might be, have beauty in relation to all the other parts. Together they make up the whole, which is the important thing. If this does not happen, the architect, for all the beautiful parts he has created, has failed and his building has failed.

In our narrative on St. John's Abbey Church, we have tried to give the reader a way of looking at any and all other buildings. As we look at the great cathedrals and other monuments of the world outside, the guide provided by this description should suggest what to look for and how to see it. The religion might differ as well as the materials and setting, but the basic design problems remain constant. When looking at architecture, the viewer should remember the limitations and expectations that have been placed upon the architect; a knowledge of these will contribute to our appreciation of his creative solution. In the building of a church he must give consideration to the beliefs and "articles of faith" of the clergy and the congregation; the ritual and ceremony that will take place within the walls determine the form that the architecture can take; however, there are conditions that he must meet with imagination and originality.

Comparison with our first example of the very broad view of art in a small community reveals some notable differences. In the one case there were so many facets of visual experience that it was very difficult to see the "forest" because there were so many "trees." The unity of the whole was more difficult to perceive. In the other the problem was to screen out a few good items from a mass of confusing data. Different sets of visual-perceptual skills were needed for each situation. Together they are the core for the development of aesthetic awareness.

REFERENCE GUIDELINES FOR ART AWARENESS

The development of aesthetic awareness starts from the perception of the work of art itself. But the spectator must integrate material from many and varied sources in order to achieve an intelligent appreciation of these results from artistic-creative behavior. These sources include: (1) biographical data on the object and the artist; (2) knowledge of the historical situation and the social context in which the object was created; (3) considerations of the working method; and (4) the immediate purposes of the artistic production. This seems reasonable for a specialist and scholar who devotes all of his time to this goal; however, for the general spectator and the beginning student there should be some answer to the question: How do I connect up all the seemingly unrelated information that I hear and read about art?

There are many widely distributed publications that concentrate upon biographical data of the artist and the art object. Many of these integrate information about the broad historical and social context in which the work was created.[4] This book is concerned with the working method and purposes of artistic production.

Are there any principles or basic concepts that can serve as guidelines for the observer when he sets out to appreciate or become aware of art?

The idea of guidelines that provide the spectator with a framework for more effective appreciation is valid. When one has a frame of reference, new experiences can be met with confidence and can be brought into harmony with previous encounters with art. To build a useful structure of this kind for an art appreciation that incorporates an awareness of the past, a recognition of the present, and a faith in the future, certain basic understandings can be developed out of an examination of the process of art and the process of art appreciation. The following guidelines for art appreciation start with the recognition that this depends upon: (1) the perception of an object; (2) the characteristics of the person doing the perceiving; and (3) the interaction of these personal characteristics with the properties of the work of art which is being perceived. This suggests that guidelines for art appreciation should incorporate aspects related to the viewer as well as to the art object.

THE SPECTATOR: LOOKING AT THE WORK OF ART

There are certain generalizations which apply to the viewer. First, all people have the potential for aesthetic awareness; it is not limited to a few gifted individuals. This removes a false barrier and allows the spectator to approach the work of art with freedom and expectancy. Next, appreciation of art grounded in perception has two dimensions: feeling and knowing. Both are important and call into play distinct aspects of personality.

Special conditions for the perception of a work of art are open-mindedness on the part of the observer and concentration of his attention upon the object being observed. An attitude of open-mindedness clears the way toward a willingness to take out of the work that which has been put into it by the artist. When there is a concentration of attention almost to the point of isolation of the self from other things and events in the surroundings, the spectator is ready to function efficiently. This, then, is the kind of attention one should practice when looking for the values or significance in an art object.

In looking at art the goal is to sense the special kind of order that characterizes art expressions rather than to make immediate sentimental associations. It should be kept in mind that in appreciating or developing an awareness of art the viewer is expected to react to it. Reacting, not evaluating, is the important action. In the processes of looking at art and

---

4 See such publications as **The Color Slide Program of the World's Art, The Color Slide Program of the Great Masters**, and **Landmarks of the World's Art**, all published by McGraw-Hill Book Company; the Time-Life **Library of Art**; and the **Metropolitan Seminars in Art** (John Canaday, ed.).

reacting to it, the spectator will compare and rate the new experience against the background of his previous and familiar experience with art; however, a fine distinction of good, better, and best need not be made before an appreciation of the qualities of the art object can be obtained.

CONCEPTS FOR ART APPRECIATION

From our references to what the artist does and how he does it and to examples of works of art which have been used to clarify aspects of this process of art, the following generalizations may be made. These are broad concepts that will help the viewer unify new experiences with others he has had. The old and the new are meaningfully related to the main- stream of art through the course of time. These concepts are presented as examples; one need not be limited to them.[5]

ART REPRESENTS VISUALLY THE CULTURE AND ERA IN WHICH IT WAS PRODUCED

A culture or civilization has used art in accordance with the purposes and values deemed important by that culture. The philosophical and aesthetic premises dominating the era find their visual equivalents in the work pro- duced by its artists. The preoccupations, the vital concerns, the values placed on the individual, and the scientific notions of the people and the age in which they live are all to be found in the works of art of that place and time. The visual representation of space in sculpture, architecture, and painting has changed as people and their thinking have changed; the struc- tural plans for compositions and even the superficial subject matter helps to place a work in its correct frame of reference and helps the viewer to understand why it looks as it does.

The most immediate example of art as a visual representation of an era can be found in the art of our own time. We know only too well what is happening today in our own country. When scientific discovery is of great magnitude, and when the course of political, economic, and social events bear down on us with great intensity, it seems reasonable that the artist who is being affected by these same forces will produce the kind of art that is part of our twentieth-century scheme. It is at the same time exploratory, visionary, and subject to rapid change. This parallels the pat- tern of our era. The artist lives in his own time and cannot help but be affected by and reflect the era with which he is identified.

ART IS A VISUAL STATEMENT OF FEELING, NOT OF FACT

The major role of art has been the expression of feeling in order to trans- mit an understanding of things and events that have happened to the artist in his interaction with his environment. Thus art and its validity can best

---

[5] A set of concepts as a frame of reference for the development of art appreciation has also been suggested by James Schinneller (see bibliography).

be measured as a statement of *feeling*, rather than for its merits according to the yardstick of *fact*. We should expect a personal element distinguished by the individual sensibility of the particular artist. We react to a work of art and should be moved by it. The artist is interested in ideas, but what he communicates are his feelings about them.

To many spectators fact and reality are made up of events and things as they have seen them with their own eyes. For the scientist, fact is something that can be measured accurately with his instruments or which will occur again when all conditions are exactly the same. Yardsticks of this nature give us strange measurements when applied to art. The artists of the twentieth century and at times in the past have changed the measurements distorting them to emphasize the feelings they wished to express. Arrangements of the parts and groups of things associated in compositions move away from the facts of visual or measured reality, to create a new reality where feeling is the paramount issue.

RETENTION AND REJECTION MARK EACH PERIOD

Sometimes, when we look back into the history of art, we have the somewhat mistaken impression that in times past things were safer and stabler. As man has vitality and the desire to improve his way of living, the art of man is also characterized by this same tendency. Thus one art movement replaces and follows another. Our example can best be seen in the art of the last twenty years. In this short span of time we have seen one movement arise and another replace it as the first invention is superseded by another. This has been confusing to many observers who have seen a succession of art tendencies erupt on the scene.

Abstract expressionism was dominant for a time, only to be replaced by pop art, op art, and kinetic art, with all manner of subtendencies coming into play at the same time. Ways of working and attitudes toward materials, space, and what previously constituted important content have undergone transformations which seem almost diametrically opposed to that which preceded it.

Often one must search diligently for some universal qualities with which to relate one of these tendencies with another or to find its links with the past. Art developments of the last thirty years were surveyed in Chapter 1; sources out of the past were traced for each of the "new movements." Although the sources are not exactly similar to the new, enough has remained to give familiarity to the new. For example, the efforts of the pop artists become familiar when considered with the work of the Dadaists; kinetic art is easier to understand if reference is made to futurism, which arose almost fifty years earlier.

THE SUBJECTS AND MATERIALS USED BY ARTISTS ARE UNLIMITED

Appreciation of the work of the artist is not based upon an idea that certain subject matter is better than some other or that an art product formed out of one particular material is necessarily more valid than one made with some other choice of material.

Art in the twentieth century has reflected developments in science, exploration of space, psychological attitudes and uncertainties concerning nuclear warfare, as well as the contrast of abundance in one part of the globe with scarcity and privation in others. The art of the caveman and primitive peoples reflected their anxieties regarding natural forces and supernatural beings. Subject matter concerned nature, fertility, myths, and gods. The period of the Renaissance had logic and a rational approach to science and life; the subject matter, the art, the materials employed, and the manner of presenting space on a flat surface reflected the ongoing conditions of that time.

The materials of the artists have seldom been limited. He has used all that was available to him. In contemporary art we find the resources and the discards of our civilization employed as media by the artist; in other cultures and at other times we have found the artist taking advantage of materials from his natural environment — porcupine quills, rattan, silk threads, and the refined metals of his culture.

Plastic, steel, ferroconcrete, and other products of technological and scientific advance are the twentieth century's art media. We should also expect the artist to utilize the machinery and tools of his own culture. Today, the use of light as a new medium for the artist should not startle the spectator, since electric power, motors, neon tubes, lenses, and light-projection equipment are part of everyday existence. It is not that one material is superior to another artistically and that the work of art made from those materials should automatically be classed as superior for appreciation; rather, attention should be directed to how well the particular medium becomes the effective tool for the expression the artist wishes to convey.

At various times we have tended to equate bigness with goodness. At the present time there is some danger that the viewer of art might get the impression that there is something particularly admirable about the fact that a particular artist has painted a canvas on a very large scale, and that it should be admired for this reason. There is nothing unusual about the canvas that is 30 by 10 feet in dimension when we consider that the ceiling of the Sistine Chapel was larger. The work of Michelangelo did not depend on scale for its effect on the viewer. A piece of sculpture 60 feet high should not be considered admirable for this reason alone. The sculptured heads on Easter Island, which are comparable in scale, were made under primitive conditions without the aid of machine tools or pieces of heavy equipment to assist the artist with problems of construction and placement on the site.

ART NEED NOT BE DISTANT IN TIME AND PLACE

This brings attention to the tendency of the spectator to assume that art products of the distant past or from foreign lands are somehow more worthy of appreciation than those by artists of the present time who are from the same region or country as the observer. Artistic merit for appreciation is based not on the time and place of either the artist or observer but on the expressive quality of the work. It is natural that the spectator may prefer an art product of a particular period in history. Preference is, however, only a narrow dimension of appreciation; aesthetic sensitivity is a much broader concept in which preference may be a special case.

Because of today's communication facilities, one finds a great deal of artistic cross-fertilization between nations. For a period of time in the past, artists of one nation tended to exert a great influence on others; art and artists in the United States found inspiration and direction in European sources. We also know how much the prints and other art from Japan influenced European artists at the beginning of the twentieth century. Now national boundaries are once more being crossed, and there is a free flow of ideas among nations. Perhaps abstract expressionism and pop art developed more rapidly here and then spread outward, but many people in European and other nations have investigated optical and kinetic art with equal speed and depth. As communication between artists and nations improves, art will have more of a universal character.

ART IS THE CONTROLLED PRODUCT OF THE ARTIST'S EXPERIENCE

Art is purposeful and is directed by the intentions of the artist to an end. His goal may not have been completely and finally set at the beginning of his work, but there is a sense of direction which motivates the efforts of the artist.

During the 1960s randomness and the "happening" have been exploited as a replacement for art as the controlled concept of the artist's experience. Minor efforts and clichés have been declared significant. There has been a tendency to substitute literary declarations for quality of expression. Much of this has come about because of a misunderstanding of the role of accidents and "chance" in artistic production. Certainly the artist with skill and intuition will take advantage of things that happen during the course of his work, but he bends and shapes these to his own purposes. He does not stop or depend upon "good fairies" to provide a masterpiece. It has been said that if a group of monkeys were placed at typewriters and allowed to type at random, the combination of letters coming out of their efforts might, by the laws of chance, eventually approximate something of great literary merit.

There is much speculation about some artist's methods, such as those of Jackson Pollock and his preoccupation with dripping paint on canvas; it must be noted, however, that the way he dripped paint on the canvas was highly controlled. The method used to get paint on canvas was merely a substitute for brushwork. The artist who spread paint on canvas by running his automobile tires through a vat of paint and then onto the canvas was in a way using the brayer (a rubber or gelatin roller used for spreading ink on a printing surface) as a tool for painting on canvas.

Random happenings will continue to be enjoyed, but as transitory events. As these are not purposeful efforts of the artist, it seems appropriate to use the power of the language to make distinctions and call them what they are — random happenings or experiences. Other than that, they are not art.[6]

---

6 See Sylvia Angus in **It's Pretty But Is It Art?**, *The Saturday Review*, (September 2, 1967), pp. 14–16.

CONCEPTS WITH SPECIAL REFERENCE TO THE TWENTIETH CENTURY

No doubt there are additional concepts similar in level and intent to those mentioned above. Those which have been stated provide support and direction for the individual who becomes involved with the appreciation of art. They offer a thread of reference and continuity that links one period of art with another. Specific works of art, styles and movements in painting, sculpture, and architecture have a relationship to each other when they are considered in terms of concepts which link them together as part of the total experience of looking at art.

Continuing with this idea of a basic set of understandings, we are still faced with the particular problems that more specifically refer to the art of the twentieth century. As examples of certain concepts relevant to twentieth-century art, two are suggested. One concerns the erosion of boundary lines that have separated one form of art from another (for example, painting from sculpture). The second refers to the new dignity that the crafts have attained in the contemporary scene despite almost total mechanization of industrial production.

TRANSCENDING BOUNDARY LINES

Inventions, novelties, innovations, and the use of new and old materials in new ways have gradually eroded the conventional boundaries between one art form and another. Flat paintings with a collage of things glued on the canvas can be considered a kind of relief sculpture. Going a step further, painters have prepared their canvases in such a manner that the painting surface is no longer flat but in bas-relief. This is done by stretching the canvas over ingeniously contrived ribs or supports which raise or lower the surface and add a real third dimension that thrusts the painted image out into space.

Sculpture has often become a pictorial tableau combining flat, painted appendages with three-dimensional forms. At other times it has encroached upon the domain of architecture when total environments have been created in the cause of sculpture.

Printmakers have produced deeply embossed surfaces by adhering thick chunks of metal and other objects to the plates. These are forced through the press and produce prints with deeply embossed and textured surfaces with a variety of depth levels. The result is a true relief print. The line between print making and painting was cut when painting incorporated the techniques of silk-screen printing as a major method; printmakers have sometimes borrowed the collage technique from painting.

Pottery has been made by other means than the traditional method of coil building and wheel throwing: it has been sculptured from slabs. Wheel-thrown pieces are cut apart, reassembled, shoved, twisted, and reshaped into complex constructions that have little in common with the pure, simple forms of classic ceramics (Figs. 12-45, 12-46).

Adventuresome craftsmen have broken down the barriers separating arts and crafts. Jewelry is small sculpture; there is little to separate it from sculpture except scale and its function of personal adornment instead

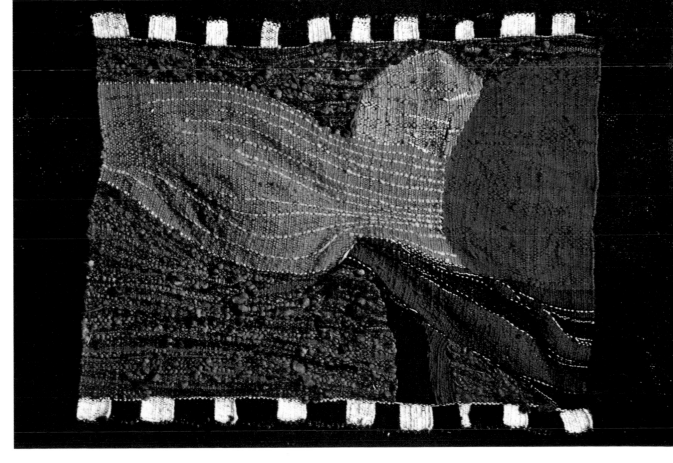

12-45

12-46

12-45
Larry Golden. Slab Pot I.

12-46
Larry Golden. Slab Pot II.

12-47
Three-dimensional effect achieved in weaving.
Janice Bornt. Hanging. St. Paul Art Center.

12-47

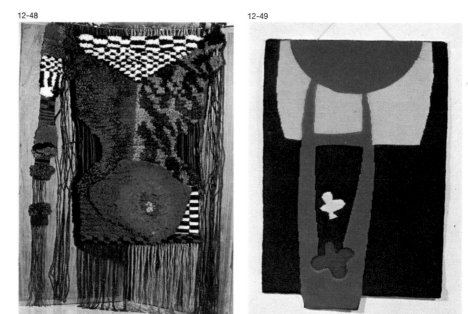

12-48
**Three-dimensional effect
achieved in weaving.**
*J. Rodono-Brown. Hanging.
St. Paul Art Center.*

12-49
*Terry Illes. Hanging.
St. Paul Art Center.*

of landscape or building enrichment. Weavers of tapestries and rugs as well as the ceramicist have become sculptors. Hooking knotted tufts of yarn into rugs give them a three-dimensional appearance (Fig. 12-47); woven wall hangings and screens move backward and forward in space, and strips of wood veneer and "found" materials like grasses, fibers, wood chips, feathers, and shells are included in their design. A light, airy feeling is obtained by gathering the yarn and dividing and shaping the material as it is suspended from heavier rods. Weaving without a loom and "creative" stitchery have freed this form of design from conventional procedures and patterns of folk art; the craftsmen have become painters with yarn (Fig. 12-48).

These are only a few examples that illustrate the dynamics of contemporary art as it has taken on a new look through a combination of evolution and revolution.

A NEW DIGNITY FOR THE CRAFTS

For quite a long time unwarranted distinctions have been made between the so-called "fine arts" and the crafts. The assignment of various art forms to one category or the other has been rather arbitrary and inconsistent, without regard for any acceptable criteria or clear definitions related to aesthetic merit. Activities such as jewelry, ceramics, and weaving have, by some system of mental gymnastics, often been assigned to a secondary position. It was decided that painting, sculpture, and architecture have some rare, special qualifications that things designated as crafts did not possess. The classification system went on despite the fact that many of these art forms designated as crafts had qualities that could evoke an aesthetic response equal to that for products of the fine arts. The creators have been men taken seriously for their accomplishments as painters, sculptors, and architects; the architects Marcel Breuer and Frank Lloyd Wright also designed furniture, and many of our jewelers and potters have also been sculptors.

The man-made object as shaped by a craftsman has given us the record of mankind from prehistoric times to the present era. The first tools and utensils were restricted to the consideration of utility and were shaped accordingly; later their shapes were refined and decorated. As man learned and improved there was a steady evolution of the shape or form of the object; choices had to be made. These decisions did not affect the utilitarian functioning of the object; they rested upon aesthetic values. When we learned to make a variety of tools capable of shaping vessels for holding grain or water, the decision among them was an aesthetic choice since all could perform the original intended function. The formal element present in the craftsman's products which surround us has had great impact upon the formation of taste and the customs of peoples. With the advent of almost total mechanization the creative and imaginative ability of the sincere craftsman stands forth. The products of his craft are cherished and bring a fine sense of beauty to the beholder.

Kazuhiko Egawa has summarized the fundamental elements of Japanese object making as simplicity, functionality, and spiritualization. Although machine production may have caused the technical tradition to deteriorate, tradition in the fundamental aesthetic elements has survived in modern Japan. Designs of craft products from the Scandinavian countries have similar qualities. The same holds for small but highly productive groups of craftsmen in the United States and England. These men and women have kept in touch with tradition and have attended to process and materials. But they have also, through the exercise of judgment, broken away from conformity to think originally and to create work in which their own personal qualities come through. They are aware of the qualities inherent in materials and bend them for their own purposes; they understand the demands for functionality but modify the rule of "form follows function" by expanding upon the limitations of structure and materials. The craftsman becomes an artist when the thing he makes expresses or excites feelings.

Contemporary craftsmen use ancient processes, but they refine them and make such applications as are in keeping with the ideas and thinking of the modern world. Thus, many of the traditional craft processes have been revived; the artist does not hide from history, but with flexibility and imagination he directs these processes to a higher level of individuality. Batik is an ancient method of applying color and design to fabrics. By using a dye-resistant wax, the artist can control the areas and shapes that receive color. With this old process, the modern artist has created both subtle and exotic patterns and has added a new dimension of individuality where conformity to tribal habits had been the standard. Other textile design processes including block printing and tie dyeing have been combined to give us products that are consistent with our time (Fig. 12-50). The processes of mosaic, glassblowing, and enameling have been revived with innovations to fit into the present era. The influences of other times and civilizations have survived in the way we experience the work of our contemporaries (Figs. 12-51–12-53).

12-50
Sister Mary Remy. Fabric.
Block print and tie dye.
St. Paul Art Center.

394   ENCOUNTER WITH ART

12-52

12-53

12-51
Northwest Coast Indian.
Chilkat blanket for a doll.
St. Paul Art Center.

12-52
Northwest Coast Indian.
Whale-motif shirt.
St. Paul Art Center.

12-53
Northwest Coast Indian.
Chief's rattle.
St. Paul Art Center.

Our artist-craftsmen, like others before them, take the best from the past and added contemporary understanding in order to create and evolve new forms. Workers in metal and wood design furniture that is sculpture large enough to sit on. Chests, doors, and other pieces are formed with the acetylene torch; surface treatment of the steel or other metals includes welded units, chemicals applied and burned with the torch. Layers of gold or silver are added during the execution of the design.

Usually the craftsman works with the simplest of tools and, using the oldest of materials, directs all of the work himself from design through execution. The three aesthetic factors attributed to artists' products — materials, structural form, and underlying meaning — have equal reference to the craftsman's work. The considerations of materials and design organization are generally the same whether the artist creates a painting or a tapestry; the craft product may have to meet functional requirements that are not expected from the painting unless it is a mural (Figs. 12-54–12-62).

CONCEPTS AS A GUIDE FOR APPRECIATION

The value of such a set of concepts is that they can be employed by the individual as a frame of reference into which his new experiences of looking at art can be meaningfully integrated. His new experience fits effectively into his whole collection of prior separate contacts. Reasonable relationships can be established; what is seen for the first time is brought into the appropriate context of all other art he has seen before. Novel solutions of one century maintain their unique qualities, but there is enough connection with the past and the future for the viewer to be secure and confident.

Perhaps it is with the art of his own time that the person interested in developing art appreciation has his greatest difficulties. This art has not gone through the tempering process of time itself. This winnowing process of retention and rejection helps to consolidate random trends or tendencies into styles; it eliminates "novelties" or puts them in their place in the main current of art. This period of the twentieth century has its own special problems, some of which have been discussed elsewhere in the text. Among them are the preponderance of technical innovations,

12-54   12-55

12-54
Claude Conover. Bottle.
St. Paul Art Center.

12-55
Sheldon Carey. Weed pot.
Collection of Ruth Roach.

12-56
*Thomas Shafer. Branch pots.
St. Paul Art Center.*

12-57
*Robert Arneson. Vase.
Applied decoration.
St. Paul Art Center.*

12-58
Warren MacKenzie. Bowl.

12-59
Alix and Warren MacKenzie. Vase.

12-60
Marie Woo. Vase.

12-61
Lyle N Perkins. Stoneware jar.
St. Paul Art Center.

12-62
Toshiko Takaezu. Twin-spout bottle.
St. Paul Art Center.

12-59

12-60

12-58

12-61

12-62

the expression of change just for the sake of change, the conflict between newsworthiness and validity as art, and the misunderstanding about scientific and technological advances as the hallmark of our time and culture. These are but a few of the factors that confuse and retard the person who is striving to bring into focus the art and the artist of today.

How can a set of concepts contribute to an appreciation of the art that is now being produced? Mostly by eliminating the irrelevant considerations and by allowing us to concentrate our attention upon the work of art itself. We can then react to it without confusing and peripheral considerations.

The concept that art represents visually the culture and era in which it was produced tells us that valid American art of today will reflect the character and concerns of our own time and the values of our culture. These are diverse, so we can expect the art to have this diversity. Thus it is not surprising to find pop art side by side with op art. The right to dissent, so cherished by a free society, should be expected from its artists. They as people will see only a part of the total picture. Some will be interested in pointing out our wasteful excesses; others will seek security in the logic and orderly measured rationale of the scientists.

Add to this a second concept, that retention and rejection mark any period, and you then know that everything that goes under the name of art doesn't have to be accepted as such. People will do the accepting and rejecting; the art reviewer and critic can suggest what, in his opinion, has merit and should be given attention. Each spectator must do his own appreciating.

The concept that there are no limits to the subjects and materials used by artists means that no preferential treatment need be given a work of art just because the subject matter or the materials used in it happen to be currently popular or novel. Appreciation should be based upon consideration of how well the artist has succeeded in presenting a visual statement that brings meaning to the spectator and a responsive reaction from him. This reaction is to the total form of the work, not to one factor among many. There is certainly a provocative attraction for the spectator when he is confronted for the first time with a product made of unusual material — plastic bags filled with air, neon tubes, flashing lights, or a squashed automobile. But there can be both good and bad art made from these things just as there have been exciting and dull paintings made with oil paint or sculptures from stone and wood. It is how well the materials have been used by the artist and the significance of his statement, not that he made it out of "rags, bone, and a hank of hair." When the artist has nothing to say, glamorous materials and computerized light sequences will not create a message.

It has been stated that art is the *controlled* product of the artist's experience. This helps us to separate art products from the accidental happening or event. Each is placed in perspective; each can be appreciated for what it is. The other stated concepts can help the appreciator cut through the surrounding fog and look to the work of art for a significant statement rather than for a miscellaneous expression of physical dexterity or a momentary whimsical tour de force. In the following chapter we will examine the process of making value judgments on works of art.

Chapter 13

ART JUDGMENT, PREFERENCES, AND TASTE

It should have become clear that in order to attain a level of aesthetic awareness people have to see for themselves. To hear from someone else, no matter how respected the authority might be, that a work of art is "a good one, moving and exciting, much to be admired and appreciated" is hardly enough. The work of art must be perceived by the person himself if he is to feel its impact and power and thus react to it. Personal involvement and a response of some sort must take place within the person. This is why we have emphasized openmindedness (willingness to perceive), attentiveness (self-involved readiness to perceive), and empathy (feeling oneself into the act of perception) as conditions for developing aesthetic sensitivity. Reading about art in books or hearing about it from lecturers may help fill the fund of information for the thinking-knowing dimension of appreciation. But no matter how good the quality of the writing or the speech, an essential and primary dimension — feeling — is not present to a significant degree.

With the visual arts, feeling comes from seeing. The elements in the work of art have this power to evoke a personal response. The expressiveness of the color provided by the artist can excite or depress. The sweep of line can project power, action, or tranquillity; the masses of sculptured volumes can give a feeling of exaltation or puzzlement to the viewer. One cannot tell another person that this will be the case; he must see for himself and in seeing will feel it for himself. This dependence on authority and on information, not on seeing, is often unwittingly carried to an extreme.

Over the years the authors have had the opportunity to observe students in a number of art history classes. An interesting phenomenon often takes place. The students are so busy writing, taking down notes from the lecture, that they seldom take time to look at the slides. These slides have been carefully selected with much effort by the teacher to reinforce the ideas

13-1
Maurice de Vlaminck.
The Blue House. 1906.
Minneapolis Institute of Arts.

13-2
Francesco Somaini. Orizzontale.
1960. Walker Art Center,
Minneapolis.

13-1   13-2

he is presenting verbally. Perhaps the students have already seen them (which is improbable), but in any case, they are usually not seen but heard. We admit that color slides or black-and-white and color reproductions of works of art are not as good as seeing an original work. It is entirely possible, however, to derive an effective aesthetic experience from them, especially if they are of good quality.

Adults are usually more self-contained in reactions to seeing art; children are more spontaneous and overt in their response. This is repeatedly demonstrated when one is present as groups of children are exposed to art in museums, galleries, or in classrooms. When a particularly colorful or provocative reproduction is flashed on the screen, the response is immediate and noisy. A gasp and a quick united burst of sound swell from the audience. This is a reaction not in sentimental association with the subject matter but to the color and shapes presented. This is the way young children respond, especially when the art is abstract, colorful, and energetic.

With the kind of seeing — perceiving that goes beyond "noticing" and includes feeling — one can begin to take in the qualities or special kind of significance which has been put into the work by the artist. This significance reaches us from three sources: (1) the medium (matter); (2) its pure formal arrangement or structure (form); and (3) the expressive meaning of something for which subject matter has been transfigured and appears as content.[1]

13-3
Eduardo Paolozzi. Little King. Minneapolis Institute of Arts.

SIGNIFICANCE OF THE WORK OF ART

Significance of the work of art and its meaning for the spectator appear as pure aesthetic space, as in the lyrical, nonobjective paintings of Kandinsky and in many of the works called by the name optical art. Their appeal rests with the application of the medium and its visual-tactile qualities as employed by the artist. This is also the force at work in many abstract expressionist efforts. It is the major point of contact of the viewer with the art product. For the spectator the significance arises from the sensuous qualities of the marks of the brush or knife which are left in the thick impasto of pigment as it sweeps across the canvas. The paint drippings of Pollock and the confident surety of the slashes of Kline and De Kooning carry this sense of the importance of the medium and its manipulation. In sculpture it appears as the flow of metal arrested like cooling lava, as the surface patina of weathering and chemical action, as the marks of tool and torch, as the light-reflecting surfaces of polished metal contrasted with the dull, stolid heaviness of lead or iron, and as the glint of thin, tightly stretched wire of nylon with slabs of plastic or steel (Figs. 13-1–13-5).

Significance in form or in pure structural relationships is found in the works of Gabo, Pevsner, Albers, Arp, Mondrian, and Nicholson. Many

---

[1] Ralph A. Smith, **The Assent to Aesthetic Education**, *Art Education*, vol. 20, no. 2 (February, 1967), pp. 8–12.

13-4
Ernest Trova. Wheel Man.
1965. Walker Art Center,
Minneapolis.

13-5
Harry Bertoia. Wheat.
Northwestern National Life
Insurance Company, Minneapolis.

13-6
Jacques Lipchitz.
Prometheus Strangling the Vulture.
1944–53. Walker Art Center,
Minneapolis.

13-6

sculptors, such as Smith, Caro, Larry Bell, Pol Bury, McCracken, Paolozzi, and Yamaguchi, have reduced their work to a very few and exceedingly simplified basic structures. These works depend upon the significance of relationships of pure form for any contact with the viewer. The work of artists who profess an interest in a highly logical, intellectual approach to art depends upon subtle mathematical or proportional sequences as the formal principle of its design and organization. Artists who work with representational subject matter often concentrate more attention upon the formal design of their compositions than upon faithful rendering of the subject matter (Figs. 13-6–13-8). The observers must perceive this formal order to comprehend and appreciate their efforts.

Another order of significance in the work of art is to be discovered in the pervasive character and intensity of its portrayal of something in its subject matter. What appears as content is this subject matter transfigured by the artist as a vehicle for his message. A message sent by

13-7   13-8

13-7
Lyonel Feininger.
Church of the Minorites II.
1926. Walker Art Center,
Minneapolis.

13-8
Jacques Lipchitz. The Matador.
Minneapolis Institute of Arts.

Robert Hodgell. Christ Scourged.

telegram has letters and words transformed into dots and dashes of sound; a photo of the moon's surface comes to us as electrical signals that must be translated. In art the images are sometimes transfigured from their original shape or are used to symbolize some mood or feeling which has no direct visual likeness (Figs. 13-9, 13-10).

For a long time artists have relied on this third order of significance (content) to touch the sensitivities of the viewer and communicate with him. Through this channel we become aware of the mood of sadness and sorrow of Grünewald's *Crucifixion* or of the terror and foreboding of Francis Bacon's figures, distorted and encased (Figs. 13-11, 13-12). We experience the joy and exuberance of Matisse's room interior, the serenity and majesty of the Gothic and Renaissance artists' religious subjects (Fig. 13-13), and a disturbing feeling of the odd and the mysterious "unreality" of the juxtaposition of objects in the surrealistic works.

PROJECTION OF SELF INTO PERCEPTUAL EXPERIENCE

When we are dealing with the special kind of significance embedded in the content subject matter of the art product, there seem to be greater differences in the way we apprehend it. Wide individual difference in perception occurs; the projections of highly personal interpretations happen more frequently. The use of artlike pictures and inkblot as the basis of many projective tests (Rorschach, Thematic Apperception, and others) demon-

13-10   13-11

13-12   13-13

strate how people looking at the same visual image will assign a wide variety of meanings to it.

In an informal test of this phenomenon with more artlike items, a group of senior high school students were shown a reproduction of a painting and asked to study it for a short time. Then they were asked to describe what they felt the painting was about. The example chosen was a work of visual realism. It could have been used for the illustration of a story in a popular magazine like *McCalls* or *Ladies Home Journal*. In the example there was a young girl, neatly dressed and displaying neutral emotions. She was inside a building and a number of other young people were standing in groups in the background. All in all it was a neutral, unsuggestive, and placid image. Observers were quite surprised by the range, controversy, and focus of the students' statements. The students concentrated their attention (as they should have) on the obvious center of interest, the girl in the foreground. The following statements have been chosen to indicate the range of significance this one neutral image had for the group.

One member said: "She's poor. The other students don't like her. She has no friends."

Another remarked: "She's rich and stuck-up. She thinks she's too good for the other students."

Still another stated: "She's lonely. The others are talking about her but she doesn't care what they say."

13-10
Max Beckmann. The Skaters.
1932. Minneapolis Institute of Arts.

13-11
Francis Bacon. Study No. 6,
after Velázquez's Pope Innocent X.
Minneapolis Institute of Arts.

13-12
Edvard Munch. Anxiety 1896.
Minneapolis Institute of Arts.

13-13
Giotto.
Madonna and Child Enthroned
with Angels.
Ca. 1310. Uffizi Gallery,
Florence.

A fourth said: "She can have all the friends she wants. But she can't be bothered. You just can't trust people!"

Another commented: "She's waiting for her friends to get there. They're going downtown now that school's over. They're going to have a lot of fun!"

Still another said: "She just got a job in that office and she's afraid to go in. When those other people get there it will be all right."

From these remarks it is apparent that there were widespread differences in the meanings obtained by the class members from the same object. These statements disclosed a great deal about the person doing the seeing and very little about the object being observed.

Over a period of time a record was kept of the responses of spectators to selected works in a number of major exhibitions of paintings. The groups of spectators included nonart-trained college students and clubwomen. There was considerable range in the art styles and tendencies represented in these exhibitions — from works by Hopper, Wyeth, and Sheeler to abstract and nonobjective works by artists of international and national reputation. Spectators were asked to express their ideas about the significance of works by the visual realists Hopper and Sheeler and then about more abstract paintings by Max Weber and others. Keeping in mind the very rough definition of category, it may be reported that there were greater differences within each of these study groups in their responses to the realist works than in their responses to the semiabstract and abstract paintings. The realist paintings seemed to have greater ambiguity for them than those with the less distinct imagery. Also, when their statements of the significance of the works were compared with those of art-trained groups of individuals (art historians, artists, college art majors) and with available statements of the artists about what they had tried to accomplish, there were greater differences for realist works than for more abstract examples. Conclusions from these pilot studies are not final answers. More stringent methods of collecting and analyzing data should have been employed here and in some other investigations of art preferences and of looking at art. The tendency for individual reactions to vary widely and to be more uncertain when identifying the meaning and significance of art works with content of visual realism deserves further investigation.

As might have been expected, the preferences of adults without previous experience with art in our studies were overwhelmingly in favor of the works of visual realism. There was no change in this respect after exposure to the three hundred works which covered the then-current range of styles and tendencies of art and artists.

RELATIONSHIP OF ART PRODUCTION AND APPRECIATION

The operational problem for the artist in the production of a work of art, simply stated, is the achievement of a harmonious interrelationship of matter, form, and content. The materials the artist has chosen are shaped or manipulated according to an appropriate technical procedure; they are shaped in an orderly fashion, or into a designed structure which has a formal plan. The meaning or content is expressed through the materials and the way they have been structured; and this desired meaning in turn dictates, to a degree, the choice of material and the formal structure of the product.

These same aesthetic factors of matter, form, and content are the channels through which the viewer may apprehend the significance and meaning of the work of art. Significance is given to the work by the artist and perceived in it by the observer according to the same elements; the essential characteristics of aesthetic production and aesthetic response are the same.

In the production of art the artist, in accordance with his own way of working, can start from any one of the three points of departure — the materials, the formal design elements, or the idea or content he wishes to express. Before he has gone very far, however, considerations related to the others will affect, direct, and condition the course of his creative process, the decisions he will make and the "look" of the final product. In some cases, the importance of one of the three will predominate, but the others are always involved. This is important for the viewer to know.

When one is looking at the work of art, there are times when its significance and meaning, are more obviously centered around one aesthetic factor, with others playing subordinate roles. As previously mentioned, the sculptures called "primary structures" and others known as "constructivist reliefs," as well as many of the better-known paintings by Albers and Mondrian, emphasize pure structural relationships. These are the content and the form in their work. When we search for significance in the paintings of Van Gogh and Munch, we can find it in their emotion-packed rhythmic swirls of pigment; but, beyond this, the content of figures and events and the compositional design are also necessary to the total effect and meaning.

ART PREFERENCES

The remark so often made in casual conversation, "I don't know anything about art, but I know what I like!" is clearly a statement of *preference*. We have made a distinction between art appreciation and art judgment, pointing out that appreciation has to do principally with perceiving the quality significance, and power of a work of art. We have stressed that the viewer's major role in appreciation is one of reacting rather than of making a formal assessment or evaluation. It is difficult to separate the two actions completely. People with or without formal training will seriously or casually make judgments about art. These evaluations fall into two broad classes: subjective and objective.

When you say, "I like that one," this is a statement of a preference, based upon subjective factors. You are always "right" and no defense of your selection is required. You are stating what for *you* is satisfying — personal and biased as it may be. Assessment is made in accordance with your own set of values, standards, and criteria of "goodness" for art or anything else.

When after examination you say, "That is a *good* painting," or "This painting is better than that one," these are art judgments. They should be made *objectively* and according to objective standards or criteria that can be applied equally to other than the item selected. This kind of judgment can be challenged and needs to be supported.

The subject of art preference and consumer taste in general has proved an elusive one for social scientists and art scholars. The social scientists have made some broad-focused attempts to attack the problem; the art scholars have ignored it when they could. For the development of art appreciation it is an important subject for several reasons. It concerns the question of how we learn to like art objects or ideas. Our likes and dislikes have influenced our attitudes and our readiness to engage ourselves completely in the action leading to appreciation.

The subjects of consumer taste and preference for art is particularly relevant to the appreciation of products of our own time, the twentieth century. As with women's fashions, innumerable fads, novelties, innovations, and a few superior new styles have appeared on the scene. The attendant publicity has made many of them familiar in a short time. This rise and fall of fads and fancies in the marketplace of art is, to say the least, bewildering to the spectator. But because of this situation, many serious questions can be asked with reference to appreciation of both the art of the past and the art of the present. Some of these questions are: What is the influence of the extent of familiarity on the degree of liking for particular works or art styles? When does familiarity outweigh other considerations? (Novelty or familiarity it has — but is it art?) What is the effect of familiarity (repeated exposures to a type of art) upon the spectator's acceptance of a new or controversial kind of art abstraction compared with older established works by Renaissance masters? From these questions we can see how the subject of preference and taste involves not only recent and successful art tendencies but also the liking and disliking of any and all styles of art that have aroused different kinds and degrees of public reaction and appreciation.

ART PREFERENCES OF YOUNG PEOPLE

There has been fairly extensive research on children's appreciation of beauty including the recording of simple judgments of preference carried out over the past thirty years in the United States and England. These provide a picture of the development of aesthetic awareness in children of these cultures. The following is a summary of findings from the early observations of Stein and Valentine and the empirical studies of Newcomb, Meier, Dewar,[2] Burt,[3] Littlejohns[4] and Needham, Bulley,[5] Child, and other researchers in this field.

These studies give support to the idea that very young children of preschool age have genuine aesthetic experiences. Some can make system-

---

2 Heather Dewar, **A Comparison of Tests of Artistic Appreciation**, *British Journal of Educational Psychology*, vol. 8 (1938), pp. 29–49.
3 C. Burt, **How The Mind Works**, Allen and Urwin, London, 1948.
4 J. A. Littlejohns, **Training of Taste in the Arts and Crafts**, Pitman, London, 1933.
5 Margaret Bulley, **An Inquiry as to Aesthetic Judgments of Children**, *British Journal of Educational Psychology*, vol. 4 (1934), pp. 168–182.

atic judgments of beauty as early as their fifth year; their capacity for making such judgments grows steadily with maturation and learning. These young children respond with pleasure mainly to nature and natural objects. At adolescence children find beauty in the human form and features or in the products of human craft and skill. Graphic or plastic arts are not often spontaneously listed by children or adolescents as a source of beauty.[6]

Young children are not particularly sensitive to the principles of compositional unity, balance, and rhythm in graphic form. There is however a rapid development in appreciation of them in the elementary school years.[7]

With respect to pictorial art, children have expressed a preference for pictures that were familiar or which portrayed objects or situations with which they were familiar. They had a strong preference for what is representationally "clear." Their own picture making or art production has moved beyond the spontaneous, uncritical, bold delineation of their feeling about what they know of their subject to a self-critical attempt to meet through their art a standard of what looks "real." The older and more intellectually able and also the art-gifted children tended toward "more objective" reasons and attitudes when noting the causes for their preferences. Their references were to technical skill or aesthetic merit in pictures — color harmony, form, composition, and design. This spontaneous mention of aesthetic criteria and general information about art correlated substantially with the individual's capacity for putting visual products in order according to merit.[8] It has also been reported that children of six or seven make better aesthetic choices, in close agreement with expert judgment, than children of ten or twelve. Aesthetic judgments of less-educated adults and laymen more closely resemble the art judgments of children than they do those of trained and well-educated adults; however, Irvin Child has reached the following conclusion from his research:[9]

> If we may tentatively take high-school preferences as representative of those of the general adult population, our data indicate that popular taste shows some systematic tendency to disagree with the judgment of experts. Younger children, in elementary school, prefer the work experts consider better only about 40% of the time. The figure rises with children's development, but even at the last year of high school hardly reaches 50%; systematic agreement with experts would be shown by a figure above 50%.

One of the important generalizations resulting from these studies of preferences and judgments is that aesthetic sensitivity, when attained, is the

[6] Edith Newcomb, **A Study of the Appreciation of Beauty in School Children**, *Forum of Education*, vol. 2 (1924), pp. 1–14.
[7] N. C. Meier, **Studies in the Psychology of Art**, *Psychological Monograph*, vol. 45, no. 1 (1933).
[8] Irvin L. Child, **Personal Preferences as an Expression of Aesthetic Sensitivity**, *Journal of Personality*, vol. 30 (1962), pp. 496–512.
[9] Irvin L. Child, **The Problem of Objectivity in Aesthetic Value**, *Penn State Papers in Art Education* (Paul Edmonton, series ed.), no. 1, Pennsylvania State University Press, 1967, p. 10.

product of development and learning through the years from childhood. Artistic training seems to shape it significantly and suggests that education enhances aesthetic sensitivity.

FAMILIARITY AND AESTHETIC CHOICES

We know that art appreciation depends upon seeing. But we are not so sure about the conditions of seeing which will bring our appreciation to its highest level or will make us more efficient and effective in developing or attempting to develop our appreciation of art. Television commercials are often based on the assumption that numerous repetitions and perhaps loudness and other provocations can affect consumer taste and make the product more desirable. But the situation in the classroom or with individual study is different from that of the marketplace. In the first instance we are more concerned with motivating the learning of individuals toward a personal solution of the riddle of art appreciation; in the latter we are usually trying to capture the attention of a passive audience in order to create a liking for ideas or objects that may be quite trivial.[10] The art appreciator cannot be entirely passive; he must take the first step of deciding to look at art and then become involved in the process. Although there are differences between the two situations, there is a major learning factor which is common to both. This is *repetition*, or how and where exposure to art and familiarity with it contributes to the development of appreciation.

A pioneer study of how familiarity may affect our attitudes toward a variety of items from everyday life was conducted by Maslow.[11] He had only a small number of college students in the experiment; fifteen met in the same room, took the same seats for a ten-day, two-hour-a-day exposure to paintings by fifteen well-known artists. Sessions were devoted to looking at the paintings and to a number of other quite different tasks. These included trying to write down and spell correctly the names of Russian women, copying sentences containing key words, and marking true-false tests. Conditions and material in the room environment were kept constant during the experiment. Near the end of the ten-day period, the students were offered something different to do or were asked to make a judgment of personal preference. For judging the paintings, they were shown a matched series of works by the same artists and were asked which in each matched pair was more beautiful; for the other tasks a similar procedure was followed.

The results showed a general tendency to choose the "familiar." Judgments of paintings were clearly affected by familiarity; the more familiar was preferred as more beautiful. It was more surely demonstrated that familiarity was responsible for the preference of the original set when another group of students, who were not involved in the experiment or

---

10 Herbert Krugman and Eugene Hartley, **The Learning of Taste**, in Perry Bliss (ed.), *Marketing and the Behavioral Sciences*, Allyn and Bacon, Inc., Boston, 1963.
11 A. H. Maslow, **The Influence of Familiarization on Preference**, *Journal of Experimental Psychology*, vol. 21 (1937), pp. 162–180.

exposed to the original series of paintings, split their preferences evenly between the two sets.

This study demonstrated the potent influence of familiarity on preference and on what is considered beautiful in painting. In another experiment, this time with music as the subject, Krugman wanted to find what happens to liking for the general category (in his study "swing" and classical music) when one has first learned to like a single item in the category.[12] He concluded that when familiarity with items created a liking for them, then some combination of familiarity and liking could create a liking for the general category. Applied to art, this could suggest that becoming familiar with the work of a pop artist (such as Andy Warhol, who has been widely publicized) and his paintings and getting to like them could lead to a liking for pop art in general.

Another study by Hartley, this time using art,[13] reached the conclusion that familiarity with items created familiarity with the category, but that this might or might not create a liking for the category. Transferred to our pop art example, this means that becoming familiar with paintings by Andy Warhol would lead to familiarity with pop art in general, but that liking pop art also depends upon a number of other factors. Hartley took as his art categories: Oriental, floral, landscape, portraiture, and modern. The findings about modern art in the experiment were interesting in view of the definite (pro and con) attitudes people expressed about it. These were to the effect that modern paintings were seen and either liked or disliked as a category (all lumped together) without much item-by-item sensitivity. Familiarity with the category of modern paintings increased moderately, but *liking for the category increased significantly.*

INFLUENCE OF FAMILIARITY ON ART PRODUCTION

Much studying remains to be done on the developing of consumer taste for art and on learning how to appreciate it. These investigations are reported more to indicate the state of affairs and to encourage exploration than to offer definite answers about how to proceed in the education of the public. Another study which attempted to discover the influence of familiarity on behavior and learning in art was conducted in Germany with very young children as subjects. The area of investigation had to do with the effects (favorable and unfavorable) of different examples of varying degrees of aesthetic merit upon the art products of these children.[14] Although the reference is to art productivity rather than appreciation, it has been reported here because familiarity as a factor in learning is of interest in both areas.

Five groups of fifteen children took part in the study. The procedure began with this drawing assignment: We are painting a father, who is in a garden; he picks apples and puts them in a basket. The period of being

---

[12] H. E. Krugman, **The Affective Response to Music as a Function of Familiarity**, *Journal of Abnormal and Social Psychology*, vol. 38 (1943), pp. 338–392.
[13] This unpublished study was reported in detail in Krugman, *op. cit., pp.* 110 113.
[14] Wolfang Metzger, **The Influences of Aesthetic Examples,** in Gyorgy Kepes (ed.), *Education of Vision*, George Braziller, Inc., New York, 1965, pp. 16–26.

influenced lasted for four weeks; then the assignment was repeated and the results were compared. One group served as a control and was shown no examples between assignments. The examples used in the experiment were simple line drawings of the three subjects mentioned (basket, tree, and man); all other pictorial references were removed from the classrooms. The replacements for each group were the following: for Group 1, line reproductions of motifs for Egyptian sarcophagi of the 18th dynasty; for Group 2, drawings by a modern graphic artist; for Group 3, drawings from an ordinary coloring book; and for Group 4, drawings by ten-year-old children. When the results were analyzed, it was noted that the groups under the influence of the artistically valuable examples improved almost five (for the modern graphic art) to ten (Egyptian motifs) times as much as the control group. The group with the examples of questionable value improved only half or one fifth as much as the control group. Considering the situation with "good" examples, the improvement under the influence of the Egyptian motifs was twice as great as that under the influence of the modern one. This was attributed to the fact that the Egyptian motifs had a fuller delineation of artistic expression which fascinated the children and compelled them to involve themselves more deeply.

This experiment demonstrated how the ability to draw can be affected to a surprisingly high degree — both favorably and unfavorably — by the examples to which the child is exposed. The researchers also came to the conclusion that the study seemed to prove that children do possess a native sense of differences in artistic value, which, if this is true, is atrophied later on in life through overexposure to inferior material.[15]

NONAESTHETIC CONSIDERATIONS

Preferences for art, like other preferences, are highly personal and subjective. They are affected and conditioned by many nonaesthetic factors. We have already discussed the influences of familiarity upon art preference; its effect upon art production has also been noted. Something should be said about other considerations that have played an important role in establishing preferences for art. These influences are powerful agents that are subjective in nature and are easy to rule out of our consideration. They include labels, styles, the artist's name, sentimental associations, price tags, cuteness, or the superficial novelty of "fashion" and storytelling qualities.

There has been very little research that can give us definitive answers about the degree and importance of these various influences upon the establishment of the preferences and the taste of the broad mass of the consumer "public" for art. From experience with the development of consumer demand in business and fashion we know that a variety of such factors has often determined choices and the values we attribute to certain products. It is reasonable to assume that our preferences for art will also be affected by other fringe considerations that are incidental to the works of art themselves.

Dependence upon stylistic labels for the identification of an art pref-

---

15 *Ibid.*, p. 23.

erence has definite weaknesses. Assignment of works to a specific category is helpful at times but has its arbitrary characteristics. Many works of art do not lend themselves to such easy classification. When an artist has an established reputation, his name on one of his products can be some sort of guarantee of quality, but this is also limited. As is true of all people, the artist will vary in his performance from work to work. Preferences limited to the works of well-known artists can exclude quite a range of products from our inspection and deny us many fruitful experiences in our appreciation of art.

The price tags placed on a work of art by the artist, dealer and the art market fluctuate with supply and demand or with changes of fashion and popularity. One cannot help but be impressed by the fact that a painting was purchased for two and a quarter million dollars; it also seems logical that we should, in turn, have a greater preference for it than for one with a price tag of two hundred and twenty-five dollars.

Sentimental associations also play a part in the determination of our preferences for one kind of art over another. Landscapes that are associated with a pleasurable experience of a trip or that bring back nostalgic remembrances of happy carefree years long past are often given a measure of preference that is out of proportion with their artistic merit.

Some people express strong preferences for works of art that have storytelling qualities which can be followed easily through a chain of connected images. This, however, places art in the realm of literature and into things that might be accomplished more effectively through literary expression. There are also many people who prefer art that has some connection with the visual reality of objects and events as they perceive them. They prefer a kind of art that has a degree of figurative or symbolic reference that coincides with their familiar experiences.

These are representative of the subjective factors that determine the preferences of children and adults for a particular work of art. They are factors outside the work of art itself. They become involved when preference decisions are made. It is difficult, if not impossible, to exclude them completely from consideration. As a result, preferences are often subjective, and they will vary according to the differences in the individuals making the decisions rather than according to the differences in the quality of the works of art that are being selected. The lack of agreement between people who are making the judgments may be attributed to the fact that they are distracted from aesthetic evaluation by the influence of factors that ought to be irrelevant. The art preferences of all of us are to some extent linked to the influences of time, culture, and personality.

MEASURING ART PREFERENCES AND AESTHETIC SENSITIVITY

A number of standardized tests have been devised by psychologists and others to measure aesthetic discrimination. Since its development in 1950, the Barron-Welsh Art Scale has been used extensively for research relevant to topics of perceptual preferences, aesthetic discrimination, creativity. It consists of line drawings, both ruled and freehand, in black ink on a white background; the subject is asked whether he likes or dislikes the figure. In the process of developing the test it was noted that when artists were compared with nonartists there was a significant difference in their acceptance-rejection of the various figures. Significantly, the figures liked by artists were more often those that could be described as complex-asymmetrical. The figures more often disliked by artists were of the simple-symmetrical sort.

The developers of this test were primarily interested in individual differences and the personality correlates of aesthetic preferences.[16] Data collected over a period of time have revealed the following relationships between preferences as measured by the scale and personality:

1. Preference for complex-asymmetrical designs is related *positively* to personal tempo, verbal fluency, impulsiveness and expansiveness. It is also related positively to independence of judgment, originality and breadth of interest.

2. Preference for complex-asymmetrical designs is related negatively to rigidity, control of impulse by repression, social conformity, ethnocentrism, and political-economic conservatism.[17]

The designers of tests of aesthetic sensitivity have all had the problem of selecting appropriate subject matter. It is impractical to employ the works of art themselves as items for discrimination; photographs in booklets or pairs of slides showing works of art have been assembled for individual and group test situations. Standardized tests of art judgment have been employed with varying degrees of success and reliability since the 1920s. Many researchers who have investigated the question of objectivity in the case of aesthetic value believe that such a thing exists and that it is to be found by looking at the opinion of experts rather than of unselected people. For the present the agreement of experts is the only basis for objectifying aesthetic evaluation. By agreement is meant substantial, but not absolutely perfect, agreement; experts have been defined as "people whose profession indicates them to be alive to problems of aesthetic value, to be reacting to works of art as works of art, rather than in terms of purely personal appeal of various kinds." We can therefore hope that their judgments are about aesthetic value.[18]

The Child Test of Aesthetic Sensitivity (1962), used for the study of aesthetic judgment and preferences, is made up of pairs of slides for group administration and of photographic prints for individual administration; it also appears in booklet form. Each pair of slides shows two works of art that are similar in character (in kind and subject matter) but differ in aesthetic value according to expert opinion. Child has presented evi-

16 The reader is referred to the theory of Herbert Read for the parallel analysis of the personality correlates of artistic production — that is, the connection between the personality characteristics of the artist and the visible characteristics of his art products.

17 For a full report on the topic see the following publications by Frank Barron: **Complexity-Simplicity as a Personality Dimension**, *Journal of Abnormal Social Psychology*, vol. 40 (1953), pp. 163–172; **Some Personality Correlates of Independence of Judgment**, *Journal of Personality*, vol. 21 (1953), pp. 21, 287–297; **Personal Soundness in University Graduate Students**, *University of California Publications, Personality Assessment and Research*, no. 1, Berkeley, 1954, p. 32.

18 Child, *op. cit.*, pp. 11–12.

dence showing that the test does measure aesthetic judgment — the ability to discriminate degrees of merit in aesthetic products or displays. Originally, more than three thousand pairs were made up by twenty-four different people; these were submitted to a panel of fourteen independent judges. Those which were retained substantially agreed with the judgments of experts. Seven sets of such slides were assembled, each containing 130 pairs. It is not necessary to use the entire set of 910 slides. A much smaller sample, carefully standardized and representative of the larger set, can be utilized for measuring individual differences in aesthetic sensitivity and judgment.

N. C. Meier, a pioneer in the field of art-judgment test construction, had envisaged a battery of three tests to provide a fuller, more complete, and more varied measurement of the facets of aesthetic sensitivity. The Art Judgment Test (revised 1940) examines an aspect regarded as fundamental and basic; the Aesthetic Perception Test (1963) has its premise in "the greater ability or capacity as observed in artists and confirmed by them, to observe phenomena (people, behavior, objects, etc.) with considerably greater adequacy than will be experienced by the non-art person." The third test was intended to cover creative imagination. As its subject matter, the Art Judgment Test has paired examples of works of art described by the author as being of "time proven" character; in one example the work has been changed slightly from the artist's original version. For the Aesthetic Perception Test the subject ranks items grouped in sets of four; the four versions offer a gradation in aesthetic character and are based on, but not strictly copied from, works of art of various periods.

Another, the Graves Design Judgment Test (1948), has been used quite extensively by research workers. This test was devised to measure certain components of aptitude for the appreciation of art structure; it "evaluates the degree to which a subject perceives and responds to the basic principles of aesthetic order-unity, dominance, variety, balance, continuity, symmetry, proportion and rhythm." Items to be judged consist of a pair or triad of designs. In each item one design is organized in accordance with the fundamental principles stated above; other designs in the set violate one or more of the principles. Abstract or nonobjective elements are used to avoid the possibility that representational art and the ideas and prejudices associated with the objects illustrated might influence a subject's decision.

There are those who question that the tests of art judgment and aesthetic sensitivity actually measure what it is claimed they do. These critics feel that judging photocopies, which are very small and sometimes of poor quality, or facsimile drawings of works of art is quite a different matter from judging art products and involves quite different attributes than the aesthetic sensitivity and judgment involved in the experience of looking at an original work of art. The developers of the tests are convinced however that their instruments are reliable and valid indexes of the human characteristics under investigation; their tests can function much as the drawings of a man can be employed as an index for the measurement of intelligence.[19]

---

[19] See the Goodenough Draw-a-Man Test.

Chapter 14

EVALUATION AND JUDGMENT OF ART

On the surface there seems to be very little connection between judging entries in a national cereal-box coloring contest and judging the art products of sincere and qualified artists. Many people might consider it "sacrilegious" to make any comparisons between the two. But from our experience with the former, some things were learned from this unlikely source which helped to clarify many aspects of the procedure for making judgments about art.

After the contest plans were well under way, some of the company staff members came to us for advice (our main claim to being experts was that we were available). They wanted to know how it would be possible to set up criteria that would differentiate among the entries. These standards or criteria had to have certain characteristics: (1) they had to be legally defensible if a protest was raised; (2) they had to be differentiated (as much as possible) on the basis of artistic merit; (3) they had to be relatively clear and efficient in application; and (4) they had to be consistent when applied by a number of different persons (in this case, five).

These four conditions posed by representatives of a commercial concern for a coloring contest are paralleled by those which are the basis for reliable and valid judgment of the quality of a work of art. This is a judgment of artistic merit according to criteria that are clear and universally applicable. These ratings should be made according to differences in the art products and not according to the personal considerations and biases of the person making the judgment. Objectivity, not subjectivity, is expected and required. Finally, it should be a judgment that can be defended and supported.

A lot of other interesting things happened during the contest judging experience. First, the problem of numbers: there were more than one million entries. A set of preliminary judging standards had to be developed. These had to be definable on an art basis (aside from the usual contest rules, which were nonart considerations). Also, they had to be clear and simple enough to allow persons with little or no art training to apply them. The total number of entries was reduced from one million to about twenty-five thousand at the preliminary judging stage.

Next, was the problem of prizes: in all there were about fifteen hundred. The wide differences in the value of the awards required that special care be taken at the division line between awards; with ten first-level awards it was necessary to be sure that item ten was superior to item eleven.

In summary (although not in defense of coloring contests), it should be stated that when proper judging procedures are employed, the two situations of evaluation have many parallel aspects. Incidentally, and as a minor reassuring footnote to the coloring contest, even under the most negative and restrictive conditions, a rare few highly creative individuals broke through and thwarted the "system" and produced art products of high quality. This was such a very, very small number, however, that it did not in any way suggest that coloring contests, coloring books, or paint-by-number sets have anything but a negative effect upon the artistic growth and development of young people.

It would not be altogether honest to say that with all this planning everything worked out to the complete satisfaction of all, including those making the judgments. Let's end with the statement that we were as "fair" as possible. Present at all times in the minds of the judges was the thought that the decisions might have to be defended; this is not always the case when a jury judges an art exhibition.

In the normal course of experiences with making judgments of works of art it will seldom be necessary to give prizes or to award a numerical rank to the art works under consideration. For critical judgment we employ words such as "good," "bad," "better," and "worse" and then tell "why" this judgment has been made. As in the coloring contest, certain conditions are implied when these words are used in connection with aesthetic judgments. These are conditions that work toward a certain degree of objectivity on the part of the person making the judgment. Some of these conditions are as follows:

1. Judgment should be based upon the aesthetic factors in the work of art itself.

2. The criteria employed should be clear, visually identifiable, and generally applicable (for other works than those under present consideration).

3. Judgments should vary according to differences in the objects, not according to the differences in the people making the evaluation.

4. Judgments must be defended and supported if necessary.

These considerations will help to make the process of judging a work of art *more* valid and reliable. The yardsticks for art are based on *relative* measurements, unlike the *absolute* measurements essential for science. Also, art judgment grows out of perception with its two components, knowing and feeling. Because of the "feeling" part, which is always present in making an aesthetic judgment, there will always be an amount of subjectivity in aesthetic criticism.

According to psychologists, feeling is one of the most subjective experiences of man; it arises from the self's individualistic judgment. Unlike many of his colleagues, the psychologist Karl Jung considered feeling to be, in some degree, a rational state of mind. To him, feeling tells us the value of an object, a value arrived at by comparing the original with one or more other objects. Judgment arrived at through feeling is based on the emotions, and the values derived from this judgment are as rational as other forms of evaluation made by an individual.

CRITERIA FOR ART JUDGMENT

There are people who are firmly convinced that it is impossible to judge art and that there are no standards which can be applied. This belief hinges upon the meanings that have been assigned to the words "judge" and "standards." These same people go happily about the process of assigning a grade to a student's drawing or to giving him an art grade on his report card. They also have little reservation about saying, "That's a good painting" or "That's a bad one." These are all art judgments and the people making them must have had some kind of standards in mind even if they could not put them into words.

The viewer can assume that the finished work of art was in the artist's opinion the best solution he could reach for the problem which he had set himself. The finished work has been taken to the point where any changes in its composition would make it less valid as an artistic statement. When an artist is asked how he knows when he was finished, the reply is often "because it felt right." In trying to explain what the artist means, we in turn solve our problem by telling ourselves that he acted intuitively. When a person confronted with an unavoidable decision is unable to give his reasons for the decision he has made, it may often be said that he acted intuitively. He has come to a decision without any conscious activity of which he was aware. Some problems can be solved only by intuition, without orderly rules of logic. The answers come from deep inside us through patterns and processes that cannot be traced and in which we cannot reconstruct our thought processes.

Like the artist, many people assign to intuition their judgment of a particular work of art. There may be a difference, however, between the viewer's use of intuition and the artist's because the artist was involved actively and completely with the act of creating, while the viewer's involvement is partial and somewhat removed. When the artist states that he has acted intuitively, he has a somewhat different basis for this operation from the viewer who insists that his judgments were arrived at intuitively.

Art judgments, according to Gotshalk,[1] are: "The systematic application of a set of relevant standards to a work." He also indicates that in the judgment process there has been a study of the factors that shaped the work and of its major features.

When we accept his definition of art judgment, some designation of what would constitute relevant standards is required. A start on the task of establishing appropriate standards may be made by looking for areas of agreement in the related areas of psychology and philosophy. Both groups of scholars agree (1) that the aesthetic experience, and with it art judgment, is grounded in perception, (2) that in looking at art there is a search for a special kind of order, and (3) that there must be unity as well as complexity in the object experienced as beautiful.

After a thorough examination of various criteria proposed for evaluation, Beardsley [2] concluded with the following:

> To sum up, the three general critical standards, unity, complexity and intensity, can be meaningfully appealed to in the judgment of aesthetic objects whether auditory, visual or verbal. Moreover, they are appealed to constantly by reputable critics. It seems to me that we can even go so far as to say that all their Objective reasons that have any logical relevance at all depend upon direct or indirect appeal to these three basic standards.

---

[1] D. W. Gotshalk, **Art and the Social Order**, Dover Publications, Inc., New York. Reprinted in Ralph A. Smith (ed.), *op. cit.*, pp. 343, 363.
[2] Monroe C. Beardsley, **Aesthetics: Problems in Philosophy of Criticism**, Harcourt, Brace and World, Inc., New York, 1958.

These standards are admittedly broad and general. If they are to have any value for the general viewer, the meaning of each should be amplified with specific indicators of how their presence in a work of art can be noted. When traveling for pleasure, one seldom has to consult a road map or navigation chart; when a more precise objective is the goal of travel, we resort to compasses, checkpoints, and navigational "fixes" that give a bearing from two or three points. Aesthetic judgments are like this more precise kind of travel. The three objective standards — unity, complexity, and intensity — have provided the person who judges art with checkpoints from which his evaluation or position can be established and defended. A description of what might be included under each of the objective standards is given below.

UNITY

The subject of unity comes up in almost all discussions of art. One description of design is that it consists of taking seemingly unrelated elements and bringing them together to obtain an aesthetically satisfying unity. Another view of the art process suggests that the aesthetic factors of material, form, and content are brought together and interrelated. The order, or unity, to be perceived when evaluating art is, then, the interrelationship of these three factors. At the same time it is important that there should be consistency within each factor when it is considered separately.

Unity in the work of art is perceivable and identifiable even for the person who has had only a minimum of experience with art. It is one of those things that leaves us uneasy when it is not present. Like balance, it is accepted without question when it is present, but we have vaguely unpleasant feelings when it is not there. When the artistic composition has parts that are not tied together, we generally say that it "falls apart," often without being able to put into precise terminology just what it is that is not quite right.

Our discussion of the psychological base of perception pointed out that separate elements are seen as a unit when they have similarities in size, shape, color, and texture. Also we tend to unify the parts, or elements in the visual field, according to "what goes with what," as we have learned from our previous experience. Separate parts of the visual field are unified through overlapping, proximity, and their directional thrust and movement. During his work process the artist is aware of these things and uses them either consciously or unconsciously.

To ensure unity in his composition the artist often employs a procedure which depends upon prior acceptance of a structural plan of great simplicity. For example, we have the pyramidal or triangular grouping of shapes or figures found in art works produced during many periods of history. A radial principle with the parts connected to a center core, an axial plan with parts joined to the central trunk, and the spiral and other geometric motifs have the potential of unifying an artistic composition with simplicity.

The artist also obtains unity in his art product through other devices, such as modularity. A high degree of visual unity is obtained when all the elements within the composition — whether it be architecture, painting, or sculpture — have a fundamental unit, shape, or size as the basis for their structural organization. In these cases the unity is obtained because every element in the composition has a precise relationship to the basic unit or module. Color can also act as the unifying agent. When all the colors used in the composition are closely analogous and some of the same hues appear in each of them, harmony is guaranteed; this common denominator relates each part to the total.

Unity is achieved in both child and adult art when all of the forms have an exact relationship to each other, as in the horizontal-vertical line pattern of Mondrian or the triadic color harmony used by many impressionist painters. The repetition or alternation of a smaller shape or motif provides visual cohesion to the whole. The repeated lines of columns enclosing a building of Greek derivation or exterior walls of repeated long arches give the visual impact, from the architectural viewpoint, a sense of oneness (Figs. 14-1, 14-2).

Unity in the use of materials is evident when the brushstrokes in a painting or the tool marks in a piece of sculpture follow a consistent pattern or direction. When the artist mixes media in a single work, care must be taken to make the right combinations. Watercolor combined with ink works well from the standpoint of unity, especially on wet paper, because the visual character of watercolor and ink are the same — both have the same feathered soft edges. The temptation to get "carried away" by the great abundance of exciting materials available is always with the artist. Disciplined restraint is required to prevent confusion for the viewer; his attention is easily distracted from the significance of the artist's work by the employment of a variety of different media.

14-1
Child art.
Pyrotechnics.

In art production, each material has its own visual quality; each process gives its unique characteristic to these materials and to the spectator's vision of the art object. Sensitivity and judgment are required of the artist when he combines a number of processes and materials in a single work of art. Integrity in the use of materials or a lack of it can be sensed by the observer even when he cannot give a verbal description of what is right or wrong (Fig. 14-3).

The nature, type, or category of symbols employed in a work should be selected carefully. Any departure from consistency is noted by the spectator. When used together, symbols that are organic in character and those that are geometrical in character can disturb the viewer. The artist should have a very good reason for combining them. This reason is connected with the meaning he wishes to project.

Even small matters can destroy unity in a work of art. For example, one part of a composition that is very beautiful when seen separated from the rest can be quite unsuitable and detrimental to the total impact. It must be "rebuilt" or destroyed if the artist hopes to preserve the unity of his composition. Surrealists combined symbols that ordinarily were not associated with each other or meant to be together. They did this for a purpose and kept their treatment of the total composition in harmony.

These are some of the considerations that contribute to unity within the aesthetic factors that make up art. On a higher level, however, the work of art is seen as a single unit whenever interaction of the aesthetic factors of materials, design, structure, and meaning are directed toward a single concept. This means that there should be not only unity within each of these three factors, but also that there must be an extension of

14-2

14-2
*Minuro Yamasaki.
Northwestern National
Life Insurance Building,
Minneapolis.*

14-3
*James Wines. Frontier Wall.
1961. Bronze and concrete.
Walker Art Center,
Minneapolis.*

14-4
*Ocotlán Cathedral,
Tlaxcala State, Mexico.
Ca. 1750.*

this unity whenever the three are interacting with one another. The artist must select and use his materials and processes with integrity and in a manner that is appropriate for the meaning he hopes to convey. At the same time the design or structural arrangement must also meet the characteristics of the significance or meaning he hopes to embody within his work. Certain materials give the artist greater facility and flexibility, and whenever these are important to his purposes, the choice of such materials would be the best that he could make.

We also know that repetition of or emphasis upon a particular structural arrangement can convey a mood to the viewer more effectively than some other selection. A composition that emphasizes diagonal lines or thrusts conveys quite a different meaning to the viewer than does one that stresses the horizontal. One gives a greater sense of power and action, whereas the other has more stability and is more suggestive of peace and rest. When the standard of unity is under inspection in the judging of art, what we are looking for is a total cohesiveness in which the visual metaphor and symbolism of the language of the artist is united with the materials and design structure of his work.

COMPLEXITY

From the viewpoint of the spectator there must be enough complexity in a work to hold his attention and stimulate his interest. At the same time there must be enough economy in the treatment to convey the meaning without the confusion of conflicting and miscellaneous information. The artist's problem has been to strike the right point of balance between complexity and simplicity. He can fall into error by moving across the line in either direction. During different periods of time, in accordance with the ideas and thinking of the people, art has taken quite different views of what was appropriate in terms of complexity for artistic compositions. At one time, emphasis has been placed upon the excitement, enrichment, and dynamics of an energetic art expression, as in the rococo and baroque (Fig. 14-4). In other historical periods, the nature of the times and its people dictated that the artist would work better in terms of classic simplicity and order, which eliminated excess articulations of the surfaces, forms, and shapes.

In a work of art complexity may be encountered when the number of units in the composition is large; it may also be found when only a few simple forms are used. In the latter case the complexity lies in the subtle interrelationships of these few simple forms with one another. Another kind of complexity is to be discovered in the treatment of surfaces in painting and sculpture or in the undulation of light and shadow across a surface.

When complexity is overdone, the viewer becomes confused or disturbed by the battery of images that meets his eyes. At the other extreme, excessive simplicity often becomes so uninteresting that the viewer's attention is lost and he remains at a level of indifference.

In the 1960s groups of artists have returned to what has been called minimal art or primary structures. What is often overlooked is that there is no great achievement in simplicity for its own sake. The artist gains little from verbal denunciations of his fellowmen or from promotion of his own work through extravagant literary support of his concept. The importance of the work of art lies within itself and the viewer must see and feel it. The viewer is not obligated to carry press clippings of interviews with the artist to reinforce the work of art which he is looking at. A cube may be a pure and static form and in itself beautiful, but to be a work of art something else must be contributed by the artist. How he uses the cube or what he does with it are important factors in determining the meaning that results from his creative artistry. Some artists who work with primary forms have managed to impart a modest amount of complexity to their products through their use of shadow, light, and color (Figs. 14-5–14-7). A large sculptured block becomes interesting to the viewer when it is tilted at a precarious angle that leaves its structural stability in doubt.

Connected with this issue of complexity in art is the need for a center of focus or interest. In a pictorial composition this brings the spectator constantly back to one area as the center of interest; time after time, as he looks at the whole canvas, his attention comes to focus here. The artist can locate an important element of his composition at this center of interest — one that has importance to the meaning he wishes to convey to the viewer in his work.

14-5
*Gio Pomodoro. Eucalyptus.
Minneapolis Institute of Arts.*

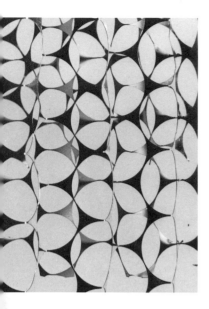

When complexity is being judged, the person making the judgment will arrive at a decision in terms of the richness of contrasts in the meanings, materials, and forms found in the work of art. His decision also depends on whether the art product lacks variety and is simplified to the point of dullness by a belaboring of the obvious.

INTENSITY

Examination of a work of art with attention to whether or not it is unified or complex is less difficult and perhaps more objective for the viewer than our third criterion: "intensity." The critic is also less likely to disagree with others on matters of technique and the structural or formal properties of a work of art than on its expressiveness. The aesthetic qualities that determine the intensity of the work of art play more upon the feelings and emotions of the viewer than upon his intellectual cognitive characteristics. This brings about greater differences among individual responses to the expressive intensity that the artist has put into his work.

In some instances this intensity or pervasive quality is achieved by sacrificing some of the unity in the composition. This decision is made by the producer and must be weighed in the overall evaluation process. When the artist has chosen to give up something to obtain a greater degree of intensity, the viewer must decide whether too much was given up to obtain too little in return.

A good aesthetic object must have some defined qualities that affect the viewer; it cannot be empty and offer nothing. The quality of intensity expected of the work of art covers a very broad spectrum and gives the artist great freedom to affect the viewer's emotions. It can be extremely calm and still or almost unbearably energetic and loud. The key word here is "unbearably." On occasion artists have chosen to depict an imagery that goes beyond the boundary of human endurance for horror, indignity, degradation, and disgust. The most open-minded viewer will rebel against these as subjects for contemplation. The act of contemplation is essential for appreciation and critical judgment. These works could have a quality of intensity, but this alone does not make them *good*. Standards in critical evaluation are subject to the limits of those qualities which we already value in human beings.[3]

EVALUATION OF A WORK OF ART

These reasons or criteria — unity, complexity, and intensity — can serve as focal points, or reference guides, for identifying characteristics that we can meaningfully appeal to in judging an aesthetic object. In evaluating a work of art we also need to arrive at a procedure through which we can obtain some relative measure of the degree to which the artist has achieved these criteria. For judgment, the work of art is measured against something.

[3] *Ibid.*, p. 324.

A FRAME OF REFERENCE

In our discussions of perception it has been noted that the meaning given to a "new" experience in seeing is related and associated with previous sensations to which we have given meaning. In much the same fashion a new experience in judging art is related to the previous contacts we have had and the meanings we have given to them. Out of our past encounters with art we have built up a reference base or model against which the new work of art under consideration can be measured; the work of art is measured against something, and that something is the cumulative background of our contacts with art. The critic or expert has achieved his position through the amount and depth of his experience with art, which allows him to draw our attention to what we ought to appreciate. As individuals we have the right to dispute, accept, or reject what we "ought to appreciate." When we move into the realm of evaluation and judgment, the course we decide upon should be dignified by the presentation of a valid

14-8
Edouard Manet. Olympia. 1863. Musée de l'Impressionisme, Paris.

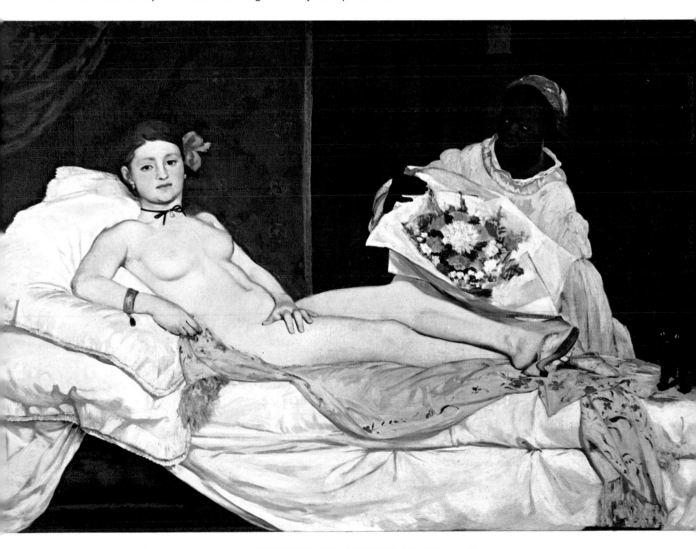

and reliable basis for our action. It is at this point that a distinction appears between appreciating and evaluating.

Critical judgment of art is quite a different matter from the casual evaluation which goes on in the normal course of appreciation. The work of art under consideration is compared with one or others that form the frame of reference of the judge or critic. The selection of suitable examples that, taken together, form the yardstick for evaluating the aesthetic merits of any product requires study, attention, time, and experience on the part of the critic. Usually, the person qualified to make judgments of art from his background of experience has built up more or less systematically such a frame of reference based upon the study of those works of the past which have a quality of excellence.

From the study of the history of art one becomes aware that certain art products stand out from the others. They have significant characteristics that distinguish them from other works of their time. For the critic or art judge they tend to act as distinguishing landmarks that show the development of artistic efforts through time. These works have some or all of the following characteristics and can be thought of as (1) *summating*, (2) *bridging*, or (3) *anticipating*.

Summating works of art are those that somehow bring together trends that have been developing for a period of time. A bridging work of art is one that incorporates elements of the past but also introduces elements quite different from those of the past. Edouard Manet's *Olympia* (1863) has this quality (Fig. 14-8). Anticipating works of art are those that break sharply with the tradition in which they are produced. They may seem strange and sometimes weird to contemporary tastes Picasso's *Les Demoiselles d'Avignon* (1907) was such a work (Fig. 14-9). Some works meet all three of these qualifying conditions.

It is quite natural for the critic, or even the general public, to refer to such identifiable and outstanding examples of man's creative effort and to relate new experiences to them. When taken together, this kind of collection of reference works represents a formalizing of the procedure that is employed quite informally by any spectator as he looks at examples of the work of artists in painting, sculpture, and architecture.

The selection of examples for constructing the scale against which new experiences can be measured is done with deliberation and after a great number of art works have been inspected. Such a reference framework will vary in detail from person to person. It is neither a very formal nor a standardized scale marked off in numbers like the Kline-Carey Free Hand Drawing Scale, or the Palmer Handwriting Scale of the 1920s. One does not slide the new work of art along the scale until a matching item is found and then transfer a number from the scale to the corresponding work of art. Instead, the individual's reference framework is employed somewhat informally and even semiconsciously, but references are made to past experiences with art when new ones are evaluated. This reference framework serves as a series of connecting links from one period of art to another and is illustrative of the concept that the art of any period is an outgrowth of previous times and has its roots within a historical background. The artist who has produced a work has been affected by contemporary sources and has his roots in all of man's heritage from the arts through

14-9
Pablo Picasso. Les Demoiselles d'Avignon.
Spring, 1907. Museum of Modern Art, New York.

the ages. He has learned about his art from the artists of the past.

The problem of establishing a valid and reliable scale for evaluating the works of art of the past is somewhat easier than that of developing a scale for evaluating those of our own time. A great part of the job of deciding upon a set of exemplars against which the new experience with historic art may be measured has already been done for us. Through some process of decision making certain works of art of an age are preserved and others disappear. What is left for us are those which have been valued as artistically important by the critics or art experts and those which have been valued by the general public because they speak more directly about the great themes of man, such as love, death, sacrifice, and victory. According to Broudy, "Works of art achieve greatness, (as distinct from aesthetic goodness, merely) as some aestheticians have noted only when they touch the nerve of man as critic and as man." [4]

EVALUATING CONTEMPORARY ART

In the present time the usual process of rejection and acceptance has not been carried out to its conclusion. The selection process is at least temporarily affected by factors such as fashion and publicity that can have a contaminating affect upon aesthetic decision making.

Although it is much closer to us, contemporary art (from 1945 to the present) often seems more difficult to evaluate, and we raise many questions about the condition of art today. The problem of judging the art of our era has been complicated by its rapid change and expansion with numerous styles and tendencies that have been launched by the artists. There has been a great deal of publicity and conflicting information distributed about current developments in the arts.

The study of art from the past can prepare one for contemporary art. The modern art specialist, as judge and critic, should find it both comforting and helpful to explore the past before judging and criticizing the present. The art of our time is woven into the fabric of all art. The innovations of pop art become understandable when given the background of the older Dadaist movement; the eye trickery of the optical artist has more than fifteen hundred years of history behind it, and the motion resolved by kinetics has long been a subject of artistic exploration.

Because of the factors mentioned above — rapid change, multiplicity of emerging styles and tendencies, plus publicity from competing dealers, and the lack of the leveling influence of time — the evaluation of works of art produced within the last twenty years poses a more difficult problem. The person who makes a judgment has many challengers. Honest questions are raised by people who make no claim to expertness, but who wish to know how judgments are made. Questions are asked, such as: how can you tell a good abstract expressionist painting (or a pop art painting or sculpture) from a bad one? These are fair questions and deserve some answers as long as the answers do not pretend to make experts of all

---

4 Harry S. Broudy, **Art Education in the Secondary School**, *Art Education*, vol. 18, n. 6 (June, 1965), pp. 24–30.

of us in one easy lesson. We should also realize that everyone will not be completely satisfied by our answers.

It should be noted that even in the evaluation of works in the contemporary art field there has been a substantial area of agreement among those making judgments (quite a satisfactory degree of interjudge reliability). In most situations where more than one judge has been involved there has occurred little or no disagreement about works that fell at the ends of the scale and were rated good or bad. It is also true that in the judging of art shows by a panel of experts the most original productions are not given first prize. First prize is often awarded to a less unusual entry on which all members of the jury panel could agree. That there is, however, some sort of basic artistic principle and preference to which all judges adhere is attested to by the many research investigations which have produced high-level correlations between the ratings of judges.[5]

AESTHETIC PARADOXES

The task of making objective judgments of the aesthetic merits of a work of art is not easy, even when the work has existed for a long time. In this situation we have an advantage. There is the accumulated evidence of the views of critics and experts who have studied it and the supporting information of its antecedents, the manner of its creation, and the culture that spawned it. Also, there are other works that serve as reliable references against which it may be compared.

Judging art of the contemporary period is a more difficult and complicated endeavor, partly because of the paradoxes that have been presented to the critic by the artistic innovations of the last twenty-five years.

Frohlich[6] has pointed out the new relations and the paradoxes that have arisen between contemporary art and the person concerned with aesthetics or the observant observer. The two poles of contemporary activity were defined as pop art and abstract expressionism. At one pole, pop art, the outward appearance of the urban environment is selected and accepted as creation; at the other extreme, the act of painting itself is offered to the viewer as the subject for aesthetic contemplation. For the viewer, both these art forms have raised questions that are almost unanswerable with logic. At one extreme, the artist has taken over the role of the critic, selecting objects and, in effect, stating that they "ought to be" appreciated. At the other pole, by making his own action the subject matter of his art, the artist is raising questions about whether his art product should be evaluated in the realm of aesthetics or in the field of philosophy that is concerned with ethics and human action.

Is a soup can, a washbasin, or a crushed automobile a better work of art depending upon who says it is? If a painting is a kind of self-exploration, how does the artist (or how do we) know whether he has succeeded when he does not know (or you do not know) what he set out to do? These

[5] See I. Child, op. cit., for a comprehensive review of evaluation of art products by expert judges.
[6] Franchon Frohlich, **Aesthetic Paradoxes of Abstract Expressionism and Pop Art**, in Lee Jacobus (ed.), Aesthetics and the Arts, McGraw-Hill Book Company, 1968, pp. 236–244.

artists are working on the opposite edges of the impossible. This can be seen in the works themselves — in the quality of concentrated intensity and involvement of abstract expressionism as opposed to the "coolness" and detachment of pop art.

This identification of some of the paradoxes that confront the person interested in aesthetics and the evaluation of contemporary art has come about as a result of scholarly inquiry. It has been a logical, intellectualized analysis about art in general and contemporary art in particular. Personal experiences with practicing artists over a long span of time has led to the conclusion that very few of them indulge in this sort of intellectualizing. Being a creative person, the abstract expressionist painter could overcome the ambiguity of working toward an undefined goal; he could know when he had succeeded even without knowing what he had set out to do.

The philosopher for his own purposes was not only defining the poles, or extremes, of a long continuum of artistic activity, but he was also describing individuals and actions at these poles. The way of working of the artists associated with abstract expressionism has been described in Chapter 5 as the intuitive-spontaneous strategy. A review of this could be useful prior to evaluating abstract expressionist paintings; however, what is being evaluated for its aesthetic worth is the work of art itself and its inherent qualities. It is good or bad art because of these and not because the artist said it was art, or because he, the artist, could justify his actions on the basis of some personal code of ethics.

CRITERIA FOR JUDGING ABSTRACT EXPRESSIONISM

How can a work of contemporary art in the style of abstract expressionism be evaluated? Perhaps it might be more prudent to avoid the issue, but it is one that will not conveniently go away. Judgments have been made about the aesthetic merits of such works, so it should be possible to examine some of the factors that have implemented these judgments. Also, this provides an unusually good opportunity to test the objective reasons submitted by Beardsley and to find out if his criteria of unity, complexity, and intensity apply to judgment of this highly personal form of expression.

First, an appeal was made for expert opinion. We discussed this problem of judgments of art in the abstract expressionist category with a number of art museum directors and teachers of art history and with men who are considered knowledgeable in the arts. There is considerable agreement on the factor which contributes most to their judgment of products done in this manner; this factor is that good abstract expressionist painting should have and convey a forceful impact upon the observer — the same "force" that we discussed earlier as the intensity of a work. In judging one abstract expressionist's work as being better than another's, this would be the most important factor. It is something which is readily perceivable by experienced persons and can be identified as such. When we consider the nature of abstract expressionist paintings and the objectives of their creators, as well as records we have of their ways of working, it can easily be understood why this factor is given foremost importance. These artists are interested in expressing their feelings with directness through all the power of their medium. This is uppermost in their intentions.

For any evaluation (a rating of goodness or badness) of a work in the manner of abstract expressionism, the person undertaking the judgment will make comparisons with the works of some of the people who have already achieved a reputation for the quality of their products. This personal frame of reference may not be resorted to in a completely systematic way, but the measure of the new perceptual experience is in some manner fashioned by associations made with these previous experiences.

Intensity. When we look over the work of the recognized leaders and innovators in this style of art, we can easily perceive differences in the

14-10
Willem de Kooning.
Woman and Bicycle.
1952–53. Whitney Museum of American Art,
New York.

"look" of their finished products. But among them all, and sometimes in different ways, there is this consistent ability to provide an impact upon the sensibilities of the viewer. Pollock with his dripping and splashing of paint seems to some observers to be wrapped in violence and, to others, to be highly controlled and organized, quite deliberate in where he splashed or dripped paint (see Fig. 1-1 for his painting *Number 1*, 1948). When the argument is finished, one thing remains certain — that his work had a very direct impact upon the viewer.

Mark Rothko had quite a different way of working and produced paintings with two or three hazy rectangles of color (see Fig. 1-2; *Mauve and Orange*, 1961). In his other paintings these ribbons of luminous color expressed a range of emotions from restful calm to brooding hostility. The feelings of the viewer are aroused, but in a different manner than they are by the work of Pollock. Kline, with his bold, powerful strokes of dark pigment that stand out against the plain background of lighter color, leaves the viewer with the sensation of the power and motion that caused the artist to place slashing strokes across the canvas (see Figs. 11-9, 11-10).

Some of the paintings by De Kooning, Hofmann, Still, Gottlieb, Motherwell, Tworkov, Guston, and Francis fit into this personal frame of reference, giving it range and variety. The images, colors, and technical mannerisms are different; the intensity and impact upon the viewer remains constant (Figs. 14-10–14-13). By comparison, less successful works are seen as such because they lack this quality of intensity for the viewer. They may imitate some of the surface mannerisms and superficial technicalities, such as dripping paint (even to the point of piercing plastic bags of liquid pigment with a rifle bullet). The painters may also have studied Zen Buddhist literature or practiced spiritualism, but these surface attributes of spontaneity and inner light are not enough. The feeling, significance, and meaning of their work for the viewer is dim by comparison with the products of the artists mentioned above.

Unity. When art is the subject for discussion, words such as order, organization, form, and unity are employed in the discourse. The "special kind of order" described by the psychologists and philosophers as being inherent in the experience of looking at art is one in which unity is the fundamental characteristic. As all art worthy of the name has this quality of unity of organization, so abstract expressionism as art must have it too. When we look for the unity in the organization of an abstract expressionist painting, it may be necessary to make some adjustment in our thinking away from traditional and customary expectations obtained from historical examples of pictorial composition. The formal modes of organization that occurred in the past will not be found here; the time and needs of the artist are quite different from those of the past. We should expect, however, to find unity in their structural designs — not to be classed as better or worse but as a different kind of unity. One should be able to make value judgments about the work and answer the question, does this work hold together as a unit or does some part break away and detract from the total? Since it is abstract, we cannot expect to find figures and objects composed in neat structural patterns of pyramids and spirals or in unifying axial arrangements; since the artist's way of working depends on spon-

14-11
Robert Motherwell. Mural fragment.
1950. University of Minnesota Gallery,
Minneapolis.

14-12
Conrad Marca-Relli. The Joust.
1959. Walker Art Center,
Minneapolis.

14-12

14-13

14-13
Grace Hartigan. Human Fragment.
1963. Walker Art Center,
Minneapolis.

taneity, a formal order was neither sought nor desired. What, then, will be the unifying devices that he has invented?

The most obvious example of a mode of unification was that employed by the most renowned of the abstract expressionists, Jackson Pollock. A special kind of unity was obtained through the swirling paint that dominated his compositions. This interwoven tract of pigment superimposed over masses of color holds his compositions together and guides the spectator's eye over the whole canvas. Likewise, Rothko's subtle overlapping of bands of paint laid on in parallel rows holds his compositions together. The soft edges of the painter's strokes allows colors to overlap unevenly.

Other proponents of abstract expressionism have taken advantage of the way the viewer tends to unify separate elements in his visual field. The spectator sees things as a unit when they are similar in size, shape, or direction; the painter often groups elements loosely and allows the spectator to bring them together into a tighter organization. At other times the prominent marks left in the thick impasto give the viewer a track pattern to follow that unifies separate symbols even when the symbols themselves are not recognizable.

Complexity. Usually, with works in the abstract expressionist manner the question is not whether there is enough complexity but whether there is too much. These artists have often been accused of painting in a language so personal that they speak only to themselves. Part of the complexity of their visual statements is counteracted by the large scale of their canvases. Complexity in works of abstract expressionists is encountered at two levels: (1) the mysterious, intimate, and personal character of their symbolism; and (2) the spontaneous-intuitive character of their way of working, even in the application of the paint itself.

As a reaction to abstract expressionist imagery, we have the pop artist who employs symbols that are easily recognized and far from mysterious; in contrast with the sometimes furious application of pigment by the abstract expressionist, we have the hard-edge painter's flat, carefully defined and restricted contours and the artist who presents a minimal form of geometric shapes.

In looking at abstract expressionist paintings, one must again return to answer the question, is it complex enough to hold interest and stimulate curiosity, or is it so complex as to be an overstatement of something that could have been said more simply?

Summary. When judging a work of art in the style of abstract expressionism, one looks first for its power and forcefulness. The intensity of a good work pervades our senses and acts upon our emotions. When we look at it, we "feel" something. We describe the work and our feelings towards it as having qualities of vitality, forcefulness, movement, calmness, or depth. It can be described as having provoked intense feelings that range from serenity to hostility.

When we consider the degree of unity in these compositions, we must decide whether they are well organized with an inner logic of structure and style or whether they are lacking in these qualities. As far as their complexity or simplicity is concerned, one must take into account that, although they are usually developed on a large scale, there should be a degree of richness in the contrasts and something subtle and imaginative for the spectator to find.

Comparisons should be made with other experiences that we have had with products of abstract expressionism and other historical examples of art. From this comparison we can establish the kinds and degrees of intensity, complexity, and unity that are present in the new experience.

Abstract expressionism has been selected as our example for the procedure of judging art because many people find its evaluation more problematic. Art products of this category are very personal visual statements, and in their time there are few historical precedents with which comparisons can be made. For an evaluation of other works of art, different in style and from other historic periods, the strongest features are first impressed upon the visual mechanism of the judge or critic. In some cases, this may be the formal structural unity of the composition; in other cases this is immediate apprehension of the richness in contrasts or the lack of them. In looking at art objects made by men who are strongly motivated to express their feelings and emotions directly through the object they are creating, the judge or critic should perceive and feel the intensity of these at the outset. Starting with this strongest force and reason, other objective factors are taken into account and appealed to in the judgment of aesthetic objects. The personal frame of reference, consisting of the individual's past experience with art, serves as the background for more explicit evaluation.

IN CONCLUSION

Man the artist, as a creator and producer of objects of aesthetic quality, and man the spectator, as appreciator and evaluator of these products, has been our subject. The expressions in objective form of the response a man makes to his environment — the world outside transformed as it is taken into the world within him — are man's most sublime creations. Art is the record of what man has valued most in the entire span of his existence. With his art he has created a more personal world for himself and for others who will take the time to look before moving on.

To open the door for looking, we have taken the reader through the experience of making and seeing, of producing the work of art and looking at what has been made. This is one door: there are others. Through an understanding of what an artist does and how he does it, perhaps the strangeness of visual statements will seem more familiar and the encounter with art will have personal rewards and satisfactions. As some of the language of art becomes comprehensible, communication through its language of symbol and metaphor can take place between artist and viewer. Through the art objects that have been created today, yesterday, and tomorrow, there will be a linking of its present with its past and future for all of us.

APPENDIXES

1. Allport's Event-Structure Theory. Allport has examined thirteen major theories of perception as well as a number of related viewpoints and has concluded with a theory of his own. His theory of *event-structure* is a completely unified system in which all subunits of experience are interlocked with all other experiences. It has a kind of design which is clear and understandable to the artist who tends to design and think in terms of patterns that are unified. A summarization of this theory follows:[1]

> *A perceptual act is a dynamically operating structure in that it presents a picture of a self-delimitated and self-contained structure of on-goings and events. The two types of elements which operate to form a structure are: (a)* Ongoing processes; *receptor activities, nerve impulses, muscular contractions, and the like. In the art situation, viewing and forming involve at an elementary level some form of motion and an on-going through space and during time. (b)* Events; *the junctions or points of contact where on-going processes which go before an encounter are linked with those that come after.*

This theory has particular interest for the artist and the art teacher because of its concept of a structure with its cycles of ongoings and events, with each ongoing element related to the others to form a complete and potentially repetitive cycle. This is in turn connected tangentially with other events and cycles to form a system (a cycle of cycles of ongoings and events).

2. The trapezoidal window frame experiment. The experiment with the rotating trapezoidal window is described by Allport as follows:[2]

> *The rotating trapezoidal window frame is a dramatic masterpiece of ambiguous stimulation. It produces effects as uncanny as any to be found in the whole repertoire of perceptual illusions. Viewed with a single eye at about ten feet of distance, the window, though actually rotating,* is seen to oscillate back and forth. *A small cube attached to one side, however, is seen to move in true circular fashion, and in part of its course, to leave the frame to float through the air and pass in front of the oscillating "window" and return finally to its original point*

---

1 Floyd H. Allport, *Theories of Perception and the Concept of Structure*, John Wiley and Sons, Inc., New York, 1965.
2 *Ibid.*, pp. 276–277.

of attachment. A straight tube of paper thrust through one of the apertures of the frame is seen in part of its course to rotate in the direction opposite to the movement of the window. When the two meet, the tube is seen to bend about the window frame, and then with further turning of the latter to straighten itself out again.

In the first of these effects (seeing "a window as oscillating back and forth instead of rotating in a circle") we assume that the window like most of the windows in our experience is rectangular. Since it is perceived as rectangular the physical difference in length of the two vertical sides is interpreted as due to perspective changes in the window when it is in a turned position. But the perspective indications will not "ring" true if the window turns completely around (as is actually the case). Reversal of direction at a certain point is phenomenologically required in order to make size and perspective changes "come out right" and thus tally with our assumption (false) of the window's rectangularity. The rotating window is therefore seen not as rotating, but as oscillating. The perceived circular travel of the cube is explained by perceiving the change in apparent size under the (correct) assumption of the movement of an object toward us and away from us. We see the tube "bend" (incorrect) because the cue of overlay is so strong. We must assume either that it does bend or disregard the fact that it overlaps the window frame and see it as passing through gaps in the mullions of the window (a less probable assumption). The cube, however, can be seen as "cutting through" the window frame if we are told it is made of a "rigid material." We hold on to certain presumptive concepts and relinquish others; and indications to which we cling are said to be the ones which on the basis of experience have the greatest "prognostic reliability" with respect to our potential action in the situation.

This experiment has been reported in detail because it illustrates how assumptions which an observer brings to a new situation can lead to erroneous and misdirected conclusions. In the case of the trapezoidal window frame the observers were not given advance knowledge that the window frame was trapezoidal in shape. Therefore they assumed according to their past experience (perceptual constancy) that the window was rectangular. Thus the stage was set for their subsequent deception and for happenings which could not be harmonized with their assumption.

3. The Basic Course of the Bauhaus. The Basic Course at the Bauhaus had as its goals the following principles for the direction of students:

> 1. *To experience through the senses:* This brought all of the senses into action. In this manner the visual data was supplemented by direct tactile contact and by any other of the senses that might be useful in bringing more information about the subject or object to the student.

> 2. *To objectify rationally:* This brought into play the thinking mechanism of the student in order to organize the information he had received through the senses and to

give it objective form through pictorial and structural designing.

3. *To realize as a synthesis:* This forced the student to resolve learnings obtained in some of his contact periods with the problem and to emphasize his discovery that gave substance to his exploration.

4. McFee's Perception-Delineation Theory. The McFee *Perception-Delineation Theory* could become a more useful explanatory aid for the art educator if a consideration of appreciation were included within its framework.

In the field of art there are two separate bodies of knowledge and experience. One relates to the production or creation of art forms—that is, delineation; the other is concerned with critical analysis of art works—that is, the capacity for making aesthetic judgments and appreciating the art forms which have been created.

Perhaps the Perception-Delineation Theory could be extended and made even more comprehensive by adding one more "point" to the four already detailed by McFee. This new point could be labeled something like Appreciation or Aesthetic Awareness. With this we would have a perception-delineation-appreciation theory, which would involve the observer or the viewer as well as the producer.

Almost without exception, all the variables or factors which may affect individuals during the process of creating art forms, including those listed under Point I, Overall Readiness and Preparation to Perceive, Point II, Psychological and Cultural Environment, and Point III, Information Handling, also affect the individual during the process of appreciating art forms. It is only for certain factors under Point IV, Delineation, that we might not be able to find application to the individual when he is engaged in appreciation of art.

Even this last category could not be discarded entirely from a proposed perception-appreciation theory because there are many people who believe, with some justification, that appreciation can be fostered through experiences involving production of art. For many years the art program in public schools has been based upon the assumption that appreciation of art could be implemented through activities which involved the student in producing art at his own level. One avenue for appreciation of art is participation, that is, working with the media and on the same problems that are faced by the mature artist. Also programs for museum directors, for which a high level of connoisseurship and critical evaluation is required, have included courses in which the learner was expected to work with media in the style of selected artists for the purpose of increasing perceptiveness and awareness of the qualitative skills evidenced in the products of master artists.

Under our Point V, Appreciation, are included such factors as (1) knowledge of the art heritage (the history of art), as well as development of knowledge and skill related to (2) intelligible standards for aesthetic judgment, (3) tools and materials of the artist, and (4) the repertoire of vi-

CLASSIFICATION OF ART WORKS BASED ON PSYCHOLOGICAL TYPES

SCHOOLS OF ART	FUNCTIONAL TYPES (JUNG)		CHARACTERISTICS OF ART EXPRESSION	DESCRIPTION OF ART EXPRESSION
REALISM	Thinking (craft)	EXTROVERT	ENUMERATIVE	Descriptive, controlled by object. Artist unable to relate to it any sensation of wholeness or atmosphere.
		INTROVERT	ORGANIC	Objects placed in organic relationships; mind penetrates form and function of external object.
SUPERREALISM	Feeling (poetry, drama)	EXTROVERT	DECORATIVE	Primarily concerned with color and two-dimensional form.
		INTROVERT	IMAGINATIVE	Contents from subconscious; purely fanciful theme. Artist uses capacity for provoking memory and eidetic images.
EXPRESSIONISM	Sensation (design)	EXTROVERT	EMPATHETIC	Imaginative projection of one's own consciousness into another being.
		INTROVERT	HAPTIC	More personal and subjective.
CONSTRUCTIVISM	Intuition (dance, music)	EXTROVERT	RHYTHMICAL PATTERN	Repetition of quantities or measures; begins with idea of external object. Artist develops original motifs to construct rhythmical forms.
		INTROVERT	STRUCTURAL FORM	Absolute relationship of individually distinct forms. Artist begins with formal motif, adapts subject to this form.

sual symbols, language and intent of the artist, and many other competencies. These points have been discussed in the last three chapters of this book.

5. Read's theory of visual and personality characteristics. The table shown above is a condensation of the theory given by Herbert Read in his book, *Education through Art.* This theory makes a connection between the visual characteristics of the art product that is created and the personality characteristics of the person who produced it. This connection is drawn for

ELEMENTS AND PRINCIPLES OF DESIGN

Elements	Major Principles	Minor Principles	Resulting Attributes	Supreme Attainment
LINE	REPETITION	ALTERNATION	HARMONY	BEAUTY
FORM	RHYTHM	SEQUENCE	FITNESS	
TONE	PROPORTION	RADIATION		
TEXTURES	BALANCE	PARALLELISM		
COLOR	EMPHASIS	TRANSITION		
		SYMMETRY		
		CONTRAST		

mature artists and for children. The functional types of personality are those described by Carl Jung. Read suggested that the personality chararateristics of a child could be determined by an analysis of his work (this is not a new idea). For example, if the child's art work was identified as having "objects in organic relationships in which the child-artist's mind penetrated the form and function of the external objects," he could be described as having a *thinking-introvert* type of personality.

6. Interest in ways of working and learning. More than twenty years ago Lowenfeld reported on the existence of two distinct creative types and developed his tests for visual and haptic aptitudes.[3]

There was a subsequent adjustment of Lowenfeld's visual and haptic types by investigators who worked closely with him at Pennsylvania State University. These types became the basis for spontaneous and deliberate "ways of learning," [4] and they can be seen later in the spontaneous and divergent strategies or "ways of working" which creative individuals use. This transition has been discussed by Michaels.[5]

Kenneth Beittel and Robert Burkhart have pursued the investigation of working strategies with college and high school art students. They make distinctions related to the potential or level of creativeness exercised by individual art students within their strategy groups, which are labeled as spontaneous, divergent, and academic. The spontaneous and the divergent ways of working in art encourage innovation and discovery, while the academic way of working has by definition less creative potentiality.[6]

---

[3] Viktor Lowenfeld, **The Nature of Creative Activity**, *American Journal of Psychology*, vol. 58 (1945), pp. 100–111. See also Lowenfeld, **Creative and Mental Growth**, The Macmillan Company, New York, 1947.
[4] Robert Burkhart, **Spontaneous and Deliberate Ways of Learning**, International Textbook Company, Scranton, Pennsylvania, 1962.
[5] John Michaels, **Art Experience During Early Adolescence**, *Art Education* (64th Yearbook of the National Society for the Study of Education), University of Chicago Press, Chicago, 1965, pp. 86–114.
[6] Kenneth R. Beittel and Robert Burkhart, **Strategies of Spontaneous, Divergent and Academic Art Students**, *Studies in Art Education*, vol. 5, no. 1 (Fall, 1963), pp. 20–41.

A different kind of research and philosophic inquiry in another type of investigation has attempted to establish methodological generalizations about artistic processes. Ecker [7] identifies two kinds of problem solving, the scientific and the qualitative, as being involved in the artistic process. Although Ecker does not refer specifically to the spontaneous and divergent strategies of Beittel and Burkhart, there is a close parallel between scientific problem solving and the divergent strategy and correspondingly between qualitative problem solving and the spontaneous strategy as these are described by different writers.

7. Elements and principles of design. The table (p. 444) shows the elements and principles of design as presented in the 1920s by a committee of art educators. This was an attempt to standardize terminology for writing and speaking about art and design.

---

[7] David Ecker, **The Artistic Process as Qualitative Problem Solving**, *Journal of Aesthetics and Art Criticism*, vol. 21, no. 3 (Spring, 1963), pp. 283–290.

BIBLIOGRAPHY

Aesthetics and Criticism in Art Education, Ralph A. Smith (ed.), Rand McNally and Company, Chicago, 1966.

Allport, Floyd H.: *Theories of Perception and the Concept of Structure*, John Wiley and Sons, Inc., New York, 1965.

America's Arts and Skills, compiled by the editors of *Life Magazine*, E. P. Dutton and Co., Inc., New York, 1957.

Anderson, Donald, M.: *Elements of Design*, Holt, Rinehart and Winston, Inc., New York, 1961.

Arnheim, Rudolph: *Art and Visual Perception*, University of California Press, Berkeley, Los Angeles, 1954.

————: *Picasso's Guernica*, University of California Press, Berkeley, Los Angeles, 1962.

The Artist in America, compiled by the editors of *Art in America*, W. W. Norton and Company, Inc., New York, 1967.

Attneave, Fred: "Some Informational Aspects of Visual Perception," *Psychological Review*, vol. 61, no. 3, pp. 183–193, 1954.

Barr, Alfred H., Jr.: *Fantastic Art, Dada, Surrealism*, Museum of Modern Art, New York, 1936.

————: *What Is Modern Painting?,* Museum of Modern Art, New York, 1956.

Barron, Frank: "Complexity—Simplicity as a Personality Dimension," *Journal of Abnormal and Social Psychology*, vol. 48, no. 2, 1953.

————: "The Psychology of Imagination," *Scientific American*, vol. 199, no. 3, September, 1958.

Bauhaus: 1919–1928, edited by Walter Gropius, Museum of Modern Art, New York, 1938.

Baur, John I. H.: *Nature in Abstraction*, Whitney Museum of American Art, New York, 1958.

Beardsley, Monroe C.: *Aesthetics: Problems in Philosophy of Criticism*, Harcourt, Brace and World, Inc., New York, 1958.

———: "On the Creation of Art," *Journal of Aesthetics and Art Criticism*, vol. 23, no. 3, Spring, 1965.

Beittel, Kenneth, and Robert Burkhart: "Strategies of Spontaneous, Divergent and Academic Art Students," *Studies in Art Education*, vol. 5, no. 1, Fall, 1963.

Bell, Clive: *Art*, Capricorn Books, G. P. Putnam's Sons, New York, 1968.

Broudy, Harry S.: "Aesthetic Education in the Secondary Schools," *Art Education*, vol. 18, no. 6, June, 1965.

Bruner, Jerome F.: *The Process of Education*, Harvard University Press, Cambridge, Massachusetts, 1961.

Burt, Cyril: "The Psychological Aspects of Aesthetic Education," *Art Education*, vol. 20, no. 3, March, 1967.

Chabet, Bernard: *Artists at Work*, Webb Books, Inc., Cambridge, Massachusetts, 1960.

Child, Irvin L.: "Personal Preferences as an Expression of Aesthetic Sensitivity," *Journal of Personality*, vol. 30, 1962.

———: "The Problem of Objectivity in Aesthetic Value," *Penn State Papers in Art Education*, no. 1, Pennsylvania State University Press, University Park, Pennsylvania, 1967.

——— and Rosaline S. Swartz: "Personality and the Appreciation of Art," *Art Education*, vol. 20, no. 1, January, 1967.

Collier, Graham: *Form, Space and Vision*, Prentice-Hall, Inc., Englewood Cliffs, New Jersey, 1963.

Collingwood, P. G.: *The Principles of Art*, Oxford University Press, Oxford, England, 1965.

Conrad, George: *The Process of Art Education in the Elementary School*, Prentice-Hall, Inc., Englewood Cliffs, New Jersey, 1964.

The Creative Process: A Symposium, Brewster Ghiselin (ed.), University of California Press, Berkeley, 1952.

Creativity and Psychological Health, Michael S. Andrews (ed.), Syracuse University Press, Syracuse, New York, 1961.

Dewey, John: *Art as Experience*, Minton, Balch and Company, New York, 1934.

Eisner, Elliot: *Think with Me about Creativity*, F. A. Owen Publishing Company, Dansville, New York, 1964.

————: "The Typology of Creative Behavior in the Visual Arts," in E. V. Eisner and D. W. Ecker (eds.), *Readings in Art Education*, Blaisdell Publishing Company, Waltham, Massachusetts, 1966.

Fleming, William, *Arts and Ideas*, 3d ed., Holt, Rinehart and Winston, Inc., New York, 1968.

Giedion, Sigfried: *Space, Time and Architecture*, Harvard University Press, Cambridge, Massachusetts, 1956.

Gilot, François, and Carlton Lake: *Life with Picasso*, McGraw-Hill Book Company, New York, 1964.

Gombrich, E. H.: *Art and Illusion*, Pantheon Books, Inc., New York, 1965.

Goodrich, Lloyd, and John I. H. Baur: *American Art of Our Century*, Frederick A. Praeger, Inc., New York, 1961.

Guilford, J. P.: "The Structure of the Intellect," *Psychological Bulletin*, vol. 53, 1956.

————: "Creative Ability in the Arts," *Psychological Review*, vol. 44, 1957.

————, R. C. Wilson, and P. R. Cristensen: "Factor Analytics: Study of Creative Thinking," *Reports from Psychological Laboratory*, no. 8. University of California Press, Los Angeles, 1952.

Haggerty, Melvin: *Art, a Way of Life*, University of Minnesota Press, Minneapolis, 1938.

Harris, Dale: "Aesthetic Awareness: A Psychologist's View," *Art Education*, vol. 19, no. 5, May, 1966.

Hospers, J.: *Meaning and Truth in the Arts*, Archon Books, Hamden, Connecticut, 1964.

Huxley, Aldous L.: *The Art of Seeing*, Harper and Brothers, New York, 1942.

Itten, Johannes: *Design and Form: The Basic Course of the Bauhaus*, Reinhold Publishing Company, Inc., New York, 1964

Janson, H. W.: *History of Art*, Prentice-Hall, Inc., Englewood Cliffs, New Jersey, 1963.

Kaufman, Irving: *Art Education in Contemporary Culture*, The Macmillan Company, New York, 1966.

Kneller, George F.: *The Art and Science of Creativity*, Holt, Rinehart and Winston, Inc., New York, 1965.

Knobler, Nathan: *The Visual Dialogue*, Holt, Rinehart and Winston, Inc., New York, 1967.

Krugman, Herbert, and Eugene Hartley: "The Learning of Taste," *Marketing and the Behavioral Sciences*, Percy Bliss (ed.), Allyn and Bacon, Inc., Boston, 1963.

Kuh, Katherine: *The Artist's Voice*, Harper and Row Publishers, Inc., New York, 1960.

Landis, Mildred M.: *Meaningful Art Education*, Charles A. Bennett Co., Inc., Peoria, Illinois, 1951.

Langer, Susanne K.: *Problems of Art*, Charles Scribner's Sons, New York, 1957.

Larkin, Oliver W.: *Art and Life in America*, rev. ed., Holt, Rinehart and Winston, Inc., New York, 1960.

Liberman, Alexander: *The Artist in His Studio*, The Viking Press, New York, 1960.

Lowry, Bates: *The Visual Experience*, Prentice-Hall, Inc., Englewood Cliffs, New Jersey, 1964.

Luckeish, M.: *Visual Illusions*, Dover Publications, Inc., New York, 1965.

McFee, June King: *Preparation for Art*, Wadsworth Publishing Co., Inc., San Francisco, 1964.

Malraux, André: *The Voices of Silence,* Doubleday and Company, Inc., New York, 1953.

Moholy-Nagy, László: *Vision in Motion*, Paul Theobald, Chicago, 1947.

Muller, Joseph Emile, and Frank Elgar: *One Hundred Years of Modern Painting*, Tudor Publishing Company, New York, 1966.

Munro, Thomas: *Towards Science in Aesthetics*, Liberal Arts Press, New York, 1956.

Myers, Bernard S.: *Art and Civilization*, 2d ed., McGraw-Hill Book Company, New York, 1967.

Osborn, Alex F.: *Applied Imagination*, Charles Scribner's Sons, New York, 1954.

Pearson, Ralph: *How to See Modern Pictures*, Dial Press, Inc., New York, 1925.

Read, Herbert: *A Concise History of Modern Painting*, Frederick A. Praeger, Inc., New York, 1962.

————: *A Concise History of Modern Sculpture*, Frederick A. Praeger, Inc., New York, 1964.

————: *Education through Art*, Faber and Faber, London, 1958.

————: *The Meaning of Art*, paperback edition, Penguin Books, Inc., Baltimore, 1964.

Report of the Commission on Art Education, Jerome Hausman (ed.), National Art Education Association, Washington, D.C., 1965.

Salome, Richard A.: "Perceptual Training as a Factor in Children's Art," *Art Education*, vol. 20, no. 9, December, 1966.

Schinneller, James: "Art: Its Present Condition," *Art Education* (64th Yearbook, National Society for the Study of Education), University of Chicago Press, Chicago, 1965.

————: *Art: Search and Self Discovery,* 2d ed., International Textbook Company, Scranton, Pennsylvania, 1968.

Segall, Marshall H., Donald T. Campbell, and Melville J. Herskovits: *The Influence of Culture on Visual Perception*, Bobbs-Merrill Company, Inc., Indianapolis, Indiana, 1966.

A Seminar in Art Education for Research and Curriculum Development, Edward L. Mattil (ed.), Pennsylvania State University, University Park, Pennsylvania, 1966.

Smith, Ralph A.: "The Assent to Aesthetic Education," *Art Education*, vol. 20, no. 2, February, 1967.

Taylor, I. A.: "The Nature of Creative Processes," in P. Smith (ed.), *Creativity*, Hastings House, New York, 1959.

Torrance, E. Paul: *Guiding Creative Talent*, Prentice-Hall, Inc., Englewood Cliffs, New Jersey, 1962.

————: *Rewarding Creative Behavior*, Prentice-Hall, Inc., Englewood Cliffs, New Jersey, 1965.

————: "Scientific Views of Creativity and Factors Affecting Its Growth," *Daedalus*, vol. 94, no. 3, Summer, 1965.

Tumin, Melvin. M.: "Education, Development and the Creative Process," *Aesthetic Form in Education*, Syracuse University Press, Syracuse, New York, 1958.

Vision Plus Value, Gyorgy Kepes (ed.), 6 vols. (*Education of Vision*; *Structure in Art and in Science*; *Module, Proportion, Symmetry and Rhythm*; *The Nature and Art of Motion*; *The Manmade Object*; *Sign, Image, Symbol*), George Braziller, Inc., New York, 1966.

Whitehead, Alfred North: *Symbolism: Its Meaning and Effect*, Capricorn Books, G. P. Putnam's Sons, New York, 1959.

Wright, Frank Lloyd: *Architecture, Man in Possession of His Earth*, Doubleday and Company, Inc., Garden City, New York, 1962.

Yochim, Louise D.: *Perceptual Growth in Creativity*, International Textbook Company, Scranton, Pennsylvania, 1967.

INDEX

INDEX

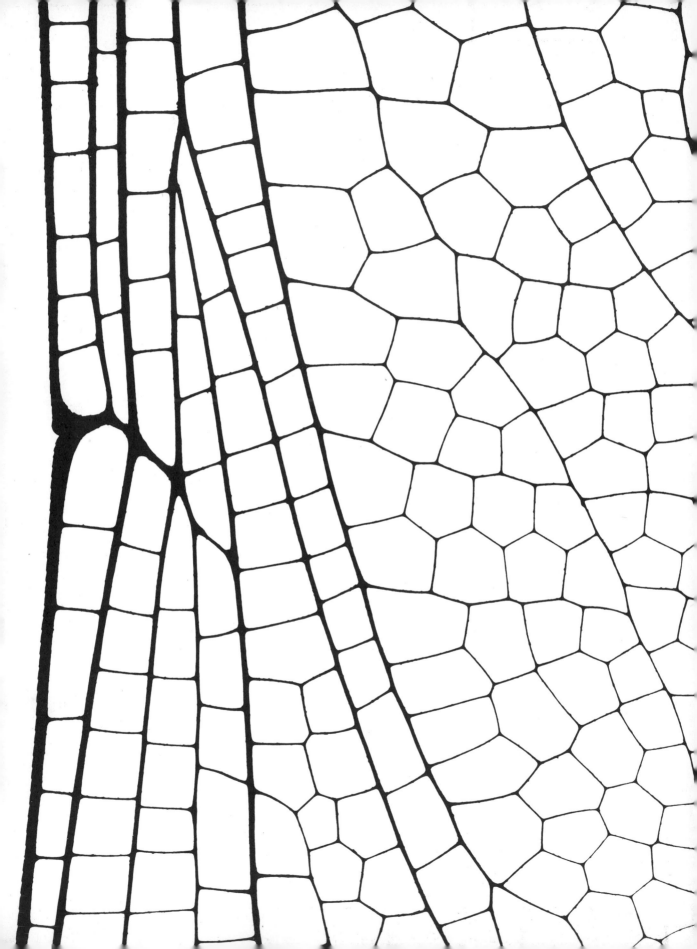